The Final Voyage of the *Central America*

The *George Law*, renamed *Central America*
Courtesy, The Mariners Museum, Newport News, VA

*For Mike
With my best regards,
Normand E. Klare*

The Final Voyage of the Central America 1857

The saga of a gold rush steamship, the tragedy of her loss in a hurricane, and the treasure which is now recovered.

by
NORMAND E. KLARE

KLARE-TAYLOR PUBLISHING COMPANY
Ashland, Oregon

Copyright 1992, by
NORMAND E. KLARE

All rights reserved including the rights to
translate or reproduce this work or parts
thereof in any form or by any media.

LIBRARY OF CONGRESS CATALOG CARD NUMBER 91-71134
ISBN-0-97644-03-0-X

KLARE-TAYLOR PUBLISHING COMPANY
P. O. Box 637, Ashland, OR 97520

LIBRARY OF CONGRESS CATALOGING-IN-PUBLICATION DATA

Klare, Normand E., 1921-
　　The final voyage of the Central America, 1857: the saga of a gold rush
steamship, the tragedy of her loss in a hurricane, and the treasure which
is now recovered / by Normand E. Klare.
　　278 p.　　cm.
　　Includes bibliographical references and index.
　　ISBN-0-97644-03-0-X (hard : alk. paper)
　　1. Voyages to the Pacific Coast.　2. Central America (Ship)
3. Steamboat disasters—United States—History—19th century.
I. Title.
F864.K59　1991
910'.9164—dc20   91-71134
                                                                  CIP

To my wife,
WINONA VERNER KLARE
with thanks for her support, patience
and many hours of research and computer time.

Contents

ACKNOWLEDGEMENTS	11
INTRODUCTION	13
FOREWORD: California Gold and the Steamship Route	15
I. A Company and Its Steamer	19
II. A Master For a Steamer	29
III. The Voyage	37
IV. A Change in the Weather	63
V. Hope, Struggle and Loss	77
VI. A Welcome Stranger	85
VII. Calm Desperation	107
VIII. A Change of Course	121
IX. On the Brig	127
X. Reunion	135
XI. All Ashore	145
XII. Rumblings Among the Passengers and Public	155
XIII. The Gulf Stream and A Lifeboat	165
XIV. California Reacts	177
XV. The Hurricane and Other Causes of the Disaster	181
XVI. Lost Specie and Treasure	195
XVII. Heroes of the Disaster	203
APPENDICES	
A: The Treasure of the *Central America*	219
B: Aftermath—Personnel	225
C: Passengers and Crew	245
SELECTED BIBLIOGRAPHY	261
INDEX	269

Illustrations

The *George Law*, renamed *Central America*	frontispiece
Steamer Route, San Francisco to New York	14
Side-view and deck plans of *George Law*	18
William Lewis Herndon	28
San Francisco from Rincon Point, 1856	38
Steamer Day in San Francisco	40
The *Sonora*	41
Ansel Ives Easton and Adeline Mills Easton	42
Alonso Castle Monson	43
Robert Turnbull Brown	43
Theodore Payne and his company sales room	45
Thomas W. Badger	46
James E. Birch	47
Francois Pahud and Rosalie Rimboust Pahud	49
Rufus A. Lockwood and family	50
Terminus at Aspinwall	56
Typical steamer cabin	56
Edward W. Hull and William H. Hull	61
Passengers bailing the ship	71
Rigging of the *Central America*	75
Hiram Burt and the brig *Marine*	84
Lowering the women into the lifeboats	87
Ansel Easton's note to his wife	103
Captain Herndon on the wheel-guard	106
The steamer plunged at an angle	111
A giant wave engulfed the *Central America*	113
A solid mass of men tossed and tumbled	115
Captain Anders Johnsen	120

Hot tea on the *Marine*	129
John Tice, Alexander Grant, and George W. Dawson	164
Dawson reaches the hurricane deck	170
Tice and Grant rescue Dawson	172
Rescue by the bark *Mary*	173
The silver cup	175
Position report on the *Central America*	194
David Raymond	209
Tiffany silver serving tray of James Birch	228
Augustine Pahud Renault, 1934	241

Acknowledgments

We offer our genuine appreciation to Dr. J.S. Holliday, author of *The World Rushed In*, for his early advice, constructive criticism and encouragement.

We are grateful to the late John Haskell Kemble, Professor of History, Emeritus, Pomona College, Claremont, California, for his review of the early manuscript and for his recommendations. His books, *The Panama Route* and others, were invaluable sources of information.

More than fifty historical societies and libraries throughout the country and overseas have provided valuable assistance to our research. Foremost among those institutions are the following: California Historical Society, San Francisco, California; California State Libraries, Sacramento & San Francisco (Sutro); Church of Jesus Christ of Latter Day Saints Genealogical Libraries: Oakland, California, and Salt Lake City, Utah; Library of Congress, Washington, District of Columbia; National Maritime Museum (J. Porter Shaw) Library, San Francisco, California, Irene Stachura; Naval Historical Center, Washington Navy Yard, Washington, District of Columbia, Paula Murphy, Librarian and Kathy Rohr, Operational Archives Branch; Oakland Museum and Library, Oakland, California; Oakland Public Library, Oakland, California, California History Room; San Mateo County Historical Association, San Mateo, California, Marion Holmes, Archivist; University of California, Berkeley, California, Bancroft Library, Department of Materials Science and Mineral Engineering, Judy Roberts, Business Manager, Main Library, Newspaper Room.

Other important sources of information were the following organizations: Aust-Agder-Museet, Arendal, Norway, Ruth Hamran, Curator; California Pioneer Society, San Francisco, California; Columbus-America Discovery Group, Columbus, Ohio, Judy Conrad, Historian; Fredericksburg Area Museum and Cultural Center, Fredericksburg, Virginia, Mary H. Dellinger, Collections Manager; Herndon Depot Museum, Herndon, Virginia, Virginia Clarity, Secretary, Herndon

Historical Society; National Archives, San Bruno, California and Washington, District of Columbia, John Vandereedt, Archivist; Norsk Sjofartsmuseum, Oslo, Norway, Else Thorstvedt, Librarian; United States Naval Academy Museum, Annapolis, Maryland, James Cheevers, Senior Curator.

Introduction

One of my vivid memories from the age of nine years, is of hearing my elderly grandmother saying "It was terrible, it was terrible!" as she recalled her shipwreck experience at her own age of nine. I knew nothing more of her story until 1976, my interest again being aroused when my cousins, William G. Fahy and John F. Ewing, discovered an old newspaper item saved by our grandmother. Augustine Pahud Renault, her mother, Rosalie Pahud, and two younger brothers, had been passengers on the *Central America*.

While this account got its start as a family history, the ensuing research and the captivating stories of the passengers suggested many questions. What sort of experience was it to travel from San Francisco to New York City during the gold rush era? Who established the steamer routes and the land connection between the Pacific and Atlantic Oceans? What kinds of vessels were in use during the 1850s? One question led to many, and before long the information found developed into a manuscript.

On the final journey of the Gold Rush side-wheel steamship *Central America*, her 491 passengers represented at least 13 countries and most of the 31 States of the Union. I have assembled the available information, integrating the comments from the biographies and statements of more than two hundred passengers and crew members of the steamship, and from masses of other collected data.

The purpose of this writing has been to consolidate into a single narrative the stories surrounding the greatest loss of life on a commercial passenger vessel of the nineteenth century, a disaster that befell many worthy people of a fascinating era. For those living during that time period, it was equivalent to the *Titanic* disaster of 1912.

Not only is this incident historically worthy of note, but many of the people involved were interesting as individuals, and played a significant role in the development of the West.

NORMAND E. KLARE

For more on the early life of William Louis Herndon, read author's <u>Herndon and Gibbon</u> – the first North American explorers of the Amazon Valley.

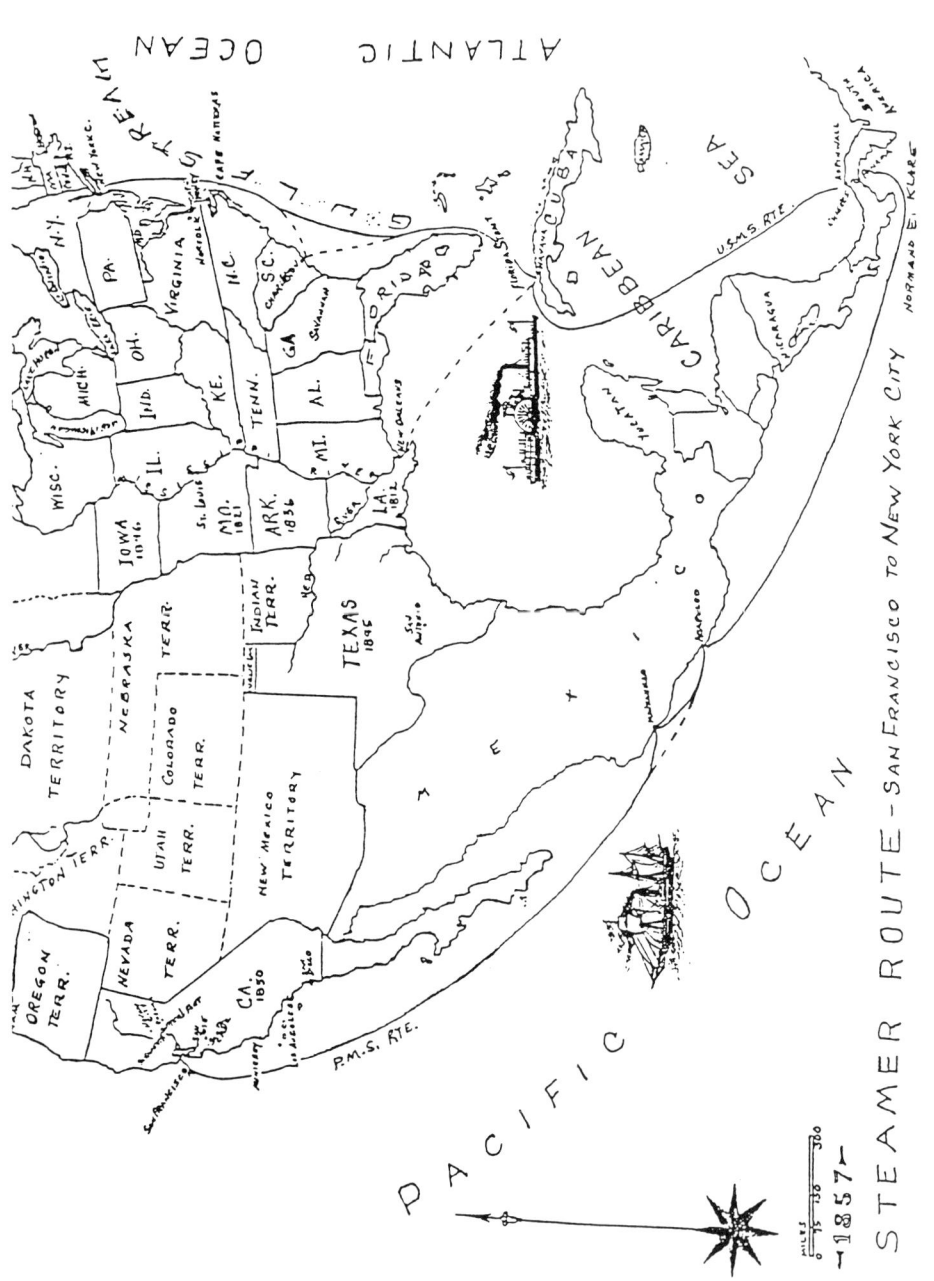

FOREWORD

California Gold and The Steamship Route

On January 24, 1848, James Marshall's discovery of gold near Sutter's Fort, California, became an international event. When the news spread to the United States and other countries of the world, men by the tens of thousands, by land and sea, headed overland and by sea to seek fortunes and adventure.[1]

Coastal currents and prevailing winds lengthened the journey from New York via Cape Horn to California because ships sailing north to San Francisco had to make a wide westerly sweep nearly as far as the longitude of the Hawaiian Islands,[2] thus greatly extending the time and distance for sailing vessels. The desirability became obvious for taking a short-cut across Central America and for traveling both legs by steamer rather than by sailing vessel.

Two crossings were developed. The first, an old passage used by Spanish explorers, crossed Nicaragua, part of the long trek being eased by water transport over Lake Nicaragua. Commodore Cornelius Vanderbilt, a wealthy and enterprising New York ship owner, envisioned a canal across Nicaragua but his plans became mired in competition with previous interests of Great Britain in the area. While California-bound immigrants continued to use this passage, a route across the Isthmus of Panama became the preferred crossing, it being about 60 miles in length, compared to 165 via Nicaragua. The two just about balanced out in terms of difficulty.

Although sailing vessels called ships, barks, brigs, schooners and clippers[3] continued in extensive trade, improvements in steam vessels

---

[1] J.S. Holliday, *The World Rushed In.* [Full citations on all noted publications are given in the bibliography following the text.]

[2] John Haskell Kemble, *The Panama Route, 1848-1869,* 37.

[3] BRIG: A two-masted vessel square-rigged on both masts. BARK: A vessel with three or more masts, square-rigged on all but the after-most mast, which is fore-and-aft rigged. A barkentine is square rigged only on the foremast, the others are fore-and-aft-rigged. SHIP: a large, ocean going vessel with three or more square-rigged masts, with jibs, staysails and spanker on the aftermost mast. SCHOONER: A sailing vessel with foremast, mainmast, sometimes more, and having fore-and-aft sails on all lower masts. When first observed, someone said "see how she scoons." This type has since been a schooner. CLIPPER: a fast sailing vessel with fine lines, an overhanging bow, tall raking masts, and a large sail area.

and ship design provided more passenger comfort, somewhat easing the stress of the passage between New York and San Francisco.

Early steamers bound for Panama, then a part of the republic of New Granada, docked at the port of Chagres, a town of about 700 inhabitants. For a two to five dollar fare, travelers made their way by dilapidated canoe-like boats called bungos, propelled by natives with crude oars or poles, along the narrow Chagres river to Gorgona, and by mule or foot over jungle trails for the final leg to Panama City on the south side of the Isthmus. No accommodations existed along the way, and the tropical heat was often punctuated by torrential downpours of rain during the three day trek.

During the early years of the Gold Rush, the sea journey from the eastern states to California took physical strength, courage, stamina and an adventurous spirit. Often beset by measles, smallpox, cholera, yellow fever, dysentery and other maladies,[4] thousands pressed on to endure the hazards of unsafe ships, distasteful and sometimes vermin-infested food, swampy trails, bandits across the land routes and frequent loss of life.

"Passengers down the river," said a weary traveler, "are constantly arriving. They complain of hard fare and being swindled at every turn." Their experiences were disheartening and sometimes fatal. Swindles, robberies and murders were commonplace. Organized bands of bandits, in many cases from other areas of Central and South America, found promising prospects for illegal booty by attacking the mule trains crossing the Isthmus, and in waylaying travelers all along the trails. One later complained of a recent attack on a specie train in which a large amount of dust "was stolen, . . . murders along the river, and no investigation instituted by the American Consul to discover the perpetrators."[5]

In 1849, adventuress Lady Emmeline Stuart Wortley, of England,[6] said of the Chagres: "It winds and twists about like a brilliant serpent, most gracefully and changefully. The enormous variety and inconceivable profusion of queenly palms was beautiful beyond expression." Although at times some travelers found compensations, the land crossing became the weak link in the chain of the route to the West.

Known until 1847 as Yerba Buena, San Francisco grew with the

---

[4] Oscar Lewis, *Sea Routes to the Gold Fields*, 196.
[5] Holliday, *The World Rushed In*, 437.
[6] *Panama Star and Herald*, 20 Oct 1851, 1-1. [Pg 1-Col l]; Mrs. Henry (Nina) Cust, *Wanderers . . . 1849-1855*. London, 1927.

times, her bay being ever crowded with vessels transporting immigrants to the gold fields. The city became a focal point for many men of questionable character, causing a disillusioned '49er, Robert Anderson,[7] to describe early San Francisco by saying:

> Nothing here but a parcel of rogues and thieves. It is no place for an honest man to be. You cannot trust a man you know as far as you can see him. There is not a night but some house or store is broken open and robbed, or someone killed in the streets. In fact, it is not safe to be in the street late of night . . .
>
> Business is very dull and the place is filled with idlers. They have got up another humbug which will take off a great many of them. I heard of a gold mine where they can pick up a fortune in a few days. They brought down a lot of the sand to show. We had some of it aboard the ship and tried it last week and there was not a particle of gold in it, but lying and humbuging are virtues here that they glory in.

Nevertheless, the city continued to grow and many found other attractions sufficient to establish their homes in the new western state.

California gold became a critical element of the United States economy. The public demanded the best possible ships and land transport, and entrepreneurs rushed to meet the demand. The *Central America's* saga began to unfold.

---

[7] The letter to his brother, dated February 14, 1851, is displayed at the Oakland Museum, CA.

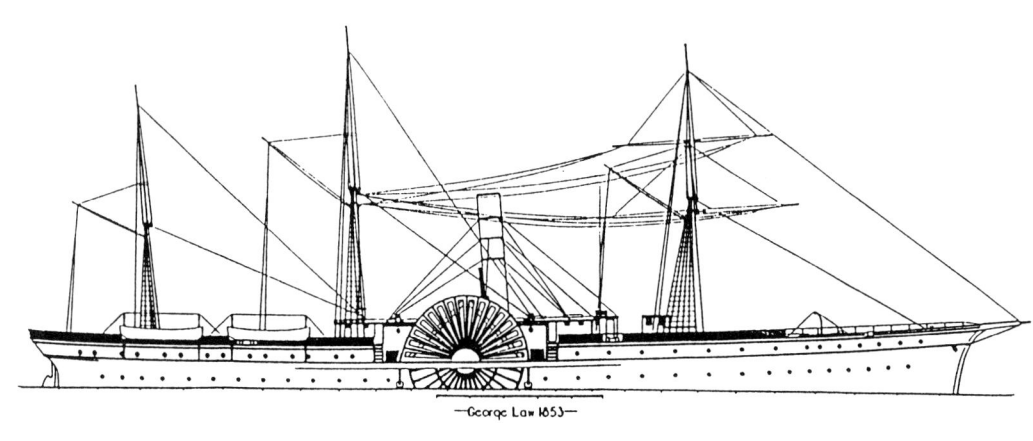
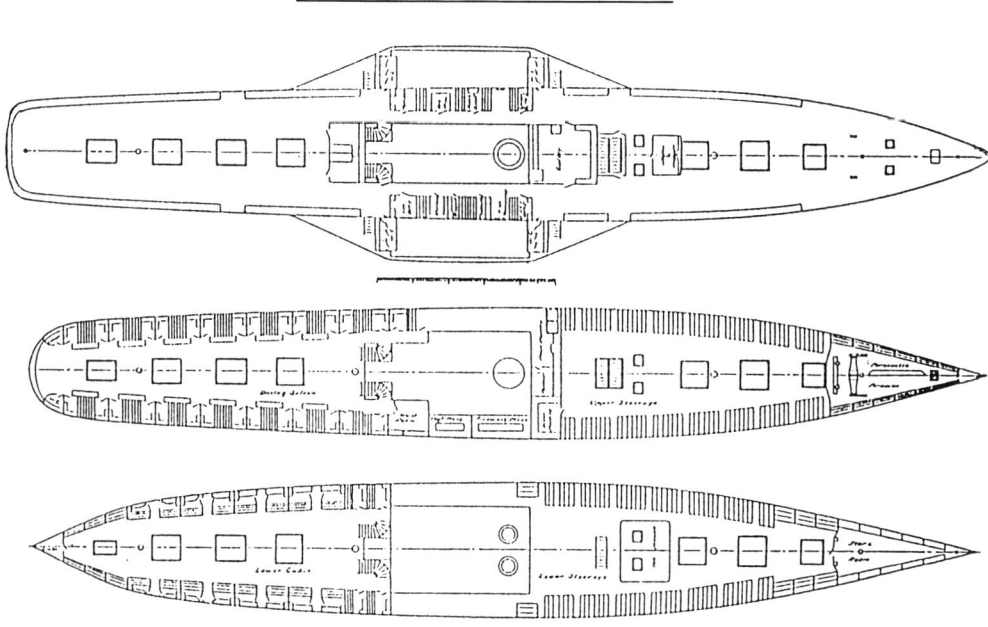

Side-view and Deck Plans of *George Law*, 1853
From Ridgely-Nevitt, "*George Law*," *American Neptune Qtly.*, X (1950), p. 304.

CHAPTER I

A Company and Its Steamer

To facilitate the westward movement and quicken the pace of the settlement of California, the 29th Congress of the United States, called for the building and equipping of five first-class sea-going steamships of not less than fifteen hundred tons burden, to provide mail and passenger service between New York and Chagres, New Granada (Panama). The 1847 bill, signed by President James Knox Polk, required that the ships be propelled by engines of not less than one thousand horsepower each, to be constructed under the superintendency and direction of a naval constructor in the employ of the Navy Department.[1] Attached to the United States Navy, the ships must be constructed so that at the least possible cost they could be converted into war steamers of the first class.[2] The Navy reserved the right at all times to exercise control over the steamships, take them for exclusive use and service of the United States, change machinery and internal arrangements as necessary and determine a proper compensation to the contractor.[3]

While granting an annual subsidy of $290,000, the congressional act directed that the Secretary of the Navy contract with Albert G. Sloo, of Cincinnati, for the transportation of mail twice monthly between New York and Chagres and return, touching at Charleston, Savannah, Havana and New Orleans.

Kentucky-born Albert Sloo had established a reputation for business acumen in streamlining and economizing the postal service and in promoting the establishment of a steamship line on Lake Pontchartrain, Louisiana, between New Orleans and Mobile, Alabama. The line gained the reward of a sizable mail contract, and this successful experience made him a logical choice to promote the New York to Chagres route. But when the task proved beyond his financial capability, Sloo assigned the contract to other experienced, capable and monied hands.

---

[1] George Minot, Esq., ed. *Statutes at Large and Treaties of the United States of America,* (Vol IX, 1851) Section 4.
[2] Ibid., Sections 1 and 3. This conversion was later accomplished for many of them during the Civil War.
[3] Ibid., Section 6.

With Marshall O. Roberts[4] and Bowes R. McIlvane as junior partners, George Law[5] formed the United States Mail Steamship Company (USMSC), and assumed the federal contract that had been assigned to Sloo. Law had participated in contracts to build canals and bridges, had interests in New York railroads and owned the New York Dry Dock Bank. Roberts' interests lay in river steamboats and railroads, and he recognized the potential of these modes of transportation for the gain of untold profits in moving large numbers of passengers. He had a reputation for being a shrewd businessman with political know-how. Better educated than Law, he moved in the right political circles to obtain contracts and otherwise attain his business objectives. Law, on the other hand, was a self-educated man, possessed of boundless energy. Both were ruthless in their business dealings. They worked together to put in place the line of steamers, with Law as president of the USMSC.[6] Roberts handled the business and the political maneuvering. Law supervised the construction of the steamships to meet the requirements of the Navy.

The congressional act did not name shipbuilders. That selection responsibility fell to George Law. However, Navy inspectors monitored the construction progress and Congress required a final acceptance of each ship by the Secretary of the Navy. Major hull constructors of the early steamers included William H. Webb, Smith and Dimon, Bishop & Simonson and William H. Brown—all New York companies.[7] Engine and boiler builders included Morgan Iron Works, T.F. Secor Co., Hogg & Delameter and Stillman, Allen & Co., also of New York.

A major purpose of the steamship routes was to transport mail to the west coast, and destinations with the most settlers were designated as ports. The 1847 Act of Congress directed the Secretary of the Navy to contract for transportation of mail from Panama to "any such port as he may select in the Territory of Oregon." The small settlement of Yerba Buena, the California town on the bay soon to be known as San Francisco (population less than 1000), would shortly become the busiest and most populous west coast port.

Congress offered a choice between steam or sailing vessels, "as shall be deemed most practicable and expedient," for the monthly connection with the Panama route. No contractor being named, the enterprise was left open to bid, and because of the lack of significant commerce

---

[4] Dumas Malone, *Dictionary of American Biography*, Vol. XII, 11.
[5] Ibid., Vol. VI, 39.
[6] Kemble, *Panama Route*, 15-16.
[7] John H. Morrison, *History of New York Shipyards*.

between the east and west coasts, little enthusiasm existed among prospective investors. This attitude changed quickly with the discovery of gold.

After a number of developments, including the decision of Commodore Morris, U.S. Navy, to exclusively use steam vessels between New Granada and the northern terminus at Astoria, Oregon Territory, William H. Aspinwall, another successful New Yorker, became the founder and first president of the new line of ships called the Pacific Mail Steamship Company (PMSC). In late 1850 the USMSC in New York City, and PMSC in San Francisco, agreed to remain on separate sides of the Isthmus.

Mid-century paddle-wheel steamers evidenced the transition between sail and steam by including sails for auxiliary power and control. On long runs, furnace stokers were delighted to see the sails raised, because the assistance from wind power meant a significant reduction in the need for coal. Too, sails afforded an economy of fuel, added power for the relatively low-powered steam engines of the day and provided a bit of insurance for having an adequate supply of coal between ports. The steamer *Falcon*, a vessel of this class, brought the first load of passengers attributed to the news of the gold discovery in December 1848, carrying 178 persons to the docks at Chagres, Panama. The PMSC steamship *California*, having successfully made the trip around Cape Horn, arrived at Panama City to make the western connection with the *Falcon*.

Besides complaints of unpalatable food and a scarcity of it, many travelers were terror-stricken by the danger of shipwreck, and bitterly criticized the USMSC for the inadequacy of lifeboats. An 1851 passenger recalled that his steamer conveyed two lifeboats with a capacity for fifty persons, but transported a load of six hundred passengers.[8] The chances of survival with such a passenger-to-boat ratio were nearly hopeless. Adding to the dangers on these trips, the ever-present fear of cholera, yellow fever and other contagions was sometimes enhanced by vessels carrying twice the number recommended by the shipbuilders. This proximity of bodies, often requiring three per berth in steerage, assured the spread of fatal diseases which claimed the lives of many passengers. Some were committed to the sea. Many died at the Isthmus.

In 1851, more passengers than could be handled had been sent to Chagres, and after weeks awaiting transportation across the Isthmus,[9] were further delayed at Panama City, where hundreds crowded the Grand Plaza. The crossing of the Isthmus, however, continued to be

---

[8] Holliday, 442.
[9] *Panama Star and Herald*, 9 Feb 1851.

improved, first, by construction of a new port, about nine miles from Chagres, named Aspinwall in honor of the PMSC president; second, by the construction of the Panama Railway, another Aspinwall project.[10] The port of Aspinwall, a filled swamp, became the southern terminus for the USMSC.

Passengers departing San Francisco in 1851, and debarking at Panama City, spent another three days of time in reaching Chagres, but by 1852, work on a Panama railroad had progressed to the point where on July 13th of that year *The Panama Herald* commented: "By a new advertisement in our columns today it will be seen that the cars are running to Barbacoas, a few miles from Gorgona. It is coming like the steady march of its own locomotive onward and will probably be in Gorgona by the first of September."[11] By 1855, the crossing of the Isthmus had been tremendously facilitated by completion of the railroad, so that upon the arrival of a steamer at Panama City, its passengers debarked, boarded the railroad, and within "a little more than three hours" were at Aspinwall. In 1857, a load of passengers could board the train on the Pacific side of the Isthmus of Panama in the morning, and be on the Caribbean side within those few hours.

The PMSC became the most prosperous of the two steamship lines, with more care and attention given to personal comfort and reliable schedules.[12] A number of steamships, such as the *Sonora*, were constructed and in service. The popular *Golden Gate*[13] entered service for the PMSC in November 1851.

Thought to be primarily interested in profit, the USMSC was from time to time accused of flagrantly disregarding the welfare of its passengers. On the route east of Aspinwall, although the seas and weather were

---

[10] Aspinwall foresaw the need for a railroad across the Isthmus and, despite general predictions of failure, succeeded in securing a charter from the New York legislature, granted to him, his brother Lloyd, Samuel W. Comstock, Henry Chauncey and John L. Stephens. Under engineers George M. Tooten and John C. Trautevine, forty-nine miles of road were completed in five years. In 1849, Aspinwall, two New York uncles, G.G. and S.S. Howland, Chauncey, Richard Alsop, and Edwin Bartlett founded the Pacific Mail Steamship Company. Malone, Vol. I, 396.

[11] Neville stated that in 1854 the tracks ended at a "point called Summit," requiring an eleven-hour trip on mule-back between there and Panama City. Amelia Ransome Neville, *The Fantastic City*, 29. E.W. Wright, *Lewis & Dryden's Marine History of . . .* , 188.

[12] During the decade of the 1850s the following steamships were among those employed by Pacific Mail in service between San Francisco and Panama: *Golden Age, Golden Gate, Panama, Sonora, John L. Stephens, Tennessee* and the *Winfield Scott*. Kemble, *Panama Route*, 88.

[13] The *Golden Gate* was built in New York City in the William H. Webb shipyard, the "Gate," a 2000-ton wooden side-wheel steamer with three decks and nearly 270 feet long. She made the passage from Panama City to San Francisco in eleven days and four hours, a record which held until 1855. In 1861, Richard Henry Dana revisited San Francisco as a passenger on this steamer. Kemble, *Panama Route*, 228. William H. Webb, *New Era in Shipbuilding and Plans of Wooden Vessels . . .* Vol. I.

often considerably rougher than conditions on the Pacific side, from December 1848 until the fall of 1857, the USMSC established an excellent safety record. During hundreds of sailings, only two ships were lost: the *Cherokee*, burned in her wharf at New York when a boiler exploded (a common problem with the early steamers), and the *Crescent City*, ran on Manatillan Reef near Nassau, Bahamas. Although a total wreck, most of her freight was saved, and no lives were lost.

The steamship *George Law*, later renamed the *Central America*, was built to be applied against the five ship congressional requirement of 1847, and was the last acquired to satisfy the contract. George Law personally superintended the construction of the steamer, and as an honor to him, the ship was given his name. However, in March 1853, after a disagreement,[14] Law and Roberts parted company. Law sold his nearly one-half of the outstanding shares of the company to Marshall Roberts for the sum of eighty thousand dollars, and Roberts then became president of the USMSC.[15] He yearned to change the name of the steamer that bore Law's name, but at that time could not do so, the change of any vessel's name being prohibited by law.

By November 1852, the Navy had accepted the vessels *Ohio*, *Georgia*, *Illinois*, *Star of the West* and *George Law* for the New York to Aspinwall run.[16] From PMSC Roberts bought at a cost of $225,000 the *Empire City*, a 1,750 ton steamer which, like the *George Law*, had been constructed by William H. Webb, New York. She ran between New York and Aspinwall until 1856, when she joined the *Crescent City*, *Cherokee* and *Falcon* in serving on the New York-Havana-New Orleans route.[17]

The *George Law* had been launched October 28, 1852, but did not enter service until nearly a year later. She left New York on October 20, 1853, for her first of many trips to Aspinwall. In December, she returned to New York with 467 passengers, $877,000 in specie or treasure, and with San Francisco mail dated November 16, 1853. On leaving Havana the ship had encountered a near-hurricane which

---

[14] In 1852, Law became involved in a dispute with President Millard Fillmore over allowing the purser of the *Crescent City* to enter Havana harbor after being forbidden by the captain-general of Cuba to do so. Fillmore had urged Law to avoid trouble, but the combative Law's disregard for the President's wishes brought about the removal of mails from the steamers of the USMSC. This led to his problems with Roberts. Malone, Vol VI, 40.

[15] Kemble, *Panama Route*, 88.

[16] United States Navy, *Aspinwall Line*, 130.

[17] The *Philadelphia*, originally purchased by Howland and Aspinwall in 1850 for the New York to Chagres route, was purchased by USMSC in January 1851 for about the original purchase price of $190,000. The USMSC line later purchased the *Ariel*, *Northern Light*, and *North Star* from Cornelius Vanderbilt, the *St. Louis* from the N.Y. Havre Steam Navigation Co., and had constructed for its service the *Granada* and *Moses Taylor*. Kemble, *Panama Route*, 215-247.

extended along the Atlantic Coast, and which she weathered well to arrive in New York December 12th.[18] Then, in February 1854, the Navy accepted the steamer as complying with the conditions of the government mail contract.[19]

A three-masted side-wheel steamer of the first class, eleventh of twenty-five ocean-going steamships built by the Webb firm, the ship was first known simply as Hull 71. Webb built her hull 278 feet 3 inches in length by a width of 40 feet and a depth of 32 feet, with an unburdened weight of 2,141 tons.[20]

The Morgan Iron Works built her machinery, which included two engines of the inclined, oscillating type, with sixty-five inch cylinders and a stroke of ten feet. All the working parts were wrought iron, and very heavy; her crank pins, for instance, were 13 inches in diameter, and said to be as large as those of the giant trans-Atlantic steamship *Persia's*. Morgan installed two boilers, two steam Worthington pumps (a direct-acting steam pump), two or three hand force pumps and life-preservers for a full load of passengers.

The steamer had three masts, three full decks, orlop decks (temporary decks) at each end, a round stern, and no cutwater (the forward edge of the stem, dividing the water as it advances). Her keel below timbers was 15 inches, draft forward 8 feet 1 inch, draft aft 7 feet 2 inches; mean draft 7 feet 7½ inches.

The spar deck,[21] described as an expanse of planking, was broken by a series of large hatches which gave light and ventilation to the accommodations below. An open rail surrounded the deck, with a rope netting lashed to it. There were wooden benches built against its stanchions. Aft of the foremast, the wheel house,[22] housed a large double steering wheel, and "abaft of that, two small hatches gave access to an insulated compartment on the third deck for perishable provisions and ice. Then came a companionway leading to the steerage forward." The galley

---

[18] Erik Heyl, *Early American Steamers*, Vol 1, 171.

[19] Kemble, *Panama Route*, 86.

[20] William M. Lytle, *Merchant Steam Vessels of . . .* , 74. Webb, *New Era . . . and Plans of Wooden Vessels*.

[21] An unsigned, contemporary model of this steamer is in the U.S. Naval Academy Museum at Annapolis, Maryland. Historian Cedric Ridgely-Nevitt, found that detailed deck arrangement drawings are very rare for any ships of the period. Since neither hurricane deck (upper, light deck) plans, sail plans, nor profile of the ship were available, he used the model as a guide in reconstructing those items. Cedric Ridgely-Nevitt, "The United States Mail Steamer *George Law*," 307.

[22] The term "wheelhouse" has been occasionally applied to the paddle box, which is the paddle wheel housing. Normally, the wheelhouse is the pilothouse, which contains the steering wheel of the vessel. When a person was said to be standing on the wheelhouse, as has been the case in some newspaper descriptions, he was standing on the paddle-box (wheel-guard).

(kitchen and cooking apparatus), just forward of the stack, "and the central deck-house formed part of the machinery space with a pair of curving stairways leading to the cabin aft and the captain's stateroom in way of the mainmast." Quarters for the other officers, the doctor, purser, and baggagemaster were next to the paddle boxes. Water closets were found on the guards and two more aft of the first cabin area for men and women. Ashes could be dumped overboard through a scuttle (small opening or hatchway, large enough to admit a man) in the inboard side of the paddlebox.

"On the second deck, the crew berthed in the bow, with a center-line bulkhead[23] separating the black gang (stokehold crewmen) from the deck force. At the after end of the forecastle were the windlass and bitts[24] for the anchor chain, but while this arrangement for anchor handling gave the passengers an unobstructed upper deck for their pleasure, it did nothing for the cleanliness, dryness, and comfort of the crew."[25] Steerage passengers were carried forward on both the second and third decks in three-high tiers of berths against the side of the ship with the center portion of the second deck kept clear for messing space. Pantry space, underneath the galley, was connected to it by a dumb-waiter serving both the steerage forward and the dining saloon aft.

The cabin passengers were carried aft in staterooms on the second and third decks. Based on the interior appointments of other Webb steamers, such as the *Empire City*, it is likely that the *George Law* had rosewood furnishings, richly colored damask upholstery, ornamental columns with gilded Corinthian capitals, doors decorated with nautical scenes, and murals on the bulkheads. The overhang of the light hurricane deck protected windows in the deck-houses from sun and rain. All the large hatches shown on the main deck were repeated on decks below for the triple purpose of admitting light, air and cargo. Orlop decks fitted in the holds aided in the stowage of cargo. The original plan provided for four lifeboats, two more being added at a later date.

The black hull had its lower wale painted red and the forward fancy rail varnished. All deck houses were varnished, paddle wheels red, funnel black with a red band at the top, and the paddle boxes black except for gold semicircles at their centers. To keep her free of worms, she was coppered below the water line.

Accommodation plans provided space for 110 cabin passengers,

---

[23] Bulkhead: any upright partition separating compartments.
[24] Forecastle: that part of the upper deck forward of the foremast. Windlass: a device for hoisting or hauling, usually with a crank. Bitt: a vertical timber or metal casting for securing ropes, etc.
[25] Ridgely-Nevitt, "*George Law*," 309.

based on berths two high, about 40 of them being second cabin spaces in the lower cabin. The ship could accommodate 384 steerage passengers (based on double bunks three high), 16 officers and a crew of 36. Nevertheless, on May 24, 1855, she arrived in New York with 817 passengers on board.

Congress required that officers of the United States Navy, not below the grade of lieutenant, command the mail steamers sailing between New York and New Granada. They were selected by the contractor with the approval of the Secretary of the Navy, the latter ensuring that these services would be "suitably accommodated without charge to the government."[26] The assignment as captains of the steamers became a highly desirable one for United States Naval officers as considerable experience with steam vessels could be gained and put to future use in the "steam Navy."

On her maiden voyage to Aspinwall, the *George Law* departed New York City October 20, 1853, under the command of Captain John N. McGowan. She continued on a departure schedule from the New York port on about the twentieth of each month with the exception of an eighteen month period between August 1854 and February 1855, when her departure date was the fifth of each month.

On occasion she stopped at Havana, Cuba, or Kingston, Jamaica, and at a speed of approximately eleven knots (12.65 miles per hour) made the Aspinwall to New York trip in about nine days. The record of her sailings was excellent, she having remained in New York only once beyond the normal period for routine repairs and overhaul.

In February 1855 the vessel hosted "sixteen guests who had been invited to attend the opening ceremonies of the Panama Railroad from Chagres to Panama. As she came into the harbor the crew decorated the steamer with flags and bunting. The guests of honor and four-hundred-and-fifty-seven additional passengers landed to board the gaily decorated train of nine coaches and a baggage car." At 9:00 A.M., the train left Chagres, "stopping at the meeting place of the east and west sections where various public and private dignitaries gave speeches, accompanied by the obligatory rounds of toasts. A public reception was tendered at Panama, followed by a banquet, grand ball and other festivities. Then the guests returned to Chagres, sailing later to New York."[27]

---

[26] The Congressional Act of 1847 provided for the assignment to each steamer of four passed-midshipmen of the United States Navy, to serve as watch officers, and one agent, to be appointed by the Postmaster General, who would have charge of the mails to be transported. Minot, 187. The passed-midshipman requirement was not enforced.

[27] Heyl, 171. Navy Historical Center Archives.

In June 1857, the ship was thoroughly overhauled on dry dock in the Webb Yard. Her boilers were repaired and her bottom partly recoppered, the main portion of the hull being found in good order. With a recent congressional decision permitting such a name change,[28] the Secretary of the Interior approved Roberts' request, and the *George Law* became the *Central America*. It had taken five years for USMSC president Marshall Roberts to find the legal means of effecting the change. During June and July 1857, she made her first trip to Aspinwall with her new name.

Although President Polk, the 29th Congress and capable contractors laid the ground work for easing a heavy migration to California, the unprecedented demand for transportation between the East Coast and California gold could not have remotely been foreseen. In spite of problems and discomforts, it became the world's most profitable route.

Until 1855, the *George Law* sailed under the command of four different masters. John McGowan commanded her for the first six trips; Lt. Gustav V. Fox, (Secretary of the Navy during the Civil War) for the 7th through 14th, and again the 17th through 19th trips; Lt. McKinstry, the 15th and 16th; Alfred G. Gray, her 20th through 24th round trips.[29] Beginning with the 25th trip, Lt. William Lewis Herndon became her captain.

The character of the steamship commanders led Lady Emmeline Wortley to observe that "the captains of the steamboats appear a remarkably gentlemanly-like race of men in general, particularly courteous in their deportment and very considerate and obliging to the passengers." On an 1856 voyage with her husband, British Army Captain Brent Neville, Amelia Ransome Neville, of San Francisco, said "Captain Herndon of the *George Law* . . . with all the gallantry of a Navy officer, gave us the daytime use of his cabin when we sailed into hot weather. Doctor Tennison and the first officer, Mr. Van Rensselaer, also helped to make this part of the voyage a happy memory." Indeed, Lieutenant Herndon, U.S.N., a remarkable person, had in recent years become a national figure.

---

[28] Minot, Chapter IV, March 5, 1856.
[29] Ridgely-Nevitt, "*George Law*," 313.

Commander William Lewis Herndon
Courtesy, United States Naval Academy Museum

CHAPTER II

A Master For a Steamer

William Lewis Herndon, descendant of seventeenth century settlers from England, entered this life on October 25, 1813. The fifth of seven children, he grew up in Fredericksburg, Virginia. He was named for his uncle, Captain William Lewis, U.S. Navy, who in 1815 died on the U.S. brig *Epervier*. His father, Dabney Herndon, Esq., a respected citizen of that city, in 1805 became the magistrate for the corporation of Fredericksburg, and later, cashier of the Farmers Bank, a position he held until his death, December 20, 1824. The family resided on the second floor of the brick bank building.[1]

The eleven-year-old son, known to his family as Lewis, was left an orphan when his mother, Elizabeth Hull Herndon died on April 20, 1825.[2] The boy then became the ward of William I. Roberts, cashier of the office of Discount and Deposits of the Bank of Virginia, in Fredericksburg.[3]

In 1827, projecting the wish of Dabney Herndon for a naval officer's career for his son, Roberts requested an appointment for Lewis as a midshipman. From persons who knew him, five additional letters[4] accompanied Roberts' letter to the Secretary of the Navy, all highly praising Lewis as "a youth of fine habits," "very promising," "highly deserving," "a young gentleman of a mind of a superior order, . . . of good moral character, and a youth of great promise." The letter from B.R. Wellford prophesied: "If you grant this request I feel no hesitation in saying that he will at a future day reflect credit on the administration which introduced him into our navy."

There was not yet a naval academy, future naval officers being required to spend a number of years at sea under the supervision of a ship's master. At such time as he deemed it appropriate, the master recommended for his charge a commission in the grade of "passed

---

[1] John Goodwin Herndon, *The Herndons of the American Revolution*. Matthew Fontaine Maury letter to The Honorable Isaac Toucey, Secretary of the Navy, Washington, D.C., 19 Oct 1857.
[2] *The New York Times*, 19 Sep 1857, 1-1.
[3] William I. Roberts, Fredericksburg, VA, letter to The Honorable Samuel Lewis Southard, Secretary of the Navy, (Washington, D.C.), recommendation for warrant as midshipman, 25 Nov 1827.
[4] Navy Historical Center Archives.

midshipman." That period of time varied with the captain under whom the candidate served, taking from five to ten years, or longer.[5]

At the age of fifteen, Lewis entered the Navy as a midshipman, and on his first voyage, embarked on the frigate *Guerriere* for a four year cruise to the Pacific. This was followed by another three year stint in the Mediterranean on board the frigate *Constellation*, and then, on the ship *Independence*, a cruise to the coast of Brazil. He became a passed midshipman on June 14, 1834, at the age of 20. On February 26, 1841, the Navy promoted Lewis to the grade of lieutenant. By this time he had proven himself a capable and skilled naval officer.

The Seminole Indian war erupted in Florida, and Herndon volunteered for duty in support of that effort. In August 1841 he was placed in command of the Revenue Cutter *Jefferson*, at Indian Key, and for two years, made penetration missions into the Everglades, "driving Indians from the recesses of the swamps to the arms of the waiting troops on shore."[6] He supported the troops of Generals Winfield Scott and Richard Keith Call, and for bravery during the campaign his home state of Virginia awarded him an elaborately engraved sword.[7]

Lieutenant Matthew Fontaine Maury, cousin and brother-in-law of Lewis Herndon, was a very unusual man. Being an experienced naval officer of extraordinary intelligence, about eight years senior in age to Lewis, Maury exerted a profound influence on his career. Disabled for active service, Matthew Maury spent several years at Fredericksburg in study and in preparing a series of articles for publication. These writings, which he called "The Lucky Bag," under the pen name Harry Bluff, appeared in the *Southern Literary Messenger*. They "wrought a revolution in the Navy Department, and led to the establishment of the Naval Academy, the Memphis Navy-Yard, and the general warehousing system."[8]

With data which he collected from sea captains, he charted the sea lanes and the Gulf Stream. In 1842, by appointment, he became Superintendent of the Depot of Charts and Instruments in Washington, which, under his direction, became the National Observatory.

---

[5] In the Navy of the 1850s there were no grades of ensign, lieutenant junior grade or lieutenant commander. The progression was passed midshipman, lieutenant and commander. Navy Historical Center Archives.

[6] *The New York Times*, 19 Sep 1857, 1-2.

[7] In August 1857, Lieutenant Herndon left his sword and several boxes containing effects with James C. McGuire, New York auctioneer. *The New York Herald*, 26 Sep 1857, 8-2, quoting *Washington Union*, 24 Sep 1857.

[8] Maury's paper on the enlargement of the Illinois and Michigan Canal brought special thanks from the state of Illinois. Matthew F. Maury, *The Physical Geography of the Sea*, 226-249. Peter Karsten, *The Naval Aristocracy*, 284. *Descendants of John de la Fontaine*. Adelaide R. Hasse, *Tentative Biography of Matthew Fontaine Maury*.

Maury made many scientific contributions which included pilot charts, deep sea studies (making him a forerunner of modern oceanography), reorganization of the Navy administration into bureaus, and many more. He furnished plans for the Atlantic cable, and was the father of the modern science of torpedo and mine laying. Some thought his greatest works were the charting of the winds and the Gulf Stream. He received honors from universities and learned societies, and decorations from emperors, kings and popes.

A foremost scientist of the day, he exerted considerable influence on Herndon. Maury discountenanced the Seminole War. He wanted to remove Lewis from the operation, and proceeded, in late 1842, to effect his reassignment to the newly formed National Observatory where, intermittently until 1847, Herndon worked diligently under an exacting taskmaster, Maury. Often required to make round-the-clock astronomical observations and to spend long hours on masses of scientific details in a type of assignment he disliked, he found himself emotionally ill and very much discontented.[9]

When the Mexican war broke out, Commodore Matthew Calbraith Perry (early proponent of the steam navy), then in the Gulf of Mexico, asked for an intelligent officer who could speak the Spanish language. Lieutenant Herndon received orders from the Secretary of the Navy to fill this requirement. Placed in command of the *Iris*,[10] (1847) a small war steamer, he successfully carried out dangerous assignments between the American squadron and the troops on shore.

After the Caribbean assignment Herndon spent another year at the Washington Observatory, where he "traced the seasonal migration of right and sperm whales."[11] From there he joined the Pacific Squadron's sloop-of-war *Vandalia*.

Again Maury exerted his influence on Herndon's career. He presented to the secretary of the Navy a plan for the exploration of the Amazon River and valley, and recommended Lieutenant Herndon for that very difficult and important assignment.[12] Said Herndon:

Attached to the United States ship *Vandalia*, of the Pacific Squadron, I

---

[9] Frank V. Rigler, "William Lewis Herndon," 1.

[10] The *Iris*, under the command of Herndon, delivered food to American refugees, reported to be starving on the beach at Campeche, Yucatan. Samuel Eliot Morison, *"Old Bruin": Commodore Matthew Calbraith Perry*, 247-8.

[11] Edward F. Heite, "Scientist on the Bridge," 4.

[12] Maury feared that slavery could bring about the disintegration of the Union, his answer being to find another home for the American slaves by selling them to the Amazon planters. Once done, this, to his way of thinking, would enable the U.S. to outlaw slavery. "The southern states," he wrote in 1850, "may emancipate just as New York and Massachusetts." James P. Reddick, Jr., "Herndon, Maury and the Amazon Basin," 56-63. William L. Herndon, *Exploration of the Valley of the Amazon*, (1854), xiii.

received a communication from the Superintendent of the National Observatory, informing me that orders to explore the Valley of the Amazon would be sent me by the next mail steamer. The ship was then bound for the Sandwich Islands, but Captain Gardner, with that kindness which ever characterized his intercourse with his officers, did not hesitate to detach me from the ship, and to give me permission to await, at Valparaiso, the arrival of my instructions.

Herndon left no doubt of his fondness for his navy career and his comrades, saying:

On the 6th of August, [1850] I unexpectedly saw, from the windows of the club-house at Valparaiso, the topsails of the ship mounting to the mastheads. I saw that she must needs make a stretch in-shore to clear the rocks that lie off the western point of the bay, and desirous to say farewell to my friends, I leaped into a shoreboat, and shoved off, with the hope of reaching her before she went about. The oarsmen, influenced by the promise of a pair of dollars if they put me on board, bent to their oars with a will, and the light whale-boat seemed to fly; but just as I was clearing the outer line of merchantmen, the ship came sweeping up to the wind; and as she gracefully fell off on the other tack, her royals and courses were set, and bending to the steady northeast breezes, she darted out of the harbor at a rate that set pursuit at defiance. God's blessing go with the beautiful ship, and the gallant gentlemen, her officers, who had been to me as brothers.

[Concerning Navy life, he said:] My residence in Valparaiso had made new friends and established new ties, that I found painful to break; but this is the lot of the navy officer: separated from his family for years, he is brought into the closest and most intimate association with his messmates, and forms ties which are made but to be broken, generally by many years of separation. Taken from these, he is thrown among strangers, and becomes dependent upon their kindness and hospitality for the only enjoyments that make his life endurable. Receiving these, his heart yearns towards the donors; and my Valparaiso friends will readily believe that I was sad enough when compelled to leave them.[13]

Lieutenant Herndon's orders were delayed by the death on July 9, 1850, of President Zachary Taylor, "Old Rough and Ready," followed by a subsequent change in the Cabinet as Millard Fillmore succeeded him. Herndon spent the time at Valparaiso in improving his use of the Spanish language and in gathering essential information regarding his route of exploration, of which he said "I probably could have got nowhere else."[14]

---

[13] Herndon, *Exploration* . . . , (1854), 1.
[14] From the commander of the English naval forces in the Pacific, Admiral Hornby, Herndon obtained all writings on the subject of the Amazon which had been stored in the naval library. He

The Navy Department, on February 15, 1851, issued to Lieutenant Herndon explicit and detailed orders for the pursuance of the Amazon exploration. William Alexander Graham, Secretary of the Navy, instructed him to cross the Cordilleras (the Andes and its component ranges) and explore the Amazon from its source to its mouth, gathering information on the condition of the Amazon valley, navigability of its streams, data on inhabitants, trade and products, its climate, soil and production, undeveloped commercial resources, condition of the silver mines at Peru and Bolivia, and a number of other facts.[15]

To accompany Herndon, the Navy selected Passed Midshipman Lardner Gibbon, "a prudent and intelligent officer." In addition to his exploration of Amazon tributaries, Gibbon made many exceptional drawings of the scenery, flora and fauna along the route.

Because of the "geographical situation and commercial position of the Amazon," Graham emphasized the importance to the United States of free navigation on the river. This was a sensitive assignment because the government of Brazil, for national reasons, had not opened the Amazon as an international waterway, a major objective being for Herndon to probe this possibility.

It was characteristic of Herndon that he did not waver, did not deviate from his objectives or his principles. He did not allow himself to succumb to homesickness or longing for his family. Having been away on a number of assignments, he had learned to adapt himself to periodic isolation from them.

In his report, *Exploration of the Valley of the Amazon,* Herndon allowed a feeling of wistfulness. Near a settlement of Combos Indians on the Amazon, he remarked nostalgically, "It was quite a treat to see so familiar a flower as the convolvulus growing on the bank. It was not so large or so gay as in our gardens, but had a home look about it that was quite pleasing." Another occasion evoked patriotic feelings. While on a very tedious ascent of the Catalina River, he walked, gun on shoulder, for miles along the beaches.

> My greatest pleasure is to watch the boat struggling against the tide. This is always accompanied with emotions of pride, mingled with a curious and scarcely definable feeling of surprise. It was almost startling to see, at her mast-head, the beautiful and well-beloved flag of my country dancing

---

consulted with other knowledgeable individuals concerning their particular specialties. Herndon, *Exploration . . . ,* (1854), 2.

[15] For the assignment, Graham agreed to honor Lieutenant Herndon's draft "for a sum not to exceed five thousand dollars, to cover your expenses by the way." Since the expenses would be "mostly for mules and arrieros [guides], boats and boat's crews," he supposed that "the sum named will be more than sufficient." Ibid., 21.

merrily in the breeze on the waters of the strange river, and waiving above the heads of the swarthy and grim figures below. I felt a proud affection for it; I had carried it where it had never been before; there was a bond between us; we were alone in a strange land; and it and I were brothers in the wilderness.[16]

Maury described Lewis Herndon as "a man of slight figure, but of intrepid spirit."[17] In 1852, Herndon commented that, near Tarma, "One of our peons carried on his back, for a whole day, (fifteen miles), a bundle of alfalfa that Gibbon could not lift with ease, and pronounced, upon trial, to be heavier than I am, or upwards of one hundred and twenty-five pounds." He gave another indication of his appearance when he wrote in Huanuco, Peru: "The people are civil and respectful, and, save a curious stare now and then at my spectacles and red beard, are by no means offensive in their curiosity."

For a man of his physique, the journey was particularly fatiguing. After many months of trekking, Herndon considered exploring the Purus River, but said "I am compelled to acknowledge that when I arrived at Barra, near the mouth of the Purus, I was broken down, and felt convinced I could not stand the hardship and exposure necessary for a thorough examination of the river." The journey was extremely strenuous, fraught with dangers from nature, men, animals and food.

Near the end of the trek, at Para, Herndon said, "I was so worn out when we arrived that, although I had not heard from home, and knew that there must be letters for me, I would not take the trouble to go to the consul's house to seek them . . . . I anchored in the stream, and, wrapping myself in my blanket, went sullenly to sleep."

Herndon revealed himself to be an astute leader in the management of men. Once, when ready to depart the Mission at Tierra Blanca, his oarsmen were drunk and unwilling to leave. His native assistant, Don Manuel Ijurra, angered, "demanded a gun, that he might bring them to obedience." Said Herndon:

> I soothed him, however, and went up to the house, where, by taking a drink with them, and practicing the arts that I have often practiced in getting off to the ship refractory sailors who were drinking on shore, I succeeded in getting off a sufficient number of them to work the boat, and shoved off with as drunken a crew as one could desire, leaving the small boat for the others to follow; this they are sure to do when they find that their clothes and bedding have been taken away.[18]

---

[16] Herndon, *Exploration* . . . , (1854), 200.
[17] *The New York Times*, 19 Sep 1857, 1-3.
[18] Herndon, *Exploration* . . . , (1854), 199.

Herndon emerged from his Amazon adventure even more a proponent of steam vessels than before. Convinced of their necessity in Amazon navigation and trade, he encouraged American employment of steamships to conduct operations up the vast river to Peru, a development eventually accomplished in 1867.

As the first American to explore the Amazon River from its source to its mouth, a distance of over 4,100 miles, Lieutenant Herndon had carried out his direction with enthusiasm, perseverance and skill. Returning to the United States in 1852, he spent several months in Washington, preparing the report on his expedition. In an interesting style of writing, his account of the journey and observations arrived on the desk of President Millard Fillmore, who sent it to the House of Representatives. When congress published it in 1854 as a House Document, Herndon received wide international acclaim, and the writing has been described as a "scholarly interpretation of the meteorology, anthropology, geology and natural history of the Amazon."[19] According to historian Basso, Mark Twain said that Herndon's report inspired him to write *Life on the Mississippi*.[20]

On March 9, 1836, at the age of twenty-three, Herndon had married Francis Elizabeth Hansbrough, of Virginia, and their daughter, Ellen, was born August 30, 1837. The absence of Lewis on naval assignments often interrupted their happiness. The time spent in completing his Amazon report enabled Herndon to spend the remainder of the year 1852 with his family. To the pleasure of her father, Ellen had become distinguished for the loveliness of her singing voice. Miss Herndon, it was later said, "has a fine singing voice, and is considered one of the best private singers in the country."[21]

The Navy soon gave Lieutenant Herndon an assignment to the Baltic on the steam frigate *San Jacinto*, then another on the *Potomac*, under Commodore Paulding. Whether at home or at sea, the exemplary character and integrity of Herndon were in evidence. His pleasant and gracious personality endeared him to many. In 1842, he became a member of the Episcopal Church and often read the service on board ship. "The humblest sailor was not committed to the deep without the burial service read over him by his captain."[22] Herndon was the

---

[19] Heite, "Scientist on the Bridge," 5.
[20] "Mark Twain, reading its [Herndon's] pages as a young man of 21 was so carried away that he determined to seek his fortune in South America . . . caused him to go down the Mississippi for the first time . . . subsequently led him to describe Herndon's book as one of the turning points of his life." Historian Basso refers to "Turning Point," a 1910 article by Twain. Herndon, *Exploration* . . . , (1952), ix.
[21] *The New York Daily Tribune*, 19 Sep 1857, 5-2. *The New York Herald*, 19 Sep 1857, 1-3.
[22] *The New York Times*, 19 Sep 1857, 1-2.

personification of Richard Henry Dana's ideal sea captain—a man of intelligence, firm, with a religious sensitivity, and with a fair judgment tempered with mercy.[23]

On September 14, 1855, he was promoted to the grade of commander, and placed on extended leave of absence to accept command of the steamer *George Law,* with home port in New York. There he and his family resided while he made monthly trips to Panama in transporting passengers and mail. His first round-trip to Aspinwall was the twenty-fifth for the steamship.[24]

In June 1857 the *George Law* was renamed the *Central America,* and Herndon made a July voyage to Aspinwall and return to New York. In early August 1857, Captain Herndon left his home in high spirits, anticipating a speedy return from Aspinwall. He bade good-bye to his wife, Elizabeth, and daughter, Ellen, who followed him to the door "and in a merry whim threw after him an old slipper—traditionally a good luck gesture to a parting friend. He turned and smiled at her, and waving his hand pleasantly, left his home."[25]

---

[23] Observing and experiencing the brutality of some sea captains, Dana completed an interrupted study of law and became a defender of the seaman's rights. Richard Henry Dana, *Two Years Before the Mast,* 3.

[24] On the steamer's 39th trip, Lieutenant Hunter commanded in place of Herndon. Cedric Ridgely-Nevitt, *American Steamships on the Atlantic,* 313.

[25] *The New York Times,* 19 Sep 1857, 1-3.

CHAPTER III

The Voyage

While Captain Herndon and his crew sailed from New York, August 20, 1857, on the *Central America's* forty-fourth trip, more than four hundred people in the western city of San Francisco purchased tickets for departure, the same date, on the steamship *Sonora*, destined for Panama and transfer to the *Central America* at Aspinwall.

San Francisco had been several times destroyed by fire. Each reconstruction of the city saw improvement as it progressed from a city of canvas to one of wood, then to a metropolis of bricks, a thriving port city.[1] By 1853 she was called the "Queen of the Pacific." She had 160 hotels, 18 churches, 10 schools, 3 hospitals, 14 fire companies, 19 banking firms, 13 foundries and more. Built over piles in the water were two and one-half miles of streets and twelve wharves. There were planked roads and a few of cobblestones. Around the two major public squares were a large number of elegant and substantial brick and stone buildings with such fire-proofing as exterior window-shutters and doors of thick wrought-iron.

By 1854, the United States Mint had opened, streets were lighted with coal gas, and amusement parks, such as Russ' Gardens, were developed where out-door concerts and other entertainments were enjoyed. Two omni-bus lines ran to the Mission district. Population pressures continued. In 1855, more than thirty-one thousand persons and eleven-hundred-fifty vessels arrived from all over the world, leading to the establishment of over twenty-seven foreign consulates by 1857.

And, by 1857, San Francisco proudly included several new buildings of respectable size, housing government, professional and business offices. Riddle's Building, on the south side of Clay Street, between Sansome and Leidesdorf, housed the *California Chronicle,* published by Frank Soulé. The Customs House Block, described as a large and elegant building at the south-east corner of Sansome and Sacramento

---

[1] Frank Soulé, *Annals of San Francisco,* 494-548. John S. Hittell, *History . . . of San Francisco.*

San Francisco from Rincon Point, 1856
Courtersy, California State Library

streets, contained the Custom House, Naval Office with related offices, stores and at least ten importers including Swiss importer Francois Pahud (pronounced pa-hyoo). One of the few survivors of the 1850 fire, Howard's Building, on the west side of Montgomery, between Clay and Commercial streets, housed the state supreme court and a number of attorneys.

Capable of coining about thirty millions of dollars yearly in different kinds of pieces, the San Francisco Mint, another three-story structure on Commercial Street between Montgomery and Kearny, had prepared a shipment of gold bars and coins destined for New York City banks. The treasure would be transported to Panama on the steamship *Sonora*.

Pioneers often left wives and families in eastern homes until their return but, despite the hardships, many wives and children crossed the Isthmus to join their husbands in the West. A surprising number of men and women made periodic trips to visit families back home, and some men made regular business trips to the United States. Others went home to marry, then returned to California with their brides. Many went home with only enough money to make the trip, having either failed to find the wealth they had sought, or lost all they had, sometimes by an unlucky poker hand or throw of dice. The many thousands of California bound men crossing the North American plains virtually always made the return trip by sea via the Panama route.[2]

California real estate values appreciated drastically, as did the prices of all commodities. For travelers, the original first cabin fare between San Francisco and Panama was set by the PMSC at $250; second class, or lower cabin, at $200; steerage $100. However, scalping of tickets often raised the prices, and single steerage tickets in 1849 sold for as much as $1,000.[3] Some ticket agents used other devious schemes to exact higher prices. For example, by convincing the purchaser that all tickets were sold out, an agent would come up with some at a higher rate, and pocket the extra cash. In 1857, laws were enacted in an attempt to prevent such swindles. Nevertheless, on June 15, 1857, a complaint against the cost of steerage passage to New York appeared on page one of *The Sacramento Union*, indicating that the PMSC then charged $300 for first cabin, $250 for second and $150 for steerage. The *Union* editorialized that the steerage price was beyond the reach of the most needy classes of people—merchants, traders, miners and farmers.[4] The Panama Railroad Company, in the *Panama Star and Herald* of September 15, 1857, advertised freight rates across the Isthmus at $1.80 per cubic foot.

West of Aspinwall

Steamer Day!!! Californians excitedly swarmed the San Francisco waterfront for the bi-weekly arrival and departure of the steamships. This day it was the Vallejo Street wharf where all residents gathered to see old friends or relatives depart.

The Daily Alta California of August 20, 1857, announced the departure of one of the steamers of the Pacific Mail Steamship Company: "The mail steamship *Sonora*,[5] Whiting, Commander, takes her depar-

---

[2] Holliday, 464.

[3] Kemble, *Panama Route*, 37. Lewis, *Sea Routes*, 194.

[4] "A simple field hand is able to save by extraordinary exertion $8 per month in the Eastern states. To enable him to come to California he must have at least $175 [including] $10 for incidental expenses, baggage charges, Isthmus money &c., and $15 wherewith to arrive here, so as not to be thrown absolutely destitute on our shores." *Sacramento Daily Union*, 15 Jun 1857, 1-4.

[5] In June of 1854, the new steamer *Sonora* was being outfitted at Benicia, California, to depart on June 16th for Panama. She was built at Westervelt's yard in New York, at a cost of about $260,000, and was said to be a vast improvement over most steamers of the day. Captain R.L. Whiting commanded the vessel on her first run to Panama, and he continued as her master. *Daily Alta California*, 10 Jun 1854, 2-4.

Steamer Day in San Francisco
Courtesy, San Francisco Maritime National Historical Park

ture from this port at nine o'clock this morning for Panama. She carries down a small load of passengers, but amongst them are the names of several prominent citizens. Their absence, we are pleased to say, will be but temporary." One of the "prominent citizens," Dr. Bates, a former senator and State treasurer, was placed under arrest, being charged with drunkenness and embezzlement. He missed his passage. Judge Heydenfeldt, detained by some last-moment business, decided to take the next steamer, but Judge Alonzo C. Monson,[6] having two days previously resigned his judgeship of the 6th Judicial District, Sacramento, prepared to return to his home in New York. In Sacramento, *The Evening Bee* reported on the sponsoring of a banquet for him "by the members of the bar and merchants of the city, at which one of the most brilliant assemblies of notable men in the history of the State gathered." Earlier, the judge, an inveterate gambler, had lost his Sacramento home (at 2nd and O Streets) to Paul Morrell, proprietor of the *Sacramento Union*, when his luck failed him during an off night at cards.

Merchants dispatched their orders and letters, and more than one hundred mail bags were closed. The gold shipments of San Francisco

---

[6] Alonzo Castle Monson, age 35, was born in New York. He graduated from Yale University in 1840 and Columbia Law School in 1844, at age 22. He came to California on the *Tarolinta* in 1849, was active in California politics and, in January 1857, declined an appointment to the state Supreme Court. *San Francisco Chronicle*, 2 Jan 1902, 2-5. C.W. Haskins, *The Argonauts of California*, 449.

THE VOYAGE

The *Sonora*. Courtesy, The Mariners Museum, Newport News, VA.

consignees,[7] with a total value of 1.6 millions of dollars, were securely stored in the hold. Most of the shipment was destined for the New York banks, some to England. Besides bars of gleaming yellow, there was a large quantity of coins freshly struck at the San Francisco Mint, as well as money of private coinage. The shipments of treasure were eagerly awaited in New York to meet the ever-growing need for specie. Additionally, passengers carried a great amount of gold in their hold and hand baggage.

A large crowd of well-wishers followed a wedding party from the Howard Street Presbyterian Church. Ansel Ives Easton[8] and Adeline

---

[7] *The New York Times,* 19 Sep 1857, 1-2: The consignees of the shipment from San Francisco and the amounts insured were as follows:

American Exchange Bank	$300,000.
Wells, Fargo and Company	300,000.
Duncan, Sherman and Company	200,000.
W. Hoge and Company	140,000.
Robb, Hallett and Company	150,000.
Howland and Aspinwall	110,000.
W.T. Coleman and Company	50,000.
Sundry Consignees	250,000.
Philadelphia Consignees	100,000.
Total Shipment:	$1,600,000.

[8] Ansel Ives Easton, age 38, was born in New York, and since 1847 had kept the Croton Hotel in New York City until he went to California in 1850. Wm. Starr Easton, *Descendents of Joseph Easton, Hartford, CT 1636-1899* (St. Paul, MN, 1899), 65.

Mills had been married earlier that morning by '49er Rev. Samuel H. Willey.[9] New Yorker Easton had gained considerable wealth with his steam laundry on Washerwoman Lagoon[10] and his manufactory of mattresses for the Pacific Mail Steamship Company. Also from New York, Adeline Mills had come to California with her brother, Darius Ogden Mills,[11] who established a banking business in Sacramento and in some of the mining towns. The Easton's were starting on their European honeymoon cruise, and their carriage to the wharf was laden with gifts of food and wine.

One of the Easton's friends at the wedding, Robert T. Brown,[12]

Ansel Ives Easton and Adeline Mills Easton
Courtesy, San Mateo County Historical Association

---

[9] Rev. Samuel H. Willey, Howard Street Presbyterian Church, arrived in California on 23 Feb 1849; he was the second Protestant clergyman in California; chaplain to State Constitution Convention at Monterey. Soule, *Annals . . .* , 690, 697.

[10] The only fresh-water lagoon in San Francisco was filled in with the rubble from the 1906 earthquake. Now called the Marina District, it was the site of great damage in the 1989 earthquake, and the home of a Pahud descendant.

[11] Darius Ogden Mills came to California, at age 23, from New York via Panama, in December 1848. Trading up and down the San Joaquin and Sacramento rivers allowed him to prosper. By 1850 he had established banks in several cities and mining towns. On one of his many trips for goods in 1852, he brought his sister, Adeline, now age 28, and other family members to Sacramento. Rockwell D. Hunt, *California and Californians*, Vol. II, 106.

[12] Robert Turnbull Brown, age 36, was born in New York and, in early 1850, established his business at Sacramento. U.S. Census, California, Sacramento City, 2 Jun 1850, 138. Samuel Colville, *Directory of the City of Sacramento*, CA, 1853-4, 13 and 25.

Judge Alonso Castle Monson
Courtesy, California State
Library

Robert Turnbull Brown
Courtesy, California State
Library

a Sacramento dry goods and clothing merchant, made occasional business trips to New York for Brown, Henry & Co.

Another Easton friend, Samuel S. Shreve,[13] with his partner, George Shreve, owned a jewelry firm in San Francisco. Shreve, a member of the Second (Pine Street) Baptist Church, played a key role in organizing the San Francisco Young Men's Christian Association. His thoughts now turned to his own coming marriage in Massachusetts.

William and Virginia Birch[14] were also newlyweds, having been married the preceding day. "Billy Birch," a widely known San Francisco minstrel, had performed for over a month at Maguire's Opera House, the advertisement of July 29, 1857 saying: "The San Francisco Minstrels will appear this evening in the 'Inauguration Ball,' the scenes of 'Dutch Drill,' 'Arabian Bros.,' and various other burlesques, besides music and song."[15]

After being her guardian for several years, William McNeil and nineteen-year-old Anna Maria Mullen were married in Oakland the previous May by Rev. James Pierpont.[16] William, a '49er, had recently terminated his partnership with Francis DeLong in their hardware business, and decided to take his bride to meet his family in Lockport, New York.

---

[13] Samuel Stillman Shreve, age 27, was born in Salem, Massachusetts, the son of Captain Samuel V. Shreve. His partner, George C. Shreve, was an uncle his same age. Samuel's fiancee lived in Danvers, Mass. Shreve, *The Genealogy and History of the Shreve Family*, private printing, n.d. Cooke & LeCount, 1854 *Directory of the City of San Francisco*, 122. Colville, *San Francisco City Directory*, 1856-7. *The San Francisco Bulletin*, 23 Oct 1857, 2-2.

[14] William "Billy" Birch, age 26, was born in Utica, New York, and had been a professional Minstrel since age 15. He had been associated with the original Christy Minstrels. They alternated seasons between there and New York, and had traveled as far as Australia. Constance Rourke, *Troupers of the Gold Coast*, 108. *San Francisco Theatre Research*, Vol 13, Minstrelsy, 50-56, 60-69.

[15] Billy Birch: "Just think of it; those big open-hearted diggers enjoyed paying their dollar's worth of dust to us to see us cut up our monkey shines, and at that very period here in New York City a man could get into the same class of entertainment for a quarter. I never in my life saw such easily amused men as those old California miners were. They did not try to suppress their hearty laughter when any of us said a good thing or did anything funny. And their appreciation encouraged us to accomplish our best. But they had a rough way of judging when our performance was not quite up to the mark and they didn't hesitate to hiss when they didn't like anything. Well, after making our circuit of the mining camps, which generally consumed about six weeks, we would return to Frisco with a clean profit above expenses of any where from $500 to $2000. Backus would get back to town with an equally good, if not better showing. During our absence our city patrons would begin to miss us, and wish us back to the old stand, and so when we began another engagement in Frisco we were certain that we would not play to empty benches. We continued in this manner for several seasons in California, and finally decided to come East." *San Francisco Call*, 6 Oct 1890, 3-5.

[16] William McNeil, age 33, born in Niagara County, New York, crossed the plains in 1849, and returned home again in 1853. A partner in the house of DeLong, McNeil & Co., he was noted for his "industry and incorruptible integrity." *Daily Alta California*, 23 Oct 1857, 4-2. *San Francisco Daily Evening Bulletin*, 4 May 1857, 3-1.

Theodore Payne (above), and Company Sales Room
From Frank Soule, *Annals of San Francisco*

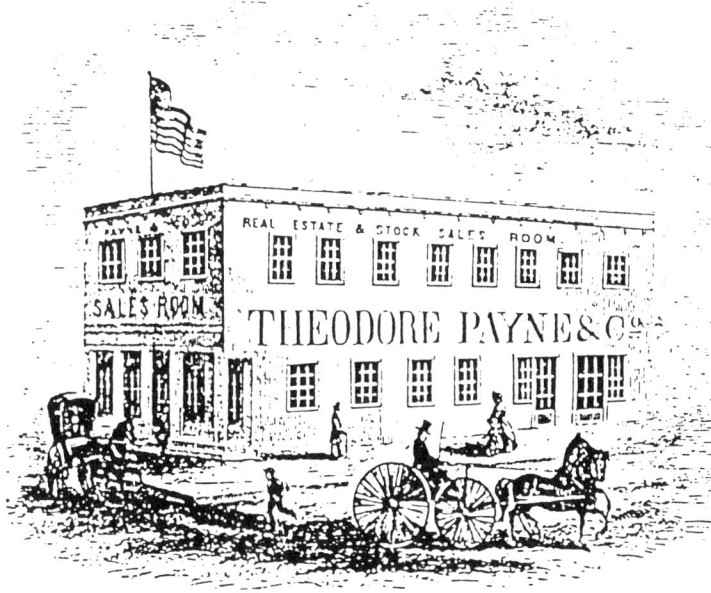

Captain Thomas W. Badger
Courtesy, Oakland Public Library,
California Room

Passenger Captain Thomas W. Badger and his wife, Jane, had been married less than a year.[17] Badger, a '49er from Virginia, an experienced and successful sea captain, owned several vessels. Jane, also a pioneer, in her namesake, the barquentine *Jane A. Falkenburg,* sailed around the Horn with her first husband, Charles Falkenburg, arriving in San Francisco from Boston on New Year's Day, 1855. After they had set a speed record to Manila, they were preparing for a trip to Sydney, Australia, when Captain Falkenburg died in a carriage accident. Jane subsequently married his friend and partner, Thomas. They decided to live in Virginia.

Despite a nurseryman's complaint that the acid fumes were destroying his plants, Marcellus Farmer[18] took great pride in the success of Farmer,

---

[17] Badger, age 30, was born in Northampton County, Virginia. He was named Thomas Chearn but was always known as Thomas W., his father's name. Thomas sailed from New York to California on March 3, 1849 as a passenger in the schooner *James L. Day,* arriving in August. Jane A. Fitzgerald, age 22, was born in England. In December, 1856, Jane Falkenburg and Thomas Badger were married at the International Hotel by the Reverend Dr. Andrews. Daughters of the American Revolution of California, *Vital Records from San Francisco Daily Bulletin,* 1856-7, 21. Haskins, 427. "Badger Family History," n.d., typewritten ms.

[18] Marcellus Farmer was about 36 years old and had first come to California in 1853. With Horace Greeley, he had been one of the early proprietors of the *New York Tribune,* and for several years edited the *Norfolk Tribune.* In 1854 he was associate editor of Frank Soule's 1853 newspaper, the *California Chronicle.* Returning east, he brought back considerable capital for his investments. He was a "good trader and manager of business—a clear, forcible writer, and a man of strong moral feeling." *San Francisco Daily Evening Bulletin,* 23 Oct 1857, 2-2.

Chase & Co., his chemicals manufactory at the Mission, the United States Mint being his foremost customer for acids. The plant proved to be much more lucrative than his previous newspaper business, but he enjoyed keeping his hand in by writing news items for the *San Francisco Bulletin*. He now looked forward to a reunion with his wife and family in Syracuse, New York.

At a nearby wharf, the propeller *Santa Cruz,* Captain Dame, had arrived earlier in the morning, after a seven hour trip from Santa Cruz. With him, and a bi-weekly load of lime, came Dr. and Mrs. Francis M. Kittredge,[19] Almira Kittredge was returning east for a family visit to Lowell and Chelmsford, Massachusetts, where her husband had practiced medicine for twenty years. Dr. Kittredge remained in California, where he managed the wharf at Santa Cruz.

James E. Birch,[20] recognized by many amid the throng on the pier,

James E. Birch
Courtesy, California State Library

---

[19] Dr. Francis M. Kittredge descended from a family of medical doctors in Massachusetts. When he came to California in 1849 he gave up his practice but continued to give medical advice. He served as a State Senator from 1853-4 and wrote extensively under the pen name of "John Dimon." Almira Mead Kittredge, age 39, had lost one child at age 3 and another at age 8 days. Their 18-year-old son, Ruel, lived with them at Santa Cruz. *Illustrations of Santa Cruz* . . . , 8. Rev. Wilson Waters, *History of Chelmsford*, 803-4. Bancroft, *History of California*, 1849-1850, 675.

[20] James E. Birch, age 28, had come to California in early 1849, and on July 21st, with four horses and a buckboard, started his first stage route with a 50-mile trip to Coloma. After his early success, he returned to Swansea, MA, and married Julia Chace. By 1855, with new Concord coaches, his routes covered 3000 miles. By 1856, the California Stage Company ran 80 Concord coaches, 125 Concord wagons, and employed 1,100 horses over 24 main routes, the daily distance traversed by the different stages being 1,474 miles. Mary McLennon and Alfred D. Gallucci, *James E. Birch*, 3-26. William and George Banning, *Six Horses*, 33. Ralph Burch, "California's First Stagecoach King," 26-31. Joseph H. Jackson, *Anybody's Gold*. Mae Helene Bacon Boggs, *My Playhouse Was a Concord Coach*. Thompson & West, *History of Sacramento*, 206.

made frequent trips between San Francisco and New York, and had been back in San Francisco less than a month. Known as the "California Stagecoach King," he had established most of the stagecoach routes to the California mines. Upon his current arrival in San Francisco, he sent to his wife $60,000 in gold bars.[21] The previous evening, while still at the International Hotel, John Andrews, one of his partners, surprised Birch in presenting to him a silver cup. The cup, crafted for Andrews by San Francisco jeweler, John W. Tucker, and engraved "To Frank from John," delighted James as a gift for his baby son. Birch, a shrewd business man, and a rather handsome young fellow of twenty-eight years, had just been awarded a government contract for the San Antonio and San Diego mail.

George Dawson,[22] a tall sturdy mulatto enroute to visit relatives in Rochester, New York, had been a porter at the St. Nicholas Hotel in Oroville, a James Birch coach stop. He and Birch must have recognized each other as they boarded the steamer.

Separate eastern visits by husbands and wives were relatively common. Madame Rosalie Pahud,[23] petite and attractive, with striking blue eyes, the wife of Francois Pahud, a Swiss importer and investor in San Francisco real estate and California mining claims, was accompanied by her three children. Francois would remain in California.

Mrs. Lucy Thayer,[24] wife of Benjamin B. Thayer, owner of a San Francisco drug firm, planned to return to their South Boston home, Benjamin remaining in San Francisco. Their black nurse, Susan Pettorous, assisted Lucy with her two children. Susan's husband, Charles Pettorous, a successful storekeeper in San Francisco, accompanied the family.

---

[21] The gold bars were transported on the *Illinois*, two weeks before Birch departed. Julia Birch then sent them to the New York assay office for refining and stamping. *Baltimore Sun*, 28 Sep 1857, 1-3. *New York Daily Tribune*, 26 Sep 1857, 7-1.

[22] George W. Dawson was born in Rochester, New York and was about age 35. He had worked as a seaman and was on the *Crescent City* when it wrecked in the Bahamas, and he had been in California for about two years. *The New York Times*, 6 Oct 1857, No. 1887, 1-2; *The Richmond Enquirer*, 9 Oct 1857, 1-6; *New York Daily Tribune*, 6 Oct 1857, 5-3,4.

[23] Rosalie Rimboust Pahud, age 34, was born in France. She and Francois, age 40, had lived near the Louvre, in Paris, before coming to New York in Oct 1849, with baby Augustine. Henri Edouard was born in New York City on April 29, 1850. Francois went to San Francisco, and Rosalie established a dressmaking business at 459 Broadway, New York City. About 1853, she and the children arrived in California, where their second son was born. Author's family history file.

[24] Benjamin B. Thayer established his San Francisco drugs and medicines business, Thayer & Little, at 127 Montgomery, in 1852. Lucy W. Phillips Thayer, age 25, was born in Massachusetts; she and their two children, Lizzie and Herbert, came to join him in 1855. Bezaleel Thayer, *Memorial of Thayer Name . . . Richard and Thomas Thayer*, (Oswego, New York: R.J. Oliphant, Steam Book & Job Printer, 1874), 97. *Daily Alta California*, 21 Jan 1855, 2. A.W. Morgan, *San Francisco City Directory*, 1852, 58.

Francois Pahud and Rosalie Rimboust Pahud
Courtesy, descendant Lawrence B. Gibbons.

Forty-niner Frederick S. Hawley,[25] a wholesale hardware merchant, with his wife, Elizabeth, and their two young sons, Charles, two years, and Willy, five months, looked forward to a family visit in Bridgeport, Connecticut. Frederick was a Deacon of Mr. Lacy's First Congregational Church and represented his church on the board of the San Francisco Young Men's Christian Association.

A prominent citizen of San Francisco, Theodore Payne,[26] was the proprietor of a real estate auction house he established in October, 1850, and which occupied a building on the southwest corner of California and Montgomery streets. Payne actively took part in civic affairs including the Vigilance Committee, Fire Department and Masonic Lodge. He now traveled to join his wife, Nancy, and their two sons,

---

[25] Frederick Hawley, age 35, was born in Bridgeport, Connecticut. He came to San Francisco on the *Tarolinta*, January 1849 with several relatives named Sterling. They established a dealership in hardware and provisions, etc., on Sacramento St. Elizabeth De Forest, age 29, was born in Connecticut. Their sons were born in California. Haskins, 449. *Tri-Weekly Alta California*, 5 Jan 1850. U.S. Census, 1860, Connecticut, Fairfield Co, Bridgeport, Pg 217 (385). Elias S. Hawley, *The Hawley Record*, (Buffalo, NY: E.H. Hutchison and Company, 1890), 322. Mrs. Robert W. DeForest, *A Walloon Family in America*, Vol I, (Boston & New York: Houghton, Mifflin Co., 1914), 282. Clifford M. Drury, *San Francisco YMCA, 1853-1953*, 24.

[26] Theodore Payne, age 41, was born in New York. He arrived in San Francisco on October 28, 1849, without means, having lost all his baggage at Panama. Soule, *Annals*, 800. *California, 1900*, 227. Harry C. Pendleton, *History of the San Francisco Fire Company Department, 1849-1900*.

who in July had preceded him to New York. Payne, well known along the Panama route, made occasional trips East.

In recent months, Mrs. Harriet Lockwood and their three youngest children had come west to visit her husband, Rufus A. Lockwood.[27] Lockwood, a nationally known attorney with a reputation for being a brilliant eccentric, currently represented the mining affairs of the nationally known explorer and politician, Colonel John C. Fremont. His family had remained on their Indiana farm while he roamed the world. In March 1857, their children, Rose Alice, fifteen, Rufus A. Jr.,

Rufus A. Lockwood and Family, 1856
Courtesy, California Historical Society

[27] Rufus A. Lockwood, age 46, was born in Connecticut. He settled in Indiana about 1836, and was admitted to the bar in that state. He came to California in the fall of 1849; practiced law; gambled; went to Australia in 1853, returned in 1855. Harriet Hill Lockwood, age 45, was born in Canada West. She operated their large farm in Tippecanoe Co, Indiana, and raised their five children. U.S. Census, Indiana, Tippecanoe Co, Wabash Tnshp, P.O. Lafayette, 14 Jul 1860, 677. Robert P. Hastings, "Rufus A. Lockwood," 97-110, 239-63, 333-40. Oscar T. Schuck, Bench and Bar. (1889) 234-260. John E. Richards, The Mystery Man, 1-2.

twelve, and Harriet, eight, were baptized at Saint Mary's Roman Catholic Church in San Francisco. Lockwood planned to be in Washington, D.C. on business concerning Fremont's gold mining claims, while his family returned to Indiana.

The hired hand-cartmen trundled the many trunks up the gang planks, and the families arranged their belongings in their cabins. Miners, anxiously trying to get to the steamer, thronged the wharves. More than 350 men boarded at San Francisco—interesting and colorful men from all walks of life, most of them having been to the gold fields. There were newspapermen, tavern and hotel keepers, merchants, engineers and a variety of tradesmen. Less than a fourth of the spaces were in first and second class, most passengers occupying the steerage berths.

Miners boarding the *Sonora* had spent long periods of time near towns bearing such descriptive names as Rough and Ready, Hell-Out-for-Noon, Gopher Hill, Seven-Mile, and so on. At White Rock Springs, a stage stop between Sacramento and Placerville (Hangtown), '49er Daniel Hudson C. Chapman and his wife established a hotel after their six-month overland journey from St. Louis.[28]

The majority of miners were young men in their twenties and thirties, but a number of older men also were returning to their homes and large families. Daniel Beaver, age fifty-six, of Hamilton, Ohio, in 1849 and 1855 had led parties to the gold fields and was mining at Mameluke Hill in El Dorado County. In November 1856, during a hard, cold winter near Georgetown, California, Beaver wrote to his wife and twelve children saying that he had not yet made enough money to return home, and added: "I would like to see you all once more on this side of the grave if it is the will of God, but if He has otherwise appointed, I hope that we may all meet again in Heaven where there is no parting again."[29]

Others of the relatively older miners included Jacob Quincer, age fifty-five, and Robert Wade, Jr., age forty-eight. English-born Wade had migrated to Michigan in 1829; his wife and eight children waited for him on their Indiana farm.[30] Mr. Robertson, a '49er from Massachu-

---

[28] Daughters of the American Revolution, California State Society, comp., *Records of the Families of California Pioneers*, Vol XXIII, (Sacramento, CA: n.p., 1956), 33. *The Bay of San Francisco: A History*, Vol II, (Chicago: The Lewis Publishing Co., 1892), 180-1.

[29] His family continued to operate their tavern, The Beaver House, which was a stopping place for teamsters who hauled their products from the west to the Cincinnati markets and on their return were loaded with dry goods and groceries for the merchants of country towns. Letters of Daniel Beaver in possession of descendant Stephen Beaver. Rev. I.M. Beaver, *History and Genealogy of the Bieber, Beaver, Biever, Beeber Family*, (Reading, PA: by the author, 1939), 448.

[30] Letter from family descendant Dale Wade. *Brunswick Sun Times*, Community Life, 19 Oct 1989, Sec B. 1850 U.S. Census, IN, La Grange Co, Town of Springfield, 7 Sep 1850, 69. *The Columbus Dispatch*, 18 Sep 1989, 1-3.

setts, a disheartened, unsuccessful miner, boarded the *Sonora* to return to his mentally ill wife.[31]

River-boats of all descriptions plied the waters between Sacramento, Stockton, and San Francisco. On one of these, John O. Stevens arrived from Stockton several days early to secure from his old comrade, Attorney Robert Simson, sketches, notes and paintings left in his care by John Woodhouse Audubon. The drawings reminded Stevens of the long trek they had endured years ago, across Mexico.[32] Audubon, son of the famous naturalist, led a party to California in 1849, and during his western adventure made many drawings. On his return to New York in 1850 he left about two hundred of them in the care of Simson. Stevens stayed in California and, with three of his Audubon partners, traded, mined and developed the first orchards in the San Joaquin Valley. For the visit East, he booked his passage on the *Sonora*. In San Francisco, complying with Audubon's wishes, he received from Simson the portfolio and carefully stored it in his trunk.

From a British vessel, Robert Levich and a partner, of England, had jumped ship at San Francisco, made money in real estate, and now he headed home for a visit. Lewis Wood, of Prussia, keeper of a bookstall on the corner of Montgomery and Commercial streets in San Francisco, wrote a report on the rise, progress and result of Vigilance Committees. He carried with him, to be published in New York, the only copy of his manuscript.[33]

There were several veteran mariners boarding—Charles McCarty, the former chief engineer on the *Golden Gate;* Second Mate Charles Tayloe and Peter Brown had been employed by the PMSC; and Navy Purser John V. Dobbin had just returned from a tour to Shanghai on the U.S. sloop-of-war *Portsmouth*. Tayloe and Dobbin agreed to share a cabin.

From "contra costa," across the Bay, in one of the smaller boats, George Lee[34] arrived at the docks. He had left his thriving nursery

---

[31] *The New York Daily Tribune*, 21 Sep 1857, 7-6. *The New York Times*, 22 Sep 1857, No. 1875, 8-1.

[32] John O. Stevens, age 32, was born in New Jersey. He joined the Audubon Company in New York, which proceeded through Mexico to San Diego and then north through the central valley to Stockton. Ill, Stevens later followed from San Diego by sea via San Francisco. They traded goods in the mining camps, mined and settled into agricultural pursuits. His partners were John H. "Jack" Tone, David Hudson and Charles Valentine. John W. Audubon, *Audubon's Western Journal 1849-1850*, 70-1, 162-195, 242-3. Alice Tone Gibbons, *My Pioneer Grandfather, John Henley Tone*, 23-115. Jeanne Skinner Van Nostrand, "Audubon's Ill-Fated Western Journey," 308.

[33] *The San Francisco Daily Evening Bulletin*, 23 Oct 1857, 2-2 and 31 Oct 1857, 3-3.

[34] George Lee was from Philadelphia, Pennsylvania, and had arrived in California on the steamer *Alabama* on July 19, 1849. Haskins, 479. *Daily Alta California*, 4 Apr 1857, 2-2.

business, Lee's Gardens, in Oakland, where his specialty was strawberries this year.

To the International Hotel, Dr. James Travis brought his wife and two children across from Alvarado for their return trip to their home in New York City. Dr. Henry Yanney's sister was stricken with an incurable ailment, and wished to see him before she died. He was hurrying to Johnstown, New York.[35]

Mexican War hero Lieutenant John Dement,[36] member of the first United States military unit in Oregon Territory, made several trips to the East Coast. His two-month-old son was too young for the trip, so Dement's wife and baby remained in Oregon City. Another Mexican War veteran, Major Jacob Brown Clark,[37] of the Missouri Volunteers, a '49er, had mined and made more than one trip back, was now headed east for a family visit.

Arriving from the most far-flung location, F.A. Bokee, a merchant had returned only a few days previously from Hong Kong, China, on the clipper *Mary Whitridge*.[38]

Charles S. Saroni, a San Francisco hat manufacturer of Saroni, Archer & Co., planned to visit his brother in Boston. He had been active in civic affairs, and in 1855 was a member of the Grand Jury, investigating interference in the proper expression of public opinion by the legislature, and its control of fraudulent elections. Saroni must have been pleased to meet not only a fellow Hebrew but a fellow German, Albert Priest.[39] At sixty years of age, Priest was the oldest man boarding

---

[35] *San Francisco Herald and Mirror*, 20 Aug 1857, 2-6. *The San Francisco Daily Evening Bulletin*, 23 Oct 1857, 2-2.

[36] John D. Dement, age 31, was born in Washington, DC. In 1846 he enlisted in the U.S. Army and served under Gen. Scott in the Mexican War. For heroism he was awarded a commission and assigned to 1 Artillery and to Oregon Territory. His brother, William C. Dement, had come overland with the first wagon train to Oregon in 1843. Charles H. Carey, "Theodore Talbot Journals, 1843, 1849-52," 326-337. Francis B. Heitman, *Historical Register . . .* , 366. James Willis Nesmith, *Two Addresses* (Fairfield, WA: Ye Galleon Press, 1978), 26.

[37] Jacob Brown Clark, age 46, was born in Tennessee and had moved to Missouri when a child, later served in the Mexican War. His brother lived in Polk Co., Missouri. *Williams Farmer*, 17 Sep 1898, 3-4.

[38] *San Francisco Daily Evening Bulletin*, 14 Aug 1857, 2.

[39] Albert Priest was born in Hamburg, Germany, in 1797. He was, in 1843, one of the early pioneers to travel west to Oregon. There he helped establish the first saw mills in Oregon City; he was associated with Dr. McLoughlin and John Dement's brother, William. In 1845, he shipped the first load of lumber to San Francisco. In September 1849, in San Francisco, Priest was a leader in conducting the first observance of Rosh Hashanah. Hubert Howe Bancroft, *The History of California*, 1848-1849, 269 and 304; *The History of Oregon*, 1834-1848, 466. *Pioneer Register*, 292. *Daily Alta California*, 25 Jun 1857, 1-1. Thompson & West, *History of Sacramento*, 124. Samuel Colville, *Sacramento City Directory* 1853-4, 1, 2. Irena Narell, *Our City: The Jews of San Francisco*, 48. William M. Kramer and Norton B. Stern, "The Search for the First Synagague in The Golden West," 3-4.

the *Sonora* and had been one of the earliest sojourners to arrive in El Dorado. In 1848, at Fort Sutter, he and his Oregon partners established Priest, Lee & Co., a mercantile outlet. Although their enormous profits ranged from 50% to 200% on most goods, he realized the greatest fortune by being in the right place at the right time and in investing heavily in the embryonic City of Sacramento. The partners immediately built a new and larger store at Second and J streets. Land values appreciated so rapidly that he very profitably sold all of his holdings by April 1850, and returned to his wife and home in Jamaica, Long Island, New York. He had made a return visit in 1851 and now in 1857.

Many of the other passengers had also left foreign shores. Gaitano Festu mined with three friends, Thomas Ravenna, Joseph Capello and Domecio Casta; they now anticipated the return to their home town, about twenty-five miles from Genoa, Italy.

Several French-Canadians had mined at Mokelumne Hill and now headed home to Montreal. An elderly English couple, John and Mary Ann Rudwell, had been operating a public house in Grass Valley. German, Henry Rummell, from Hesse Darmstadt, had been mining for three years on Irish Flat, about six miles from Georgetown, and was on his way to visit his brother in Tazewell County, Illinois.

Professional gamblers enjoyed traveling on the steamers; there were many idle hours to pass in gaming, and many miners willing to risk their gold.

Addie Easton saw Frank Jones as a "handsome young fellow. Some said he was a large landed proprietor of Kentucky, and some that he was the cleverest gambler in San Francisco."[40] Jones had arrived in San Francisco on the *John L. Stephens* only a month ago, and now headed back with $6,000 in gold. Passengers knowing him as a New York socialite included Joseph Bassford,[41] a shipwright from Benicia, Califor-

---

[40] During the 1850s and 60s, hundreds of gamblers worked the steamers. This activity extended to the steamers of the PMSC and USMSC. Although discouraged by the captains, gambling was difficult to control on the long, boring voyages the games becoming more and more interesting and the stakes higher and higher. Oscar Lewis, *Sea Routes*, 83, 190. Olmsted-Lincoln, *Wedding Journey*, 15.

[41] Joseph McDonald Bassford, age 36, was born in New York City. At age 11, he was sent to Moravian School, Nazareth Hall, Pennsylvania, for two years. Returning to New York, he worked on the family farm and also learned the ship joiner's trade; in 1845 he married Julia Sprague. On January 9. 1850, he sailed as a ship's joiner on the steamer *Carolina*, Captain Marks. He located at Benicia, later and briefly the capitol city of the new state. On July 1, 1851, he brought his wife and two small sons to San Francisco on the steamer *Sarah Sands;* two more sons were born in California. *A Memorial and Biographical History of Northern California* (The Lewis Publishing Co, Chicago, 1891), 601. Rasmussen, *Ships Passenger Lists*, 170.

nia, and Charles Reed, who, with Jones, had been on the *Yankee Blade* in 1854, when it foundered about twelve miles off Point Conception, California, enroute to Panama.

Having made seven or eight previous trips, Jones had brought his wife and child on at least one of the journeys. His black servant, Charley traveled with him. Southern families, when going west, would often bring one or two slaves; some were given their freedom and wages in the "new country."[42] Bassford had traveling with him another Charley, a free black.

Amid the final bustle on the Vallejo Wharf, much hand-waving to and from the steamer, shouts and tears, the *Sonora* departed on schedule. Men with barrows and shovels steadily fed coal to the ship's furnaces, and with a good head of steam from the boilers the steamship slowly moved away from the dock, her whistle blowing a farewell to those on shore. The Pahud children waved to Papa.

The trip to Panama City, about one-half again the distance from Aspinwall to New York, took nearly two weeks. The passengers, on the first night out, were served turtle soup. Oliver Manlove,[43] heading homeward, satisfied with his California experience, watched the dressing of the "great ocean turtle. It was quite palatable," he said, "but I believe that I would prefer oysters or chicken." At Gopher Hill, Plumas County, Oliver had worked for Warner Meeks and three other partners in a hydraulic mining operation in which they moved "tons upon tons" of dirt to extract gold, "filling our sluice boxes." Men like these provided the gold shipped to New York on the steamers of the PMSC and USMSC. Other men, like Albert Priest, of Priest, Lee & Co., received the gold from the miners, issued drafts, and sent the metal to the mint.

Henry O'Connor,[44] a young man of seventeen years, accompanied

---

[42] Neville, *Fantastic City*, 29.

[43] Oliver Perry Manlove, age 26, was born in Rushville, Schuyler Co, Illinois, and lived on his father's farm in Muscoda, Grant Co., Wisconsin. In 1854 he spent five months driving oxen to arrive in Plumas Co., California. Tall, at five feet eleven inches, Manlove could walk 28 miles in the California mining country in five hours. Oliver Perry Manlove, "*Autobiography of Oliver Perry Manlove,*" typewritten ms., 1915, courtesy of descendant, Robert T. Manlove. *Richmond Daily Dispatch*, 21 Sep 1857, 1-4. *New York Daily Tribune*, 21 Sep 1857, 7-1. *The New York Times*, No. 1874, 3-1. *Waukesha County Republican*, WI, 24 Oct 1857, 1-1. *History of Grant Co* . . . , 804, 967.

[44] Henry T. O'Connor worked as a printer at O'Meara & Painter. With his mother, Eleanor, he came to San Francisco in 1854; she established a dressmaking shop, earning about $3. per day. They saved about $2,000 for his and his six-year-old brother's education, and were returning to their Albany, New York, home. *The New York Herald*, 21 Sep 1857, 2-5, 6. *Albany Evening Journal*, 23 Sep 1857, 2-3.

The Steamer Terminus at Aspinwall
From Otis, *Illustrated History of Panama*

Typical Steamer Cabin
Courtesy, California
Historical Society

his mother, Eleanor, and a "fine bright little boy," Louis Bonneau, sent in her charge by his widowed father, Thomas Bonneau.[45] Henry found the weather fair down to Manzanillo, Mexico. After a stop there of about a half hour, however, and just as they were leaving, a squall had struck. "It rained violently, but the rain soon subsided and the sea ran very high." "In coming out of the harbor," said Manlove, "we came very nearly being blown on the rocks by a 'white squall' . . . it came suddenly, piling waves up before it six or eight feet high, and for ten minutes it meant business and made everything rattle."

From there they enjoyed pleasant weather down to Acapulco. "We left Acapulco about 7 o'clock the next morning," said O'Connor, "after taking on coal."[46] Addie Easton recalled the voyage on the *Sonora* as "one long delight, with smooth waters, sunny skies, and a joyous, congenial company."

The *Sonora* anchored in the Gulf of Panama at 8 P.M. on September 2nd, the passengers remaining on board until daybreak. Small steamers, one called the *Tobega*, towing a baggage barge behind her, carried the passengers from deep water to shore, some four miles distant. Sometimes passengers preferred to ride on the barge, seated on trunks and enjoying the harbor view.[47]

"The Isthmus is healthy," the *Daily Alta* had reported on June 16, 1857, "and the railroad was never in better condition than at present. The iron bridges are now nearly all completed, and the vessels of war, both at Aspinwall and Panama, render the transit of the Isthmus perfectly safe."

Along forty-seven miles of single track to Aspinwall the hundreds of passengers from California passed through tropical swamps and jungle, over land-fills, trestles and a bridge across the Chagres River. To an earlier traveler, the rail trip was made "in toy cars," and breakfast at the Howard House, Aspinwall, was "a sad meal, gastronomically speaking."[48] Oliver Manlove said that his trip across the Isthmus took six hours. "The railway," he said, "was a rickety affair which, we were told, was built on men's bones, there having been such a great death rate in its construction." Addie Easton thought the rail passage across the Isthmus "uneventful and all too short."[49]

---

[45] Thomas C. Bonneau was a barber in San Francisco. His wife, Ann, had been the proprietress of the Fairhaven House, at 41 Sansome, until her illness and death in April 1857. She died of heart failure at age 34. Their eleven month old daughter, Janet, died July 22, 1857. *San Francisco City Directory*, 1854, 27. *San Francisco Daily Evening Bulletin*, 6 Apr 1857, 1-3. *Daily Alta California*, 7 Apr 1857, 2-9. *The New York Herald*, 21 Sep 1857, 3-5. *Sacramento Bee*, 24 Jul 1857, 3-3.
[46] *The New York Herald*, 21 Sep 1857, 2-5.
[47] Neville, *Fantastic City*, 30.
[48] *Ibid.*, 28.
[49] Olmsted-Lincoln, *Wedding Journey*, 11.

The trip from Panama City to Aspinwall took about three and one-quarter hours—for some of them. The crossing required at least three trips in the nine small railway cars over the single track, causing considerable waiting time for many of the passengers. The trains wound through green country, the thick foliage of tropical forests brushing the windows of the cars. A siding at Matachin allowed the trains from either terminus to pass along the single rail, and during the delay natives took advantage of the time to transact a little business in cakes, native candy and an assortment of fruits of the region. There, too, a native "saloon served very good English beer, French claret, crackers and cheese," and other interesting items.

From there the rail passed over sturdy iron bridges and "luxuriant woodland, where the delicious wild mango, the zapote, the nispero, and the guava" are found.[50] Passing further through fertile plains, along rivers and across wild mountain scenery of the tropical rain forest, the passengers arrived at the Caribbean shore.

At Aspinwall, some who went "to the hotels for dinner were afraid to eat meat," thinking it "might be cooked monkey." Manlove said that many of them had been observed "climbing trees and swinging in their branches."

The *Central America* had arrived from New York on September 2nd. She fired her customary salute to the departing westbound passengers, and soon unloaded an unusual cargo. On this the second trip under her new name, she transported on her deck in eight sections, a small steamer named the *Explorer*.[51] The craft was destined for use by Lieutenant Joseph Christmas Ives, a first cousin of passenger Ansel Ives Easton, and commander of an expedition to explore the Colorado River.

The steamship also carried with her a grieving widow. Mrs. Ann Redding's husband had become ill and died enroute from New York. She remained on board to return home.

The American Consul at Aspinwall placed in the care of Captain Herndon a rather frail, unwell young lady and her infant daughter. Mrs. Ann Small was the widow of Captain Benjamin Small, of Newburyport, Massachusetts. On his first trip as Master of the *Augustine Heard,* they had sailed to the Chincha Islands and loaded a cargo of guano, a natural

---

[50] F.N. Otis, *The Panama Railroad,* 116.

[51] The *Explorer,* fifty feet in length, with a beam of sixteen feet, was the first steamer to be transported across the isthmus. She was built for the United States government by Reaney, Neatie Co., of Philadelphia. *Panama Star and Herald,* 5 Sep 1857, 2-2. Arthur Coon Ives, *Genealogy of the Ives Family* (Watertown, NY: Hungerford-Holbrook Co., 1932), 64, 160-1.

manure composed chiefly from the excrement of sea birds. Becoming suddenly and seriously ill, Captain Small put his ship into Callao and directed the crew to proceed without him. Hoping to reach home before his illness became worse, he and his family boarded the regular steam-packet to Panama City, where he died at Aspinwall House on August 26th, and was buried there. Friends at Panama had persuaded Mrs. Small to avoid the confusion of the steamer crowds on the railroad by going to Aspinwall a day early.[52]

F.M.B. Smith, leaving for his home in New York, mourned his brother, L.W. Smith, the proprietor of Howard House, Aspinwall, who had recently been shot to death.[53]

Gabriel Brush, retiring baggagemaster of the Panama Railroad Company, known and recognized by a number of the passengers and crew, boarded the steamer to return to his wife and four children in New York.

Thirty-three additional passengers boarded the *Central America* at Aspinwall, including three of General William Walker's men: William Bourne, Robert Christy and Thomas Matthews, who were allowed to work their passage.[54] Several Latin diplomats also boarded. They were Ange Richon, Belgian Consul at Lima, bearer of a dispatch to Paris; Jose Seguin, Peruvian Minister to the United States; and his secretary, Nichollas Tirado. Pasqual Esquerra, of Saragossa, Spain, and Valparaiso, and J. Thorne, Ship's Chandler at Callao, were with the Peruvian party. The passenger group from Lima also included Enrique Ayulo, Adolpho Ollague, age twenty-seven, and his eleven-year-old brother, Ricardo, the brothers being enroute to Paris for the completion of their educations.

East of Aspinwall

Captain Herndon greeted the travelers as they boarded the *Central America*. The captain, the steamer's master for more than two years, spoke to many of his passengers and assured to them the provision of every available comfort.

Meticulous and experienced, and with a well-qualified crew of officers and men, Herndon busied himself in ordering the detailed preparation

---

[52] *The New York Times*, 20 Sep 1857, No. 1874, 3-4. *The New York Daily Tribune*, 21 Sep 1857, 6-3.
[53] *The New York Times*, 22 Sep 1857, 8-1.
[54] General Walker was a self-styled, would-be conqueror of Nicaragua. *New York Daily Tribune*, 21 Sep 1857, 7-5.

of the steamer for departure. Provision of coal for the furnaces of the steamship, food for the passengers, stowage of rigging for the masts of the vessel, medicines, medical instruments and supplies, and general inspection of the vessel, were part of the routine to be accomplished. Essential preparations had been taken care of before cast-off from New York harbor, but rechecks and replenishment of supplies at scheduled stops were always required. The assurance that all scheduled passengers were accounted for prior to departure was a routine necessity. At 4:15 P.M. on September 3, 1857, with all in order, the *Central America* set sail for Havana and New York.

Losses of vessels at sea, such as the *Arctic, San Francisco* and *Yankee Blade,* created a constant fear of disaster. Any unusual circumstance presented a cause for suspicion. On boarding the *Central America,* Easton remarked to Captain Herndon that he thought it bad luck to change the name of a vessel, but Herndon emphatically stated he didn't believe in bad luck.

A blue sky with scattered puffs of cumuliform clouds, air mass conditions typical of the area, greeted the passengers and crew as they sailed from Aspinwall. September in the Caribbean is a season for hurricanes, but as the paddlewheels of the *Central America* propelled her across the blue waters of the calm sea, there was no indication of anything but beautiful cruising weather. Indeed, the leg to Havana was uneventful, the steamer arriving at port at four o'clock, Monday afternoon, September 7th.

The crew immediately made arrangements for taking on coal and other supplies. A few of the passengers went ashore, but many were deterred because yellow fever raged. The Spanish fleet had anchored in the harbor, and some sixty to eighty crew members daily were being destroyed by the fever.[55] More than three hundred would be lost. Soon the port would be closed and the stop instead made at New Orleans.[56]

Another USMSC steamer, the *Empire City,*[57] was at anchor. She had entered the Havana harbor at six o'clock on the morning of Tuesday, September 8th, having left New Orleans on the 5th. Her captain, John McGowan, first commander of the *George Law,* anchored close by.

As a pleasant-faced man came on board the *Central America,* Easton

---

[55] *San Francisco Daily Evening Bulletin,* 4 Nov 1857, 3-4.

[56] Mr. H.D. Barrows had at the last moment canceled his passage on the *Sonora/Central America* voyage. Two weeks later, on the *Northern Light,* he found the port of Havana closed, and stopped at New Orleans. H.D. Barrows, "The Foundering of the Steamship *Central America,*" 70-75.

[57] This Webb-built side-wheel steamer of over 1750 tons had three decks, three masts, round stern, dragon head, with a side-lever engine built by T. F. Secor & Company. She was modeled for speed and very strong. Kemble, *Panama Route,* 224.

remarked to Addie: "Well, there's Captain McGowan." Acquainted with Easton from previous trips, McGowan exchanged pleasantries, asking if it was too late for them to change passage to the *Empire City*. Easton again commented about the change of name, but thought it too difficult to move the trunks and "those hampers."[58] McGowan went to visit with Herndon.

Colonel A.B. Gray, a passenger on the *Empire City*, thought there were about six hundred passengers on the *Central America*, a considerably larger steamer than his, there being sixty passengers on the *Empire City*. Gray and others were eager to learn the west coast news, and were delighted to see Purser Edward Hull[59] and Dr. Joseph Tennison, Surgeon of the *Central America*, board the *Empire City* by a small boat, bringing an August 20th copy of the San Francisco newspaper *Daily Alta California*.

Many of the men took advantage of their short stopover by securing a

Edward W. Hull, Purser, and William H. Hull, Storekeeper, of the *Central America*. Courtesy, Ruth Hull Falk.

---

[58] Olmsted Lincoln, 14.

[59] Edward W. Hull, age 32, and his brother, Ship's Storekeeper William H. Hull, age 26, were born in New York. Edward was formerly a clerk in the firm of Howard & Sons, and was a purser of the California lines of steamships since they were established. His dispatches were always written with concise precision and business ability, and promptly delivered. He was a purser on the *Empire City* in 1851 when the consolidation of the Atlantic and Pacific lines was effected. He was married and had two children, Anna and William. William H. Hull was single. *The New York Herald*, 19 Sep 1857, 1-3. Ruth Hull Falk, descendant of Edward Hull.

supply of several brands of the best cigars to be found anywhere. One hundred fifty millions of the famous Havanas were annually exported to the United States. Captain Herndon enjoyed a good cigar, and in his *Exploration of the Valley of the Amazon* had written of the delight of relaxing with a good one after a long day's trek.

Small boats "scudded around on all sides" of the several ships at anchor, manned by native Cubans peddling their "fruit and shells." Oliver Manlove, for ten cents, "bought a very large orange . . . . It was double the size of any one that I had ever seen before. I wanted it for a specimen to take home."[60]

The bark *Vespasian*, with a load of coal, had wrecked on Old Providence Island, Bahamas. The survivors were stranded there until some natives from nearby islands came and took them to a port from which they got passage to Havana. There they were placed in charge of the American Consul who put them on the *Central America*. The crewmen were Thomas Fryer, James Gallaher, Alexander Gardner, William Green and James Smith.[61]

At Havana, J.C. Lenea,[62] a young man connected with the press in Cuba, purchased a ticket for New York on the *Central America*. Lenea having returned to the hotel to get his baggage, the steamer departed without him, and he was forced to embark on the *Empire City*. Another man, Mr. Jacobs[63] asked for passage on the *Central America* but his request had to be refused because the berths were all occupied.

Satisfied that all scheduled passengers and cargo were on board, Captain Herndon gave the sailing orders.

---

[60] Manlove, 73.
[61] *The New York Times.* 22 Sep 1857, 8-2.
[62] *The New York Herald*, 19 Sep 1857, 1-6.
[63] *Baltimore Sun*, 24 Sep 1857, 2-5.

CHAPTER IV

A Change in the Weather

The *Central America* drew considerable attention and admiration, particularly from the officers and passengers of an English steamer from Vera Cruz, and from the *Empire City*. Colonel Gray, a passenger on the latter vessel, observed that she was "trimmed and ballasted apparently to perfection. She sat on the water beautifully, and as she hauled out and steamed past us there was a universal teeming of pride manifested in every countenance on witnessing so noble a specimen of American skill."[1]

The *Central America* sailed for New York at 9:25 A.M. on Tuesday, September 8th, steaming past the old Spanish landmark, Morro Castle, as she left the harbor. The *Empire City*, following in her wake, sailed less than an hour later. Because she was a faster vessel, the *Central America* was out of sight by sunset, and the last Colonel Gray saw of her "was a trace of smoke floating along the horizon." On the *Central America*, James A. Forster[2] noted that "at dark on that evening we saw the smoke of the *Empire City* about fifteen or twenty miles in the rear."

At about 11:00 P.M. on Wednesday, September 9th, a large steamship, steering south, exchanged signals with the *Empire City*. Captain McGowan identified her to Gray as the *Star of the West*, coincidentally commanded by the colonel's brother, Alfred G. Gray, an earlier commander of the *George Law*. Captain Gray now continued enroute to Aspinwall with passengers and mail.

The *Central America* put out to sea, steered for the Strait of Florida, east of which she would continue to New York via the sea lane in normal use for that route. In the pilot-house, Second Officer Frazer observed the weather to be very good, with moderate breezes. Others on deck

---
[1] *New York Daily Tribune*, 21 Sep 1857, 8-2.
[2] James A. Forster, a 35-year-old engineer from Harrisburg, was born in Pennsylvania. He had been working at Murphys, Calaveras Co., CA, and with his partner, G. Washington Montgomery, of Muncy, Lycoming Co., PA, planned to obtain stock and to return overland to California. He had about $9,000 with him. 1850 U.S. Census, PA, Dauphin Co, East Ward of Burrough of Harrisburg. *Baltimore Sun* 21 Sep 1857, 2-4.

watching the progress of the steamer included Captain Badger, a strong-built man above the medium height, with a full crop of dark hair, beard and mustache. He was often taken for more than his thirty years. As captain of his own ships, sailing the seas of the world and in West Coast trade, he took great pride and pleasure in knowing what was going on when on board of any vessel. Badger had made three trips on the steamer under her original name, and considered her "as staunch as any ship afloat," an opinion shared by passenger Bassford, a shipwright.

Herndon's officers were dependable and experienced. He knew them well. A keen analyst of individual behavior, Herndon was well aware of the capability and general character of his subordinates.

First Officer Charles Van Rensselaer[3] had been with the USMSC for three years, and, as executive officer of the ship, enjoyed the complete confidence of Captain Herndon. Because of the first officer's love for the sea, Herndon had urged him to purchase a ship of his own and sail whenever and wherever he wished, but Van Rensselaer preferred to remain with the captain. A New York *Times* reporter who had spent much time at sea in sailing vessels and steamers, and having previously sailed with Herndon and the first officer, said that he had never seen a ship "sailed so scientifically as the *Central America*. Observations were constantly made, and no expedient of seamanship was untried."[4]

Second Officer James M. Frazer had been employed by the company for a number of years, serving as a mate under several different captains. Third Officer Charles A. Myers[5] had served with the USMSC for several years, and Dr. Joseph T. Tennison[6] had been a surgeon on the line since 1851.

Chief Engineer George E. Ashby, five feet ten inches—well above the average height of the day—sturdy-looking, thirty-six years old, an Englishman by birth, was hired by the line in 1851. He and his first assistant engineer, John Tice, rather slightly built man, five feet six inches tall, had been on the *George Law/Central America* since she was launched.

The passengers enjoyed the comfortable cruise and excellent weather

---

[3] Charles Watkins Van Rensselaer, age 34, a native of Albany, New York, was a son of General John S. Van Rensselaer. He had been a Lieutenant in the Revenue Service; he was single. Florence Van Rensselaer *The Van Rensselaers in Holland and In America*, (New York: American Historical Company, Inc., 1956), 53-4.

[4] *The New York Times*, 2 Oct 1857, 4-6.

[5] Charles A. Meyers was married and had a family. *New York Herald*, 19 Sep 1857, 1-3.

[6] Joseph T. Tennison was single; his mother and brother lived in New York. *New York Herald*, 19 Sep 1857, 1-3.

by strolling about the promenade deck, reading books[7] and newspapers, playing whist and other games,[8] getting acquainted with fellow travelers, listening to the churning of the paddle wheels, and whatever they could devise as a way to pass the hours. Thoughts of many, during those quiet hours, turned toward home, to the return to loved ones, some of whom they had not seen for years. From string and harmonica they heard on board some of the popular tunes of the day, such as "Oh, Susanna" and "My Old Kentucky Home," composed by their contemporary, Stephen Foster. The Californians looked forward with great anticipation to their reunions. It was a time for quiet reflection and contemplation of the days ahead.

For the Tuesday evening meal, Captain Herndon arranged to have the Eastons at his table. This pleased Addie, as she thought him to be a "delightful man." The Captain related some of his Amazon experiences, one of his many stories describing the Brazil nut:

> The tree that gives the Brazil-nut is not more than two or three feet in diameter, but very tall; the nuts, in number about twenty, are enclosed in a very hard, round shell, of about six inches in diameter. The crop is gathered in May and June. It is quite a dangerous operation to collect it; the nut, fully as large and nearly as heavy as a nine-pounder shot, falls from the top of the tree without warning, and would infallibly knock a man's brains out if it struck him on the head.[9]

The conversation turned to shipwrecks. In speaking of some vessel lately wrecked, Addie was impressed by the expression on Herndon's face as he said, "Well, I'll never survive my ship. If she goes down, I go under her keel."[10]

On Wednesday morning, the 9th of September, Samuel Shreve remarked to Easton that the ship hadn't sunk yet, in spite of his concern. "Well, Sammy, we haven't reached New York yet,"[11] replied Ansel.

In his log, Second Officer Frazer noted that at 5:30 A.M., Cape

---

[7] *Uncle Tom's Cabin* by Harriet Beecher Stowe, *Robinson Crusoe* by Daniel DeFoe and *Two Years Before the Mast* by Richard Henry Dana, were popular reading, the latter because Dana had written the best available description of early California.

[8] An anonymous, possibly fictitious, "returning miner," on this trip of the *Central America*, told of playing cards with California friends. "We began with stakes of $2.50 . . . we soon made them twenties . . . An open basket of champagne stood beside us," he said, "one or two of the party sang hilarious songs . . . I won several hundred dollars, perhaps thousands, I hardly know." Gaming was a favorite pastime. Monson and Lockwood had been fond of the sport, and Frank Jones had a gambler's reputation. *Harper's Weekly*, 3 Oct 1857, 365.

[9] Herndon, *Exploration* . . . 283

[10] Olmsted-Lincoln, 15.

[11] Ibid., 16.

Florida, seen from aloft, bore west seventy-five nautical miles, that at noon there was a fresh breeze and head sea, and that in their first twenty-six and one-half hours the *Central America* had traveled two hundred eighty-six nautical miles, following the Gulf Stream, and steering about NW 1/4 W.

On this Wednesday, passengers noted a change in the weather. Although the day had begun with fresh breezes, the ladies noticed a strong wind, increasing in fury, developing into a gale, and forcing them to head for the shelter of their cabins. Madame Pahud observed the storm to be so heavy that most were too sick to eat anything. Henry Childs, the senior partner of the firm Childs and Dougherty, of New York City, a fuel oils business, termed the condition a hurricane.

The larger and speedier *Central America* had left the *Empire City* far behind. The purser of the latter vessel, Charles H. Denison, was still amused by lingering thoughts of bantering at Havana between the officers of the two steamers, as to their speed. At sunset on the 8th, he saw barely visible on the horizon the smoke from the stack of the *Central America,* and next morning she was completely out of sight. On the 9th, Denison noticed that the wind blew fresh from northeast.

Wednesday evening, September 9th, at the regular evening whist game in the ship's cabin, Captain Herndon and Judge Monson sat as partners. Monson, brother-in-law of Robert H. Morris, former Justice of the United States Supreme Court, "had been an old acquaintance of his, and occupied a seat at his left at the dining table."[12]

Dr. Obed Harvey,[13] a physician from Placerville, California, was going East for a visit. When on the 10th, the ship's physician, Dr. Tennison, became ill with a fever, Harvey prescribed for him and agreed to assume his duties aboard the *Central America.*

In steerage, Barney M. Lee,[14] a mulatto, traveled with his uncle, Daniel Mahoney. Lee had been a miner, and recently the proprietor of a hair dressing salon in Nevada City, California, while Mahoney operated the Magnolia Saloon there. Lee, in his berth during the very

---

[12] *New York Herald,* 27 Sep 1857, 1-1.

[13] Dr. Obed C. Harvey, age 32, was born in Wayne Co., New York. He graduated from Rock Island Medical School, Illinois, in 1849, and practiced medicine in that State until 1850; he then came to El Dorado Co., California. Thompson & West, *History of Sacramento Co,* CA, 256.

[14] Barney M. Lee, age 28, was born in Washington, DC. He had lived in Pitt Township, Allegheny County, Pennsylvania, with his mother, uncle and other family members. In 1852, he mined and, by 1856, he and his uncle were in Nevada City, Nevada Co., California. 1850 U.S. Census, PA, Allegheny Co., Pitt Tshp, 20 Jul 1850, 12. 1852 CA Census, Nevada Co, 114. *Directory of Nevada City, CA,* 1856.

early hours of Wednesday morning, became aware of an increase in the rate of wind, but thought the gale would soon subside. By Wednesday noon, however, it had worsened, and he heard some of the seamen call it a storm.

Wednesday night, Lee climbed into his bunk thinking the storm would probably be over by morning. "Down below, nothing could be heard but the crying of children, or the moans of those suffering from seasickness, and rising above all the sounds that [emanated] from the inside of the vessel was the continued dashing and splashing of the waves against the sides of the ship, and the howling of the storm as the wind swept through the steamer's rigging."[15] Amid all of those noises, Lee fell asleep. He awoke early in the morning only to find the storm had increased even more in intensity, and on that day, Thursday, the 10th, it was a hurricane. There appeared to be no concern for danger among the men, but he thought the women were becoming apprehensive because they were unable to go on the upper deck.

In the first cabin, Robert Brown had been completely satisfied with this trip on the *Central America.* "The steamer behaved beautifully." As the vessel proceeded toward the Strait of Florida, his observations of the increasing intensity of the storm were essentially the same as other passengers. On Friday, the 11th of September, he sat all morning watching the storm's progress, and noticed how well the steamer performed—always head to the sea—no obvious strains—not a creak in her timbers. "I made up my mind," he said, "to wait two weeks for her at any subsequent time that I should wish to go to California."[16]

Thomas Badger, a thorough seaman, went about the steamer with a keen eye peeled for irregularities, his purpose being neither idle curiosity nor to challenge decisions of the ship's officers. On Thursday, Badger felt the fresh northern breeze increasing until evening. He noted the mercury in the barometer going up slowly.

He arose at 6:00 A.M. and, on deck with Jane Badger at seven-thirty on Thursday, September 10th, he noticed that excess steam was being allowed to escape, it apparently having been made faster than needed. Upon the noise made by its release, he saw George Ashby leave his room "hastily, being only partially dressed, and looked down into the engine room." At the same time, Theodore Payne saw Captain Herndon rush from his cabin to the engine room. The engines and boilers of the ship were in perfect order, and had been working well, carrying an average of

---

[15] *New York Herald,* 21 Sep 1857, 2-1.
[16] *Daily Alta California,* 23 Oct 1857, 1-3.

fifteen pounds of steam. The maximum working power was twenty pounds to the inch, but Ashby seldom let it reach that pressure "even under the most favorable circumstances."

Because of the heavy sea, the engine labored, had to be "worked very slowly by hand, and men properly placed to push the cranks to keep them from catching on the center."[17] At about 10:00 A.M. he again met Ashby "walking about the ship on deck;" Ashby said that he "had a man stationed at the starting bar" to ease the motion of the engine over the center, the added manual pressure being sufficient to move the crank-shaft rod through the sluggish part of its cycle. At that time the ship worked easily.

Captain Badger, having gone below during the forenoon, at 1:00 P.M. observed the engines "moving still more slowly than before." He could see through the hatchways to the bottom, and detected no water in the ship. "She was perfectly dry, lay head to the wind, and was making very fine weather."

James Frazer, on duty in the pilot-house on Thursday, found strong breezes with a head sea and head wind from north and eastward. Frazer steered north, and at 8:00 P.M. placed their position in the bend of the Gulf Stream, having run 215 miles that day,[18] and sailing in the normal off-shore position for the steamer, about 75 miles to sea.

Captain Herndon had appeared at the table for the last time on Thursday morning, and cancelled the evening games. The storm "raged all Thursday night, and Friday was no calmer." Stewardess Lucy Dawson asked Mrs. Easton if she wanted any food, but Addie was too seasick to think of eating.[19]

On Friday morning, September 11th, Badger found the ship "free from water, with head to the wind, laying very easy, and engine working slowly." The passengers were quiet—for the most part feeling sick because of the pitch and roll of the ship.

At nine o'clock Chief Engineer Ashby saw the ship taking water, and reported the condition to Captain Herndon. At ten, on orders from the captain, Ashby started the Worthington Pumps and bilge injection on steam from the main boilers. Water had entered the starboard (right side) bilge,[20] where, heated by the steam pipes, it became very hot. The leeward pump worked but failed to prevent a gain of the water level. The larboard (port, or left-hand side) pump, being above the water because

---

[17] *Richmond Daily Dispatch,* 21 Sep 1857, 1-2.
[18] *New York Times,* 22 Sep 1857, 8-3.
[19] Olmsted-Lincoln, 16.
[20] That part of the ship's underwater body extending to the point where the sides rise vertically.

of the ship's list, could not be used. Ashby inspected the pipes, connections, and deadlights. He found them all tight.

The violence of the sea and list of the ship made it impossible for the coal passers to use the wheel barrows. The chief engineer reported the situation to Captain Herndon, and then started all hands of the available crew to passing coal to the engine room in buckets and baskets. The captain ordered all waiters to assist in this activity and, in a further attempt to keep up steam pressure, sent an organized male passenger brigade to assist the crew.

The steamer remained in the trough of the sea. Dr. Harvey told engineer Ashby that "something was giving way in his room,"[21] and Ashby found that the starboard paddle-box and guard had settled several inches. As a result, a leak had developed around the starboard shaft. This leak was nearly stopped with blankets, and crewmen wrapped a sail around the shaft, outside, between the paddle-wheel and the ship. Problems were compounding.

At 11:00 A.M., on Friday, Captain Herndon gave the first indication to the passengers of the seriousness of the situation at hand when he appeared in the first class cabin area, quietly asking the male passengers to stand by with buckets and some blankets. These, he added, would be immediately needed to bail the ship and keep down a leak. "The engines have stopped but we hope to reduce the water and start them again," he said, "she's a sturdy vessel and if we can keep up steam we shall weather the gale."

Herndon's attendent, William Garretson, and Thomas Badger went with Captain Herndon in making the rounds to alert all of the male passengers on board. Badger also aided Herndon in organizing gangs to pass coal in the engine room and bail water from the steerage area. Herndon seemed to be everywhere—in the cabins and about the ship cheering and inspiring passengers, in the pilot-house directing action in an attempt to control the ship. He sought anyone or anything usable to fight the emergency.

"Danger makes faces grim and stern and hardens the nerves," said Manlove. "Everyone realized our position, and in every heart there was a hope." He wondered if he would ever again see the faces of his brothers and sisters, who awaited his arrival. "Would those eyes be dimmed with tears?"

Soon the ship gave a sudden lurch to starboard, and when Addie looked toward her port-hole, she saw "that it was entirely under water."[22]

---

[21] *New York Times*, 22 Sep 1857, 1-3.
[22] Olmsted-Lincoln, 17.

Herndon called upon the passengers to come on deck, as he needed their assistance. There he ordered all to stand on the port side of the steamer in order to help right her, which it did to a minimal extent.

The immediate responsibility for maintaining steam power and engine operation rested with Chief Engineer George Ashby. Uneasily, at noon, he saw the water overflow the coal-bunker floors, both forward and aft, the water becoming very hot by its contact with the boilers. Most of the oil lamps in the engine room had been extinguished by water vapor, and the men could no longer work there. He reported the problems below to Captain Herndon, who ordered steam gotten up in the repaired donkey boiler. Responding, Ashby called to First Assistant Engineer John Tice to fire the boiler, which was situated on deck. Then, with the aid of Thomas Badger, he organized another gang to break up steerage births for fuel.

Since the lower deck was swamped, the waiters attempted at one o'clock on Friday to set the table on the next level for the steerage passengers. Instead of the usual twelve, only two tables were set, the sea being so rough that it was with great difficulty that even those were prepared. "Very few thought of eating," observed Judge Monson, and "when those who chose to eat had eaten," an attempt was made to set the regular two o'clock table for the first cabin passengers. "No one cared for food, seemingly. Those who were not suffering from seasickness manifested no disposition to eat." Badger and Monson insisted there was no necessity for setting table, and the attempt was abandoned. Only hard crackers and water were then available.

Although the staterooms had been rendered unusable by waves breaking over the steamer and large amounts of water entering them, most persons on board had not recognized the danger presented by the inability of the crew to stop the leak, and the consequent loss of control of the vessel.

Almira Kittredge noticed that when Captain Herndon called all hands to help in bailing, two of the little girls, Harriet Lockwood and Augustine Pahud, "got their dinner nevertheless, and had a merry time over it. The sea tossed the steamer about very violently, but the girls laughingly told us how they braced themselves to the table and ate away. When the dishes flew about smashing and crashing as they fell to the floor, the girls laughed merrily, thinking it was rare sport. They were decidedly jolly, little realizing the danger in which they stood." The following day, September 12th, would be Augustine's ninth birthday, and although this day was not ideal for a celebration, the two girls enjoyed a delightful party in the dining salon.

Passengers Bailing the Ship
From *Frank Leslie's Illustrated Newspaper*

Returning to the deck, Herndon ordered Third Officer Myers to set the storm spencer,[23] or spanker, close abaft a lower mast in an attempt to help stabilize the ship and keep her head to the wind. The sail disintegrated. Captain Herndon stood by the wheel-house directing the procedures. He and his officers had had little rest since entering the storm and, as it increased, again striving for stability and control, he brought down the foreyard. When he could not bring the ship head to the wind, he spread canvas and sails in the main and mizzen[24] rigging, but with the ship so high out of the water, all such attempts failed.

When Frazer again relieved Myers at noon on Friday, he found the gale heavy, but the sea had subsided a little. He spoke to the captain about trying to get the ship head to the wind. Herndon explained that he had been attempting for all the forenoon to do just that, but could not effect it.

The captain and his officers knew that in a storm, in order to keep the

---

[23] A trysail (spanker, fore-and-aft sail), behind the foremast or mainmast.
[24] Mizzen mast: the third mast from forward. On this ship, the aftermast.

vessel from falling off in the trough between waves and from suffering irreparable damage to the wooden hull, the vessel had to be kept head to the wind. To accomplish this, it was imperative that coal be rapidly passed to the engine room, and the fires continuously kept burning in order to maintain steam pressure. Without steam for the engines there would be no power to control the steamer unless the sails could be manipulated. They could not.

The captain, turning to Frank Jones, remarked jokingly, "you must take off your broadcloth and go to work." Jones immediately "borrowed a pair of sailor's pantaloons, red shirt and coarse boots, and with the glazed cover of a cloth cap on his head reported himself in working costume." Amanda Marvin said that Frank "had been very sick, but on Friday he went to work with great energy."[25] Before doing so, he handed to Mrs. Easton his valuable watch, asking her to take care of it while he joined the bailing crews. She gladly accepted it.

Both Billy Birch and Joseph Bassford also left their watches in the care of Addie Easton. Birch and Jones went to check the water level, and were dismayed to find it up to the second cabin floor. I.N. Van Hagan[26] handed his watch to his wife, Hannah, telling her to keep it as a memento if he perished.

In the first cabin area, the Hawley family, all of whom had been ill, were attempting to eat, when Garretson rushed in saying "All hands below to bail!" Frederick Hawley immediately pulled off his coat and went to work with the bailing crews. In their stateroom he found a rope needed for use in rigging the buckets on the pulleys. He told his wife, Elizabeth, that he had found the water up to the knees of the men, and gaining. At the moment the order came, Jabez Howes,[27] a San Francisco commission merchant, seated at the table with them, "pulled off his coat and went to work."

Dr. Harvey continued providing medical service. The Ship's Steward, N. McBride, "was taken with excessive hemorrhage of the lungs. I gave him such medical attention as was in my power."

---

[25] *The New York Herald*, 27 Sep 1857, 8-3. *Frank Leslie's Illustrated Newspaper*, 10 Oct 1857, 297.

[26] I.N. Van Hagan, from Binghampton, New York, had operated a public house at Rough and Ready, in Penn Valley, CA. Hannah Van Hagan, 30, was born in New York; one child accompanied them. *Baltimore Sun*, 21 Sep 1857, 2-1.

[27] Jabez Howes, age 26, was born in Yarmouth, Massachusetts. He and two brothers had established a commission merchant firm, Geo. Howes & Co., in 1852. Their father was a widely known and competent old-time trans-Atlantic packet-ship commander. Jabez was very interested in yachts. Robert M. Sherman, comp. *Yarmouth, MA, Vital Records to 1850* Vol I, (Society of Mayflower Descendants in State of Rhode Island, 1975). Frederick C. Matthews *American Merchant Ships, 1850-1900*, 173-7. Karl Kortum, An Old San Francisco Firm. *San Francisco Call*, 31 Jul 1897, 14-5.

Robert Brown had observed the spanker set, and in an hour he saw it blown away. He went downstairs to talk to Easton and very shortly Badger called for all hands to get the buckets ready. Two lines were formed from the lower well-hole, near the cabin, to the deck. There were about fifty men in each line, and fifty more bailing from the well-hole on the steerage at the forward end of the ship. Brown and the others "worked assiduously and laboriously, and succeeded in preventing the water from increasing upon us by the rapid use of the buckets." Until dark the water in the hold was still shallow enough to see the pig iron ballast on the bottom of the steamer's hold. Soon, however, the water gained considerably and continuously.

Captain Herndon concerned himself with both the safety of the ship and the well-being and peace of mind of the passengers. When not on deck directing the progress of the vessel he was in the cabin giving reassurances to the passengers. Mrs. Jane Harris, another young mother whose husband had stayed in California, noticed that "during all the time of the storm the captain kept coming down into the cabin, and going all around the ship, to cheer the spirits of the passengers and to quiet their fears. I do not mean that he could quiet our fears," she said, "no one could do that, . . . He did not try to disguise the danger, but he made us all look more cheerfully at it than some other men might have done."

At 1:00 P.M. on Friday the engines stopped for want of steam. They were soon restarted but, Ashby noted, with only port fires and the starboard side under water, steam was soon exhausted. Because the coal was wet, the boilers were then fired with wood, and Herndon ordered all cabin doors readied to burn for fuel. But, at about 2:00 P.M., the port boiler fires were extinguished by water. Bail gangs were at work in the after cabin hatches and lower steerage, but in spite of the efforts, by 4:00 P.M. the rising water extinguished all of the fires in the boilers.

Wind from the northwest had driven the ship off course to the southeast, and the *Central America* was taking on an increased amount of sea water through the leak. Van Rensselaer ordered Frazer to rig the forward and afterdeck bilge pumps. Frazer saw the sea running high with heavy rain at 4:00 P.M., and it still ran high when Myers relieved him at the helm.

Herndon strove to keep the ship under control. He attempted to set the fore staysail with the helm hard to port, but before it could be hoisted, the staysail blew away. Seeing the futility of using the sails, he ordered the crew to haul down the remaining canvas and bolt ropes.

Van Rensselaer suggested that the jib[28] be moved and bent onto the forestay[29] for a staysail. Captain Herndon said: "We will try the foresail by reefing [shortening] it and lashing the clews [lower corners] to the deck, and heave up the yard[30] with the yard tackle[31] and forelifts." This attempt, to lower the center of gravity and make the sail less vulnerable to the wind, failed. No sooner was it started up when the sail blew to ribbons. The captain then ordered a drag (to increase draft toward the stern) put overboard to try and bring the ship head to the wind. Without delay, the crew rigged the foreyard with a heavy kedge anchor hanging to it. "The foreyard had a seven or nine inch hawser [large rope] fast to it and we payed it out about 40 fathoms [240 feet] at first," said Frazer. At 5:30 P.M. on Friday the ship remained in the trough of the sea.

In an effort to right the ship (Maury described her as having "not a little top hamper,[32] and therefore an ugly thing to manage in such a situation") the captain ordered the foremast cut away. Said Badger, "At five o'clock, after consulting with Captain Herndon, I assisted in cutting away the foremast." By this time the ship listed to leeward, and people could not walk on deck. Captain Herndon, with the chief engineer, crawled along the deck to inspect the after pumps. With the mates and Ashby, Herndon discussed "everything that experience could suggest, or the extremity of their condition devise."[33]

The foremast being secured by a hawser to its stump, Frazer, John Black and Badger cut away the rigging and let the foremast go over the side. As the rigging went over, it became entangled with the cathead[34] and anchor. This caused the foremast to be pulled under the ship, forward of its original position, and where for some period of time it thumped the bottom of the oak hull.

The Worthington Pumps continued to operate under power from the donkey boiler until 8:00 P.M., with a few short stoppages to free from obstructions the boiler feed-pipe. The donkey engine (auxiliary steam engine) stopped because the feed-pipe became so clogged that it had to be cut and repaired.

---

[28] A triangular sail set upon a stay, extending from the foremast to the bowsprit or the jib boom, a spar extending the bowsprit.

[29] A large, strong rope (stay) from the foremast head to the deck, to support the foremast, and to which a sail may be mounted (staysail).

[30] A long spar, tapered toward the ends, to support and extend a sail.

[31] The rigging, an assemblage of ropes and pullies, etc.

[32] Rigging, spars, etc., not needed for the time, and hence in the way.

[33] *The New York Times*, 22 Sep 1857, 1-3.

[34] A projecting piece of timber or iron near the bow, for holding the tacks of jibs or stays. The cat is a tackle used in hoisting the anchor to the cathead.

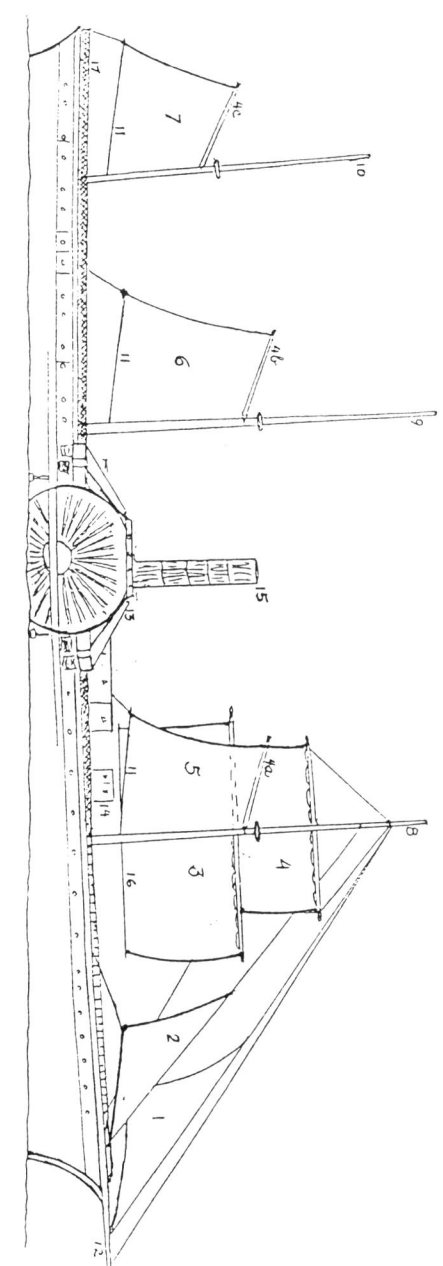

Rigging of the Central America
The sails and other parts of the *Central America* named by Captain Herndon, First Officer Frazer, and Captain Badger: 1. jib; 2. fore staysail; 3. foresail; 4a. fore Yard; 4b. main yard; 4c. mizzen yard; 5. fore spencer; 6. main spencer; 7. mizzen spencer (spanker); 8. foremast; 9. mainmast; 10. aftermast (mizzenmast); 11. boom; 12. jib boom; 13. paddle-box (wheel guard); 14. wheel house (pilot house); 15. funnel; 16. spar; 17. taffrail. Drawing by author.

Herndon had tried every means at his disposal to head the vessel into the wind and here is found an ironic parallel to feelings of uneasiness he experienced in traversing the intersection of the Amazon and Madeira rivers.

> I always felt some anxiety in crossing so large an expanse of water in such a boat as ours, where violent storms of wind are of frequent occurrence. Our men, with their light paddles, could not keep such a 'haystack' as our clumsy, heavy boat either head to wind or before it, and she would, therefore, lie 'broadside to' in the trough of the sea, rolling fearfully, and threatening to swamp. I should have had sails fitted to her in Barra.[35]

He must have found his situation on the *Central America* to be quite similar, the steamer being very clumsy to manage without steam, and the sails that he had available in this case being quickly destroyed by the powerful gale.

The captain turned his efforts toward attracting passing vessels to the rescue of his passengers and crew.

---

[35] Herndon, *Exploration* . . . 87-8.

CHAPTER V

Hope, Struggle and Loss

At daylight on Saturday, Captain Herndon ordered the flag hoisted at half-mast, union down, the signal of distress. Being in a frequented part of the ocean, he considered that if the ship could be kept afloat, a vessel would come to their rescue, and he encouraged the passengers with this hope.

On the *Empire City*, far behind the *Central America*, Purser Denison found "the wind increasing tremendously with a heavy sea running and, on Saturday, the 12th, blew a hurricane. The force of the gale at this time," he said, "exceeded anything in my previous experience. I can compare it only to the roar of steam from an escape pipe."[1] A low, gloomy, cloudy sky overhead shut out the sun and stars, and the wind drove a heavy mist of spray over a plane of foam.

On the *Central America*, some men refused to go to work. George Ashby came to the ship's cabin, "pulled men out of their staterooms" and said they should go or he would throw them overboard. Mr. Ashby came down stairs thus several times and entreated or forced the men to go up to work. He said he had a "mother in New York, and was as anxious to see her again as anyone could be to see his mother, and the only way to be saved to see them was to keep the bailing active."[2] Charles McCarty, Chief Engineer of the *Golden Gate*, a passenger on the *Central America*, assisted Ashby, and demanded the men should go up to work, or they would be thrown overboard because the lives of all depended upon the exertion of each. Ange Richon "saw Mr. Ashby work faithfully with others in trying to bail the steamer,"[3] but in spite of all the bailing efforts, the water level continued to increase until she now listed 45° to the port side, with portholes under water. Water gushed in through the ports; Monson, Taylor and others "tried to stop it with blankets," without much success.

Jones said it was "a novel experience to see the men at work, many of whom had never been in the habit of physical labor, taking hold with

---
[1] Escape pipes allowed excess steam to escape from the boilers to the deck.
[2] *The New York Herald*, 27 Sep 1857, 8-3, *Frank Leslie's Illustrated Newspaper*, 10 Oct 1857, 297.
[3] *Baltimore Sun*, 21 Sep 1857, 2-1.

strength and willingness equal to the heartiest. After a while the work began to be rather a serious affair for the strength and muscles."[4]

When Elizabeth Hawley looked down the companionway on Saturday morning, she saw the water level nearly up to the floor of the second cabin.

Mrs. Kittredge noticed that some of the men declined to work. Mr. John Fell,[5] a miner from McAdam's Bar, Siskiyou County, California, was one of them; his young wife, Jane, and two sons were with him. One child was very sick, and he considered it necessary to conserve his strength in order to ensure their safety.

Several passengers convinced Fell that the "lives of all depended upon the efforts of each man." Jane Badger took his sick baby and assured him she would take the best care of him. John Fell went to work, and did so with determination, joining Captain William H. Marvin, an agent for Michigan Central Railroad in Chicago, who by that time had worked so hard that he could hardly speak to his wife, Amanda. Marvin rested a moment, then resumed bailing.

The captain obtained Monson's permission to leave his instruments in the Judge's stateroom because, in its position on the upper deck, the captain's stateroom could be blown away with everything in it.

Captain Herndon continued to encourage the bailers. Going below to where Robert Hutchinson and other men labored, he said: "Work on my boys, we have hopes yet. Then he would ask us if we wanted any fresh water, and whenever we did, he had it brought to us. He was very active all the time," said Hutchinson. "He told us to relieve each other like men, and not to suffer any one of us to drop down while another man stood idle."[6]

About eight o'clock he told Monson that there was no hope for them unless the storm abated soon or some vessel hove in sight. Monson presumed he was the only person on board in whom Herndon confided this concern.[7] "The captain was perfectly calm, and intimated that it

---

[4] *The New York Herald*, 21 Sep 1857, 3-2.

[5] Jane Miller was 17 years old when she married John Fell at her home in Glasgow, Jefferson Co, IA, January 1853. Three months later they started across the plains, arriving in California on 5 Sep 1853. Their two sons were born in California, and there they had saved $6,000. Daughters of the American Revolution, Log Cabin Chapter, *Jefferson County Records*, Vol II, Fairfield, IA: 1962-1963. *Fairfield Ledger*, Iowa, 14 Apr 1926, 2-5. *The New York Herald*, 27 Sep 1857, 8-3, *Frank Leslie's Illustrated Newspaper*, 10 Oct 1857, 297.

[6] *The New York Times*, 22 Sep 1857, 8-5.

[7] Monson had made a number of trips between the east and west coasts, and had become well acquainted with Herndon. "Three consecutive times," said Monson, "it has been my misfortune in journeying from California to the States, to get caught in the equitorial storm. . . . For the fourth time I found myself on board ship, off Cape Hatteras, in one of the most terrific storms, probably, that ever stirred the angry water off that Cape, a more dangerous place than which, in a heavy gale, is not on the whole Atlantic coast." *The New York Herald*, 27 Sep 1857, 1-1.

(the encouragement he gave) was but to keep up the courage of the passengers and crew until the last moment."

Addie Easton earned the admiration of many by encouraging the passengers and crew members engaged in bailing. Because the storerooms were filled with water, no meals had been prepared on Friday. At about eleven o'clock, she thought of the many bottles of wine and biscuits that had been given to her and Ansel as gifts in San Francisco. She reached their stateroom "with great difficulty," and brought them to where her husband, his friend Robert Brown and others bailed. All "eagerly took the crackers and wine, stopping only long enough to eat them and then going on with the work of bailing."[8] She "was altogether an angel of mercy." During the night, at intervals, she made the rounds among the men until they had eaten all the food.

On Saturday morning Herndon appeared at the door of the dining saloon, saying: "If we can keep the ship afloat for three or four more hours, we shall certainly see a sail and help will come. You remember the *San Francisco* floated eleven days."[9] Mrs. Easton "responded to his bright influence and felt more hopeful."

"On Saturday morning," said James Forster, "there was a lull of the gale, the sun shone out, and all hands went to work with the hope of being saved. Strenuous efforts continued. All available materials, including blankets, mattresses and counterpanes were stuffed into the area of the leak, but nothing worked."[10] Frank Jones said: "The main leak, which admitted the largest volume of water, could not be discovered." Chief Engineer Ashby and other crewmen thought the principal leak to be around the starboard paddle wheel shaft, but water also entered the ship from other locations.

At about ten o'clock Saturday morning, Captain Badger went to Captain Herndon's room, remarking that the storm appeared to be abating but the water was gaining rapidly, and the steamer must go down. Captain Herndon agreed, adding he had made up his mind to it; that he found it very hard to leave his family thus, but it could not be helped. At that moment George Ashby entered the room and Badger said to him, "The ship will sink." The remark startled Ashby, who earnestly replied, "She shant sink, I'll be d____d if she shall. We must all go to work and bail her out." Badger replied that he "wished talking in that style would do it, but he and all the rest on board had been hard at work all night bailing, but without avail."[11]

---

[8] Olmsted-Lincoln, 21.
[9] *Ibid.*, 22.
[10] *Baltimore Sun*, MD, 21 Sep 1857, 2-4.
[11] *The New York Times*, 23 Sep 1857, No. 1876, 1-1.

Captain Herndon ordered the use of beef and pork barrels with tackle for bailing larger quantities of water. Frank Jones, John Dobbin and Charles McCarty joined others in rigging the pulleys over the hatchways, hoisting the water-filled barrels with ropes on the pulleys, and in emptying them overboard, convinced that this activity, in addition to the bailing parties lining the companionways passing water up, helped to keep the ship afloat. "Four hundred gallons of water per minute were thrown out of the ship," Ashby estimated.[12]

Two lines were formed from the lower well-hole, near the cabin, to the deck. There were about fifty men in each line, and at the forward end of the ship fifty more bailed from the well-hole on the steerage.

> The labor of the men at the buckets and barrels was very severe and trying, [said Joseph Bassford.] Everything was done to keep up the spirits, and to give impetus and encouragement to the work, a large number sang while laboring. The voices of the workers rose merrily and powerfully above the din of the storm and the lashing of the steamers sides by the waves. The song was a stereo type couplet, sung with a sailor-like melody and vivacity -Heave O, Heave O, jump and go, We'll be jolly blather, O.[13]
>
> [The men] became so completely tired out, [continued Bassford,] that after a time they had to give up work. Some fell down exhausted and fainting in their steps. At this crisis some of the ladies behaved most generously and nobly — several of them volunteering to take their place at the buckets; but the men, tired as they were, had too much gallantry to allow this. The offer . . . gave renewed encouragement to the men.

Assistant Engineer Henry Keefer cut off the escape pipes and rigged them as manual pumps,[14] and early Saturday morning, the 12th, Brown worked for three hours on them, but he and the others could see no water being drawn up. With no progress seen on the reduction of the water level, the pumps were repaired, and the men spent about three more hours in pumping, without apparent results. "There was a row of ten men working at the pumps," said Henry Kimball.[15] Every man worked to the best of his ability. "and each man had his life-preserver by his side," but the pumps still did not appear to remove water. Barrels and ropes were then put into service and hauled up through the skylight.

Second Officer Frazer, learning of Brown's complaint about the

---

[12] *The New York Times*, 23 Sep 1857, 1-3.
[13] *New York Daily Tribune*, 21 Sep 1857, 6-7.
[14] Ridgely-Nevitt, *"George Law,"* 315.
[15] Henry Kimball was from St. Laurence Co., New York. *The New York Daily Tribune*, 21 Sep 1857, 7-6, and *The New York Times*, 22 Sep 1857, No. 1875, 8-1, *The Sacramento Daily Union*, 26 Oct 1857, 1-6.

pumps, quickly sought the cause. He could not see the discharge pipe of the after pump because of its location below the deck, out of sight. Going forward, he saw the lee forward pump heaving water. The time on the pumps had contributed to the bailing effort, but the ship took on water faster than it could be removed. Then Frazer found that the chamber of the forward weather pump had burst just below the discharge pipe.

After examining the pumps, at 5:00 A.M. Frazer "went below decks to have two whips[16] rigged between decks in order to hoist water to the upper steerage for discharge through the scuppers."[17] Crewmen rigged pulleys to run barrels to lower steerage, where they were filled with sea water, hoisted and emptied as quickly as possible. Gangs of fifty men manned the pulley ropes, Jones and Willard Fletcher[18] being among them.

Frazer found the freight room one-half to two-thirds full of water, then found whips had been rigged in the engine room and men heaving out water with tubs. He counted a total of nine whips with tubs, and three gangs bailing with buckets.

Henry O'Connor saw on the larboard side waves sliding off as far as several building stories, and on the starboard side just as high and as steep. The ship was "in the trough of the sea all of the time." O'Connor, as did all of the men, observed the call to bail the vessel. The negative aspects of the situation weighed heavily on his young mind—the water gaining because the pump would not operate, the donkey engine's failure to work, the seeming futility of the bailing by buckets, and the retardation of this process caused by the mass of floating materials which rose to the surface of the water in the ship. He overheard discussions concerning the possibility of "constructing box pumps, such as used in the California mines" [boxing the existing pumps in order to keep them free of obstructions], and although there were carpenters among the passengers who could build them, no tools could be found. The ship had no carpenter assigned to her crew, and any tools that may have been on board were below decks and consequently inaccessible.

Considering that the steamer must soon sink, Henry decided to do his best to save himself. With his life-preserver around him, he went

---

[16] A center pulley block arrangement to permit water containers to be hoisted with ropes.

[17] *New York Daily Tribune*, 23 Sep 1857, 5-3, *The New York Herald*, 23 Sep 1857, 1-1.

[18] Willard F. Fletcher, age 20, was enroute to his home in Bloomfield, Maine, where he was born, and planned to establish a home there. In 1852, at age 15, Willard went to San Francisco, by the Nicaragua route; he mined at Timbuctoo on the Yuba River. In 1853 he mined in Columbia and Gold Springs with two other Fletchers. *Oakland Tribune*, Alameda County, CA, 202. Heckendorn's *Directory of Tuolumne Co, CA, 1856:* Columbia, CA, 11. *New York Daily Tribune,* 21 Sep 1857, 6-5. *Baltimore Sun*, 23 Sep 1857, 1-2. *Richmond Daily Dispatch*, 24 Sep 1857, 1. *New York Herald*, 27 Sep 1857, 8-8. *Baltimore Sun*, 28 Sep 1857, 1-3, quoting *The Boston Journal*.

upon the paddle-box where he had a brief encounter with Chief Engineer George Ashby. "The chief engineer," said O'Connor, "drew his bowie knife on me and attempted to cut away my life preserver, but someone [a young man from New York, whom some of the passengers called 'handsome Harry'] interfered by seizing his arm, and would not allow him to do that."[19] While Henry thought Ashby to have been "crazy or drunk," the chief engineer, in his coarse manner, continued his efforts to assure that all able-bodied males were kept at work in bailing the ship.

Below, a determined passenger named Miller took a position at the top of the companionway leading to the steerage. He drew his revolver and threatened to shoot down any man who attempted to go up on deck or refused to work. John Taylor[20] saw him strike one person a sharp blow in the face. After a while, Miller relaxed his watch. Taylor proceeded to rouse as many men from their bunks as he could.

Almira Kittredge watched Amanda Marvin "pull up a little Irish boy and girl named Fallon,"[21] second cabin passengers. Their cabin was half full of water. "These children said they dared not go upstairs, because the men were passing water up the stairs."[22] Unable to stand on the listing, rolling deck, Amanda succeeded in pulling them up through a hatch by holding onto a table leg with all her strength.

Jane Badger made a last minute effort to rescue some of the gold that Thomas had brought from San Francisco, and which was stored in a trunk in their cabin. She "crawled along the floor" to reach the place to which it had shifted as the ship listed to her starboard side. From Theodore Payne she borrowed a universal trunk key, "took out the gold, which she had sewn up in toweling in three pieces, placed it in a carpet-bag," and finding it too heavy to handle, made her way back to the deck and "reported to Thomas what she had done, greatly to his astonishment." Jane had found in her husband's coat, hanging in the state-room, his "memorandum book containing notes and other evidences of debts owing to him in New York," and amounting to "some thousands of dollars." Thomas told her to throw away her jewels, but she refused, instead putting them into her pocket.[23]

---

[19] *The New York Herald,* 21 Sep 1857, 2-5,6. *Albany Evening Journal,* 23 Sep 1857, 2-3.

[20] John C. Taylor, age 26, was born in New York. His home was in Cohoes Falls, Albany Co., New York. He had been a tradesman in California, and had saved $300. *The New York Times,* 21 Sep 1857, 8-2, *New York Daily Tribune,* 21 Sep 1857, 7-3.

[21] Seventeen year old Winifred Fallon's mother had died the previous February in Connecticut. In April, she and her brother, James, age 3, went with their father, Lawrence Fallon, to San Jose, CA. They stayed four months with her uncle and were now enroute home. *New York Daily Tribune,* 21 Sep 1857, 6-2.

[22] *The New York Herald,* 27 Sep 1857, 8-3.

[23] *The New York Times,* 21 Sep 1857, 8. *Daily Alta California,* 23 Oct 1857, 1-6.

Annie McNeil noticed that

> owing to the violence of the storm there was considerable suffering from sea-sickness among the passengers on the steamer, but as soon as the danger became imminent all symptoms of sea-sickness disappeared. The men, especially the first cabin passengers, had worked hard all night long, their strength now fast failing. Sometimes they had to give up, and lie down flat on the deck for a moment with half recovered breath, again to rise to battle for life and death against the encroaching waters. Many of the men had been quite sea-sick, and had not eaten anything for three days, but the peril recalled their strength and avidity, and they, or at least many of them, did all that human power could do to save the ship.[24]

Captain Herndon sent word by Ansel Easton to Second Officer Frazer, telling him to stop near the rocket-box and send up a flare every half hour, "thinking, no doubt," said Frazer, "that the ship would go down before morning." The wind still blew heavily in squalls, and the water in the ship rose rapidly. Herndon carried on his untiring exertions to cheer the men to their work, and inspired the passengers and crew-members alike. He continued to be ably assisted by Captain Badger. Mrs. Kittredge remarked, "Captain Herndon called on Captain Badger a great deal and wanted him to do this thing and that."

Jane Badger began to lose hope, and thought she must prepare herself to die. When her husband came to comfort her, she said: "I am prepared to die. It is hard to die in this way—but we may be in a happier world tomorrow." Jane wept bitterly, but silently, fearing to affect others with her grief. Turning to the ladies in the cabin, she assumed, as well as she was able, a cheerful countenance, and said to one who sat near her, "The Lord is merciful. It is not 12 o'clock yet. Perhaps some vessel will come in sight before that time, and we may be saved yet."[25]

I.N. Van Hagan, a hard worker, leaving his work for a moment, ran to his wife in the cabin to encourage her and others who were nearby. From him they heard the first word that a ship was in sight, and on hearing that news some "cried lustily for joy." Almira Kittredge, disbelieving, remarked that it could not be possible that a ship was coming. Van Hagan replied, "Mrs. Kittredge, if the ship does not come and take us off we shall all go down to-night," and "the tears came to his eyes." It was "the first discouraging word" that she had heard.[26]

The men had bailed continuously for twenty-two hours before a sail appeared at about 1:00 P.M. on Saturday, the 12th of September.

---

[24] *Richmond Daily Dispatch*, 23 Sep 1857, 1-3. *Chicago Daily Press*, 24 Sep 1857, 2-4.
[25] *The New York Times*, 24 Sep 1857, 1.
[26] *The New York Herald*, 27 Sep 1857, 8-3. *Frank Leslie's Illustrated Newspaper*, 10 Oct 1857, 297.

The Brig *Marine* Lays by for Passengers from the *Central America*
Courtesy, Library of Congress

Captain Hiram Burt
From *Frank Leslie's Illustrated Newspaper*

CHAPTER VI

A Welcome Stranger

The brig *Marine* of Boston passed under the lee of the *Central America*, and Captain Herndon told Second Officer Frazer to contact her. On his speaker horn he called out, asking her captain to lay by. Captain Burt acknowledged, calling that he would do so, at the same time wondering why a hawser had not been thrown from the steamer to the brig. The available sturdy hawsers had been used in creating drags with the heavy kedge anchor and the foremast.

Captain Hiram Burt, youthful-looking forty-five-year-old master of the brig *Marine*, sailed toward the Port of New York, where the *Marine* was the property of Mr. Elisha Atkins, Esq. Born in 1812 and raised in Taunton, Massachusetts, Hiram had a New England boy's education until going to sea at the age of fifteen. Six years later, he mastered a ship, and before 1857 sailed in the European, West India and California trades.[1] Burt now found himself in an Atlantic hurricane with a load of molasses from Cardena, Cuba, and a storm-damaged ship.

Captain Herndon had ordered flares fired every thirty minutes, and Burt, nursing his vessel toward Cape Hatteras, sighted the distress signals of the foundering *Central America*.

"With all the calmness of an ordinary occasion," said Burt, "Captain Herndon hailed the *Marine*, saying, 'We are in a sinking condition, and you must lay by us until morning.'" This was actually the voice of Frazer, following Herndon's instructions.

Captain Burt replied, "I shall stay by you as long as I can," and as he passed by the steamer within one hundred feet of her stern, the passengers cheered, believing they were now all safe.

Herndon's first consideration extended to the women and children. He gave explicit orders for their evacuation. At about one o'clock, Garretson went to the cabin and announced: "The Captain says all the ladies must go on deck," to which they complied. On deck, they were immediately soaked as the ocean water dashed over them. Because of the list to starboard, the footing was hazardous.

---
[1] *Frank Leslie's Illustrated Newspaper*, 17 Oct 1857, 315. William Lee Burt, "Descendants of Richard Burt," typewritten, n.d.

There had been six life-boats,[2] five wooden and one metallic, but during the gale one of them was lost from its davits. Captain Herndon ordered the remaining five lowered, and two now were safely put into the rough sea.

Boatswain Black and other seamen lowered the first; Third Officer Myers, Quartermaster Finley Frazier and three men launched the second. Herndon ordered Black and Frazier to take charge of the boats.

A terrible crash startled the passengers, and "the cry ran through the cabin that the ship was sinking." On finding the noise to have been caused by the smashing of a life-boat against the steamer, the apprehensions of Almira Kittredge and others were relieved. Nevertheless, it meant the loss of a much needed boat, leaving only four for rescue operations.

Virginia Birch had listened to the cracking of timber as the heavy seas struck the steamer, and though she did not then fear for her safety, she mused that "the strongest vessels were not always proof against the storm." The Birches' stateroom lay on the starboard side, and consequently, as the vessel listed, large amounts of water entered the room, making it unusable. Suffering from sea-sickness, they passed Thursday night on the sofas in the cabin. William Birch without hesitation answered Captain Herndon's call for assistance. "When the first boat was ready," said Virginia, "my husband came to the cabin and asked me to prepare myself to go in the brig. He put a life preserver around me. As I was leaving the stateroom, I saw my pet canary in the cage, and instinctively I opened the door, took him out of the cage and nestled him in my bosom." Billy escorted Virginia to the deck for her transfer to a life-boat, with the understanding that the male passengers and crew would be transferred after the ladies and children were safely on board the brig.

Madame Rosalie Pahud groped her way to the deck with her three children. Augustine, her most treasured birthday gift now proving to be her rescue from the steamer, assisted her mother with her infant brother, followed closely by seven year old Henri Edouard. On leaving the first cabin area, "many I knew asked me to write to their families and tell them they would not live. It pained me a great deal."[3]

To effect the transfer of the woman and children to the life boats, crewmen rigged bowlines to the lee davits, and one by one lowered them into the boats, the number in each being limited to less than the normal capacity because of the treacherous sea. Thirty-foot waves made the

---

[2] The terms "life-boat" and "small boat" are synonymous.
[3] *New York Daily Tribune*, 21 Sep 1857, 6-2.

Lowering the Women into the Lifeboats From *Frank Leslie's Illustrated Newspaper*

boats difficult to control, requiring the utmost skill of experienced hands to manage them.

The ladies very reluctantly left their husbands on the steamer. Annie McNeil considered that if her husband were lost she would not want to be saved, and not wishing to be separated from him, decided to remain on board. William had different intentions. To assure her safety, he told her he would go with her, accompanied her to the deck, and assisted her into the boat. There he bade her goodbye, saying he could easily take care of himself. With her went all of her jewelry and $17,000 in drafts.

Mrs. Jane Harris carried to the deck in her arms her small child. The captain placed a noose of a rope around her waist, and assisted in lowering her to the first boat. As she looked up, she saw him fastening a rope around her little one and lowering her.

Stewardess Lucy Dawson, age fifty-six, a free black known affectionately as "Aunt Lucy," appearing quite frightened and unsteady, fell into the water and was rescued. Then followed Mrs. Birch, Mrs. Frances Thomas and Madame Pahud with her three children. Virginia Birch, while being lowered into the boat, was "completely saturated by the waves." The small boat had taken in a considerable amount of water, and Boatswain Black ordered Herndon's orderly, Garretson, to get in and assist in bailing. William McNeil watched the boat move away before he returned to bailing.

The captain made it clear that no one else should be permitted in the boats until the women and children were all safe. He gave his personal assistance to some and, with Van Rensselaer, closely supervised the entire transfer. "Several men stepped to get in them," said Frank Jones, "but Captain Herndon ordered them to stay back."

While Herndon's orders readied the boats, Captain Burt and his small crew struggled with the brig's rigging to keep her from drifting. The *Marine* had already suffered severe damage from the storm, and some of her spars were gone. She had lost the main spar, jib-boom,[4] her jibs and other sails. Her rigging was generally badly damaged.

There were eleven men on board the brig, including the captain, David O'Keefe, a fifteen year old Taunton lad, and two passengers. The limited cabin space had poor accommodations, with four bunks and cooking utensils for only fifteen. Captain Burt was confronted with taking on board as many as possible of the hundreds of people from the sinking steamship. He did not hesitate.

On the *Central America,* bailing continued without abate. Some of the men were so completely exhausted that, not able to endure any longer the agony of it, some were seen by Winifred Fallon to lock themselves in their rooms. Mrs. Hawley observed that others "drank themselves into oblivion."

Joseph Bassford saw several passengers "whose position and intelligence and withal . . . ought to have restrained themselves [but] drank heavily of liquors . . . probably from their own private stocks, and made themselves very noisy and troublesome. I know of two of the passengers," he said, "of high social and political associations, who refused to work, but got alarmingly drunk, so much so that their more sober companions had to put them in their berths."

Manlove observed that the minister who had conducted services before reaching Havana "did not have the courage to meet his fate squarely, but became intoxicated two days before the crisis, locking himself with a bottle of whiskey in his state room . . . Poor fellow," said Oliver, "God is his Judge." He did not identify the man.

Eleanor O'Connor said:

A great many of the passengers were so intoxicated, from drinking freely

---

[4] Boom: a long pole or spar used to extend the bottom of a sail.

of liquor and going without food, that they were unfit to do anything, and betook themselves to their berths. Among those intoxicated was Mr. _____ who was regarded in California as the greatest temperance lecturer who had visited that country. No harsh judgment, however, should be formed from these facts; being utterly prostrated from want of food and rest, they betook themselves to stimulants as a last resort.[5]

While bailing in the engine room, passengers Oliver Manlove and Richard Wilton saw each other for the first time in many years. They had been school-mates in Illinois. Wilton, age thirty-one, was from Quincy, Illinois, and had mined in El Dorado County since 1852.[6]

Captain Herndon called Alonzo Monson to his stateroom and said he was afraid there might be a rush of passengers for the small boats. "He wanted the ladies and children saved first. He wanted to organize some of the passengers to help prevent a rush for the boats—presumed that the brig had some boats which could be used in transferring the passengers—the *Central America* could not stay above water more than fifteen hours longer."

Three years earlier, Captain Herndon had been appalled when with the wreck of the trans-Atlantic steamer *Arctic* the lives of 350 persons were lost because of mass panic, which had resulted in the swamping of the life-boats when rushed by the firemen and other men.[7] He resolved to maintain order and discipline.

The chief engineer accompanied the captain to his room and, having in mind the dangerous possibility of a panic, Herndon asked George Ashby if he was armed. In a moment of desperation the ship could be swamped and consequently cost many lives. Ashby answered that his only weapon, a knife, had been given him that morning by a passenger. Herndon said he would try to borrow a pair of pistols, and asked Mr. Payne for the loan of his. The pistols were in Payne's trunk, already under water.

Herndon ordered Ashby to transfer the passengers to the brig, and to not allow a single man in the boats until the women and children were safely on board.

Second Officer James Frazer and Third Officer Charles Myers would normally have gone in charge of life-boats, but Captain Herndon told them to remain "on board the steamer until he went from her, which he intended to do after all the passengers and crew were transferred to the brig."

---

[5] *Albany Evening Journal*, 23 Sep 1857, 2-3.
[6] California Census, 1852, El Dorado County.
[7] Richard Miller Devens, *Our First Century*, 610.

As the first boat, with Boatswain John Black in charge, left the steamer, Herndon said to him, "Tell the captain of the brig for God's sake to remain by us—that I have 500 people on board and two millions of treasure."

The gale forced the sea into giant swells and white-capped mountains of brine. Through this the gallant oarsmen labored. By now, the brig, being much lighter than the ship, had drifted more than a mile to the leeward, and it required a great deal of time for Black's men to reach her. The distance between steamer and brig increased at the rate of nearly one mile per hour, and the storm damage rendered the *Marine* incapable of maneuvering into a more favorable position.

In calm weather, the main-rail or deck of the brig stood about seven feet above water level, but when the first life-boat came alongside, the waves rose higher than her deck. As the boat approached the brig, Jane Harris watched for a chance to spring at the rigging. She caught it with both hands, but being encumbered by her life-preserver, could not get between the ropes, and dangled over the side at the end of a rope. The captain seized her, cut off her life-preserver, and pulled her to the deck.

"One of the most remarkable events recorded in the history of sea expedients" ensued. Burt took advantage of the high sea, and positioned himself on deck close to the railing. He shouted to the women and children to hold out their hands one at a time when he directed. This being understood, two sailors stood by to keep the boat from being precipitated onto the deck of the brig. When the boat rose, Captain Burt stood ready, and at the agreed signal, seized one woman, hauling her to the deck. He did not stand on ceremony, saying "my only object was to get them safely on my ship." In this perilous way all were taken on board the *Marine*, but not without mishap.

Stewardess Lucy Dawson, fell in the sea three times, and was caught between the boat and the side of the brig. A heavy wave dashed the boat against the ship, and struck the poor woman a severe blow. After her hazardous transfer, gentle hands took "Aunt Lucy" below and placed her on one of the four bunks.

All the passengers were removed from the first boat and, though drenched and shaken, had gotten safely on board the *Marine*, where they found the water a foot-and-a-half deep and the sea rushing constantly over her decks. "It was a hard time for me with those three little children to save," recalled Mme. Pahud.

Boatswain Black sent Garretson on board the brig to relay the "lay by" request of Captain Herndon to Captain Burt, and through the shrieking gale he replied, "Ay, Ay, tell him I'll stand by him." Black, to avoid damage to the hurtling life-boat, prudently shoved off from the ship leaving Garretson on board. Passenger Joseph Bassford and some of the other men on the steamship assumed he had deserted his captain.

Winifred Fallon and Ann Redding had been sick in bed and without food since Wednesday. On Friday, a crewman had taken their blankets, counter-panes and mattresses to stem the inflow of water. Saturday morning at 10 o'clock they found the water three feet deep in their cabin.

"My father," said Miss Fallon, "handed me his money and told me to keep it—perhaps I might be saved and he not. This was before we came in sight of the brig. After we got in sight of the vessel I handed it back to him; I told him that it was too heavy." She feared boarding the life-boat, and said she would as soon remain on the steamer even though she noticed that part of the second cabin deck had collapsed. Henry Dean[8] escorted them to the saloon and then helped Winifred, James and Ann Redding in fastening their life-preservers. She "saw the smile of satisfaction on my father's face as we were borne away from the ship. This was the last view I had of him."[9]

Elizabeth Hawley, concerned because Frederick had been so sick and working so steadily, asked him if he was not tired, and he replied, "Yes, I am tired, but I can work forty-eight hours longer in the same way if necessary. I am working for your life—for you and my children."

Adeline Easton went to her stateroom trunk and took out the miniatures of her mother and brother, some money and her shawl. Ansel put on a suit of clothes, took his money and valuable papers. Addie sadly realized that "my watch, my beautiful ring, wedding presents and many other things I valued"[10] were in the large trunk in storage.

With Quartermaster Finley Frazier in charge, women and children were lowered into the second boat. Frazier took on board Mrs. Badger, Easton, Fell, McNeil, Misses Fallon and Elizabeth Smith,[11] Nurse Pettorous, Mrs. Hawley and Thayer, and the children. Jane Badger and Annie McNeil missed their timing on dropping into the boat, and fell into the sea. They were quickly rescued.

On getting into the boat, Jane Badger crouched down in the bottom, and had scarcely been seated when "a lady of remarkable stoutness of

---

[8] Henry Dean, a son of John Dean, a dry goods merchant in Hartford, CT, had gone to California from Fall River, MA, in the *Mary Mitchell* in August 1849. Haskins, 500. *The New York Herald*, 19 Sep 1857, 1-3.

[9] Bangor, ME, *Whig Courier*, n.d.

[10] Easton letter to sister, Jenny Page, 4 Oct 1857.

[11] Elizabeth Smith had been at Don Pedro's Bar, Tuolomne Co., California, with her father. She was going to New York to visit her brothers and sisters. *New York Daily Tribune*, 22 Sep 1857, 5-5.

person was lowered by the bowline from above in such a way as to land directly upon Jane's neck and shoulders."[12] She thought for a moment that her neck was broken. Waves missing the gunwale (upper edge of the side), dashed over her head, drenching her, but she protected about twenty-thousand dollars of Thomas's drafts.[13]

In her moment of terror on leaving Ansel and being dropped into the bottom of the boat, "a touch of the ridiculous helped to bring" Addie Easton back to reality. The contents of one of the barrels of sea water came down on her head. Ansel had "put nine hundred dollars and some valuable papers" into his overcoat pockets. This he threw to Addie and, removing the coat he wore, he also threw it to her to "put around my shoulders."[14]

The rough sea threw the life-boats violently against the steamer, thus making the transfer very difficult. Jane Badger kept her promise to John Fell by helping his wife, Jane, in saving their two children.

Accustomed to steamer travel, Lucy Thayer had for a number of years alternated time spent in San Francisco and South Boston. She and her children, Lizzie and Herbert, boarded the second life-boat, but only after oarsmen rescued Lucy from the sea after she misjudged her drop into the boat.

Ailing Mrs. Hawley did not want to be separated from her husband, and had asked him to go with them, telling him she needed his help with the children. Frederick walked to his trunk, removed his money, but made no reply. In his arms he carried to the deck their infant son, Willy. Mr. Bokee carried their two-year-old son. Elizabeth Hawley saw

> the little children passed down, the officer lowering them by their arms, until the boat swung underneath, and they could be caught hold of by the boatmen. It was frightful to see these helpless little ones, held by their tiny arms above the waves. My babe [age 5 months] was nearly smothered by the flying spray, as they were obliged to hold him a long time before he could be reached by the boatmen; but when I pressed him once more to my bosom, and covered him with my shawl, he soon fell asleep. The children did not cry, except when the salt water came over us and flew in their faces.
>
> The brig had drifted far away from us, [she continued,] and we were half an hour in getting to her. She was very deeply loaded, and rolled badly; her bulwarks were nearly level with the boat when it was lifted by the sea, and great care was necessary in going alongside to keep the boat from

---

[12] *The New York Times*, 24 Sep 1857, 1.
[13] *Richmond Daily Dispatch*, 21 Sept. 1857, 1-3.
[14] Olmsted-Lincoln, *Wedding Journey*, 24-25.

being swamped. Captain Burt, with his mate, stood with open arms and a willing heart to receive us; a rope was thrown, and in another moment the children were being passed out. Captain Burt took my little Willy, and the mate received DeForest, playfully saying as he passed him over the side, "He is all gold."[15]

At the command of Captain Herndon to First Officer Van Rensselaer, crewmen cleared and lowered the captain's gig from starboard aft, and it was nearly swamped under the guards of the steamer. The gig,[16] smallest boat of the steamer, had a capacity for twenty-one persons. By the captain's order, the thirty-year old Welshman, Quartermaster David Raymond, took charge of her, "again ran under the bows of the steamer and took in seven women, five children and one man," for transport to the brig. Just then, Seaman James Travis saw five men and three firemen jump from the steamer into the boat, and Captain Herndon "called to us to shove off, or the boat would be swamped." Manning the gig with Raymond were Quartermaster Robert Long, Seamen Edward Brown and James Travis, and passenger/seaman James Gallaher.

The crews propelled their charges through a churning ocean of thirty-foot waves and swells. The most vicious winds of the hurricane had eased, but high seas still threatened to swamp the sturdy small boats. Valiant oarsmen pressed forward to exhaustion, and passengers as well as crewmen bailed for their lives.

Before he died, Captain Small had given a parcel of papers to his wife, to be delivered to the owner of the ship in which he sailed. Mrs. Small delayed leaving the steamer until she could secure that package. With the boat ready to leave, against the warning of the passengers she waded through the water that filled the cabin, and found it.

As Ann was being lowered into the third boat, Captain Herndon adjusted her shawl and said, "Mrs. Small, this is sad. I am sorry not to get you home safely." With those words, he turned away. When mother and daughter were separated during the transfer, he sent her baby with Mrs. Kittredge in the next boat. The frail Ann Small fell twice into the sea and was rescued.

A young man, James C. Clow,[17] entrusted fifteen-year-old Rose

---

[15] *Frank Leslie's Illustrated Newspaper*, 3 Oct 1857, 286.

[16] A long, light ship's boat. The gig was 26' long and 6' 9" wide.

[17] James C. Clow, age 26, was born in Pennsylvania. He had been in San Andreas, CA, and "the readers of the *Independent* were indebted to him for some choice pieces . . . He was an active member of the San Andreas Lodge of Masons, and was regarded as a worthy member of the 'brethren of the mystic tie.'" *New York Daily Tribune*, 21 Sep 1857, 6-7. *New York Herald*, 27 Sep 1857, 8-3. *The New York Times*, 21 Sep 1857, No. 1874, 3. *The Independent*, San Andreas [Calaveras Co,] CA, 31 Oct 1857, 2-1.

Alice Lockwood with a bag of money, which he asked her to take to his mother in Pennsylvania. She promised to deliver it.

Ohioan Thomas O'Neil, a butcher in California, lowered his wife, Annie, to the lifeboat, then returned to the pumps.

Having preceded his wife by two or three months, Isaac McKim Bowly, awaited Angelina[18] in New York. She had with her their two children, Charles, age two, and Isabella, age one. Angelina Bowly thought that although the ladies were frightened, none lost her composure. "There was fear, but no panic. The rope noose was tied around me, and swung out over the water into the boat. The life-boat could not come close to the side of the steamer, and we all had to take our chance to jump at it." Some of the ladies fell into the water and some into the boat. They were either hauled up again by the rope noose, or they were caught by the sailors that manned the boats, and hauled in over the sides. At the brig, she caught the rigging with one hand and held on until a seaman helped her. In the third small-boat with Mrs. Bowly went Mrs. Harriet Lockwood, her three children, Mrs. O'Connor, O'Neil, Redding, Small, Mary Bailey, of San Leandro, California and one male passenger (probably Joseph Schuler[19]).

Black's and Frazier's boats were of the fifty-man type, but because of the roughness of the sea only a much smaller number of occupants could be placed on board. Eleanor O'Connor could not get little Louis Bonneau in the boat with her, but Henry sent him with the next load of women and children.

> After I got safely into the little boat [said Mrs. Bowly] and my baby with me, I had but little hope of getting to the brig. The peril then seemed to be greater than ever; but as the ship was in a sinking condition, the only hope seemed to be in attempting even this dangerous escape from her. The water dashed into the boat and we had to keep dipping it out all the time.
>
> Two high waves passed entirely over us, so that it seemed as if we were swamped and sunk; but the boat recovered from them both. The men rowed bravely, for their own lives as well as ours were at stake. The commander of this boat was . . . [Quartermaster Raymond] . . . he encouraged the sailors to keep every nerve steady, and told them that it would require the exercise of all their skill and courage to reach the brig in safety.[20]

---

[18] Angelina Bowly had followed her husband, Isaac McKim Bowly, to San Francisco in May 1855. He was a commission merchant in New York City and came west in 1854. *Daily Alta California*, 17 May 1855, 2. San Francisco *Grantors Index*, 23 & 27 May 1854.

[19] Joseph Schuler, of Hamilton, OH, had been seen in Georgetown, CA, in 1856 by Daniel Beaver. After returning home he was scorned by his neighbors for having escaped with the women and children. Beaver family history file.

[20] *New York Daily Tribune*, 21 Sep 1857, 5-6.

Herndon ordered the launching of a fifth, a metallic boat. This last of the life-boats of the *Central America* was successfully launched, but the heavy sea carried it under the lee guard, where it was stove and swamped, carrying Mr. Ashby down with it. He quickly regained the deck, but this left only three boats in service for repeated trips.

Amanda Marvin saw Dr. Charles Gibbs[21] helping to pull up the barrels of water; he "was white as a sheet from over-exertion." Gibbs, a thirty-two year old physician, born in Massachusetts, was returning to his residence there. He had been practicing medicine in Columbia, Tuolumne County, California, since 1852.

Working to windward, it took at least two hours for John Black to arrive back at the steamer for his second load of passengers. In order to get her into the life-boat, and as some other husbands had done, William Marvin told his wife he would accompany her to the *Marine*, and she "believed this promise until she was in the lifeboat." With Amanda went "seventeen thousand dollars in drafts, all her diamonds and jewelry. Had I not thought my husband was going with me I would not have left the steamer." After she got into the boat, William told her that he had secured her safety, and assured her that he could easily look out for himself.

Mrs. Kittredge and several other passengers waited in the captain's room. As she prepared to leave, she heard elderly Mrs. Eliza Caruthers,[22] say to A.J. Alston,[23] "Alston, I want you to save my boys," meaning Gibbs, Van Hagan and Alston. She had taken off her extra skirts, and said that if she had them she would dress him up in them and take him along as a woman. He said he wished he had "so good a chance for going."

Mrs. Kittredge said: "Later in the day Alston attempted to jump into the boat . . . but fell between the life-boat and steamer and was crushed by them, breaking his arm, dislocating his shoulder and injuring his chest." Dr. Harvey, Dr. Gibbs and Mr. Van Hagan carried him into the captain's quarters where Harvey dressed the wounds, set his shoulder and arm. He "told us he last saw him in the arms of Dr. Gibbs, breathing

---

[21] Dr. Charles Gibbs came to California on the ship *New Jersey*, from Boston, 1 May 1849. Haskins, 459. *California Census 1852*, Tuolumne Co, 187. Heckendorn's *Tuolumne Co. Directory*, 1856, 14. *The New York Herald*, 27 Sep 1857, 8-3. *Frank Leslie's Illustrated Newspaper*, 10 Oct 1857, 297.

[22] Eliza G. Caruthers, of Nantucket, Massachusetts, had been at Iowa Hill, Placer Co., California. *Baltimore Sun*, 21 Sep 1857, 1-7.

[23] A.J. Alston, age 29, was born in North Carolina; his family lived in Georgia. He came to California in 1852, was appointed Post Master of Alpha (previously called Hell-Out-For-Noon) in 1855 and now was a partner in a clothing store, Alston, Newman & Co., in Nevada City, Nevada Co., CA. *California Census*, Nevada Co, 1852, 90, *The Nevada [CA] Journal*, 13 Jul 1855, 2-3. H.E. Salley, *History of California Post Offices*, 1849-1976, 5. *The Nevada [CA] Journal*, 14 Aug 1857, 3-4.

very heavily, and without the least hope of being saved."[24]

Mrs. Caruthers and Kittredge left in the fourth boat-load, with John Black. Also boarding this life-boat were Mrs. F. Rahan, of Belleville, Illinois, and Mrs. Jane Travis with her two children, leaving her husband, Dr. James Travis, on board the ship.

Mrs. Marvin got into the "rope chair," and a noose was passed around her feet and dress. Nothing supported her back, but she seized the rope that came down in front of her. The boat approached the steamer between the waves, and she remained suspended while the waves passed.

> The women were swung off into the life boats, [said Almira Kittredge] in any way, with or without their children, just as it happened. Three children went out with me [including Anna Small, Louis Bonneau and probably John Seeger, age 3]; I put one in my lap, another between my knees, and the third I held by the collar. At length I got tired of holding the one by the collar and let him sit down in the boat the water coming clear up to his neck. He sat in that condition and never spoke a word all the time we were going to the brig *Marine;* nor did the other two children. The water dumped over us all of the time, and of course we were wet through and through.[25]

Samuel Swan helped his wife, Mary,[26] lamed and bruised, to the deck. She had been injured when thrown out of her berth by a lurch of the ship. He took her aside, bade her good-bye, saying, "I don't know that I shall ever see you again." He said that he did not care about himself, if it were possible that she and their baby girl might be saved. He promised to save himself if an honorable opportunity presented itself and, although he had been sick for three or four days, he took his place in bailing. Mrs. Swan fell three times into the water before being successfully lifted into the lifeboat, and with good reason. Her husband had "tied about my waist a belt containing about ten thousand dollars in gold dust and nuggets, saying: 'If you are saved this will be a good friend to you—if you drown, it will help carry you to the bottom.' "[27]

Raymond's boat returned. While helping a lady onto the brig, Quar-

---

[24] *The New York Herald,* 27 Sep 1857, 8-3. *Frank Leslie's Illustrated Newspaper,* 10 Oct 1857, Pg 297.

[25] *Ibid.*

[26] Mary Ann Swan, age 22, was born in England. She and her husband, Samuel B. Swan, mined and farmed at Rough and Ready, Nevada Co., California. They were going to visit his family in Pittsburgh, Pennsylvania. *New York Times,* 21 Sep 1857, No. 1874, 8-1. *Baltimore Sun,* 23 Sep 1857, 1-3. *San Francisco Bulletin,* 22 Oct 1857, Pg 3.

[27] *The Saturday Bee* (Sacramento, CA), 23 Nov 1901, 3-2.

termaster Robert Long badly injured his leg and could not continue rowing. Raymond returned to the ship short one oarsman, and a young man, William Plass,[28] offered to go. Not knowing passenger Plass, whether he was able and wanted to be an oarsman, or whether he simply sought a way to escape the sinking vessel, Captain Herndon hesitated to trust him, but asked him if he could row well. The young man said, "I have a hard hand that can row, and a soft heart that can feel." Impressed with the remark, Herndon said, "I believe you trustworthy, you can go." Plass proved himself equal to the task.

Seaman Travis counted four women in it for their second trip to the *Marine*, then "four miles dead to leeward."

Mrs. Mary Ann Rudwell, an English lady, frail and advanced in years, asked Captain Herndon to permit her husband to accompany her. Herndon "very kindly but firmly" refused, saying that no man could leave the steamer until all the women had gone. They sadly turned aside.

Barney Lee watched the loading of the life-boats. He saw the sea so high and the breakers so furious that many preferred to stay on the steamer rather than venture into the small-boats which were being wildly tossed and looked ready to capsize at any moment. His uncle, Daniel Mahoney, "an infirm old man" (a forty-seven-year old mulatto), suffered with rheumatism, and Lee was watching for an opportunity to get him into one of the boats. "We watched the boats," said Oliver Manlove, wistfully, "with throbbing hearts, as they passed from crest to crest across the dark valleys, where they were hidden from view. Sometimes we would think that the boats were swamped, and would cry out: 'Lost! Lost!' and when they came to the crest again: 'All right.'"

At 4:00 P.M. Captain Herndon, seeing the *Marine* drifting farther away, ordered the main spencer set "to cause the steamer to forge ahead as far as possible, and keep up with the brig in drifting. Between four and five o'clock the lee boiler fires were extinguished. Badger saw the engines "make a few revolutions, with the steam from them quickly exhausted, and they again stopped."

Herndon conferred with Van Rensselaer and Ashby, and they agreed unanimously that the ship could not live until midnight of that day, Saturday. Now with the last of the women passengers in the life-boat, the captain, with no direct word from Captain Burt, and seeing the

---

[28] William Plass, age 21, was born in New York. His home was in Newburgh, Albany Co., New York; he had been working in Napa Co., CA. Seaman Travis said Plass had been a whaler. He boarded the ship at Aspinwall. *New York Daily Tribune*, 21 Sep 1857, 6-7. *The New York Herald*, 25 Sep 1857, 1-1.

necessity of obtaining closer communication with him, ordered Ashby to leave with the next boat from the steamer. Herndon directed that upon arrival at the brig Ashby must request that Captain Burt send additional boats for the transportation of more of the passengers.

The captain discovered that three of the ladies in steerage, had failed to answer his call for transfer to the brig. Theodore Payne went below and escorted to the deck Mrs. Mary Rudwell, and probably Mrs. Athros Hahn[29] and Mrs. Carolyn Shaw.[30] John Rudwell took Mary by the hand and bade her good bye, adding that he would try to meet her again, but that perhaps he would not be able. He helped to lower her into Black's boat.

Meanwhile, Quartermaster Frazier returned for his third load of passengers, followed soon after by Quartermaster Raymond.

Most men, seeing the last of the women leaving the ship, sought a way to escape the unhappy end that now confronted them.

Black's and Frazier's boats were both being loaded, one fore and the other aft of the steamer. No sooner had George Ashby safely placed the three ladies in Black's life-boat when a steerage passenger, William Geary,[31] jumped from the deck of the ship into the boat, a considerable distance. Theodore Payne saw Ashby "hastily lower himself into the boat to prevent more passengers from swamping it." Then as the chief engineer got into the boat, another steerage passenger, Thomas Bride,[32] jumped from the deck and fell upon Ashby's back. Ashby seized him by the throat, and drew his dirk knife, whereupon the boatswain shoved off in order to stabilize the boat.

During the commotion, two other steerage passengers boarded the small-boat. They were Douglas Rutherford,[33] a miner from Yuba County, California, an acquaintance of Geary, and John Cummings, an English miner from Sierra County, California. Payne saw Ashby's use of his knife "as a means of deterring others who crowded the decks looking for

---

[29] Mrs. Athros Hahn was traveling with her husband and son. G. Hahn was from Cincinnati, Ohio, and Yreka, Siskiyou Co, California. Mrs. Hahn had arrived from Panama on 7 March 1853 on the *Tennessee* with three children. *San Francisco Daily Alta California*, 7 Mar 1853, 2-4. *Richmond Enquirer*, 22 Sep 1857, 2-3,5.

[30] Mrs. Carolyn Shaw and husband were from Volcano, Amador Co., California. *New York Daily Tribune*, 21 Sep 1857, 1-3.

[31] William Geary had been mining in El Dorado Co., California, and was going home to Isle of Jersey, England. *New York Daily Tribune*, 21 Sep 1857, 6-6.

[32] Thomas and his brother, Patrick Bride, had been mining in Yuba Co., CA. Thomas had $600 and Patrick had about $900. Thomas claimed the right to get into the boat because he had paid one of the engineers for the privilege. *The New York Herald*, 21 Sep 1857, 3-1.

[33] Douglas Rutherford, age 37, born in New York, left his wife and 5 children on their farm in Oakland, Jefferson Co., WI. He had been working in Yuba Co., CA, for about a year. *New York Daily Tribune*, 21 Sep 1857, 6-6. *The Richmond Enquirer*, 25 Sep 1857, 1-4.

a means of escape from the steamer, "not as using it on the passenger." The boat had been nearly swamped by the leaping men who, misunderstanding his motives, not only saw his actions as threats to their lives, but thought the engineer to be deserting the ship.

Theodore Payne had spent much time throughout the journey in conversation with Captain Herndon, and it was evident that Herndon placed considerable confidence in that gentleman. With the women and children nearly in place in the life-boats, the captain asked Payne what he thought of affairs, and the latter replied, "Thank God, the women and children are all off, and we are strong." Herndon replied, "Yes, thank God," and added, "you take the next boat." Captain Herndon then asked Payne to go to his office and get his (Herndon's) gold watch and chain, and that, if saved, to carry them to his wife.[34] Said he, "Tell her, —— ," but, his utterance choked by deep emotion, he said no more of the subject, but changed it, saying he wished Payne to see the president of the USMSC, Marshall Roberts and the agents, and communicate to them the details of the disaster.

Judge Monson asked Van Rensselaer if he would allow his fellow Sacramentoan, Priest, to be taken next. "The First Officer said yes," and Monson fetched Priest from his cabin where he had asked him to remain in order to be found. As Priest was being lowered into a life-boat, Monson gave him a message for his brother in New York, "in case I should not be saved myself." Priest said: "Never mind the message, come, Judge, yourself." Van Rensselaer said: "Certainly, Judge, it is your turn, all right, jump in." Monson was immediately lowered into the boat, and later said: "A moment previous, I had not the slightest idea of leaving the steamer then."[35]

George Ashby asked fellow engineer Charles McCarty to "go along and assist me," and he too boarded the boat.

Herndon had remained continually at his post during the entire crisis, retaining his composure throughout the ordeal, but after his comments to Theodore Payne, he moved away a few steps and sat down on a rolling bench with his head in his hands, apparently overcome. He remained in that position a few moments, and then arose to resume command.

Black worked his boat back to the steamer, and Payne, being lowered in the rope chair, bade the Captain good-bye. As the boat again pushed off, a third passenger, Joseph Bassford, tumbled into it, and as he did, a

---

[34] *The New York Times*, 22 Sep 1857, No. 1875, 8-4. *The New York Herald*, 22 Sep 1857, 1. *The Daily Alta California*, 23 Oct 1857, 1-4. *San Francisco Bulletin*, 22 Oct 1857, 3, quoting the *Herald*.
[35] *The New York Herald*, 27 Sep 1857, 1-1.

package containing $2000 in gold dust fell from his pocket into the sea. Bassford lost his gold, but he felt justified since he was just recovering from a broken hip and, had he not gotten into the life-boat, his chance of survival would have been doubtful.

Before Boatswain Black's boat pushed off, William Birch, acquainted with Ashby, called, asking him to take him on board. Ashby told William to fetch James Birch. Billy went to James' stateroom, where he found him changing his clothes. They arrived on deck too late to board the departing small boat, and as the boat pushed off, Joseph Bassford saw James Birch on deck lighting a cigar.

On Mr. Ashby's leaving the ship, Captain Herndon reiterated to him his orders to have the captain of the brig lie by the steamer all night, as closely as he could, and, if possible, get the brig's boat and a crew.

> As the boats were passing from the brig to the steamer [Barney Lee said] everyone would rush to the sides of the ship as each boat came to take away her complement of passengers. Some would look round wildly and ask for their friends before they would step into the boat which was to convey them to the brig; but in most instances no one responded to this parting call or, if they did, their voices were drowned in the general confusion.[36]

Lee saw others running for treasure in order to give it to the ladies before the boat left. "But considering the awful circumstances in which all were placed," he said, "the order that was preserved, and the desire to render mutual assistance which was manifested by all, have few parallels in the history of ship wrecks." The orderliness and self-control of the men during the emergency was exceptional when compared to many sea disasters.

Frank Jones observed that "the moment the last lady and child were lowered, a tremendous rush was made by the passengers, and as many as could, threw themselves into the boats and water. The boats were shoved off immediately to keep them from sinking, and those who remained in the water were drawn up" into the sinking steamer by ropes.[37]

Black's boat had moved but a few feet from the steamer when a young man, William Adams, from Baltimore, dove head-first from the steamer and came up the other side of the small-boat. Skillfully he put his leg over the side and got in so quickly and quietly that only one or two of those in the boat noticed him.

---

[36] *The New York Herald*, 21 Sep 1857, 2-1.
[37] *The New York Times*, 22 Sep 1857, No. 1875, 3-2. *New York Daily Tribune*, 21 Sep 1857, 6-4.

On their way to the *Marine*, a great many seas washed over them, and the lifeboat had to be constantly bailed. The brig had by now drifted two or three miles to the leeward, but they arrived safely even as a sea swept over the deck of the vessel. Mary Ann Rudwell, not as frail as she seemed, grabbed at the rigging and held on ferociously until a seaman helped her up. The others followed her.

Ashby immediately asked Captain Burt to send the brig's boat and crew. The Captain replied that he could have his boat, but that being only a yawl,[38] it could not live a minute in such a sea. Burt added that he would do all in his power to get closer to the steamer, but his vessel being in such a crippled condition, he could not work to windward.

Ashby told William Geary that he must go back to the steamer with the boat. Geary retorted that he would not, whereupon Ashby, knife in his hand, chased him around the deck of the *Marine*, saying he was a runaway sailor from the steamer. At that point, Black intervened, saying that Geary could be of no more service to him, and Ashby refrained from further coercion. Meanwhile, his small-boat being battered against the brig, Black departed without him for a return trip to the steamer.

The chief engineer "expressed his wish to return in the next boat," but when the other two arrived at the brig, the oarsmen jumped on board the vessel, leaving only quartermasters Frazier and Raymond in their boats, and refused to return to the *Central America*. Mrs. Kittredge saw Ashby sit in a lifeboat and, without success, order the men back into it; he offered $100 to any man who would return with him, but there were no takers. Others witnessed the engineer's efforts to return to the steamer, among them being Captain Burt, Mrs. Marvin, Judge Monson, Mrs. Small and Mr. Payne, who said that Ashby "implored the boat crews to return, and tried unsuccessfully to raise another crew to accompany him." Ashby had made a number of enemies, who interpreted as desertion his remaining on the brig. The men on the steamer having seen him leave in the boat, held the same opinion.

Addie Easton, with a "choking fear," had watched Raymond's boat approach the brig, and was gravely disappointed on seeing that "in it was not the one I longed to see." As the evening grew dark and she saw the boatmen refuse to return to the steamer, she put her "face down in [her] hands, too wretched to speak, reproaching [herself] that [she] had not stayed with him, regretting that [she] had not defied Captain and all when they were commanded to leave the steamer."[39]

---

[38] A small boat, jolly boat.
[39] Olmsted-Lincoln, 26.

Quartermaster David Raymond's gig soon arrived at the brig. Seaman James Travis[40] described their departure from the steamer.

> On our return to the *Central America*, Brown and myself gave up, as we were overcome with our labors both on board and in the boat. The quartermaster [Raymond] told us to lay on one oar, and both of us managed to man it. It took us two and a half hours to reach the steamer, this the third time [from steamer to brig]. When we did get alongside the boat was jammed against the side of the ship and had a portion of her gunwale knocked off and some of her timbers started. She then began to leak, and we had to set ten men to work to bail her out. Just then five passengers and three firemen jumped from the steamer into the boat, and Captain Herndon called to us to shove off, or the boat would be swamped.

During this commotion, on an envelope, Ansel Easton managed to hastily scribble a note, giving it to someone departing in Raymond's boat. In it he told Addie to ask the Captain to send a boat for him. "You can give him what he will ask."[41] She begged Captain Burt to send a boat, saying "they may all die before morning. Anything—ten thousand dollars if you will send another boat."

"My dear, dear lady," said Burt, "if I could send it, one should go without a cent of money, but a boat such as we have could not live a moment." He promised to attempt to bring the brig nearer the steamer, adding "she will probably float until morning."[42]

From the deck of the steamship, Henry Kimball observed the following incident:

> The captain was standing forward of the wheelhouse watching his gig as she neared the ship from the brig. He ordered the boat to be brought close to the ship, and as soon as it came near her side, the passengers began to drop from the rattling [ratline, webbing of ropes for climbing] of the steamer down to the boat, a distance of some twelve feet, which was almost sufficient to break the boat in pieces.[43]

Kimball had made up his mind from the appearance of the vessel that the ship could not remain afloat more than three hours. Confident that the small-boat would never return to the steamship again, and

---

[40] On 19 September 1857 Boatswain Black said that Frazier and Raymond made two trips each, and that he (Black) returned to the steamer for a third. His last leg, however, was his fourth trip from the steamer to the brig. *Richmond Daily Dispatch*, 22 Sep 1857, 1-6. *The New York Herald*, 25 Sep 1857, 1-1.

[41] Original note on a scrap of envelope was preserved by Adeline Easton.

[42] Olmsted-Lincoln, 28.

[43] *The Sacramento Daily Union*, 26 Oct 1857, 1-6.

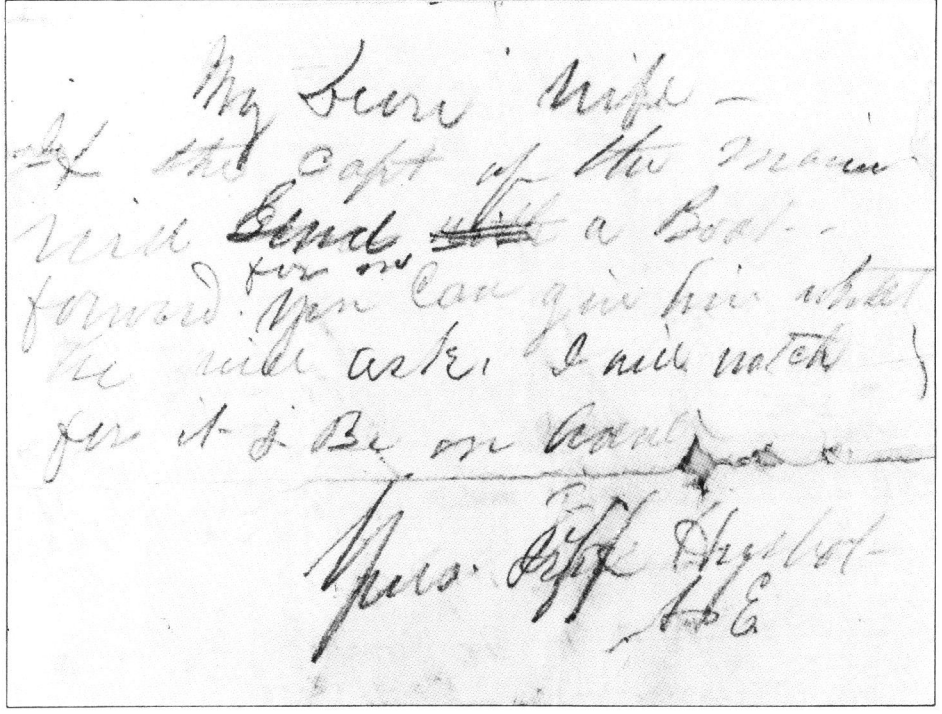

Note from Ansel Easton to his wife, Addie, written on an envelope from the *Central America*.
Courtesy, San Mateo County Historical Association

concluding that if he remained on the ship he must perish, he determined to get into it. Accordingly, after she had put off about five or six rods from the ship, he jumped into the water. After swimming to her, he was taken in.

The brig *Marine*, [said Travis,] then was six miles dead to leeward. We reached her with great difficulty, at half past six o'clock in the evening. This was our third trip. When alongside, the passenger [Plass] who had been a whaler said we could never reach the ship again, and he refused to go in the damaged boat any more. We all then got out of the boat and told Captain Burt and Mr. Ashby that she could never live to reach the ship.

The last two small-boats to depart the *Central America* contained sailors, firemen and a few male passengers, among whom were Consul

Ange Richon, Robert Hutchinson[44] and Frank Jones, who said he had "succeeded in getting into Frazier's boat." The consul, having jumped into it as it shoved off from the steamer, was the last passenger to enter a lifeboat. Boatswain John Black, quartermasters Finley Frazier and David Raymond, in a total of nine trips to the brig, carried 109 of the ships passengers and crewmembers, including the boat crews.

Lieutenant Dement, "a muscular, well-built man, rather above the average stature, with strong nerves, . . . apparently capable of retaining his presence of mind in emergencies—to which qualities he has been indebted under Providence, for the preservation of his life on several occasions,"[45] had commenced bailing on Friday afternoon. He continued to work all night until about 4:00 P.M. on Saturday, "without a morsel to eat," when he decided it was time to take care of himself. Dement "went to his trunk, removed some papers of value and some money, and with his overcoat and life-preserver went on deck and sat down on a trunk in one of the upper state rooms." Leaning back against the state-room wall, he slept.

Toward nightfall, another sail came in view and Captain Herndon ordered two signal shots fired. The schooner *El Dorado* of New York, Captain Samuel Stone, not able to be identified in the darkening night, ran about 100 feet under the stern of the *Central America*. Willard Fletcher observed her to be "rather small and clipper built, but of sufficient size to contain us all." The time was 6:50 P.M.; the position, lat. 31° 25'north, 78° 10' west.

Captain Stone could see that she was deep in the water and disabled. He gave orders to "stand by the main sheet, to heave our vessel to."[46] The helmsman steered to within fifty feet, and at that time Stone called out "Can I render you any assistance?" Sherlock, mate of the schooner, heard Herndon say in a steady voice.[47] "Lay by me until morning, for I am in a sinking condition." Captain Herndon asked him, for God's sake, to "lay by" and send a boat. Stone said he would lay by all night. The communication was brief because the *El Dorado* quickly passed the *Central America*. Stone supposed that the steamer

---

[44] Robert Hutchinson was from Fairmount, VA, had been in California, working in Kidd's Tunnel for eight months; lived in Nevada City, Nevada Co., CA; was a business partner of Thomas McNeish, of Grass Valley. *New York Daily Tribune*, 21 Sep 1857, 7 + 8-1. *The New York Times*, 22 Sep 1857, No. 1875, 8-5.

[45] Barrows, 70-75.

[46] *The New York Times*, 25 Sep 1857, No. 1878, 1-3. *New York Daily Tribune*, 26 Sep 1857, 5-2, and 25 Sep 1857, 4-5. *The New York Herald*, 26 Sep 1857, 8-1. *Baltimore Sun*, 28 Sep 1857, 1-3.

[47] Sherlock said "he spoke as if he was every inch a man and a sailor." *Frank Leslie's Illustrated Newspaper*, 17 Oct 1857, 315-2.

had good boats, while I had but one, a small jolly-boat, which would not live in the high sea then running for a moment . . . I supposed his reason [for not attempting to put passengers on board] to be . . . that he thought it advisable to await daylight, as he might (it being then near dark), lose more than he could save, while, by awaiting daylight, perhaps all might be saved. I then said. "Set your lights." By that time I had drifted out of hailing distance, and I ordered my lights set immediately.

Stone heard the cries of the passengers, and above them all, the request that he send a boat, but, as Captain Burt's, his yawl could not survive the rough sea. Herndon had no way of knowing that the schooner, being flat bottomed and drawing only seven feet of water, would have inevitably drifted to leeward. Additionally, the schooner's center board had been removed and her fore-and-aft mainsails destroyed by the storm, thus assuring an even more rapid drift. Although she could easily accommodate all on board, her only chance of rescuing them would be to make fast to the steamer, but having used at least three-hundred feet of heavy hawser during his attempts to bring the steamer head to the wind, Herndon had none left to pass to the *El Dorado*.

Barney Lee heard Captain Stone reply that he "had not a boat that he could send. Before other words could be exchanged, the fury of the storm had so separated the vessels that all hopes of obtaining relief from her were abandoned, . . . and those on board the *Central America* relapsed into their former state of gloom and anxiety."[48]

Henry Childs watched the schooner move to a distance that increased with every moment. She did not again approach the steamer. Captain Badger saw two of her lights far to the leeward. At 5:00 P.M. the second cabin had been under water, and at 7:00 P.M. the water level reached the upper saloon deck. Manlove "could hear the swishing of the water in the ship and the breaking up of the cabin floors, and outside the ship was the surging and washing of the merciless waves."

"At ten minutes of 8 o'clock," said Badger, "Captain Herndon took his position on the larboard paddle-box with his second officer, and ordered rockets fired downward, the usual signal, to the brig and schooner that we were sinking rapidly."[49]

Captain Herndon continued to reassure the 437 men remaining on the steamer, but he knew that another vessel must come along if more of them were to be rescued.

---
[48] *The New York Herald*, 21 Sep 1857, 2-1.
[49] *New York Tribune*, Monday, 21 Sep 1857. *The New York Times*, 21 Sep 1857, 1-5. *The New York Herald*, 21 Sep 1857, 2-1. *Daily Alta California*, 24 Oct 1857 1-2.

Captain Herndon on the Wheel-Guard
From *Frank Leslie's Illustrated Newspaper*

CHAPTER VII

Calm Desperation

John Black and his oarsmen, weary but intent on saving more lives, constantly bailing, labored their damaged craft on its third return toward the sinking steamer. George Ashby unsuccessfully tried to plead, coax, force or buy a crew to man another boat, and Quartermaster David Raymond, the only other man willing to return to the steamer, like Ashby, demanded and begged for someone to accompany him for another trip. Standing in the damaged captain's gig, he pleaded for help until he had to be hauled on board the brig. Black's crew would be the last to return.

Frazier's boat, in serviceable condition, and Raymond's nearly swamped, were both towed by the *Marine,* but Finley Frazier's later broke loose. The other was so badly stove that Burt's crewmen cut it loose.

As the last of her life-boats approached the steamer, Black noticed she had settled considerably in the water since his last trip. Captain Herndon ordered Frazer to fire a rocket, and as he did, the light revealed Black's boat approaching the steamer. The captain called to him to stand off, as it would be unsafe to approach because there was danger of the boat being swamped by a rush of the hundreds of passengers.

At young Alston's request, Dr. Harvey had him "removed to the hurricane deck, but he had only lain there a few moments when a huge wave rolled over the ship and carried him with it into the sea." Harvey continued to treat Dr. Tennison, who had been confined to his room some three days with fever. "Just before the steamer sank," said Harvey, "he came to me much prostrated, with his life preserver on. I said to him that he must go in one of the life boats the next trip, and that I would speak to the captain about it. He said no; it was cowardly for any one of the ship's company to leave under any circumstances."

Thomas Badger "procured a board six feet long and six inches wide, tearing it off the front of a berth, took my position on the taffrail, and held onto the after awning stancheon." He estimated there were between one and two hundred men on the quarter deck, breathlessly waiting the final sinking.

When John Dement awoke, he stepped out on deck, found himself ankle-deep in water, and quickly went to the starboard paddle-box. In order to be as high as possible, he moved rapidly to the hurricane deck. The time was nearly eight o'clock.

Captain Walter Dyer,[1] of England, and William Osborne, of Tennessee, had manned the hand-pumps, "keeping them at work all the time." Dyer now turned to Osborne, saying: "All is lost—come with me into the rigging." They ascended the mizzen mast about thirty or forty feet together, exchanged names and residences, "commended themselves to the Almighty," and waited for the probable end. Osborne removed all his clothing except for shirt and pants, and threw all his money over with his clothes so it would not encumber him in any effort for safety.

The men generally awaited their fate with composure. At about seven-thirty, James Forster saw Captain Herndon go "to his stateroom, put on his uniform, and go to the larboard wheel-house." Mr. Childs and several others went to their rooms and changed their clothes completely.

Billy Birch went to the state-room of James Birch and Mr. White and proposed joining the butchers who were building a raft forward on deck. They got as far as the smoke-stack, when the ship was struck by a "tremendous sea." Billy moved near the wheel-house, but fearing he might be "struck by the chimneys, which were abreast of the wheel-house," he went to the forward part of the ship.

Gabriel Brush, seeing James Birch without a life-preserver, supplied him with one. He offered to buckle it around his waist, but Birch refused, saying that there would be no chance to preserve life by such means—that he should perish from the cold—and that floating upon the water would but prolong his misery. He preferred to meet his fate at once, and professed his willingness to do so. Lighting another Havana, he turned aside. Dr. Harvey noticed that he had on a very heavy over-coat, which "I tried to induce him to take off. Mr. Easton afterwards succeeded in getting him to remove it, and put on a life-preserver." Stephen Caldwell saw "fifteen or sixteen men who had locked themselves up in their staterooms, saying they would rather die there than go down struggling with death in the waters. Five or six were sick in their berths."

Captain Herndon stood on the paddle-box in dress uniform, one hand on the rail. First Officer Van Rensselaer, Second Officer Frazer and

---

[1] Captain Walter G. Dyer was a contractor, carpenter and repairer of steamboats and worked for the Panama railroad line. His wife and family were in England. *The Baltimore Sun*, 21 Sep 1857, 1-4.

Third Officer Myers were near him. Nearby, clad in his overcoat, stood Ansel Easton. Shortly before, his friend, Robert Brown, had supplied him with a cork life-preserver.

Other men, whose faces were by now familiar to each other, waited anxiously yet calmly within sight of Captain Herndon. German-born Jacob Quincer, of Watertown, New York, wearing a metal life-preserver, stood only a few feet from him. Jacob and Randolph Casey[2] were difficult to distinguish from each other. From the start of the emergency, the twenty-five-year-old twins had bailed constantly, remaining at the task until it seemed probable the ship would sink. Henry Childs witnessed the parting of the Casey's who "embraced each other in tears on deck saying that each must take care of himself. They bade each other a final adieu."

Jacob Brown Clark had for several hours believed the ship must go down—that it would be only a matter of time. Clark, determined to leave the wreck before she went down, "secured a stateroom door and a life-preserver, and took my position near the bulwarks on the larboard side." As he stepped on the bulwarks the ship lurched. A sea washed over the deck, throwing a passenger and his door against Clark, catching his ankle against the helm chain and severely injuring his foot. Although momentarily confused, he forgot the pain with the next roll of the ship, and plunged out into the ocean. With him went a friend, J.F. Reed, of Petaluma, California, who also had a life-preserver and door. "Just before going over [he saw] Captain Herndon standing on the larboard wheel-house with his life preserver on."[3]

Thomas McNeish[4] had worked constantly since Friday night in the engine room where the oppressive hot water rose about six inches an hour. Although exhausted, for hours he helped rig the water barrels and hoist them to the deck. On deck, McNeish now faced the waves of the boiling Atlantic.

Assistant Engineer John Tice pried loose a good sized plank, 10' in length and 1-1/2" thick, and waited. Celebrating his twenty-sixth

---

[2] The illiterate Casey twins each had a wife and son who were awaiting them on their farms in Sebastian Co., Arkansas. *New York Daily Tribune,* 21 Sep 1857, 7-5. *The New York Herald,* 21 Sep 1857, 3-3. 1860 U.S. Census, Arkansas, Sebastian Co, Sugar Loaf Township, 26 Jun 1860, 28. 1870 U.S. Census Arkansas, Sebastian Co, Sugar Loaf Twp, 18 Sep 1870, 172.

[3] Bolivar, MO, *Courier,* 2 Oct 1857, quoted by the Sonoma County Journal, (Petaluma, CA), 29 Jan 1858, 2-3.

[4] Thomas McNeish, age 24, was born in Nova Scotia to Scottish parents. He now lived in Bloomsburg, Columbia Co., Pennsylvania, and had been a merchant in Grass Valley, Nevada Co., California. 1850 U.S. Census, Pennsylvania, Columbia Co, Bloom Tnshp, 23 Aug 1850, 302. *The New York Times,* 20 Sep 1857, No. 1874, 3-2.

birthday, Oliver Perry Manlove, who had secured a life-preserver and a piece of spar, noticed that all hands had seized some object to aid them in keeping afloat, "including pieces of spars, chairs, and life-preservers, of which there were plenty for all." He put a manuscript book of over two-hundred pages of poems (which he had written in the mining camp) in an inside pocket of his coat. He buttoned it tightly and tied a handkerchief around his waist.

John George, a thirty-year-old native of England, had spent seven years in California. He and Enrique Ayulo, of Peru, wearing life-preservers, braced themselves for a plunge into the sea.

Earlier Captain Herndon had ordered cut away the forward part of the hurricane deck (made of one inch board, covered with oiled canvas); he also ordered doors from various parts of the ship brought to the deck to be furnished as rafts for the passengers.

Henry O'Connor, on the upper deck, took two hatches from over the sky-light of the engineer's room. Young O'Connor sat beside the wheel-house, holding onto the scuttles, wearing the preserver that Ashby had threatened to remove. Earlier he had noticed some men praying, others cursing and swearing, but now he saw that all around were resigned. He waited for the final moment.

At 8:00 P.M. on Saturday, September 12th, the scene on board the *Central America* seemed calm. On deck with the others, twenty-year-old Willard Fletcher said to those around him, "There will never be as many die again as coolly. Boys, let us all die like true Californians!" David Smith, an "old man" from Bloomfield, Maine, the same town as Fletcher, had also been mining. Feeling the hopelessness of the situation, he exclaimed, "My God, we shall all perish!"

Glancing around the ship, Second Mate Frazer saw a large number of men jump overboard in an attempt to escape the pull of the sinking vessel. He could see heads bobbing in the sea. The three mates, Van Rensselaer, Frazer and Myers, and Captain Badger, having all promised to remain with Captain Herndon, kept their word. Herndon, having been at his post during the entire storm, without rest, had told Badger he would stay with the ship as long as there was a soul on board. Shortly before eight o'clock the captain borrowed Easton's lighted Havana, fired two rockets, and remained on the larboard paddle-box of the ship.

After the captain waved off John Black without his taking on any passengers, Barney Lee sadly realized that he would be unable to save his Uncle Daniel. With several others, including Fireman Alexander Grant and passenger George Dawson, he then assisted in the construction of a raft, until the steamer settled so low in the water that every wave broke over her, clearing the decks of all loose items. "The second of two seas," said Badger, "crossed the entire deck, sweeping nearly all the passengers on the main deck into the sea."

The first wave ran partly over the deck, washing John Dement between the escape pipe and the smoke stack, then receded. The second large sea from the windward side threw another man against him, forcing him "out from between the 'scape pipe and smoke stack" as the ship submerged. Captain Herndon's last orders were: "Buckle on your life-preservers. We are going down."

Lee was then swept off the deck by a gigantic wave which also cleared away the planks intended for use in making another raft. Caught in the final wave over the deck, John Taylor was swept into the rigging and spent two or three minutes in a great effort to extricate himself. He was

The Steamer Plunged at an Angle of Forty-five Degrees
This widely used sketch contains many errors. The *Central America* had only one stack, a short bow-sprit, the foremast had been cut off, and the flag had been inverted to signal distress. The brig *Marine* (background) was a two-masted vessel. Courtesy, Mariners Museum, Newport News, VA.

nearly exhausted from working hard on the pumps since Friday at 2:00 P.M. In the engine room, he had worked up to his neck in water until Saturday morning.

There were cries of despair, cracking of timbers and the rush of waters as the seas closed over the scene. Jacob and Randolph stood together as the ship gave her final lurch, and in a moment found themselves in the maelstrom.

A bright flash of lightning lit the deck, revealing the entire scene, and a tremendous sea struck the *Central America*. She shuddered, plunged stern first at an angle of forty-five degrees, and with a simultaneous cry from the engulfed mass, she disappeared.

Meanwhile, the crippled *Marine* had made a long sweeping turn, and as she again headed toward the steamer, Addie saw the rockets fired and the lights of the *Central America* disappear "beneath the waves, and all the world grew dark for me."

On the sinking steamship, William Ede,[5] was standing near the forward hatch. "Something came rolling down the deck toward me and struck my legs. It was a life buoy. I seized and adjusted it to my person. I was bailing water out of the hatchway, clinging to a rope the while for dear life, fearful every moment of being swept overboard. I raised my head once, and in the glare of a brilliant flash of lightning saw the stern sink beneath the water." His hand frozen to the rope, Ede felt himself dragged way below the surface. A blow on the back of his neck aroused him and he released his hold. Below the surface, a flash of lightning "lit up my surroundings with a phosphorescent glow. The great life buoy which I had under my arm carried me up at as rapid a rate as the rope had dragged me down." On the surface he "settled back into the life buoy with a sigh of relief, exclaimed aloud: 'Well, this thing's pretty good!'"

Though drawn down a great distance, John Dement remained conscious. The seemingly endless descent finally stopped and "his life-preserver brought him up with tremendous velocity, but, unable to hold his breath any longer, he began to strangle before reaching the surface." He cleared his throat and nostrils, saw a short plank near him, and grasped it, all of the while surrounded by struggling, desperate men, "clinging frantically to each other and going down in utter despair and exhaustion."

---

[5] William Ede, age 31, was born in Sussex, England. This was his second round trip to California. In 1850, he mined at Howland Flat, Sierra County, California; went home to Waukesha Co., Wisconsin; brought his brother, Abraham, out in 1852, and was now going home to get married. He had saved $1500. J.M. Guinn, *History of the State of California*, 451-2. Mrs. Bernice Ede Campbell. "The Five Ede Brothers," *Plumas County Historical Society Publication*, No. 20, 19, and No. 30: Abraham Ede. *Baltimore Sun*, 22 Sep 1857, 2-4.

A Giant Wave Engulfed the Central America
From *Frank Leslie's Illustrated Newspaper*

Floating near one of the paddle boxes, "with the bowing, or semi-circular side up," he swam to it, climbed on the piece of wreckage and soon was joined by Robert Brown.

Doors, planks, boards and other pieces torn loose from the ship floated and tossed on the turbulent sea, inflicting injury to some, death to others. They saved the lives of many.

Easton, carried down with his life-preserver, soon arose to the surface, where he was seized by Van Rensselaer. The first mate had no life preserver, and "it was soon apparent that one would not long sustain both." Then came a death grapple between the two. The mate tried to retain his grasp upon Easton's coat, while the latter knew his life depended upon getting free. They struggled briefly, Easton finding himself unable to shake off the hold of the first mate. By a sudden movement, he "slipped his arms from the sleeves, and left the garment in his hands! In an instant the first officer sank to rise no more."[6]

---
[6] *San Francisco Bulletin*, 23 Oct 1857, 2-2.

Oliver Manlove thought he "must have been swept through the rods of the smoke stack as my life buoys were torn off." In removing his boots, he lost his "grip on the rubbish I was clinging to," then came upon a man holding a board, and who begged Oliver not to take it from him. The fellow had a pair of life buoys, which he gave to Manlove, and Oliver quickly fastened them to himself, one under each arm.

Surfacing without mishap, Henry O'Connor saw there was no moon, the sky clear overhead, and stars shining brightly. "One passenger attempted to get on another's raft, and the occupant swore he would blow his brains out if he did not get off." For several hours Henry heard a continual cry from the struggling mass of human beings, "such as no one can imagine who was not there." The spasms in his limbs pained him a great deal, and at one time he had cramps in both legs at once.

Willard Fletcher, one of the last to go under (an estimated fifteen or twenty feet) took so long to surface that he felt he must breathe water. When he came up he found a door to cling to, and held on until three men grabbed it. Fletcher left it, swimming to warm his numb body. He saw "a good deal of desperate men struggling and fighting to appropriate articles promising the most security." A strong swimmer, he successively took advantage of getting hold of several objects to help keep him afloat. A trunk to which he clung fell to pieces, a flour barrel proved handy, and later he exchanged the barrel for a board.

Badger saw hundreds of "human beings floating out on the bosom of the ocean, with no hope but death." With this memory of the event, he struck out for a piece of wreckage. The suction of the ship drawing the passengers under water for some distance, threw them in a mass together. When they reached the surface the struggle for life was intense. Badger heard cries and shrieks for help, with those unable to swim clinging to those who could, or grabbing hold of the larger pieces of wreck, which were soon swamped by the weight of many men. They were scattered over about a mile distance. He observed a scene which "beggared description. Some were crying 'God save me!' 'God have mercy on me!' and other pious ejaculations. Some were screaming, some crying and some praying." In all his years at sea Badger had "never, never experienced such a scene before, and God forbid I ever shall again!" He estimated that three hundred drowned within the first ten minutes. Knowing that the ships to leeward could not reach them, he looked in the opposite direction.

Others fought for survival in the rolling sea, chilling wind, and seemingly endless time, hoping to see a sail or some means of salvation. They secured various floating objects, sometimes exchanging one for

A Solid Mass of Men Tossed and Tumbled and Whirled
From *Frank Leslie's Illustrated Newspaper*

another found to be more substantial. Though some fought for the possession of pieces of wreckage, others, such as James Forster and Barney Lee, were able to separate themselves from the struggling group.

After watching Captain Herndon fire a rocket from the port paddle-box to windward which went horizontally, James Frazer hardly had time to look around before being lifted by a heavy sea, "hove in amidships and back to the starboard side." He rose to the surface in time to see about ten feet of the steamers' funnel instantly sink. Seeing around him what appeared to be about a hundred men and large amounts of driftwood, he removed his overcoat and boots, and swam away from the crowd.

Dr. Harvey had a door "to which I clung with great difficulty." Finding himself in the midst of "hundreds of souls launched into the boundless sea and left at the mercy of the waves," he saw it would be "much to his best interest to get as far as possible from the rest." With the constant wave action, all were soon scattered. Harvey had a tin life preserver fastened to his body with a buckskin string, which stretching, caused it to slip around his throat, and once or twice it came near suffocating him.

Obed Harvey witnessed a memorable scene. When

> the mass of human beings had risen to the surface, one man proposed in a loud voice, 'Three Cheers!' and, like a person at a political gathering, he led off with the usual 'hip! hip! hurra!'—when the drowning multitude simultaneously fell into the wild strain, and brought out two distinct cheers—the third being nearly a failure, as a majority of them could not, on account of the rough sea, keep their heads above water long enough to fill the complement.

Stephen C. Caldwell,[7] a husky young New Yorker weighing over two hundred pounds, was swept off the deck a few minutes before the vessel lurched down and took with him the twenty pounds of California gold that he had mined. "When the vessel went down, I just laid under her bows—her bowsprit[8] hit me on the shoulder, and I should have been carried down, but she went a little aft and cleared me." Three or four men seized him, pulling off his life preserver. Caldwell submerged before he was able to extricate himself by pulling up one leg and then the other from the grip of the desperate man. Others grabbed at him as he searched for some sort of support. Swimming away from the crowd, he pulled off his boots in the water, "and a difficult thing it was, by standing in the water, which I could do, as I swim well." He had packed his gold coin and dust "in a belt around me, so that I could loose it and throw it off in a moment if I found it likely to bear me down." Support appeared in the form of a plank three feet long and nine inches wide. This he later exchanged for a cabin door to support his large frame and load of gold.

After jumping from the steamer, Major Clark swam about forty yards. Drawn into the whirlpool, he soon found himself surrounded by hundreds of men. "As they came up, there arose a heart-rending scream from nearly every one of them, which was heard far above the roar of the angry water. No language can give you the slightest conception of the scene." Realizing his "frail craft was scarcely enough to keep him above the surface," he too got away from the thrashing men. "With a desperate effort," he said, "I shoved away from those immediately near me,

---

[7] Stephen C. Caldwell, age 27, was from Phillipsport, Sullivan County, New York. He had worked as a miner in California since June, 1855. *New York Daily Tribune*, 21 Sep 1857, 7-6. *The New York Times*, 20 Sep 1857, No. 1874, 3-2. *New York Daily Tribune*, 21 Sep 1857, 6-5. *Atlas & Argus*, Albany, NY, 24 Sep 1857, 2-1.

[8] Bowsprit: a spar projecting from the upper end of the bow, for holding tacks, jibs or stays.

and grasping the knob of my door with the tenacity of a vice, I resigned myself to my destiny." The waves ran high, and it took all his strength to keep from being washed off his raft.

J.F. Reed floated up to Clark. They conversed for a few minutes when "a monstrous wave" separated them. Clark did not again see Reed, and a feeling of loneliness came over him. Twice he was washed off his door, but kept his hold on it. Occasionally, as he mounted a high wave, he caught a glimpse of a distant light, but it disappeared. About midnight he found another door, and with his neckerchief lashed it to the one he was on. Maintaining his presence of mind, he did not allow himself to "think of home or family," but kept his "mind on his present circumstances."[9]

Jacob Quincer, on discovering his metal life-preserver to be filling with water, "cut away its fastenings with a knife." He heard a number of the passengers hailing each other, and "at one time I saw one or two hundred people around me; at another I was poised on the summit of a wave forty feet high, and not one of them was in sight."[10]

The twin Caseys were separated as they rose to the surface. Randolph felt a plank nearby, grasped it, and swam with it away from the crowd of struggling men. He could hear the cries of drowning men as they grappled for the fragments of the wreck, crying "Don't hold me," "You will drown me," and similar cries. He said that, seeing the confusion, he "guessed that it would be better to get as far from the rest as possible," and paddled "the best way I could until I heard the cries and moans, at some distance." It was so dark that he could see nothing, and gradually the voices became more indistinct. "In fact," he said, "I may say that I was alone, without either seeing or hearing anything but the storm and rough sea."

R.T. Brown had secured a cork life-preserver. He noted that there were relatively few of those on board, most of the preservers having been made of tin and easily damaged when struck by solid objects. When sucked far below the surface of the water, some of the tin preservers were collapsed by the sudden force and pressure of the water. Brown tied ropes around a hatchway cover, and carried it with his life-preserver to the starboard paddle box, which he hardly reached when the gigantic wave struck. Swept off the deck, he grasped tightly one of the ropes, and remained under water until nearly strangled.

The sea was high, but less windy. Brown, freeing his eyes from water, saw no sign of the steamer. "A fearful cry, almost a yell, shrieked in my ears, which seemed to arise from all . . . the sea was literally covered

---

[9] *Sonoma County Journal*, Petaluma, CA, 29 Jan 1858, 2-3.
[10] *The Boston Liberator*, 2 Oct 1857, 3-3.

with human beings and floating objects." He was separated from the hatch-cover, but soon joined Dement on his piece of the wreckage. Dement, having left his overcoat on the steamer, became chilled in the wind, and had to keep partially submerged to keep up his body temperature. Brown, wearing his coat "stood the cold pretty well," remaining on top of their raft all of the time. They took turns keeping each other awake, all of the while hearing voices calling out.

William Chase[11] had secured two life-preservers which were lost when he submerged. Once on the surface, he found a plank and another preserver, and with these he "managed to float without much difficulty." Chase noticed that many passengers had lost hope, and when the critical moment arrived, lacked the energy to make any effort to save themselves.

Jacob Casey, on surfacing, swam to one of the hatchways, climbed on it, and was shortly joined by five others. The six held on desperately, but after several hours, three became exhausted, fell off and drowned.

Showman Billy Birch, having been severely injured in the water by loose debris, involuntarily grasped some boards, and sustained by these, reached a hatchway on which there were already three young men. Bleeding from his injuries, the plucky veteran entertained his fellow passengers by imitating sea-monsters, telling funny stories and performing Shakespearian parodies.[12]

Osborne was the last to be submerged. Captain Dyer was just beneath him, and they were discussing how the ship would go down. Osborne thought bow first, Dyer thought the stern would be first under, which proved correct. Osborne believed they were "the last above water to touch any portion of her," as she went down. "Good-bye old boy," said Dyer, and Osborne last saw him as he struck out swimming.

On regaining the surface, Osborne got on a hatch cover, drifted off to leeward, saw a light and, using a bunk slat for a paddle, headed for it. He lost the light, but suddenly heard someone call him. It was young Julius Stetson,[13] also on a hatch-cover, who asked Osborne if he would like company. They floated on together.

---

[11] William Chase was from Washtenaw County, Michigan; had been mining in Nevada County, California since 1852 and had served for 13 months on the local police force. *History of Washtenaw County, Michigan*, 1881, 1335-6. *Directory of Nevada City, CA, 1856*, 56. *The New York Times*, 20 Sep 1857, No. 1874, 3-2. *The New York Herald*, 21 Sep 1857, 3-3.

[12] *Frank Leslie's Illustrated Newspaper* 3 Oct 1857, 286.

[13] Julius Stetson, age 21, was born in Boston, Massachusetts. He was a Mayflower descendent (Brewster). He had been mining for four years at Shaw's Flat, Tuolumne Co., California, with relatives who were advertising the "Manufacture of Tin, Copper & stoves." He had saved about $400. Emma C. Brewster Jones, *Brewster Genealogy* (Grafton Press, NY, 1908), 396. *San Francisco Daily Bulletin*, 16 Apr 1856, 3-2. *Directory of Tuolumne Co, CA, 1856; Shaw's Flat*, 64. *Richmond Enquirer*, 25 Sep 1857, 1-4.

At first, Ede felt more secure in the water with his life-preserver than on the deck of the *Central America* "with the water pouring into the hold faster than we could bale it out." But when he became more aware of his situation, he changed his mind.

> The lightning played incessantly, [he said.] I was in the vortex of an immense whirlpool caused by the sinking of the ship. In the very center of this vortex there was a solid mass of men tossed and tumbled and whirled. Their groans and cries went to my heart. Presently a great wave broke over them and silence ensued. After about three hours of silence I could bear my loneliness no longer, and heartily wished for the return of the vessel and would have been glad to feel even the sinking deck beneath my feet. I cried out in agony: "Hallo! Hallo! Ahoy!" "Ahoy!" [came an answer.] "Who are you?" [inquired Ede.] "Jack Klus of Pine Grove, California," [came an answer through the darkness.] . . .

Ede asked how everything was with him, and Jack answered, "All taut, pardner," those being the last words heard from Klus.[14]

"Between two and three hours after the vessel sank, Captain Herndon floated up" to where Adolph Frederick, of San Francisco, and some others clung to a raft. "Captain Herndon was provided with a handsome India rubber life-preserver, and was floating on a piece of plank." He "seemed capable of floating in safety for a period of time." Herndon "addressed them encouragingly, saying: 'Boys, this is a poor craft to get to New York in. Have you got any brandy among you?'"[15] Lieutenant Dement also had seen Herndon during the night on a hatchway, "brave and undaunted to the last, and only feared death because it separated him from his family."

About midnight, Henry Childs was drifted near Captain Herndon. Childs hailed him, "received an encouraging answer, but did not see him again."[16]

At 1:15 A.M., after about five hours in the sea, Badger sighted a vessel "running down with a free wind." He saw her "hove to under short sail," and could see that she was a "three-masted bark."

---

[14] *San Francisco Chronicle*, 23 Feb 1896, 8-5.
[15] *The Richmond Daily Dispatch*, 30 Sep 1857, 4-2.
[16] *The Baltimore Sun*, 23 Sep 1857, 1-2, quoting *The Savannah News*. *Richmond Daily Dispatch*, 23 Sep 1857, 1-7.

Captain Anders Johnsen
of the Bark *Ellen*
From *Frank Leslie's Illustrated Newspaper*

Captain Johnsen and the Bird
From *Frank Leslie's Illustrated Newspaper*

CHAPTER VIII

A Change of Course

Captain Anders Johnsen, of the Norwegian bark *Ellen,* with a crew of thirteen men from their home port, Arendal, Norway, had set his course a little north of northeast. He had sailed from Arendal on the previous December 15th, and from Belize, Honduras, on August 17th. Laden with logwood, he headed for Falmouth, England, where he expected further orders. Because of the rough sea, the ship had made considerable water, had a broken foremast and had lost shrouds.

At just before 6:00 P.M., Saturday, September 12th, Captain Johnsen stood on the quarter deck with two crew members and the helmsman, when a bird flew around the captain, grazing his right shoulder. It flew around the vessel, then again around his head. When it flew at his face, Johnsen grabbed the unusual bird and held it by the legs.

"The bird," he said, "is unlike any bird I saw before, and I don't know its name." He described its feathers as dark gray in color, its body a foot-and-a-half in length, with wings three-and-a-half feet from tip to tip, and a beak like a small handsaw. "In capturing it," said the captain, "it gave me a good bite on my right thumb. Two of the crew who assisted in tying its legs were also bitten. As it showed to bite at everybody I had its head afterwards cut off and the body thrown overboard."[1]

Typical of the superstition found among many seamen of the era, Captain Johnsen saw as a message this encounter with the strange bird. "I regarded the appearance of the bird as an omen, and an indication to me that I must change my course. I accordingly headed to the eastward direction." The bark had been headed a little north of northeast.[2]

At about 1:00 A.M. on Sunday, September 13th, Johnsen, again on the quarter deck with his helmsman, Gustav Jacobsen,[3] was alerted by agonized cries near his vessel. He soon identified them as a large number of human voices. Presuming himself to be in the midst of a wrecked vessel, he roused all the crew.

---
[1] *Richmond Daily Dispatch,* 24 Sep 1857, 1.
[2] *Richmond Daily Dispatch,* 24 Sep 1857, 1-4.
[3] *Agderposten,* Arendal, Norway, 3 Aug 1965.

"In less than a minute," related the captain, "I found that we were surrounded with persons floating in the water. The darkness of the night made it impossible to see them; the voices calling for aid rang in my ears from every direction." Had Johnsen not changed course, his position after the lapse of seven hours would have been far to the north/northwest of the scene.

William Ede "halloed lustily." Soon the somewhat shaken helmsman bore the bark down on him, the bowsprit passing directly over his head. A crewman threw down a rope and he went up hand over hand, assisted by a sailor. The first survivor hauled aboard the bark from the sea, Ede said, "I guess I was insane with joy. I fell upon the sailor and would have bitten a piece out of his arm had I not been prevented." Captain Johnsen demanded he surrender the life buoy, which he tied to a rope and, with this apparatus, began to rescue others.

Crewmen cut the lashes of a small boat and threw it into the sea. Hardly had it touched the water when six men grabbed hold of it, turning it keel upwards. Johnsen's men soon righted the small boat, took in the men, and put them on board the *Ellen*. He ordered additional lights put up so that floating men could better be seen around the ship, and rescue work proceeded rapidly. The bark rolled unceasingly. The noise on board and the wind whistling through the ropes made it difficult to hear any distance.

Still clinging to a box top that he had found during the night, wearing his life preservers, and with "dying shrieks of some . . . [of the men] . . . still ringing in my ears," Oliver Manlove felt a chill creeping over him, and began to feel drowsy. "I knew what that meant and fought against it." Suddenly he saw what appeared to be a star ahead of him. It was the light of the *Ellen*, headed straight toward him. He called out at the top of his voice, "the drowsiness for the time was gone and the blood was leaping through my veins." With paralyzed hands he grasped with both of them the rope thrown to him, managed to pull himself up about six feet, but fell back into the sea, under the bark. His buoys brought him back to the surface, where he wrapped the rope around his arms, pulling himself up until crewmen had hold of him. He said, "I was so weak that I could scarcely stand . . . I thanked God . . . from the bottom of my heart." Through the ordeal, in a buckskin wallet in his shirt pocket, he saved one hundred forty dollars. However, his coat buttons were gone, his coat in shreds and his manuscript of poems was lost. He later contributed a twenty dollar gold piece to the fund for Captain Johnsen and his crew.[4]

---

[4] Manlove, *Autobiography*, Chp 48.

Jacob Quincer, seeing a light in the distance, swam for it. "I saw two poor fellows near me who were almost gone; I took hold of one by the hair and the other by the arm, and so kept them up as I swam along." He found the light to be a vessel, hailed her, and ropes hauled him on board the *Ellen*. With him were hoisted the two men he had rescued, "whose names I do not remember."

Mate Gustav Jacobsen and sailmaker C.A. Norlund[5] made many heroic efforts to rescue the drowning men. At great personal risk, trusting himself to the chances of being lost in the sea, Norlund sprang overboard and tied a rope around one of the thrashing passengers and continued helping others.

From his plank, Badger called to the crew of the bark, urging Johnsen to the rescue of scores of others who "were on the point of being swallowed up by the waves."

> I felt miserable with cold and weariness, but consoled myself with the thought I was not as bad off as I might be [William Chase said.] I clung to my plank and life-preserver as well as all my power would enable me, but in spite of all my efforts the former was several times swept from my grasp by the violence of the waves. Most of the men around me were able to hold on until an early hour in the morning, when a vessel appeared, which was not visible with the fog until she was close to us. One poor man who had held on to a plank close to where I was, after rising and sinking once or twice near me was seen for the last time in his life, although the vessel was on the point of relieving him.

William Chase was in the first group taken on board the bark.

At about two o'clock on Sunday morning, as the *Ellen* approached, voices called to Randolph Casey. He answered and crewmen threw him a rope and hauled him on deck, doing all possible to make him comfortable.

F.A. Wells, of Leyden, Massachusetts, managed to cling to his door. After being on it for two hours, he sighted a larger raft with five men on it. Parting with his door, he swam to them and climbed on. From time to time they were washed off the raft and had to swim to regain it. Soon one man was missing, then toward morning a sea washed all of them off and only two were able to recover the raft. More hours passed, when at about 5:00 A.M. they spotted the bark. Too weak to signal, they could hardly maintain their hold on the raft when rescued by Captain Johnsen.

Seeing someone approaching him "floating on a chair and a life-preserver," Dr. Harvey recognized a spent James Frazer, and with much exertion, Frazer transferred to Harvey's door. They held on together,

---

[5] Dannevig, "Dadenbak Medaljen," 26-7.

"supporting each other to keep above water the best we could until sighting a vessel at some distance, which we supposed to be the brig *Marine*, but which turned out to be the bark *Ellen*."

Harvey and Frazer, too weak to get on board, failed several times to cling to the rope which was lowered by the mate. Being raised a little, Dr. Harvey would let go and "plump down into the water, sometimes under the bottom of the vessel." A seaman lowered a rope ladder, and on the third attempt Harvey succeeded in tangling his foot in it, "clambered up into the ship, and found my strength completely exhausted." Frazer, being more muscular, mounted the ladder more easily. On deck at about 2:00 A.M., "both insensible, they remained in that state for about two hours." By the time Frazer recovered, many more of the shipwrecked men had been picked up.

Henry Childs found himself in the sea with many companions. The storm had subsided, and they kept together, floating with the waves and cheering each other onward. In a few hours, three who could not swim became exhausted, and soon drowned. One by one others faded from view. By one o'clock Sunday morning, Childs "felt nearly alone upon the ocean, nearly 200 miles from land." About an hour later he saw the light of a vessel which he judged to be a mile distant. With new courage, he struck out for it and arrived at the *Ellen* after having swum for six hours.

Easton, when on the top of the waves, saw John Fell. Fell never expected to be saved, and asked Easton to tell his wife, Jane, if saved, to return home, assured that she had plenty of means to live comfortably.

The first ten or twelve men were nearly all so spent that they were unable to give an account of the disaster. Only two of them were able to speak coherently. One of these, a stout swimmer, was much less tired than any other of those rescued, and had the manner and vocabulary of a seaman. He was Captain Thomas Badger. The other was Ansel Easton. Both were able to be of service in rescuing others and in ministering to those who had been rescued. Badger and Easton were rescued at about the same time, Badger having lingered in the sea to help direct the rescue of others.

Thomas McNeish, after being in the water a long time, came up with Peruvian Enrique Ayulo who gave him a share of a long board. They drifted to the leeward until falling in with the *Ellen*. Having been in the sea for about two or three hours, James Forster sighted a sail, and was rescued about five hours later. The sea then "was still high but lulling."

After seven hours in the water, Henry O'Connor felt on the point of giving up, when he saw the light of the *Ellen* suddenly appear, and a line thrown to him. Unable to hold on to the rope, he twisted it around his waist so that he could be hauled up. "A number of persons died alongside the vessel before they could get on board," he said. "The sailors were exceedingly expeditious in the work of rescue, and as kind as possible to the shipwrecked." He still wore his summer suit.

John George felt a long way, "maybe an eternity," from his native England. He went under water with the steamer, probably twenty or thirty feet, then, fortunate in escaping injury from loose timbers, rose to the surface with his life preserver still on. He seized a couple of strips of board, and was able to stay afloat. George, afloat for nine hours, was picked up at 5:00 A.M. "I never felt so thankful in all my life. I never knew what gratitude was before."

Willard Fletcher floated on his pieces of wreckage and swam intermittently for about ten hours. When he heard waves coming, he rose to let them pass over his shoulders. As he "weakened," he was drawn aboard the *Ellen*.

Osborne and Stetson drifted together for about an hour when Stetson saw a light; they started toward it. Osborne, now some distance behind Stetson, lost sight of him. He continued in the direction of the light, and as he approached, perceived the bark. After last seeing Stetson, it had taken two hours for him to reach the ship, and he was about the thirty-fifth man hauled on board. Stetson had been enfeebled by illness and said he had hardly a hope of being saved. On board, someone asked him if he had seen anyone else down that way. He told him yes, he had seen a very pleasant fellow down to leeward, who had been a companion in trouble, and would like to save him if possible. The man remarked that he had seen a noble fellow down to leeward, too, and would like to save him also, as they had floated together some time. "What's your name?" asked Osborne. "Stetson" said he. "Well, I am Osborne" said the other.

Toward morning Stephen Caldwell "felt very cold indeed, from the water dashing over me and around me, but used every effort not to yield." About five o'clock, he saw a light, swam toward it, and an hour later he and his gold were rescued. Caldwell felt no ill effects from the experience, "with the exception of being a little sore and stiff . . . I gratefully and humbly acknowledge my deep obligation to Providence for having brought me safe out of those great perils."

At about 7:00 A.M., Jacob Casey and his two companions were rescued from their hatchway by Captain Johnsen.

"There were a good many dead bodies floating about in the water. I struck against many of them. They were all provided with life-preservers, yet dead, and with their heads down in the water. It was a horrible sight," said John Taylor. He tried to get up the side of the *Ellen*, but couldn't make it without help. Along with most of his clothing, he also lost three hundred dollars in gold he had placed in his pockets. "I had not secured it with a string as I ought, and the violence of the waves had reversed my pockets, so I lost it all."

Major Jacob Clark was the forty-seventh man hauled on board.[6]

When Easton realized his friend Brown was not found, he begged Captain Johnsen to "make just one more tack."[7] Easton called: "Brown. Brown." As a small object neared, it proved to be Brown and Dement on their doors lashed together. Robert Brown and Lieutenant John Dement had been in the sea for twelve hours when rescued. Captain Johnsen explained, "They were first discovered at three o'clock in the morning, but immediately afterwards they unaccountably disappeared. At nine o'clock I saw them again, ran down for them, and threw them a rope, which they caught, but could not retain. After making one or two tacks, they drifted alongside, and I got them safely on board."[8] They were the last to be found, although "Captain Johnsen continued to search among the driftwood, tacking backward and forward," said Thomas Badger, "but found none." A sharp but futile lookout was kept for floating survivors.

After recovering his strength, Dr. Harvey found an "excellent chest of medicine" on the bark, which he "used with gratifying results."

Captain Johnsen was convinced that had it not been for the strange bird, he would not have deviated from his original course and consequently would have passed far north of the drowning passengers. In all, he had taken on board his brig forty-nine men. The final rescue was completed at 8:00 A.M. on Sunday, the 13th of September. Finding no others at 11:00 A.M., Johnsen headed the *Ellen* for Hampton Roads, Norfolk, Virginia.

---

[6] *The Missouri Republican*, 24 Sep 1857, 2-2.
[7] Olmsted-Lincoln, *Wedding Journey*, 1.
[8] *The Baltimore Sun*, 23 Sep 1857, 1-2.

CHAPTER IX

On the Brig

The first life-boat trip from the steamer to the *Marine* had taken one-half hour. Because of the strong drift and the extreme weariness of the crew, boatswain Black's last leg, an estimated seven miles, took two and one-half hours. During a nine-hour period he had made seven one-way trips between steamer and brig, across the ever-increasing distance between the vessels. The crew had rowed an estimated 23 miles in the rough sea, a herculean task. On the last two legs the crew bailed all the way, without passenger help.

James Travis explained:

> We were greatly exhausted. We could not have reached the steamer . . . for the boat which boatswain Black commanded left the brig forty-five minutes before we got alongside of her the last time, and still the boatswain did not get to the *Central America* only just as she went down. Mr. Black's boat was manned by a full crew, but in our enfeebled state we could not reach her in season.[1]

The men had not permitted the women to assist in bailing the ship, but in the small boats they had to bail to keep from being swamped. With Mrs. Lockwood, "three of the ladies bailed out the water all the way as hard as they could," and in the fourth boatload, Mrs. O'Connor "had to bail for her life."[2]

Accommodations, food and water on the *Marine* were scant items, but Captain Burt and his congenial crew did more than required in providing all in their possession to make the refugees of the *Central America* as comfortable as possible under the circumstances. This extension of hospitality included their own bunks and clean clothing.

The cabin of the brig was scarcely larger than a single stateroom of the steamer, and the passengers, consequently, were sandwiched in tightly. There were four bunks in the cabin, and three more in the captain's and mate's quarters. All were surrendered to the women and children. Shortly after they got on board, hot tea was passed among

---

[1] *The New York Herald*, 25 Sep 1857, 1-1.
[2] *The New York Herald*, 27 Sep 1857, 8-4. *Albany Evening Journal*, 23 Sep 1857, 2-3.

them, and they shared it in the ship's supply of five cups. Almira Kittredge, not having eaten since Friday morning, thought it the best tea she had ever tasted, and some hard crackers tasted good to the hungry refugees.

Mrs. Lynthia Ellis,[3] wife of Dr. Alvin Ellis, had with her four very young children; she and two of them were very sick. The women managed to fit them all in one bunk, and Theodore Payne said that when the provisions were carried round, the children "made such a chattering for food" that he called that berth the "birds' nest," and from then on it was known to them by that title. "Considering the exposure and manner of living, it was almost miraculous that no one else became sick," he mused.

Virginia Birch suddenly remembered her canary. "My first thought was that it had been crushed by the rope about my waist. I looked and found the little fellow lying quietly under the edge of my dress, unhurt. "He was soon singing cheerily in a box cage made for it by one of the sailors."[4]

It was customary for the ladies to wear several layers of underskirts. In evacuating the steamer, all of them and the children wore only their outer garments, the bulky excess clothing having been removed to facilitate swimming in the sea if necessary. This proved to be a sensible move for those who fell in the water while being transferred. With less bulk, they were able to maneuver and to dry out more quickly.

"When we came on board the brig, everything was wet, like we came out of a bath. The Captain was so good, he gave all his clothes to the ladies," said Madame Pahud, expressing gratitude for this gesture of Captain Burt. Many of them dressed in crewmen's apparel while their own dried.

"Nothing could exceed the kindness of Captain Burt and his officers," said Mrs. Hawley, gratefully. "They did everything that kind and generous hearts could prompt to relieve our sufferings."

> Each [said Payne] seemed to endeavor to make the other comfortable. Even the ladies who were separated from their husbands, and who

---

[3] Lynthia Powers Ellis, age 36, was born in Ohio; on 15 Sep 1851 in Huron Co., Ohio, she was married to Alvin Ellis, age 34, who was also born in Ohio; their children were born in California; they were Charles, age 4; Alvin, age 2; and Lillie, age 1. The fourth was a child they were caring for, identified as an infant, possibly her brother's child. Harry H. Ellis, U.S. Army, Retired, comp., *The Family of Lt. John and Elizabeth (Freeman) Ellis of Sandwich, Massachusetts*, (Dallas, TX: 1983), 67, 80. *Columbus Dispatch*, OH, 18 Sep 1989, 1-2, 3. 1850 U.S. Census, OH, Huron Co, Norwalk Twp; 5 Aug 1850, 39. International Genealogical Index, OH. Cooke and LeCount, *Directory of the City of San Francisco*, 1854, 51.

[4] *New York Daily Tribune*, 21 Sep 1857, 6-2. *Frank Leslie's Illustrated Newspaper*, 3 Oct 1857, 286-2.

Hot Tea on the *Marine*
From *Frank Leslie's Illustrated Newspaper*

frequently could not control the outpouring of their hearts, would console one another with the fact that there was a schooner near the steamer when she went down, and their husbands might have gone on board of her. Thus every hope and ingenuity was used to cheer the poor sufferers, and from my own observation I must say, that it would be quite impossible to get together again, under the same trying circumstances, a more self-sacrificing, generous, kind-hearted number of people.

At 4:00 P.M., as the fog cleared away, Elizabeth Hawley could see the steamer distinctly, thought it a beautiful sight, and not seeming in danger of sinking. But she and other wives began to despair when Raymond's boat-load arrived without husbands on board, and the crew refused to return to the steamer.

Of the thirty-two women on board, eighteen had husbands on the steamship. Some had sons, one left her father on the steamer, and all feared for the lives of the men. The women were very quiet. They watched the distant lights of the *Central America* as long as they could, then feared the worst when they could no longer be seen. "It is not to praise ourselves," recalled Rosalie Pahud, "but I think we have been very quiet, all the time there was not a word; we did not say one word."

Mrs. Swan "felt sick at heart" when, shortly after 8:00 P.M. she no longer saw the light, and wondered if Samuel had perished. Hurt and bruised by her fall from the steamer's bunk, she rested in one of the bunks.

At nine o'clock a man came on board and unceremoniously said, "The steamer has sunk, I saw it go down, and every soul on board has gone to Davy Jones' locker." A shriek arose from the women, and Jane Badger sprang to the cabin door saying, "I hear my husband's voice." For some time she stood looking out, until others assisted her back into the cabin. "It terrified us awfully," said Amanda Marvin, "we shrieked and halloaed at the loss of our husbands."

"Many of the rescued wives of the passengers, who had left their husbands behind them," said Joseph Bassford, "declared with cries of piercing agony that they would rather have stayed behind and gone down with their husbands than to have been saved without them. The scene on the boat was one to be long remembered."

One child had not arrived at the brig. Mrs. Kittredge said: "There was a little Spanish boy, Ricardo Ollague, from Lima, eleven years old, he looked like a little boy of mine, and I became very much attached to him. I took charge and care of him. He was to be put off in the boat with me; they promised to do so but did not . . . . He had an older brother, Adolpho, who came to me and beseeched me to take the little boy with me; I promised to do so, but they would not put him on board."[5] Almira Kittredge could not here refrain from weeping. No one had an explanation for young Ricardo's not being placed in the life-boat; perhaps at the last moment he refused to leave his brother.

The ladies had little sleep that night. Miserable and cold, the women sat waist deep in water on the cabin floor. Almira Kittredge remained by the cabin door, "through which the water was rushing in all night." At daylight there was no sign of the vessel. Captain Burt, soon after he got all the women on board and "put away," being very busy on every part of his ship, found that in the excitement the sailors had neglected the pumps. "In no very choice language, he called the men to account." The night was dark, and the storm still raging.

Amid the confusion of the situation on deck, and Burt's orders, the cabin door opened and "out popped Mrs. Marvin . . . a very little woman." She said, "Captain, let me pump; I'm a good hand, and can do my share of the work." She put on a suit to help the men work, supposing they would think she was a boy. Captain Burt requested her

---

[5] *The New York Herald*, 27 Sep 1857, 8-3. *Frank Leslie's Illustrated Newspaper*, 10 Oct 1857, 297.

to retire, saying that he had plenty of men to do the work. After a little discussion, "little Mrs. Marvin, with a gigantic spirit,"[6] reluctantly stepped back into the cabin.

There were forty-nine male survivors on board the brig, many of them crew-members who had transported the passengers from the steamer. Others had jumped into the water and had been pulled on board the last boats, and a few had jumped into John Black's lifeboat. Some had been permitted, or managed in some way to get on board, such as Albert Priest, Alonzo Monson, George Ashby, Charles McCarty, Frank Jones, Theodore Payne, and William Garretson.

When Joseph Bassford and Frank Jones arrived on the brig, Mrs. Easton was pleased to return to them their watches.

A number of men slept in the after hold of the brig, where they were equally as crowded as the ladies in the cabin, and more uncomfortable. The hold, loaded with sugar and tar, scarcely admitted fresh air. Hogsheads of molasses had burst and run loose, causing a nauseating odor. Many men slept on the wet, cold deck, and even in that discomfort preferred it to the close quarters of the hold. The crew provided them sails for covers and some warmth. Their diet consisted of gruel, boiled rice and molasses. Most recognized these as minor hardships when compared to those of the men who had remained on the *Central America*.

The seven berths of the brig were mostly occupied by children and those very ill or injured. There were two or three trunks and as many stools to sit on.

"The appearance of the ladies, under other circumstances, would have been very amusing." Even so, Rosalie Pahud, in her French accent,[7] said, "A great many of the ladies were dressed in gentlemen's clothes to let theirs dry. It was quite cunning to see us on board, the way we were fixed; we can't help but to laugh now." Some were in a full sailor's rig, with red shirt and jacket. Jane Badger wore the captain's undershirt, boots, and socks, and had a large blanket wrapped around her. Mrs. Lockwood, Thomas, Pahud, and Birch, as others, wore old hats, some with brims cut off, and pieces of sail. For Mrs. Thayer, Mrs. Marvin made a bonnet of a piece of flounce torn from her dress. Addie Easton wore Captain Burt's old hat.

Mrs. Hawley wore a pair of gentlemen's white drawers and socks, and a blanket having a "hole cut in it, through which she put her head, wearing it *a la Mexicana.*" Mrs. Travis could not get her shoes on, or

---

[6] *New York Daily Tribune,* 21 Sep 1857, 6-7.

[7] In quoting Mme. Pahud, a reporter said: "We give it in her own simple, unaffected words." *The New York Daily Tribune,* 21 Sep 1857, 6-2.

had lost them. Mrs. Kittredge had not had her shoes off for a week. "I lay with them on all the time." During the day the wet clothes were hung in the rigging to dry.

The odor from spilled cargo caused the air in the cabin to be stifling. Mrs. Travis could not sleep, so Mr. Payne suggested they all go up on deck for a breather. "At night we used tin life preservers for pillows," said Mrs. Kittredge, "in the cabin they put us together so thick as not to give us room to kick. During the last part of the voyage [in a calm sea] we slept on deck under a sail. We liked this very much better than the cabin."

"We had the same *good tea* in the same five cups," said Amanda Marvin. "Afterwards our fare was changed to gruel. At first we drank our soup and gruel out of soup plates, but at length we got quite aristocratic and ate them out of wooden spoons." Frank Jones carved wooden spoons for Mrs. Marvin, Easton, McNeil and Travis, who shared them with the others.

Mrs. Small's rations consisted of Indian gruel, baked or stewed beans and hard bread in three meals per day, slightly different than Mrs. Kittredge's diet of gruel, boiled rice and molasses—a little variation in their unappetizing but life-sustaining diet.

After three days, Mme. Pahud observed Captain Burt's food supply to be running low for the over one hundred hungry people. "He didn't have victuals enough for all of us." One day an unidentified survivor [probably Mr. M. Dougherty] saw Mary Swan moisten her "hard-tack" in a cup of water and feed it to her starving little girl. Approaching her, he offered his scanty ration, saying he had a wife and two children in Albany, New York, and understood her plight. Mrs. Bowly said, "There were not enough provisions even to do anything more than just to keep us from starving; and yet the captain shared them with us. I did not eat anything for nearly three days, but kept my little allowance to feed my children with. If they had not had the food they must have died."

Theodore Payne spoke in the highest terms of the kindness and unremitting attentions of Captain Burt and the crew. On Wednesday evening, a seaman sighted a sail some six or seven miles away, in a calm sea. "A boat and crew were got ready," said Payne, "and I volunteered to go and speak her." After rowing several miles in the captain's yawl, he boarded the clipper *Euphrasia*, bound for New Orleans, and from her master, Captain William Lanfare, obtained a supply of provisions. Payne described Lanfare as "one of those genuine sons of the ocean, whose hearts are ever ready to respond to the distresses of others." The captain supplied all he was asked for, and refused reimbursement, adding other items he thought necessary. Among other supplies, he provided two barrels of sea biscuit, two barrels of potatoes, three hams and six chickens.

"After loading our boat with the provisions," resumed Payne, "he sent it back to the brig, and politely lowering his gig from the quarter, he rowed to our vessel and was introduced to the captain and passengers. This little episode relieved the monotony as well as furnished a bountiful supply on which to regale ourselves." As Lanfare "left the brig," said Bassford, "three rounds of cheers were given to him."

"Captain Lanfare," reported Mrs. Easton, "said with tears in his eyes: 'Heaven knows, I'm sorry for you! You can have anything I have.'" Captain Burt was ready to ration out his last day's allowance of water, and had not an opportune supply of provisions been received from Lanfare, all would have been "driven to great straits with hunger as well as thirst."

Becalmed for three days, and because the damage inflicted by the storm, made maneuvering the *Marine* increasingly difficult, it became apparent to Captain Burt that it would be necessary for the vessel to be towed into the harbor at Norfolk, Virginia. Therefore, on Friday, September 18th, when off Cape Henry, Payne again struck out with the yawl and crew in the direction of the Cape lighthouse, near the entrance to Chesapeake Bay. Within a few miles, Payne saw a vessel approaching their boat. He stood up, waving his handkerchief as a signal of distress; the propeller-driven steamship, *City of Norfolk*, Captain Greene, saw him.

Theodore Payne described to Greene the situation on the brig, the conditions of the vessel, and asked for his assistance in towing the brig into the harbor. Green asked, "What will you give?" Payne replied, "Anything that is right," naming the sums of $100, $150 and $200. Greene said he would not do it for less than $300, to which Payne then said, "Well, we are helpless, and must submit to your terms to go out to the brig."[8] As the propeller ran alongside the *Marine*, the mercenary Greene again tried bargaining. Seeing the desperation of the circumstances, he increased the charge to $500, but finally accepted $300, and commenced towing the brig toward port. Rosalie Pahud thought that "was a shame."

With Payne on his quest for towing assistance, the *Marine* entered the mouth of Chesapeake Bay where, sadly, on Friday, September 18th, the injured stewardess, Lucy Dawson, died.[9]

---

[8] *The New York Times*, 22 Sep 1857, No. 1875, 8-4. *The New York Herald*, 22 Sep 1857, 1. *The Daily Alta California*, 23 Oct 1857, 1-4.

[9] *Richmond Daily Dispatch*, 22 Sep 1857, 1-7. *The Baltimore Sun*, 23 Sep 1857, 1-4.

CHAPTER X

Reunion

The steamer *Empire City* encountered the storm much later than the *Central America*. Captain McGowan[1] and her crew, with considerable difficulty, succeeded in keeping the vessel head to the wind, with steam up at all times. The hull of the smaller vessel held firm.

She weathered the storm, but the voyage of the *Empire City* was nearly disastrous. A passenger noted that "too much credit could not be bestowed upon the officers and men for the skill and courage they evinced during the storm." The passengers were in a state of alarm, but were reassured by Captain McGowan and his officers. Several Spanish officers complained bitterly that they had been put on board the *Empire City* in lieu of the *Central America,* and asked to be taken to Savannah or Charleston. McGowan denied the request.

On Friday morning, September 11th, the coal supply ran out and the steerage berths and all other available woodwork on the ship were broken up to feed the furnaces. That night two starboard ports were stove in by a heavy sea that struck the starboard bow. At about 2:30 P.M. the engine steam drum burst and filled the interior of the ship with steam, making breathing difficult. The engineers repaired the drum in about three hours.

By Sunday, September 13th, neither the sun nor stars had been seen for four days. Col. Gray believed that by drifting with the Gulf Stream they were "forced to keep pace somewhat" with the storm. The ability to maintain boiler steam pressure allowed Captain McGowan to hold a normal track, whereas the *Central America,* with no power, had drifted about 150 miles to the east. Looking for a recognizable landmark, McGowan ran the steamer toward land. On the afternoon of September

---

[1] Captain John N. McGowan was born in Philadelphia, Pennsylvania, December 3, 1805. He was appointed a third lieutenant in the Revenue Cutter Service, May 14, 1831. McGowan was commander of the revenue cutter *Gallatin* during the early 1830s. He served on the cutter *Jackson*, on the Florida coast during the Seminole War and, also as Herndon, served in the Squadron of Commodore Perry during the Mexican War. McGowan sailed with the Navy on the Pacific Coast between 1850 and 1855, when he entered the service of the PMSC. Being a naval officer, he qualified for service with the eastern line. Navy Historical Center Archives, Biography, 9 Apr 1918.

14th a heavy rainstorm shut in the horizon to a few ship's lengths. Suddenly, the mizzenmast of a ship came into view, and the *Empire City* nearly ran over the wreck of a bark. A lead sounding gave a depth reading of ten fathoms. Although the crew of the bark was plainly visible on her decks, no assistance could be given them because of the risk of running on a shoal. Purser Denison said that in this "frightful running sea, we lay with our decks nearly perpendicular up and down."[2] Gray said that the force of the gale was such that "our forward iron brace, some three inches in diameter, was snapped in two, and the bull's eye deadlights or footlights, an inch in thickness, were shivered and broken into pieces like panes of common glass."

In spite of concentrated efforts at cleanliness through pavement of the streets and alleys, improved drainage and removal of refuse, periodic epidemics broke out in the city of Norfolk, Virginia. During an 1855 epidemic brought in by the steamer *Ben Franklin*, the daily death rate was eighty to one-hundred persons. The city took on a deserted look, and in potter's field coffins and rough boxes were seen "piled up like cordwood as high as a man could reach. Every man, woman, and child, almost without exception, had been stricken with yellow fever, and about two thousand had been buried." Winter frost finally halted the spread of the disease.[3]

It is therefore understandable why, less than two years later, precautions were taken to prevent a recurrence. Any suspicion of the presence of a disease dictated that ships entering Hampton Roads (the channel between the mouth of the James River and Chesapeake Bay) anchor in a quarantine area, as was required of the *Empire City*, Captain McGowan, on September 15th.

The *Empire City* anchored in the quarantine zone about four miles from the port of Norfolk, and McGowan proceeded to the port by pilot boat. He sent a dispatch to the steamship office in New York: "Quarantined in port at Norfolk. Arrived at this port this morning at 7 o'clock, encountering one of the most severe gales of wind I have ever witnessed, commencing Thursday at 12 o'clock; the wind varying during the time NE to SW, around by west, and blowing furiously from each point."[4] He described the storm and the considerable damage to his ship, including the loss of a portion of the starboard paddle box, sails

---

[2] *New York Daily Tribune*, 21 Sep 1857, 8-3.

[3] Dr. Dabney Herndon, younger brother of Commander Herndon, died in 1870 as the result of treating victims of a yellow fever epidemic in Mobile, Alabama. *Descendants of John De La Fontaine*, 130. Wertenbaker, *Norfolk: Historic Southern Port*, 191.

[4] *New York Daily Tribune*, 18 Sep 1857, 3-1.

blown to pieces, all usable wood used for fuel, sidelights broken and boilers torn loose from their fittings. Herndon had encountered the storm on Wednesday, suggesting much distance, an estimated fifty miles, between the two ships. McGowan said he would "use all economy and dispatch in getting the ship to sea . . . and sail for New York, I think, about Thursday morning, 17th."

The captain had arranged for refueling and, on the 17th, a schooner came alongside the steamer to deliver a load of coal. Meanwhile, Marshall Roberts wired Captain McGowan to send his passengers to New York by railroad, take in coal, and instead of continuing on to New York, to at once proceed to sea and search for the *Central America*, now over-due at New York and presumed to be in some sort of difficulty.

Sixty passengers had sailed from Havana on the *Empire City*, and fifty of them now debarked at Fort Comfort, where they boarded railroad trains to Baltimore and their respective destinations. Others, including Colonel Gray, proceeded by steamer to Baltimore after release by the health officer. Before they departed, McGowan's grateful passengers took up a collection for the crew of the *Empire City*, in appreciation for their extraordinary efforts. Of $300 collected, $100 was given to the first officer, $100 to the engineer and firemen, and $100 to the seamen. As a testimonial of their gratitude for the attention and care he extended to them, and for his skill in guiding the steamer through the storm, McGowan's passengers made a separate subscription for him.

The *Ellen's* crew and the forty-nine survivors of the *Central America* found a scarcity of food on the bark. On Sunday afternoon, shortly after leaving the search area, they sighted, contacted and boarded the bark *Saxony*, and Captain Smith gave them two barrels of provisions. With all on board living on gruel, five of the passengers, Henry Childs, Adolph Frederick, Jabez Howes, Samuel Look[5] and Billings Ridley, gladly accepted an invitation of the captain to transfer to the *Saxony*. In passing the time, Childs composed his narrative of events.[6]

On Tuesday the 15th, farther up the East Coast, the *Ellen* met the

---

[5] Samuel Look, age 47, and his younger brother, Prince, age 40, had "spent the night together on the same plank, but Prince became so exhausted that a heavy sea swept him off before succor came. He leaves a wife and three children in Bath." Prince died on the plank. Samuel held him until he saw another man drowning, and released his brother to save the other man. This man, unidentified, wrote to Samuel every year until death. Jane Renard, descendant of Samuel Look. *The Boston Daily Evening Transcript*, 2 Oct 1857, 4-3. 1850 U.S. Census, Maine, Lincoln Co, town of Phipsburg, 2 Aug 1850, 106. 1850 U.S. Census, Maine, Franklin Co, Town of Farmington, 12 Aug 1850, 175.

[6] E. Merton Coulter, The Loss of . . . , 468.

dismasted bark, *Cuba*, bound for Gloucester, obtaining two barrels of bread. Later, sighting the propeller *Thomas Swann*, Captain Post, bound for Charleston, Captain Johnsen asked for a tow. The vessel had an insufficient supply of fuel to accommodate the *Ellen*, but "offered to take passengers to Charleston," said R. T. Brown, "but no one accepted the invitation." Johnsen asked Captain Post, on his arrival at Charleston, to report the catastrophe of the *Central America*.

At dusk on Thursday, September 17th, Johnsen's *Ellen* entered Norfolk Harbor where at daylight on Friday, September 18th, Ayulo, Badger, Brown, Easton and Birch engaged a pilot-boat to take them to Norfolk. Enroute, seeing a steamer moving through the harbor, they recognized the *Empire City* and boarded her, informing McGowan of the disaster. The captain soon relayed the information through the port of Norfolk to Marshall Roberts in New York. Until the arrival of Robert Brown and the others, Purser Charles Denison said: "No one on board doubted the ultimate safety" of the steamer. Leaving the steamer, the five men continued on to Norfolk in the pilot-boat.

Meanwhile, Captain Post, of the *Thomas Swann*, arrived in Charleston on the 17th and reported the loss of the *Central America*. This first word of the disaster was telegraphed to New York City late that evening and appeared in the morning newspapers of September 18th at about the time Captain McGowan, at Norfolk, learned of the loss.

Abandoning his previous intention, McGowan immediately got his ship under way. On nearing the *Ellen* he exchanged greetings with Johnsen by voice horn, and the former offered a New York passage to all who desired it. The majority of the survivors were then taken on board the *Empire City*, and "with a parting round of three hearty cheers for their preservers," they proceeded toward Cape Henry, still hoping to fall in with the *Marine*. Captain Johnsen and the *Ellen* went on to the quarantine zone.

Oliver Manlove, with some of the other men who accompanied Johnsen to quarantine, headed for the city and other transportation. Manlove "walked the streets . . . hatless and barefoot. I had a handkerchief tied around my waist when in the water. This I had now tied over my head to keep the sun from scalding it. We soon attracted attention and people came flocking to us to hear of the wreck . . . . I was shown a clothing store and was soon dressed in a new suit of clothes."

Within three miles of Cape Henry, the men on the steamer sighted a vessel in tow of a propeller. Anxiously leveling glasses as the ships rapidly closed together, they recognized the *Marine* in tow of the *City of Norfolk*. "Her low and confined decks were swarming with wretched-looking objects," said Denison, "many of them women and children, wringing their hands, weeping and laughing hysterically." Captain McGowan hailed Captain Greene, and asked if the passengers on board were from the *Central America*. With an affirmative reply,

> our boats were speedily lowered, and McGowan, in the first, boarded the brig in person, was caressed, embraced, and, indeed half strangled by the poor women, who threw themselves upon him as he reached the deck. [All praised] the attention paid them and the humanity displayed by the officers and crews on both brig and bark.[7]

On the *Marine*, Captain McGowan called Mrs. Easton aside and told her that her husband was waiting for her in Norfolk. Her feelings were "beyond description." Said McGowan, "Let us sit down here, for I must tell you all about it. He is safe and anxiously waiting for you."[8] To her great delight, he told her of Herndon asking Ansel to pass him his cigar to light the last rocket, of Easton and Badger assisting in saving others and Ansel's insistence on finding Brown.

Theodore Payne thought: "The ways of Providence are inscrutable, —while in the midst of the storm, many extended their sympathy for those on board the *Empire City*, thinking she would certainly be lost in the storm."[9]

> As boat load after boat load reached the ship's side and ladder, [resumed Denison,] each vied with the other in assisting them to our decks, and in a short time the greater portion were comfortably quartered in the cabin. To the bystanders the recognition and greeting between the two parties — mother claiming son and husband wife; the eager scanning of each face in agonizing fear and expectation; the joy or grief manifested as recognition or disappointment awaited the gazer—was touching in the extreme, straining the heart strings and moistening the eyes of many hitherto unused to such manifestation.

Henry O'Connor said, "I sent word to my Mother that I was safe. This was the first time she knew whether I was lost or saved, and it had been five days since we parted." Eleanor O'Connor received him as "life from the dead."[10] The Seeger family was reunited on the *Empire City*.[11]

---

[7] *The New York Herald*, 21 Sep 1857, 1-1. *The New York Times*, 21 Sep 1857, No. 1874, 1-1. *New York Daily Tribune*, 21 Sep 1857, 5 5.

[8] Olmsted Lincoln, *Wedding Journey*, 2.

[9] *Richmond Daily Dispatch*, 22 Sep 1857, 1-5.

[10] *The New York Herald*, 21 Sep 1857, 2-5, 6. *Albany Evening Journal*, 23 Sep 1857, 2-3.

[11] Ben (Bernhard) Seeger, age 33, was born in France; his wife, Mary Seeger, age 24, was born in Baden. With their two California-born sons, John, age 3, and William, age 1, they had been living at San Andreas, Calaveras Co., California. They were returning to their home in St. Louis, Missouri. 1860 U.S. Census, St. Louis, Missouri, Ward 1, 92. 1870 U.S. Census, St. Louis, MO, 2nd Ward, 13 Jun 1870, 359.

By one or more of the survivors, including Bassford, George Ashby had been described to Captain McGowan as a coward. As he attempted to board, McGowan told him not to come on his steamer. When the chief engineer asked him the reason for his refusal, McGowan told him that he had acted most cowardly in deserting his steamer, and, "assured him that if he attempted to set foot on his steamer he would blow his d——d brains to hell!"[12] O'Connor heard McGowan tell the chief engineer that if "you had been on my ship, I would have put a ball through you, or hung you at the yard arm." When Ashby attempted an explanation, McGowan said that he based his action on "reliable information" and would say nothing further to him.

Captain McGowan emotionally witnessed the scenes of sorrow and despair among those who had suffered irreparable loss. The lives of hundreds of passengers had been lost, as well as many crew-members probably known to himself and to his crew. The news no doubt left him greatly disturbed over the loss of an old friend, Lewis Herndon, whom he had known for many years in the Navy with Perry in Mexico, in the Florida campaign, and as a fellow captain with the mail steamship company. The reports, by persons such as Bassford and Harvey, of Ashby's desertion of his captain and ship must have sorely angered that steady, conscientious naval officer. With Ashby as engineer, McGowan, as master of the *Central America,* had made six trips to Aspinwall during 1853. He knew the chief engineer yet apparently believed the stories now being told about him.

Captain McGowan learned of an extortion by an oarsman in Finley Frazier's lifeboat, named Frederick Brougham. The victim, a "German" passenger, had slid down the side of the steamer and jumped into the boat. On their way to the brig, the boatman demanded all his money on pain of being thrown overboard. The German paid him all he had, about forty dollars, and thus saved his life. Brougham surrendered the money, but not until Captain McGowan threatened to put him in irons.[13]

Most of the forlorn passengers accepted McGowan's invitation to board the *Empire City.* The remaining survivors, after passing the health inspection, proceeded to Norfolk. But before departing the brig, the grateful group quickly raised a sum of money and presented it to Captain Burt and his crew—$500 for the captain; first mate $100; second mate $75; two cooks and steward $150; sailors $25. Virginia Birch said that the money had to be forced upon the captain before he would take it.

---

[12] *New York Daily Tribune,* 21 Sep 1857, 6-7. *The New York Times,* 21 Sep 1857.
[13] *The New York Times,* 22 Sep 1857, 8-5, and 23 Sep 1857, 1-6.

By pilot boat to shore, Captain McGowan dispatched a message to M.O. Roberts in New York:

> The *Central America* foundered at sea on Saturday evening last at 8 o'clock. Fifty passengers were rescued from pieces of wreck by a Norwegian bark and brought into Hampton Roads. Twenty-six females were taken from the ship *Central America* by a brig three hours previously. Officers all lost except Mr. Frazer, the second mate. I will leave for New-York with the surviving passengers at 10 o'clock this morning.[14]

"When all who wished had been taken on board," said Denison, "the *Empire City* again got under weigh for New York."[15] By going in the pilot boat to Norfolk, Badger, Birch and Easton missed seeing their wives on the *Marine*. McGowan was not aware of who had accompanied Brown, but Addie said the pilot boat captain later advised Virginia that her husband had been rescued, and Virginia went on to New York. Jane decided to seek her husband at Norfolk.

With the transfer of the passengers to the *Empire City* at Hampton Roads complete, about twenty-five *Central America* passengers remained on the brig *Marine*. Greene sent his second mate on board to see if his services were further required, and Burt said, "I want you to tow me to the quarantine." The *City of Norfolk*, Captain Greene, complied, arriving soon after dark. Burt cast off Greene's hawser and paid his fee.

Jane Badger, Addie Easton, Almira Kittredge, Amanda Marvin, Theodore Payne and others left the brig in a small boat, "were rowed seven miles to the city of Norfolk, and landed away from the usual wharf, down near a lumber yard. At seven P.M. [on the 18th of September], the forlorn little procession walked up to the hotel."[16] Women sought word of their men folk, others wished to go on by land to their respective destinations; probably all were anxious to find food, clothing and baths.

On their arrival they were quartered at the National Hotel.[17] The proprietor, Mr. Walters, and the ladies of the house immediately commenced the unremitting work of ministering to the needs of the survivors, who were all gathered in an immense parlor of the hotel. The citizens crowded in to see them and listen to their "perils of the deep."

---

[14] *New York Daily Tribune*, 19 Sep 1857, 4-5.
[15] *The New York Herald*, 21 Sep 1857, 1-1.
[16] Olmsted Lincoln, *Wedding Journey*, 36.
[17] In 1857 the National Hotel was the largest hotel in Norfolk. Located at Main and Church Streets, the four story structure was built before 1850 on the site of French's Hotel. The hotel survived until early 1958, when it was destroyed as part of the Norfolk Redevelopment and Housing Authority's Project No. 3, to clear the site for a new Civic Center. Wertenbaker, *Norfolk*, 201.

Payne described the reception of the refugees at Norfolk as simultaneously heartwarming and heartrending. The parlors of the National Hotel were thrown open to them, and

> a scene of anguish and distress was presented, which moved the stoutest heart, and bedewed every eye with tears. The ladies would cast a hurried glance around the room, and with the smothered exclamation of "my husband, or son, or brother, is not saved," would sink helplessly to the floor. The scene was distressing in the extreme, and beggars all description. —Many citizens were present, and deeply affected, as the tears which stole down their cheeks too plainly attested.[18]

On her arrival at the hotel, Addie Easton found that Ansel had become impatient and, with Captain Johnsen, had gone in a small-boat to the *Marine*. In a few hours, having passed her somewhere along the route to the brig, he returned to the hotel. Addie said: "Of our meeting a few hours later I cannot speak. Great joy is too deep for words."[19]

"Kindness loaded us with everything we needed," said Addie. One lady even gave them a trunk, which Addie declined to take, saying she had nothing to put in it. Mr. Ferguson, Mayor of Norfolk, called a meeting of the citizens, and "at eleven o'clock an immense throng assembled in the city." The townspeople adopted resolutions and subscribed the sum of $2000 for the purchase of clothing and for defraying the expense of the destitute to their homes. They presented each lady with fifty dollars, and those with children were given one hundred. "All fares were paid to New York, and not one hotel bill was charged to them."[20]

Almira Kittredge said,

> I wish it was in my power to express our gratitude for the kindness with which we were treated by the people of Norfolk. About twenty of us went in there, and stopped at the principal hotel. The ladies of the place immediately sent in great baskets of clothes to us—skirts, under-clothes, and clothes of all kinds—so that those who went there without anything came away with carpetbags full. Some one sent in and took the measure of all our feet, and then supplied us with very good gaiters. Especially are we indebted to Mrs. Walters, the landlady of the hotel, and several ladies who were stopping there.[21] Our own sisters could not have treated us with more consideration; they did everything in the world that could be done for us. We shall ever remember their kindness with the deepest gratitude.

---

[18] *Richmond Daily Dispatch*, 22 Sep 1857. 1-6.
[19] Olmsted-Lincoln, *Wedding Journey*, 37.
[20] *The New York Times*, 22 Sep 1857, No. 1875, 8-4. *The New York Herald*, 22 Sep 1857, 1. *Daily Alta California*, 23 Oct 1857, 1-4. *San Francisco Bulletin*, 22 Oct 1857, 3, quoting the *Herald*.

Said William Ede: "We were given safe passage and landed at Norfolk, where we were treated with the utmost hospitality. We were not allowed to spend a dollar for anything. We were feted and feasted and I was taken clear to my home in Wisconsin without paying out a dollar for anything. The $1500 I had when I started went down with the vessel."[22]

"A slight altercation took place here this evening, between Judge Monson and Mr. Payne," said a reporter from Richmond, Virginia. There had been an unexplained misunderstanding which had arisen at the time of leaving the ship, but which was amicably reconciled "to the satisfaction of both parties, and ended by Mr. Payne's asking "all hands to take a drink."[23]

After giving his statement to a reporter at Norfolk, Capt. Badger had remarked to him that "the old brig *Marine* would get into New York tomorrow evening, and as my wife does not know that I am saved, I am most anxious to meet her."[24] Postponing a visit to his old Virginia home and relatives, he decided to head north to find Jane.

On September 18th, at about the time the twenty-five passengers arrived at Norfolk, Thomas Badger, Enrique Ayulo, Billy Birch, R.T. Brown and Oliver Manlove boarded the night steamer Louisiana, Captain Russell of the Bay Line, to Baltimore. From there Brown and Ayulo took a through train to New York City. At 5:00 P.M. on the 19th, after resting at Norfolk, others, including George Ashby and Theodore Payne, traveled to Baltimore on the steamer *Georgia,* Captain Cannon.

Virginia Birch later traveled by rail from Jersey City to Baltimore to meet Billy, and Jane Badger, who remained in "utter ignorance of [Thomas's] fate, suffering intense anxiety," arrived at the National Hotel to find he had left for Baltimore. At Baltimore, she would find him "alive and well."[25]

---

[21] Mrs. Sally Tazewell, [Wife of Littleton Waller Tazewell, Governor of VA, 1834-36.] Mrs. A.F. Leonard, [Wife of Abraham F. Leonard, a Norfolk poet who contributed to some of the leading literary journals of the day.] Mrs. Sharp, [Wife of Charles Sharp, member of a committee of three organized to influence the extension of Virginia and Carolina railways to the Elizabeth River.] Mrs. R.H. Stevens, Mrs. A. Santos, and Mrs. R.N. Bagner. Wertenbaker, 120, 124, 277. *The New York Herald,* 27 Sep 1857, 8-3. *Frank Leslie's Illustrated Newspaper,* 10 Oct 1857, 297-1. *San Francisco Daily Bulletin,* 27 Oct. 1857, 3-4, Payne.

[22] *San Francisco Chronicle,* 26 Sep 1896.

[23] *Richmond Daily Dispatch,* 21 Sep 1857, 1-3.

[24] *Ibid.,*

[25] *The New York Times,* 24 Sep 1857, 1.

CHAPTER XI

All Ashore

Coast-to-coast news traveled at a slow pace in the United States of 1857, there being no wireless, cross-country telegraph or railroad.[1] Coast-to-coast mail service had yet to be initiated by James Birch's competitor, Butterfield Overland Mail. It took more than a month for the news of events occurring on the east coast to reach San Francisco by steamer.

The United States had a population of less than thirty million. There were in 1857 thirty-one states, only five of them west of the Mississippi River. Missouri, Iowa, Arkansas and Texas bordered the western frontier. James Buchanan presided over the nation, the election of President Lincoln, and the Civil War, being several years away.

Daily newspapers reported on some of the national problems, world events and noted personalities, and these were among the stories of the day:

Because of a shortage of money, a large trade deficit and business failures, many citizens thought a collapse of the economy was imminent.

From Mississippi came a report that officers were recruiting men for General William Walker's[2] army, destined for Nicaragua. President Buchanan was "uncompromisingly opposed to such foreign intervention." The constitutional authority for the declaration of war being vested in Congress alone, he had the support to prevent it.[3]

---

[1] There were, however, coastal and inland telegraphs. In California, on October 24, 1853, "the mountains spoke to the sea with a lightning flash over the wires from Marysville to San Francisco, a distance by the telegraph line of over 200 miles—charge for the first ten words—two dollars." In addition to the east coast terminals, by 1857, St. Louis, Missouri and other inland cities also received Associated Press messages from New York City. Colville, *Directory of Sacramento,* xxix.

[2] Colonel Slatter of New Orleans was raising the finances, and General Walker [three of whose men had been lost on the *Central America*] planned to leave for Central America in November. Sam Houston was suspected of being the instigator of the planned invasion. Walker had already been twice indicted for fitting out an armed expedition to Lower California, but had been acquitted. He had been "out to revolutionize Central America," and had "virtually conquered Nicaragua." *New York Daily Tribune,* 19 Sep 1857, 4-3.

[3] Buchanan issued circulars to the United States Marshal to arrest any attempted departures from the United States for the invasion of another country. The administration determined to enforce the neutrality laws, and on September 21st, 1857, took the initial steps for that purpose. *The New York Times,* 19 Sep 1857, 1-6.

The laying of the transatlantic cable by the Atlantic Telegraph Company had to be delayed until the summer of 1858 while the cable-laying vessel, the U.S. steam-frigate *Niagara*, Captain Hudson, had her fixtures repaired in New York.[4]

Dr. David Livingstone, famous explorer, advocated the opening of Africa to commerce, civilization and Christianity. William Lewis Herndon, after exploring the Amazon valley, had been proclaimed the "Dr. Livingstone of South America."[5]

The western frontier continued to attract pioneers. Six wagons, with as many families, passed through Lewisburg, Virginia, enroute west, while Pittsylvania County, Virginia, was visited by a hailstorm, some of the stones being five inches in circumference.

In New York City, the Committee on Finance advocated passing an ordinance favoring an issue of stock in the amount of $100,000 for the improvement of Central Park.

Citizens knew California as a land of adventure, and the city of New York as the center of elite society, business activity, entertainment and the latest news.

The owners of the *Central America* had supposed that, running short of coal during the gale, she made her way under sail along the Gulf Stream and may have put into Nassau or Key West. Their consternation grew on learning the electrifying news from Charleston.

On Friday morning, September 18th, news of the disaster filled the front pages of the New York City and other East Coast newspapers.[6] All other news items became secondary. The arrival of survivors in Norfolk left no further doubts as to what had befallen the vessel. How many survived, their identities, and who was lost became the first questions.

---

[4] "Some 200 miles from land, the cable parted in 2000 fathoms of water . . . unfortunate, unwise order of an engineer who thought it necessary to tighten the brakes [because of] the rapidity with which the cable was being paid out." Work on the cable recommenced in June 1858. *Harper's Weekly*, 5 Sep 1857, 503. *The New York Times*, 5 Oct 1857, 1-2.

[5] Virginia Magazine of History and Biography, *Genealogies of Virginia Families*, Vol IV, (Genealogical Publishing Co, Baltimore, MD, 1981), 36.

[6] In Richmond, Virginia, news of the disaster was carried in *The Richmond Daily Dispatch*, with inputs from their own reporter at Norfolk, *The Norfolk Day Book and Argus*, and an "Extra" of the *Baltimore Sun*.

News of the wreck was carried to Europe by the United States mail packet *Arago*, which arrived at Southampton, England, from New York on October 2nd. The loss of the *Central America* was considered "the greater matter in the news brought by the steamer."

Frankfurt's *Allgemeine Zeitung*, on receiving news from Liverpool, reported on October 6th that the *Central America* was missing, and on October 6th printed a brief story of the disaster.

In Paris, *L'Illustration, Journal Universal*, 31 Oct. 1857, published a dramatic depiction, covering two full pages, of the foundering and rescue vessels.

With scant information, the media erroneously proclaimed a total of sixty-five survivors.

Captain Nichols, of the brig *Mungo Park,* arrived at Philadelphia on Saturday morning, September 18th, reporting that at noon on the 11th, he discovered a large steamship, painted black, thought to be the *Central America,* steering northeast by north.

> The wind was blowing strong from the northwest, and the weather thick and rainy. Nothing unusual was observed in the motion of the ship to suggest any distress or danger. On the 12th, while scudding under close-reefed topsails, during a terrific gale, saw a steamship, supposed to be the above vessel, laboring very heavily, without steam, with no signal of distress hoisted, and remained about half hour in sight.

Nichols said that in all his experiences at sea he had never encountered such a gale.

William Tecumseh Sherman had left the Army in 1853 as a captain and had been in the banking business in California before removing to New York in 1857. In writing to Mrs. Sherman on September 18th, he said: "You will have heard that the *Central America,* our *George Law,* is lost, swallowed up in the terrible storm of the 11th. We who have been on her can fancy the terrible scene, as wave after wave swept over her, filling her, and sinking her. Captain Herndon was in command and of course is lost."[7]

Sherman, in a letter of September 18th (under Banking House of Lucas, Turner & Co., 12 Wall Street, N.Y. letterhead) to D.O. Mills, Esq., congratulated the latter on the safety of Ansel and Addie, Mill's sister. "I know if an opportunity offered that Herndon, true to the chivalry of his profession, to which let us offer its need of praises, would put the ladies and children safe first of all, and then like a man die with his ship." Sherman postulated "you cannot but feel relief that those so dear to you have escaped a death the picture of which alone makes me and all who have seen like occurrences tremble at the thought." This from the pen of the man who seven years later, would say "War is cruel and you cannot refine it," then cut a swath from Atlanta to Savannah, Georgia.

Robert T. Brown and Enrique Ayulo, the first of the rescued arriving in New York City, had traveled by regularly scheduled boat from Hampton Roads, Virginia, to Baltimore. From there, on Saturday, September 19th, they proceeded by rail to New York City, where they registered at the Metropolitan Hotel, 580 Broadway, a block from

---
[7] Sherman, Home Letters . . . , 150.

where Rosalie Pahud established a dress-making business in 1850 while waiting to join her husband in California. The men were besieged by a crowd of anxious relatives and friends of the passengers and overwhelmed with questions. Both gave an excellent account of their experiences, Brown being the first passenger to give a narrative of the disaster.

Joseph Bassford arrived in New York City wearing the attire he wore when rescued—red shirt, stockings, pants, and glazed cap. They were all he had saved, and since he had worn them for eight days, he thought that he could make it for one more—until he could have a daguerreotype photograph taken. Frank Jones, too, wore his bailing garb, old pants, red shirt and boots, in which he was coaxed to have his likeness photographed for Frank Leslie, by Fredericks.[8]

On September 16th, at Norfolk, the bark *Sarah A. Nickel*,[9] twenty-five miles west by north of Cape Henry, saw a quantity of floating mattresses, belonging, apparently, to a steamer. "Amongst them was part of a wheel-house, painted white or a very light color, the side of a cabin or saloon, with four windows lost, and a sofa bottom."

Other reports began arriving at the New York port. Mr. Simmons, mate of the steamer *Atalanta*, on Sunday, the 13th, eighteen miles northwest of Cape Lookout, had seen fragments of a wreck, comprising a steamer's wheelhouse, two or three panels of doors, and what appeared to be portions of a light cabin or upper deck.

Captain Brown, of the steamer *Falcon*, arriving from Savannah, had sighted near Cape Lookout large quantities of floating materials including the wheelhouse, berth boards in large numbers, and pieces of deck planks twenty-five or thirty feet long.

A portion of the hurricane deck, a paddle-box, pilot house and other parts of the *Central America*, had been seen on the 17th of September, about fifty miles northeast of Cape Hatteras, by Captain Slocum of the schooner *E. Townsend*, which arrived at Charleston, from New York.

A large crowd of friends and relatives of those on board the steamer gathered at the home office of the United States Mail Steamship Company at Warren and West Streets in New York City. Everyone wanted to know the exact list of passengers. One inquired "about a father on board, another a mother, another a brother or sister, and an occasional one sought information of an absent lover." But the company had no list of names until one could be delivered from

---

[8] *Frank Leslie's Illustrated Newspaper*, 3 Oct 1857, 286-2.

[9] A letter to the Baltimore Exchange Reading Rooms, dated September 16th, at Norfolk, said: "The bark *Sarah A. Nickel*, (which sailed from Baltimore, September 12th, for Montivideo) . . . on Sunday night, during the gale, lost both anchors at 8:00 P.M., [the time of the sinking of the *Central America*], . . . made sail and got to sea at 9:00 A.M. next day."

Aspinwall. Many lingered until the hour of closing, and eagerly sought information from the telegraphic dispatches received from time to time by Mr. Roberts.

During the afternoon of September 19th, Commodore Cornelius Vanderbilt visited the steamship office to inquire into the latest developments. He expressed his sympathy for the passengers, and commiserated with the company for its "heavy pecuniary loss."

When the *Empire City*, bringing seventy thousand dollars of California gold, arrived at New York, the appearance of the refugees of the lost steamer

> betokened the extreme poverty of their condition and painfully recalled the suffering through which they had passed. The men were so thinly clad that many of them feared to encounter the exposure of the deck, and the women were forced to make apologies to the visitors that came on board for their destitute and ragged appearance. The children were nearly naked, and many of them crying.

Sheets from the *Marine* had been cut up to make underclothes for the children, and rags were tied around the feet of those who had no shoes. A dozen newspaper reporters boarded the *Empire City* in the quarantine area of the harbor, interviewing many of the survivors. The "intelligent manner" in which Virginia Birch described the events of the disaster "led her statements to be sought with avidity by the reporters." She was "young, petite in form, and in personal appearance very attractive; added to this, she is possessed of a lively vivacity which renders her very interesting in conversation."[10]

Virginia Birch "did not know till it was too late" that her husband had been rescued and was at Norfolk, "or I should, of course, have proceeded there also." "Mrs. Birch," reported the *New York Daily Tribune* of September 21st, "went on last evening in the 6 o'clock train from Jersey City to join him in Baltimore."

When the passengers received word to go ashore, Mrs. Mary Swan burst into tears and, wringing her hands, said: "Where shall I go after I go ashore?" When asked, she said: "No, I have no friend in New York, nor in all the world, now that my husband is lost."[11] She and other ladies got into carriages, and the hackmen drove them to hotels, refusing to take pay.

New York City, taking their plight to heart, received the passengers with hospitality and sympathy. At a fully-attended impromptu meeting

---

[10] *The New York Tribune*, 21 Sep 1857, 6. *The New York Times*, 21 Sep 1857, No. 1874, 8.
[11] *The New York Times*, 21 Sep 1857, No. 1874, 8-1. *Baltimore Sun*, 23 Sep 1857, 1-3. *San Francisco Bulletin*, 22 Oct 1857, 3, quoting the *Times*.

of merchants "to adopt measures for the relief of sufferers," a committee of thirty persons was appointed to raise funds for the passengers, "as well as for the families of the officers who perished in the discharge of duty." The group resolved to reward "those who had been instrumental in the rescue of those saved."

The passenger group at Norfolk, Captain Johnsen among them, had departed that city at 5:00 P.M. on Saturday, September 19th, and arrived in Baltimore the following morning. There they were put up at the Barnum Hotel where, said Theodore Payne: "We were again received with every attention, and a collection also taken up for those that were in want. We left Baltimore that afternoon, reaching New York at day-break on Monday morning, 21st September."

Carrying out the directions of Captain Herndon, Mr. Payne, on his arrival in Norfolk, had dispatched to Marshall Roberts two messages relating the details of the disaster. These were sent by Mr. Lemosey, of the Norfolk telegraph office, to Petersburg, for relay to New York, but had not arrived before Payne. Eventually, on October 3rd, it became known that the messages, consisting of about 1500 words, because of their length, had been refused by the Petersburg press agent and detained.

In the lobby of the Metropolitan Hotel, Sherman heard Captain Johnsen "tell his singular story of the rescue of these passengers," and relate his account of his experience with the bird that caused him to alter his course. He described Johnsen as "a short, sailor-like-looking man, with a strong German or Swedish accent," and said he would never forget that meeting.[12]

Several groundless complaints arose. These concerned a delay in the arrival of news from Norfolk because of a closing of the telegraph office, a delay in the arrival of the *Empire City's* Havana mail, a supposed failure of the city of Norfolk to properly receive survivors of the shipwreck and the turning away of seven lady and two child survivors by the New York Hotel.

On September 21st, newspapers confirmed the total loss of the steamer, announced the rescue and printed a list of "thirty-nine men by the bark *Elise*." The *Ellen* had not yet been identified.

Mrs. Elizabeth Herndon, the commander's wife of twenty-one years, being informed of the disaster, said, "No, I cannot believe he is safe, for

---

[12] Anders Johnsen, of Kolbjornsvig, near Arendal, Norway, age 35, was employed by A.C. Juell, of Arendal. Hartvig W. Dannevig, "Dadenbak Medaljen," 26-7. *The New York Times*, 21 Sep 1857, 4-2. Sherman, *Memoirs*, 135.

I know he would be the last to leave the ship." She and her daughter were consoled by Ellen's fiance, New York State Quartermaster General Chester Alan Arthur.[13]

On September 22nd, Theodore Payne, calling on Mrs. Herndon at 82 East 23rd Street, delivered to her the gold watch entrusted to him by her husband. Later that day the *New York Tribune* reported, "Captain Herndon's wife last night received dispatches from the south greatly exciting her hopes for the safety of her husband. Mr. Frazer, Second Officer, says he is positive another large number of the saved will turn up on board the schooner seen near the steamer on Saturday night." But when no survivors arrived on the *El Dorado*, hope waned.

The story of explorer William Lewis Herndon was fresh in the minds of many. On September 5th, *Harper's Weekly,* in a concise, illustrated article had attracted public attention to the captain by descriptively recounting Herndon's Amazon adventures and scientific determinations. Now, two weeks later, the *Times* extolled "Lieutenant William L. Herndon, U.S.N.,"[14] as "a man of gifted intellect and resolute will," and lamented his supposed loss. However, hope soon revived for his safety because the captain had been reported seen by one of the passengers, floating on a plank and clinging for life.[15]

By September 26, a total of $11,518 had been collected in New York City by a Relief Fund Committee.[16] Additions were expected. Captain Johnsen said he had been offered $2,500 by the USMSC, and would therefore not accept funds from the committee, and Second Officer Frazer promptly but gracefully declined to accept any money.

James Forster also declined to accept money. Although he had saved only $100 of $9,000 that he had accumulated during his six years in California, a member of the committee pointed out that Mr. Forster

---

[13] Arthur, on the assassination of President Garfield, in 1881, became President of the United States. James Grant Wilson, *The Presidents of the United States*, Vol III, 212.

[14] In 1855, Herndon was promoted to the grade of commander, which at that time was one grade above that of lieutenant.

[15] *The Baltimore Sun*, 23 Sep 1857, 1-2, quoting *The Savannah News*. *Richmond Daily Dispatch*, 23 Sep 1857, 1-7.

[16] The committee consisted of thirty-three members, including prominent citizens and business establishments. Pelitiah Perit, a political figure and aspirant for the presidential nomination, headed the committee. Other members included Lloyd Aspinwall, John A. Stevens, Moses Taylor and Wm. H. Webb. One hundred nine contributors to the fund included Moses Taylor & Co., Duncan, Sherman & Co., G. & H. Howland (partners & uncles of Wm. Aspinwall), Wm. H. and Lloyd Aspinwall, Panama Railroad Co., John Jacob Astor, Jr., Tiffany & Co., and D.O. Mills (brother of Adeline Easton). The PMSC donated $2000 to the cause. *The New York Times*, 23 Sep 1857, 1-5. *The New York Herald*, 22 Sep 1857, 1-4.

gave that last $100 as a token of gratitude to the captain of the bark *Ellen*. These revelations won the hearts of the committee, who shook hands warmly with him, and "hoped he never might want a dollar."

Believed by many to have rescued some of the passengers, the steamer *Nashville*[17] was sighted coming up Chesapeake Bay with a schooner in tow. The report proved to be false, and the schooner *Melvina*, Captain Calhoun, also giving hope, had only a load of naval stores on board.

Matthew Maury described Captain Herndon as being "small of stature, delicate frame and constitution, and by no means robust in health. His fatigue must have been great." Adolph Frederick,[18] John Dement and Henry Childs were the last men known to have seen the captain.

Frederick, very ill at Savannah, remained there after his four fellow survivors departed for New York on September 19th on the *Alabama*, Captain Schenck. The *Savannah Republic* published the grateful acknowledgements of Henry H. Childs and his rescued friends to Captain Smith and the crew of the *Saxony* "for untiring exertions in providing for our comfort and attending to our wants and necessities . . . . We were sick, nearly naked and completely exhausted." Childs, Look, Ridley and Howes arrived at New York on the 22nd, Frederick a week later on the *Augusta*. None were charged for their passage. Adolph Frederick, a German machinist, when at Savannah, had been the recipient of more southern hospitality. Shown "every kindness," the Pulaski House lodged him free of charge, and local citizens gave him three hundred dollars. He had lost $4,000 of California gold.

Joseph Bassford, in a statement to the *Herald*, accused William Garretson of deserting the steamer. Answering the charge, Garretson related to the press his story of assisting in bailing water from the small boat, assisting in rowing, and getting off at the brig to relay for the boatswain the message of Captain Herndon to bring the *Marine* closer to the steamer.

> I started to get into the small boat to return to the steamer, but Mr. John Black, the boatswain, who had charge of her, was obliged to row off from the brig before I could get in, to prevent the boat from being dashed by the waves to pieces against the side of the brig, and, of course, I could not return. I never betrayed the implicit confidence he placed in me, and as this Bassford was not present, it was at least cruelly unfair for him to make such a statement. I worked, without sleep, for 26 hours at the pumps, and would have stuck to the boat till she went down had I been permitted, and

---

[17] *New York Daily Tribune*, 22 Sep 1857, 5-5.
[18] Coulter, *The Loss of* . . . , 469.

had it been necessary for me to do so in the discharge of my duty. The boatswain can vouch for the whole of my statement.[19]

News of Garretson's alleged desertion upset Mrs. Herndon and Ellen. On visiting the stricken family, he "was received at first very coldly, but he had been so faithful a servant, and protested so earnestly that he went in the boat by order of Herndon himself,"[20] that they reconsidered and accepted his word.

Families awaited the arrival of their sons. An anxious father, Mr. T.V. Van Ness, from Rochester, stopping at the Merchants' Hotel, waited in vain for his son who had sailed on board the ill-fated steamer. "At the Girard House," said the *New York Herald* of the 19th, "is a letter addressed to Charles H. Boyd, a sixteen-year-old cabin boy of the *Central America*, written by his father, who returned to Albany about a week since, and left this letter for his son when he should arrive." He did not.

Another father, John Dean, a dry goods merchant in Hartford, Connecticut, had been at Earle's Hotel in New York for a week awaiting his son Henry's arrival. The *New York Herald* stated, "He went back to Connecticut yesterday afternoon in great anxiety as to the cause of his non-arrival. The sad news will have reached him ere this."

Mrs. Marcellus Farmer, having waited at a New York hotel for several days for her husband, returned to Syracuse, and Mrs. Julia Birch, with her son, Frank, having waited at the Metropolitan Hotel for James, returned to Swansea. At the Astor House, a saddened brother of William McNeil met survivor Annie McNeil.

On September 25th, 1857, a letter signed by Victor Audubon arrived at the desk of the editor of the *New York Herald* saying: "Thinking your numerous readers might like to know the name of the singular bird taken by Captain Johnsen, . . . I send it you. The bird, I have no doubt, was a frigate-pelican, (also called the man-of-war bird by sailors), . . . and is figured and described in the seventh volume of Audubon's *Birds of America*, octavo edition, p. 10, where an account of its habits is given." Victor's brother, John Woodhouse Audubon had lost his many western sketches with John Stevens on the *Central America*.

On reading the statement of Theodore Payne regarding his having taken unnecessary advantage of the passengers on the *Marine*, Captain Greene, of the propeller *City of Norfolk*, gave a statement on September

---
[19] *The New York Herald*, 22 Sep 1857, 1-4.
[20] *Richmond Daily Dispatch*, 25 Sep 1857, 1. *Baltimore Sun*, 24 Sep 1857, 2-3.

22nd to *The Baltimore Sun*. He said that he had offered to tow the *Marine* into Old Point, "then distant some six miles . . . . I told them they might give what they pleased; but if I took them up to Norfolk, within quarantine, I should charge them $300." On approaching the *Marine*, and after "some half a dozen called out to know what I would charge to tow them to Norfolk," he added, "I said, jokingly, 'no more than $500.' " Greene said he was obliged to leave his course, delay his trip, and "put myself at great inconvenience to serve them." Further, he said he asked nothing more than fair compensation, and that all he received for the service "goes to the company, not to me . . . not for one cent of advantage to myself."[21] These comments were not likely to have changed the survivors' opinions.

Ten days following the sinking of the steamer, the Russian battleship *Le Fort* sank.[22] A Russian Admiral and eight-hundred men were on board the battleship, and another officer, Admiral Nordman, country unspecified, saw the ship capsize and sink within four cable lengths (less than one-half mile from him), but made no effort to save anyone. There were no survivors, even though the incident took place in broad daylight, with two other men-of-war close by, it was thought to be in sharp contrast with the ready assistance given by captains Burt and Johnsen.

On September 27th, near Portsmouth, Virginia, William Bishop picked up on Scott's Creek (a branch of the Elizabeth River) a bottle containing a slip of paper on which was written: "William Birch, San Francisco, on board the steamer *Central America*."[23] Billy's note had traveled a distance of at least 250 miles.

Questions arose concerning the cause of the *Central America* disaster, and why more passengers had not been rescued. What had become of the schooner to which Captain Herndon had "spoke"?

---

[21] *Baltimore Sun*, 22 Sep 1857, 2-2.
[22] *The Herald*, Newburyport, MA, 28 Sep 1857, 2-3.
[23] *Richmond Daily Dispatch*, 28 Sep 1857. Sherman, Memoirs, 135.

CHAPTER XII

Rumblings Among the Passengers and Public

The performance of Chief Engineer George Ashby received wide condemnation. Some of the passengers, irate and vocal over his departure from the sinking vessel, branded him a coward and deserter. His actions became the subject of discussion among the men, and severe criticisms and condemnations of him were reported not only in the newspapers of the United States but in papers of other countries.

The human tendency to find someone to blame found the fingers of the accusers pointed in four directions: The chief engineer of the *Central America*, the steamship company, the steamship itself, and Captain Stone of the *El Dorado*. Fault for loss of life centered on Stone, who, it was supposed, could have saved many lives. Although made in absolute sincerity, most accusations of the passengers and public resulted from hearsay and misinterpretations of the facts, compoundly exaggerated. Even the best of witnesses inadvertently left the impression that he was the only person on the scene.[1]

Some principal accusers, Joseph Bassford, Douglas Rutherford, William Geary and Robert Hutchinson, had experienced Ashby's threats. Bassford and Rutherford said that Ashby had begged the captain to let him go to the *Marine*, solemnly promised to return and failed to do so. The engineer had threatened several men with his knife. Hutchinson said Ashby left the steamship on a pretext and made no effort to return.

Some passengers were bitterly critical of Ashby for leaving the steamer, regardless of the reason, and branded him a coward. Among them, Robert Brown, John George, and Oliver Manlove, who said:

---

[1] Captain Badger, a highly respectable, qualified and astute witness, greatly praised Captain Herndon, yet at times left the impression that Herndon was either not present, or that he and Ashby simply reacted to Badger's suggestions. This human failing, possibly also exaggerated by the interviewing reporters, was also later overblown in the *History of Alameda County* which had Badger responsible for the rescue of all of the passengers after the crew had been lost overboard. A similar historic account held Dr. Obed Harvey as taking command of the ship. J.P. Munro-Fraser, *History of Alameda County, California,* (Oakland, CA: n.p., 1883), 54-5. Sacramento *Themis,* 17 Feb 1894, 2-3.

The conduct of the engineer is much censured by all the passengers. It was believed that better discipline in the engine room would have prevented the fires from going out and the steam getting down so low as to stop the working of the machinery and the pumps. His final behavior in seizing the first opportunity to escape before a single male passenger had entered the boats, also exciting reprobation.

John George stated: "The only act of cowardice exhibited during the whole of the trying scene was that of the Chief Engineer, Ashby." Robert Brown made similar remarks, and Bassford said that Captain Herndon told Ashby to not get into the boat. Ashby then "besought the captain to place him in charge of the boat."

His conduct had been abusive to several passengers. Young Mrs. McNeil and Mrs. Birch told the press that he had used insulting language in denying their requests to allow their husbands to accompany them to the brig.

On arriving in Baltimore, the chief engineer was dismayed when he learned of the accusations made against him. On Monday, September 21st, in an office of the *Baltimore Sun,* Ashby asked for a suspension of opinion, and declared himself ready to meet any investigation that may be ordered as to his conduct in leaving the vessel or the manner in which he performed his duties. He characterized the criticisms as erroneous and unjust, and as malicious fabrications. He "deemed it proper to refer to Mr. Payne, Mr. McCarty, Judge Monson, Captain Burt of the *Marine,* and Mrs. Marvin, all of whom are familiar with the course I pursued on reaching the brig, and the two first-named of whom heard the orders given to me by Captain Herndon."

The interviewer described him as a fine stalwart man of about thirty, with a frank seaman-like face and bearing," and recalled Ashby as "the person who distinguished himself so much during the great riot between the natives and Americans at Panama, and as the leader of those Americans who fought so bravely. He still bears marks of that fight upon his body."[2]

In New York, on September 22nd, the arrival of George Ashby "caused the most excitement." Many were interested in knowing what he would say in answer to the charges made against him. Arriving by the early train from Philadelphia, he proceeded to his residence on 9th Avenue, then to the office of the USMSC for an interview by some of its officials. "Much grieved by the impression" which prevailed, Ashby avowed that he had "obeyed implicitly the directions given him by Captain Herndon."

Explaining his actions, he said he besought the boats' crews to return

---

[2] *Baltimore Sun,* 23 September 1857, 1-3.

to the rescue of the passengers, and offered them money to do so. When the offer of money proved ineffectual, he drew his knife to enforce obedience to his orders, being restrained by Captain Burt. "Under those circumstances, there was no choice but to remain on the brig," he asserted. "Only one of the quartermasters [David Raymond] was ready to return, and two men could not manage the boat in such a sea . . . . If Captain Herndon is safe, I shall be entirely exonerated from the charges made against me, and instead of giving censure, will redound to my credit."

The chief engineer's sworn statement seems convincing if for no other reason than the fact that he made it when there was positive speculation regarding the safety of Captain Herndon, who had been seen by three men. He could at that time have been rescued by the *El Dorado*, which had not yet arrived at port. Ashby must have either been certain of the captain's reinforcement, or willing to risk career and reputation if he did not, as claimed, have the order of Herndon to leave the steamer.

A number of reliable witnesses willingly upheld Ashby's performance of duty. Principally, they were Captain Burt, Mrs. Amanda Marvin, Judge Monson, Mrs. Kittredge, Theodore Payne and a few others, all of them being reputable witnesses.

Mrs. Marvin said that on a number of occasions "he seemed to be anxious to do his duty, . . . came several times into the cabin . . . in search of passengers who had retreated to their state-rooms with a view to skulk from the labor of bailing the ship . . . He was not especially gentle or refined in his use of terms, whether addressed to passengers or crew." Ashby "was active in trying to free the ship from water, and worked as long as the best." On the brig, "Mr. Ashby entreated, saying, 'For God's sake come and help save some more of the poor men; if two men will go with me I will go back.' " Almira Kittredge reported similar remarks regarding Ashby's attempt to man the boat.

The New York Herald, on September 22nd, said:

> Another lady, whose name by her special request we do not mention, made the following statement to us on this point: The chief engineer, Mr. Ashby, called loudly from his boat to get a man to get in and help row back to the steamer. He exclaimed, "If you have any humanity in you, for God's sake, come back to the ship!" He and one boatman were ready, and if he could get another man, they would have been able to row back. He came on board and wanted the captain of the *Marine* to go nearer the steamer, and again tried to get another man to go back with him, but could not . . . . I could tell more about the conduct of Mr. Ashby, which was directly the reverse of cowardly; but have hereto-

fore refused to for fear he would call upon me as a witness if he should be tried, and I never was in a court in my life, and I never want to be. I would not tell the papers in Baltimore when they applied to me for information on this subject a single word; however, if it becomes important or necessary, I will come forward of my own free will and do justice to Mr. Ashby, by telling all I know.

Theodore Payne owed nothing to Chief Engineer Ashby. He gave a detailed, accurate account of the disaster, speaking emphatically of owing his life to Captain Herndon. If he had thought Ashby derelict in carrying out the orders of the captain, his disapproval would have been resounding. Payne reinforced the statement of Ashby, saying that as Ashby left the steamer in the life-boat, Captain Herndon, through his speaking-trumpet, reiterated his orders to have the captain of the brig lie by the steamer all night, as close as he could, and, if possible, get the brig's boat and crew. "This he did, as soon as he got on board."[3] Ashby "implored the boat crews to return," said Payne, "and tried unsuccessfully to raise another crew to accompany him."

Judge Monson described the situation:

> When the passengers had landed, one of the oarsmen jumped on the brig . . . . Mr. Ashby endeavored to make him get back in the boat, but he would not, and neither could Captain Burt or anybody else induce him to resume his place as oarsman. Ashby passed on to Captain Burt the message of Captain Herndon. Captain Burt expressed his desire and intention to do all he could, but not only was his small-boat—he only had one—unseaworthy, but the brig was disabled.[4]

Captain Burt thought that Ashby had been unjustly condemned, and spoke of him in the highest terms to the reporters of *Frank Leslie's Illustrated Newspaper*. Charles McCarty said:

> I was in the boat with Mr. Ashby, and had cognizance of his conduct before leaving the ship. The going out of the fires was entirely beyond his control, and he did everything possible for the safety of the ship and passengers. After landing the load on board the brig *Marine*, Mr. Ashby asked his boat's crew to go back with him to the ship to assist in saving more of the passengers, but they positively refused. He was then left helpless and could not have got the boat back without help.[5]

Support for George Ashby's character came from an unexpected direction. The Panama City correspondent of *The New York Times* said:

---

[3] In a later letter to the *San Francisco Daily Evening Bulletin*, Payne confirmed these facts, and the contents of his statement appeared in the November 4, 1857, edition of the *Bulletin*.

[4] *New York Herald*, 27 Sep 1857, 1-1.

[5] *Baltimore Sun*, 21 Sep 1857, 1.

Ashby may have been lax in the details of the duties properly belonging to his department on the steamer. That I know nothing about. But that he is a coward, or acted in a cowardly manner when danger surrounded him, no one on this Isthmus who knows him believes. Besides, Theodore Payne's testimony is conclusive, to my mind, in his favor. I know Mr. Payne—have known him for eight years—and no man's character or veracity stands better on this coast than his. If Captain Herndon is saved, and I pray God he is, he will bear ample testimony to Mr. Ashby's good conduct after the disaster, and relieve him from the odium that is now sought to be attached to his name.[6]

George Ashby, confident that his honor would be redeemed, while at Portsmouth, Virginia, directed a letter on September 19th to the editor of the *Transcript,* designed to "place his conduct before the public in its proper light." In it he described his activities on board the steamer, including his being directed by Captain Herndon to personally communicate with Captain Burt, and drew attention to the fact that the steamer had sunk in "much less space of time than predicted." He wrote a detailed account and presented it in a sworn statement on September 22d, before Notary Public Charles A. Rapallo.

Captain Badger said: "Captain Herndon laid nothing to Mr. Ashby."[7]

On September 24th, 1857, the newspaper *The Boston Traveler* reported the arrival from Galveston, Texas, of the schooner *El Dorado.* She had experienced a hurricane on the 11th of September in lat. 29° 40', lon. 78° 20', had lost fore and mainsails, and had incurred other damage. At 6:50 P.M. on the 12th, at lat. 31° 25', lon. 77° 10', Captain Samuel Stone had spoken the steamer *Central America,* and at the time a gale blew from the northwest with a heavy sea running, and laid under her lee until 9:30 A.M.

When the *El Dorado* brought no survivors to New York, the newspapers printed accusations against Captain Stone and his crew for ignoring Captain Herndon's request for assistance. The willful disregard and neglect of the opportunity to save the lives of many of the passengers and crew of the stricken vessel, was contrary to the laws of the sea.

Because of the darkness at the time of contact between the vessels, the schooner could not be identified, and the appearance was that she had slipped away, her crew not wanting to become involved. Willard Fletcher recalled that at about dusk on Saturday two guns were fired from the steamer and "the captain spoke a schooner, telling her to lay by, as we expected to sink every moment. But she went off." Enrique

---

[6] The New York Times, 17 Oct 1857, 2-1.
[7] *The New York Times,* 23 Sep 1857, 1-1.

Ayulo and Robert Brown spoke of witnessing the same event, Brown adding: "Her captain replied that he would lie by; but on the contrary, they passed on, and we saw nothing more of them. She passed so quickly that we could not ascertain her name. She was rather small, and clipper built, but of sufficient size to have contained us all. At that time the storm was not severe."[8]

To his many detractors, Captain Stone replied that he had "steered for the spot" where the steamship had sunk, but must have miscalculated her position, and drifted farther than he and his crew had supposed, because they found "no vestige of the steamer, made sail," and "wore ship every two hours during the night . . . and at dawn placed two men at the mast head with directions to look for anything belonging to the steamer."[9] He observed then that three other vessels were in the area, a brig and two barks. They were the *Marine*, the *Ellen*, and the *Saxony* which he saw to the south, and believed southbound.

From the deck of the brig, as she worked during the night toward the place of the wreck, George Ashby had seen "nothing whatsoever in the water, except the light of a schooner several miles distant." In the morning, he saw the schooner just visible.

Stone declared that the crew had taken a deep interest in looking out for the steamer, and had preferred to be aloft rather than below. He "left the spot with a heavy heart."

The failure of Captain Stone to rescue anyone was widely condemned by many, including Thomas W. Badger, Henry H. Childs, A.I. Easton, and Obed Harvey in a condemning statement appearing in the *District of Columbia Intelligencer*.

> The schooner was under balance-reef mainsail, storm foresail and reefed jib. After hailing us he stood along under our lee, and ranged out ahead of us, apparently running off, not close hauled. At the time of the ship's sinking he was still on the starboard tack, distant some three miles. Captain Stone, as a nautical man, must certainly have known that keeping his vessel under short sail and wearing ship every two hours he was losing ground and driving to leeward four times faster than people who were floating in the ocean . . . by daylight next morning he was some eight miles to leeward of the floating pieces of wreck and the spot where the Norwegian [bark *Ellen*] rescued his passengers. He also says that he stood directly over the spot where the steamer sunk. Had he done so, many hopes would have been realized, as he was anxiously expected.[10]

---

[8] *Daily Alta California*, 23 Oct 1857, 1-3.

[9] *The New York Times*, 25 Sep 1857, No. 1878, 1-3. *New York Daily Tribune*, 26 Sep 1857, 5-2, and 25 Sep 1857, 4-5. *New York Herald*, 26 Sep 1857, 8-1. *Baltimore Sun*, 28 Sep 1857, 1-3.

[10] Nearly 40 years after the disaster, memories were still vivid, and at least one opinion was as

Each spoke from his own perspective. Some echoed the comments of others. Captain Johnsen said that if he had had the fore-and-aft schooner which approached the steamer before she sank . . . he might have saved three times the number he did.

In reply to the above complaints, the pilot who took the *El Dorado* up Boston Harbor said that the schooner, being flatbottomed and drawing only seven feet of water, would have inevitably drifted to leeward. Although she could have easily accommodated all on board, her only chance of rescuing them would have been by making fast to the steamer.[11]

Badger and Johnsen had no lack of understanding of controlling and maneuvering ships, but they had no way of knowing that the *El Dorado's* center board had been removed, or her fore-and-aft mainsails destroyed,[12] thus making her more rapid drift inevitable. In recalling his experience, Badger had commented, that when afloat in the sea, "we knew that the ships to leeward could not reach us, and turned our gaze in the opposite direction."

Finally, withering under the load of the confrontation, Stone said:

> This is certain: I drove my vessel to the windward all I could in that heavy sea and wind; and if I fell to the leeward, I could not help it, and could not under like circumstances again. My heart and soul, and those on board with me, responded freely to the call of our suffering fellow creatures, and we gladly did do all in our power to rescue them, and did not square away until after the brig and the *Saxony* did; then I was almost crazy at the thought of so many of my fellow creatures perishing so near me and I not able to save them, when I had been so sure that I should save them all. The disappointment was so great that for ten days I was unfit for duty and have not been a well man since, in consequence of the shock to my system.

---

strong as ever. William Ede had made a public statement in 1857, and again in 1896. Although, in 1857, he had made no statement on the *El Dorado*, the *San Francisco Chronicle* of February 23, 1896, printed the following comment of the San Francisco capitalist concerning the schooner incident: "About that hour the schooner *El Dorado*, cotton laden, passed so close to our stern that a hawser was tossed upon her deck and she was begged to stay and save us. Her captain was a coward, threw the hawser overboard, and continued on to Boston, where he told the details of a dreadful wreck and claimed to have spent three days in attempting to rescue passengers." No one else mentioned a hawser being thrown. Considering the lapse of 40 years, this detail is questionable, the remarks colorful but doubtful. *District of Columbia Intelligencer*, 30 Sep 1857, 3-3.

[11] *District of Columbia Intelligencer*, 1 Oct 1857, 3-3.

[12] The *El Dorado* is a schooner of 212 tons. She is a square built, broad beamed vessel, well calculated for much stowage and dull sailing. She labors heavily in a bad sea, and ships her water over the quarter rail. On her late voyage she was loaded down to her chains, and the peculiarly shaped barnacles of Matagorda Bay are visible upon her hull, almost up to her chains. She sprung her bowsprit so badly in the late gale that she leaked, and her cotton is damaged with water. Her foregaff was carried away, her foresail split to rags, her bulwarks stove, and she was badly strained. She must be put on the ways for thorough repairs on her return to New York. *Frank Leslie's Illustrated Newspaper*, 17 October 1857, 315-1.

The *Central America* and the United States Mail Steamship Company came under fire, her recent change of name being characterized as a cover-up in an attempt to disguise an old patched-up unseaworthy hulk, and to present it as a new and modern steam vessel.

In restaurants, counting rooms and offices, the *Central America* became the major topic of conversation. "Why, she was the old *George Law*, a condemned ship, totally unseaworthy," many exclaimed, and very indignant were the speakers in believing that, under a change of name, she should have been imposed upon the public as a worthy sea-going craft. "There has nothing been known like it since the sinking of the *Arctic*," others exclaimed. "And in view of the loss of specie, this is even a worse calamity, occurring as it does during the present pressure on the money market."

The *Central America*, being only one of many vessels in trouble during the hurricane, the steamship company described her as "one of the best and staunchest sea boats afloat, and her disastrous loss can only be attributed to circumstances completely beyond human control." As the result of the gale, there had been numerous other disasters on the Atlantic, and the *Times* referred to the storm as one of the "most violent ever known on the coast."

In a statement issued by the steamship company to Horace Greeley, editor of the *New York Tribune*, Marshall Roberts noted that doubts had been "expressed by some in respect to the sea-worthiness" of the *Central America*, the public not being informed of their source, comments by "men wholly uninformed upon the subject, and who have not taken the pains to become instructed."

Roberts asked for the containment of idle speculation until the particular cause could be determined, and pointed out several factors regarding the vessel which he considered the pride of the fleet. The ship "was built under the active superintendency of the officers appointed by the U.S. government;" Before acceptance, she was "thoroughly examined as to the character and sufficiency of her construction, by Commodore Kearny and Captains Bell and Skiddy." The USMSC president stated that, in departing New York, the vessel was in perfect condition, but claimed no defense against natural disasters. As to the discipline of the ship, he claimed no knowledge beyond the fact that though the ship was sinking, all the women and children were safely transferred to the *Marine*, and that this event sharply contrasted to the panic on board other vessels in similar circumstances. This "reflects unusual glory upon her officers," he concluded.

Roberts attached a copy of Secretary of the Navy James C. Dobbin's[13]

---

[13] Secretary Dobbin was the brother of Navy Purser John V. Dobbin, who went down with the steamer, but had just died in Aug. 1857

letter, dated February 13, 1854, attesting to the satisfactory acceptance by the Navy of the *George Law* under the act of Congress of 1857, and included a copy of the cover letter to the report of the Examining Board, dated October 15, 1853, signed by Lawrence Kearney, Charles H. Bell, Commander, and William Skiddy, Constructor, representative of W.H. Webb.

William H. Webb, builder of the *Central America*, on September 19, 1857, issued to the press a statement attesting to the strength and seaworthiness of the ship, giving emphasis to her construction. "The frame of the ship," he said, "was of the best materials known in the country, the top timber and end frame being live oak, and the entire frame double diagonally braced with long iron bars reaching from the floors to the top of the ship."[14]

Newspaper reports placed the value of the *Central America* at from one hundred forty thousand to three hundred thousand dollars.[15] The "character of the ship for seaworthiness and popularity was never at any time greater than at the moment the change was made," and it was "not conceivable that any of the parties concerned could have intended that the public should be deceived." As an indication of the confidence held by the company in the reliability of the steamer, Roberts added, "the company were willing to stand their own insurers, and at the time of her loss there was not one dollar of insurance upon her, although policies could have been effected at the lowest current rates of A-1 steamship risks."[16]

The seemingly endless discussions and deliberations over the causes and results of the loss of the *Central America* were interrupted during the first week of October by news from the bark *Laura*, which arrived from Scotland after passing through the eastern extension of the Gulf Stream.

---

[14] *The New York Times*, 21 Sep 1857, 8-6.

[15] Ridgely-Nevitt, *The George Law*, 316. *Frank Leslie's Illustrated Newspaper*, 3 Oct 1857, 281-1. *Daily Alta California*, 23 Oct 1857, 1-6.

[16] Public opinion may have been somewhat assuaged in 1857 by the assurances contained in the above statements, but in Augustine Pahud Renault's preserved copy of the *San Francisco Chronicle* of February 23, 1896, there appeared a rather irresponsible report on the lost steamer. "The *Central America*," said the *Chronicle*, "was an old wooden steamship which was launched under the name of *George Law*. She was then owned by the well-known steamship man whose name she bore; and after serving him long enough to have entitled her to an eternal rest in the boneyard, she was sold to the Pacific Mail Company, rechristened the *Central America* and put on the Atlantic end of the California route. The change of name was a subterfuge resorted to for the purpose of deceiving the traveling public, a subterfuge which an act of Congress now very properly forbids." Although residing in Oakland, California in 1896, Captain Badger was not interviewed at that time, and no reference to his opinion of the vessel was made in the newspaper account.

Above, left: John Tice, Second Engineer

Above, right: Alexander Grant, Fireman

Left: George W. Dawson, passenger
From *Frank Leslie's Illustrated Newspaper*

CHAPTER XIII

The Gulf Stream and A Lifeboat

Equatorial currents carried into the Caribbean Sea waters derive their motion in part from the trade winds and the prevailing easterly winds, moving them against the western shores. The level of the Gulf of Mexico is slightly higher than that of the Atlantic. These and other forces move the water toward the Straits of Florida, passing through and occupying the entire forty-mile width and four hundred eighty fathom depth of the channel at surface velocities of sixty-nine to one hundred nautical miles per day.

From the straits, this ribbon of warm water, the Gulf Stream, moves northward about one hundred nautical miles off the East Coast, over a rocky bottom about two hundred seventy to four hundred sixty fathoms in depth. Off Cape Hatteras, North Carolina, the stream approaches the coast to a distance of thirty-five miles, with a width approximating forty miles. On leaving the Cape Hatteras vicinity, it makes a gradual change of direction to due east.

When the *Central America* foundered, the Gulf Stream was moving at approximately three miles per hour, and at that rate, in a week's time, a floating object traveling with the stream covered more than five hundred miles.

Alerted by a signal from an approaching vessel, Captain Wilmsen (Williamson) (Wilmonson) of the bark *Laura* immediately hove to. The day was September 28, 1857. Captain Colin Shearer of the brig *Mary*, of Greenock, Scotland, hailed the bark on his speaking trumpet, advising Wilmsen that on September 21st he had taken from the water three men. The *Mary* was bound for Ireland, and Shearer requested the transfer of the three rescuees to the *Laura*, which was headed for New York.

Wilmsen ordered a small boat lowered, and when the oarsmen got it alongside the *Mary*, they assisted on board Assistant Engineer John Tice, Fireman Alexander Grant, and passenger George Dawson, of the *Central America*. Soon the haggard men were carefully taken onto the *Laura*. Their stories, after they were able to speak, were of hardship, starvation, heartbreak, despair, tenacity and survival. They had been at sea for nine days before they were rescued by the bark *Mary*. During those days, Dawson and Grant had seen their companions die one by one, hoping for a sail to appear.

Captain Wilmsen transported them to the Port of New York, anchoring in the North River. One of the boats of the bark carried them ashore at Castle Garden depot, where they were met in a carriage by George Ashby and Mr. Hollister of the Battery Hotel. The meeting between Tice and Ashby was very affecting, Tice being so overcome by it that he had to be helped to the carriage. His first question was "How many of the crew and passengers of the steamer have been saved?" Ashby answered his questions, and then, according to the *Times*, Tice, in 19th century fashion, said, "Captain Herndon, the noble and gallant commander of the steamer, I fear we shall never see again, and Van Rensselaer, the First Officer, one of the bravest and most generous fellows that ever lived, I fear he has gone down with the Captain." He remained silent for several minutes as the carriage proceeded to the home of his friends on Avenue D, and then began to tell of his experiences.

John Tice had worked without let-up during the period of crisis on board the *Central America*. When it appeared to him the steamer was lost, he seized a plank, and as the deck neared the surface, he made a plunge as far away as he could get and struck out in hope of avoiding the suction. This maneuver, he found, did not help much, for he was carried down what seemed an unfathomable distance under water. He rose to the surface to find the sea covered with pieces of the wreck, and hundreds of men grasping for them.

Resting his chest across his plank, he floated away, none of the desperate men interfering with his progress. He made several attempts to reach the glimmering lights of what he supposed to be either the *Marine* or the schooner to which Captain Herndon had spoken shortly before the steamer sank, but the lights disappeared below the horizon.

Purser Edward Hull[1] had been active in getting the women and children into the boats. Subsequently, while constructing a raft, a

---

[1] Shortly before the last voyage of the *Central America*, Purser Hull purchased a handsome $8000 house on Taylor Street, Brooklyn. He had moved his wife, mother, and two children into it before leaving home. "On the morning of the day on which the ship sailed, Mr. Hull remarked to an old friend, Mr. Fairchild, treasurer of Williamsburg Ferry Company, that 'parting with his wife was painful, and he had fully made up his mind to leave off going to sea very shortly.' Fairchild remarked that, if he did not take care, he would go once too often—until the fever took hold of him and carried him off, to which Mr. Hull playfully remarked, that he guessed there was no danger of that." *The New York Herald*, 26 Sep 1857, 8-1. *Richmond Daily Dispatch*, 21 Sep 1857.

heavy timber had fallen on his back, severely injuring him. Now, in the water, Tice saw Hull, who, despite his injury, appeared in good spirits and spoke encouragingly to him, urging him to "hold fast to his plank, as some vessel would doubtless soon come along and pick them up." During the night Tice exchanged words of hope and consolation with several other struggling survivors, soon separated by the waves. The sea continued to roll heavily during Saturday night and Sunday.

There was no further hope in sight on Sunday morning. At about noon, Tice was again discouraged on seeing the *Marine*, after making another tack, disappear beyond the horizon.

The sun was now shining, but it only added to his discomfort as the heat became nearly intolerable. Night found him alone on the sea. Although exhausted, he determined to survive, and clung tightly to the plank. Fatigued, he fell asleep from time to time, and would suddenly awaken to find himself firmly gripping his plank.

Tice spent all day Monday in solitude in the endless expanse of unpotable water. Occasionally he saw fragments of the wreck, and, on the waves, a life-preserver or two, all of which seemed to bespeak a story of despair and death. Tice was a strong swimmer, and when on Tuesday he spotted at some distance a dark object, he pressed forward toward it, and was elated to find it to be one of the life-boats of the *Central America*.

Three or four hours of great effort passed before Tice was able to get hold of the side of the boat, and he clung to it for some time before he could muster enough strength in his exhausted body to hoist himself over the side. He found the boat half full of water, but also found in it three oars, a pan, a pail and three coats. He used the pail to bail some of the water, and raised one of the oars with a coat tied to it as a signal. Tice thought he recognized the boat as the one "which was swamped in being launched before [the *Central America*] went down."[2]

Although suffering from thirst, the Assistant Engineer now found himself in a considerably better position than when in the sea with only his plank, but he realized that he was a long way from safety. As night approached he fell into a troubled sleep, and drifted on.

---

[2] There were six lifeboats on the steamer. One broke loose from its davits during the night of September 11th, a day before the ship sank; another was smashed against the steamer and lost; a third boat was stove and swamped, Mr. Ashby nearly being lost with it. This left three for trips to the *Marine*, and of these, Black's was scuttled, Raymond's and Finley Frazier's were lashed to the brig, but the latter broke loose during the night the *Central America* sank. Considered unsalvagable by Burt's crew, Raymond's boat was cut loose. The contents of the boat strongly suggests that it had been in use, oarsmen leaving items behind when they declined to make another trip. Most likely, Finley Frazier's boat rescued the three men.

All day Wednesday he continued to drift with the Gulf Stream at the rate of about three miles per hour. An agonizing hunger and thirst seemed to engulf him through Wednesday, and raging throughout the night unrelentingly, allowing no deep sleep, but only dreams of water, food, and rescue, and his awakening to find himself alone.

At about mid-morning on Thursday, Tice saw another object in the distance and, using an oar, moved toward it. As he approached, he saw it was a piece of wreckage.

About fifteen minutes before the steamer sank, Fireman Alexander Grant,[3] who had been laboring during the storm with more than a dozen other men, set to work to build a raft. Toward this end they cut away part of the hurricane deck. Just as he cut the last rope that held it to the ship, he was astonished to see the steamer move away from him and submerge, leaving him floating on the sea on his raft. He was quickly surrounded by debris, struggling and drowning men. Ten or eleven others were able to join Grant on the hurricane deck and together they floated away to the leeward.

The raft would not support them all in a sitting position, and it was necessary for them to lie down with their feet in the water, their heads raised, and holding on to the ropes. In that position, and with the sea constantly washing over them, they were compelled to swallow large amounts of salt water.

The ten survivors thus spent the first night in that manner, hoping and praying for one of the vessels in the area to find them. Grant recognized Third Assistant Engineer George Buddington, Coal Passer John Banks, Fireman Patrick Carr, Coal Passer Patrick Evans, Coal

---

[3] Alexander Grant was referred to as a 'Bluenose,' that is, he was born, in 1831, in the Gut of Canco, in the British province of Nova Scotia. As a child he was extremely fond of the sea, and was said to be "the best swimmer" of the area, "and absolutely lived in the cold water of the Gulf; no boy or man could remain so long in deep water as he." At age 13, "he went to sea in a blind Nova Scotian fishing schooner, with cold nights, hard work, poor pay, bad fare, and every discomfort in prospect." His rescue in the Atlantic was the fourth such experience for him during his thirteen years at sea. The first was on the brigantine *Atlas*, of Windsor, Nova Scotia, bound for Fall River, Massachusetts. The vessel was crippled in a storm, one hundred miles at sea, and sank just after his rescue by the *Amazon*, of Holland. The second, when he escaped from the steamer *Arctic* after she had collided with another steamer. He had seized a fore-hatch and threw it overboard a few moments before the *Arctic* sank. After fifty-two hours in the water, he and a companion were rescued by the *Cambria*, Captain Luce, bound for Quebec. After the second rescue, Grant married "a pretty young girl of his acquaintance," then went to sea again, as a fireman on the USMSC steamer *Crescent City*, only to find himself fast on a reef off the Little Bahamas. "There were sharks in abundance all around, and very evidently there was no chance for any one who got overboard there." Fortunately, wrecking vessels from the Bahamas arrived to take off all on board the steamer, including, coincidentally, George Dawson. *Harper's Weekly*, 17 Oct 1857, 1. *New York Daily Tribune*, 6 Oct 1857, 5-4, 5. *San Francisco Bulletin*, 3 Nov 1857, 2-2.

Passer John Kinnelty, and Officers' Mess Boy Richard Gilbert. The others were passengers whose names he did not know. At daybreak the *Marine* was in sight, but all efforts to signal her failed.

It was almost unbearable for Grant to call forth his recollections of the scenes that followed. All the first day and night they saw others struggling in the sea around them. They searched the horizon for signs of a vessel, but there were none, and as darkness fell on Sunday night, hope faded. From exposure, thirst, and the buffeting of waves, some grew delirious. The weight of those on it held their raft about a foot under water, keeping them all partially submerged.

George Dawson, with others on the steamer, had been busy trying to construct the raft. When he saw the second floor burst up to the first level, he reached for a plank, but it was claimed by another passenger. Then, as the steamer plunged, he grasped hold of the gang-way near the pilot-house, and was drawn under the sea head first. He let go, rose to the surface and found the support of a life-preserver. As he looked for a piece of wreckage, one of the passengers, drowning, seized him by the neck. Escaping this danger, he found three pieces of board and put them together for support.

He was within one-hundred feet when the *Ellen* was engaged in picking up survivors, and frequently called for help, but his cries were lost in the noise of the sea. Soon the bark disappeared, leaving him and many others to their fate in the darkness on the surface of the water.

During the early hours of the morning, Dawson saw Grant and the others on their submerged raft and, with considerable effort, he reached them, but was unable to get on board for fear of submerging the whole group. He remained nearby, supporting himself on his planks, and clinging to a rope on the raft. Dawson did not recognize anyone on the raft.

About noon on Monday, eighteen-year-old John Banks became exhausted and sank swallowing sea water. Three more died before nightfall, and just before dark, another nearly spent survivor who had been supporting himself on a piece of plank, was pulled onto the raft. By this time all were nearly wild from hunger and thirst. Many gazed with vacant stare in a vain search for a sail.

During the night, four more died, and floated off in the sea. Dawson, by this time, had joined the others on the raft, and was instrumental in cheering his mates. In the afternoon, Jacob D. Gillead, black barber of the *Central America*, floated into view, seated on one of the life-buoys which had hung on the steamer's starboard side. Gillead did not wish to

Dawson Reaches the Hurricane Deck
From *Frank Leslie's Illustrated Newspaper*

leave the buoy, and saluting Dawson as he floated by, he wished him a good journey and soon disappeared from view. On the following day, Dawson sighted the buoy without its occupant.

Later on Tuesday another passenger came into view, floating on the door of the captain's room. He seemed in fair condition, and asked how the four remaining on the raft were getting along. The young man, about twenty-two years of age, had his legs through a hole in the upper panel of the door, hanging in the water. Having been in a sitting position since the steamer sank, he joined the men on the raft at their invitation, but remained only long enough to stretch his legs. After cheerful conversation with the others he again mounted the door and released it from where he had tied it to the raft. Paddling to the life-buoy, he laid it on the door, and saying he felt comfortable, was soon lost to view, never to be seen again.

The men had been on the raft three days, said Dawson, and weak from starvation, they "became deranged in mind, and would talk about such things as going to the pantry in order to get dinner, and conversing with the steward. Their bodies finally dropped along the raft, or they would fall asleep, lose their hold and be washed into the sea. The sleepy ones became troublesome because they had to be so often roused. Every effort possible was made to cheer them, but it was of no avail. The delirious ones often came near upsetting the raft by their conduct, and had to be held down by someone pressing their arms over their backs."

They were separated at nightfall by a strong easterly wind which caused the sea to become heavier. John Kinnelty, became deranged and unaware of his situation. During the night, he and another died. With the weather improving, the two survivors, Dawson and Grant, remained on the raft, which was now at the surface.

The two suffered extremely through Wednesday. Although many pieces of the wreckage were seen, nothing to eat was found. They saw small fishes around the raft, but had not been able to catch any. Dawson finally snagged a dog fish by striking it with an oar, grabbing it by the tail, and dashing it against the boards, killing it. Grant cut it up, but though they were starving, it was too tough to eat, so "by fastening it to a rope and exposing it to the sun, we managed to eat a little of it, then threw the rest into the sea."

Thursday was the fifth day after the shipwreck. That morning they floated near a passenger who was supporting himself on a plank. He swam to the raft, and the two assisted him on board.

> His Christian name was Frank, and he had a large ring on his finger marked F.B. [F.A. Bokee or F. Barr]. Frank, however, was exhausted, he having floated on the plank for four days and a half, and he too soon became delirious. His companions tried to cheer him up, but so intense were his sufferings, that he was unmindful of their encouraging words and he soon after laid himself down and died.[4]

Later that day, Grant saw a boat that appeared to be about three miles away, but could not tell if anyone was in it. Determined to reach it, he removed all clothing but his underwear, tied a life-preserver around himself, and though weak and spent from days without food and water, he struck out, hoping to be able to improve their position and chances for reaching safety. Dawson remained on the raft.

Grant could not remember how long he struggled toward his goal, but as he neared it he saw a man sitting in the boat, trying to scull it toward him. As Grant reached the boat, John Tice reached out to help him in, and after a joyful moment of meeting, the two surviving crew-members combined efforts to rescue Dawson from the hurricane deck. Dawson stripped off his wet clothes, but kept a wet cloth over his head. They left lying upon the raft the dead body of Frank.

The eighth night brought heavy rain. Using their bailing gear to

---

[4] *New York Daily Tribune*, 6 Oct 1857, 5-3, 4.

collect water, they drank freely. Grant said they would have killed themselves with it if their supply had not soon run out.

For the first time they discovered a sail. Hopes were raised, and an attempt made to reach the vessel, which at one time was not more than two miles distant. In two or three hours, the vessel sank out of sight and left them in despair.

Captain Colin Shearer and his crew, hauling a load of molasses and sugar from Cardenas, Cuba, to Cork, Ireland, spotted the life-boat and coat-flag of the wanderers. The three men were not far from death when on the ninth day after the sinking of the *Central America* their hopes were once again cautiously kindled.

They saw the bark unfurl, set her topsails for maneuverability, then turn her bow upon them. Grant and Dawson grasped their oars and began feebly to row; they seemingly had lost all feeling in their emaciated bodies. As they neared the vessel's side, lines were thrown to them and weakly seized, anything more being beyond the capability of their exhausted bodies. A sailor jumped down, carefully placed more lines around them, and lifted them one by one to the deck of the *Mary*—at last rescued from their torturous ordeal.

Dawson said that the sailors hoisted them "with the greatest care, being careful that their emaciated bodies did not strike against the timbers" and, when on deck, they were carried in the arms of the crewmen into the cabins.

First they were refreshed with a glass of warm claret with sugar, which seemed to them the greatest delicacy of their lives. But still they yearned

Tice and Grant Rescue Dawson
From *Frank Leslie's Illustrated Newspaper*

Sailors on the bark Mary hoist the survivors.
From *Frank Leslie's Illustrated Newspaper*

for water, "which the captain very judiciously refused, . . . [acting toward them] . . . as a father would to his children." Later, they were allowed a little gruel, but only in small amounts, then, when the time seemed appropriate, they were allowed to eat a little food. In this manner they began to regain their strength.

Aboard the Mary the three survivors were so prostrate that they were not able to communicate much of their nine-day ordeal. They could scarcely move a hand or speak; their flesh was wasted, and their skeleton forms unpleasant for anyone to see. They were covered with small boils which were opening into painful ulcers. Their feet were swollen and tender. Captain Shearer and his crew treated them with great humanity, and supplied their clothing needs.

Although Grant had recuperated sufficiently to tell his story while on the *Laura,* but "of the 400 odd German passengers and crew of the *Laura,* only the mate and one passenger spoke English."[5]

John Tice was in such a very weak state that he fainted several times on the day they arrived at Castle Garden. They were advised by their physicians to open their mouths only to eat, and statements were gleaned only from occasional conversations.

Dawson, impatient of the attention given him by the crowd that greeted them, found an opening and limped away. George Dawson was described as "a mulatto man, about 35, tall, and stout built, though now much wasted in flesh." He was a native of Rochester, New York, and since a boy had spent his life at sea. He now proceeded to the home of a friend, Henry Sampson, at 12 Leonard St., New York City. He, Sampson, and Alexander Grant had been employed on the steamer *Crescent City,* and the three were on that vessel when she was wrecked on Manatillan Reef, December 7, 1855.

Dawson had suffered terribly. His hands and fingers were worn from holding tightly to the ropes. On his face were large seaboils, and he had the same kind of eruptions on other parts of his body. Dawson reported that he had lost all he had except a gold ring on his finger and the clothes on his back. He had one other item on his person—a silver cup.

James Birch had surveyed the situation on board the sinking *Central America* and considered the desperation of it. His business success was at least in part due to his ability to calculate accurately his chances of coming out on top in a given situation. Dawson was employed as a porter at the St. Nicholas Hotel in Oroville, California, one of Birch's stage-coach stops. Birch concluded that his own chances of survival were questionable, and to the strong, muscularly-built Dawson he entrusted the silver cup, requesting him to take it to Mrs. Birch in New York.

By recovering the cup from his stateroom, Birch missed his opportunity to board the life-boat with Ashby, and forfeited his life. The cup was important to Birch as a final remembrance for his son. He gave the cup to Dawson before the steamer sank.[6]

Throughout his ordeal, Dawson protected the cup. Although a non-swimmer, he carried out with dogged determination the request of James Birch, who, in the final analysis had picked the right man. When Dawson recovered, he paid his respects to Mrs. Julia Birch in Swansea,

---

[5] New York Times, 6 Oct 1857, 1-1. *Frank Leslie's Illustrated Newspaper,* 17 Oct 1857, 305.

[6] *Sacramento Daily Union,* 19 Nov 1857, 3-3. Contrary to some later references on the subject, a private letter of May 18, 1857, from Julia Birch, advised the *Union* of the history of the cup, stating that "Mr. Birch gave it to this man [Dawson] to preserve *before the ship sank."*

The Silver Cup
Courtesy, University of
California, Berkeley,
Department of Materials
Science and Mineral
Engineering

Massachusetts—and delivered the cup.[7] He "received a reward from her for his care and diligence."[8]

After hearing the news of her husband's safety, Mrs. Grant for some time did not believe it, being indignant with the person who informed her that he survived, thinking he was trifling with her feelings. Her joy and thankfulness were beyond description when he arrived in a carriage at their door at 36 Vandam Street. There reporters found him improving and busy making up for lost meals. However, he complained of not feeling very well. His lips, which had been blistered, were still swollen and covered by a black scab.

---

[7] On September 26, 1986, while viewing a display of silver masterpieces at the Oakland, California Museum, this author noticed a large tureen and platter, part of a collection with scenes of the Gold Rush, commissioned by one James E. Birch to be made in New York by Tiffany. There, on a card, was a brief account of Birch being shipwrecked "off of the Carolinas," and having given a silver cup to George W. Dawson to deliver to his wife for their son. This discovery led to the research on Birch and Dawson.

[8] Swansea, *The Harvester*, MA, 25 Sep 1954, 2-5.

A reporter of The New York Times described the appearance of Grant as looking like

> one who, having been brought to death's door by a scorching fever, had just passed the crisis of the disease. His large, manly face was white and almost fleshless, showing the bold outlines with ghastly distinctness, and his black, scarred lips looked as though in his agony he had frequently bitten them through . . . his eyes wore a fixed, straining sleepless expression, as though still looking from the frail raft along the dreary horizon for a friendly sail.

The joy of Mrs. Grant added only grief to Mrs. Wilson, another wife living on the same floor, whose husband, George Wilson, a steerage waiter, was lost. News of Grant's safety renewed her hope, but on learning he had no news of her husband, "she swooned, and continued from one fainting spell to another for several hours before she was able to compose herself."

The twenty-seven year old John Tice seemed to have recovered more rapidly than the others. He had been an engineer on the *Central America* from the time she was launched until she sank. The small but sturdy Tice was escorted to the Battery Hotel by George Ashby, but before that, he and Grant were driven in a carriage to 177 West Street, where they went upstairs to see and report to the officers of their steamship company. Both walked with difficulty, and said that they could not have continued alive many hours longer.

On Monday, the 14th, two days after the sinking of the *Central America*, Tice and Dawson had seen a number of passengers clinging to pieces of wreck, and it seemed strange to them that Captain Stone, who claimed to have remained in the area of the disaster until the following morning, should not have been able to see some of the survivors. Their judgment was against the schooner.

In fairness to Captain Stone and First Mate Sherlock of the *El Dorado*, neither the *Ellen* nor the *Marine* had been able to find any more survivors on the Sunday morning the search was abandoned.

The speed of the current had not been given full consideration by any of the searchers. By 8:00 A.M., Sunday, September 13th, at the rate of three knots per hour, the Gulf Stream carried survivors and debris thirty-five miles or more from the position of sinking. Other survivors, including Captain Herndon, must have been carried away from the paths of the rescue vessels.

The survival of the last three men had been made possible by an unmanned life-boat of the *Central America*.

CHAPTER XIV

California Reacts

On October 22nd, thirty-five days after the news broke in New York City, California learned of the loss of the *Central America*.

The eastern mails and dispatches arrived at Aspinwall on board the steamer *Northern Light*, which had departed New York Harbor on September 21st. The steamer *Panama* departed Panama at 6:00 P.M. on Friday, October 2, and carried to San Francisco, on Thursday morning, October 22, the mails and passengers from New York and New Orleans. The first report appeared in the *Daily Evening Bulletin* of the 22nd. On the following morning, five weeks after the New York headlines, the *Daily Alta California* horrified the people of San Francisco with its announcements. Black-bordered news columns reflected San Francisco's state of mourning.

> Total Shipwreck of the Mail Steamship *George Law*
> Loss of Four Hundred Returned Californians
> and $1,500,000 in Treasure
> Minute Details of the Awful Calamity
> Statements of the Saved
> The Hurricane
> Cowardice of the Chief Engineer
> Causes of the Disaster
> Gallant Conduct of the Passengers
> Deplorable Condition of the Survivors
> The Ship—Her Officers and Crew
> Interesting Incidents
> The Very Latest Telegraphic Dispatches
> List of Passengers, Memoranda, &. c.

With the arrival of the *Panama*, three husbands, Francis Kittredge, Francois Pahud, Benjamin Thayer, as well as many other family members and friends, first learned of what had befallen their loved ones. The news from New York included the list of rescued and lost persons and, no doubt, many letters to families and friends arrived with the awesome news. "Strong hopes," said the *San Francisco Herald and Mirror* of October 23rd, "are entertained of Capt. Herndon's safety."

Commencing October 22nd and 23rd, reports of the disaster appeared in the *Daily Evening Bulletin, Daily Alta California, Herald and Mirror* and other San Francisco newspapers, the *Bulletin* referring to the steamer as a "miserable hulk."

Westerners had waited long for the latest news from the eastern United States, but now on October 23rd, an inside page of the *Alta* lamented: "of minor importance to us now are all the detail of the Eastern news . . . All is swallowed up and lost in the heart-rending catastrophe."

"There has been an unmistakable gloom prevailing throughout business circles today," continued the *Daily Alta*, "the effect of the deplorable intelligence which reached us by the mail steamer. Quite a number of those thus suddenly perishing were prominent business citizens of this city, and the calamity seemed to fill men's minds and mouths."

After the initial shock of the news, the question asked was "Who is to blame?"

Attack upon the eastern steamship company now ensued: The "responsibility" for the disaster, said the *Evening Bulletin* of October 23rd, "rests on the avaricious company, which made money by the hundred thousand, . . . at the expense of passenger comfort," and the editor directed a part of the blame to the PMSC for sharing in the profits. The harangue against the USMSC continued, but interestingly, a comment on Chief Engineer Ashby said: "The passengers who blame the chief engineer were not in our opinion competent judges, and might have been influenced by common rumor on ship board, during the exciting scenes."

> There is blame elsewhere, [pursued the *Daily Alta* on the following day.] Why were the pumps out of order? . . . There was no carpenter attached to the ship . . . where the lives of four or five hundred passengers may depend on the nailing of a single plank. [The USMSC] cannot be held blameless for thus risking human life, for the purpose of saving a few dollars annually in the coffers of a heartless, soulless monopoly.

On October 24th, the *Daily Alta California,* pressing to influence Western public opinion against the United States Mail Steamship Company, said: "Of all corporative bodies, proverbially soulless, this one has always seemed to us to possess the least degree of conscience or heart." And regarding the *Central America:*

> The first serious gale she encountered was the one which ended in disaster and demonstrated what everybody who was acquainted with the history of the *George Law* believed as to her condition was true—namely, that

she was absolutely unseaworthy—as rotten a hulk as the steamship *Pacific* proved herself to be when she was struck a glancing blow by a lumberladen schooner and dropped apart as if she had been so much gingerbread.

The *Daily Alta California* continued its barrage, complaining: "But for the catastrophe of the *Central America,* doubtless we should have had the present line of rattletraps introduced to us under fictitious names, after a course of tar and oakum, to give a semblance of repairs." The *Alta* called on Mr. Aspinwall to "break up the disgraceful contract with Roberts and Company."

There seemed to be a mind-set against the company and its steamer, ignoring all significant testimony to the contrary. A San Francisco reporter commented: "From the many statements of passengers we select that of Captain Badger, as being the most accurate and reliable. It is clear, straightforward, and comes from a thorough seaman, who remained cool, determined and energetic to the last. His opinions seem to be authoritative and unbiased." Badger had made three trips on the *Central America,* and the crux of his opinion of her was: "I considered her staunch and safe as any vessel afloat."[1]

Several weeks later, the subject remained active. On November 23d: "The distressing condition of affairs in the East is already beginning to have its effect upon the immigration to California as also to decrease visibly the number of passengers leaving our State." The situation, being reduced to dollars and cents: "the loss of money through an inability to handle the passenger traffic, or through a loss of passenger confidence [would] surely have a contractual effect."

Given the proper construction, seaworthiness and reliability of the *Central America,* the acceptance of authoritative testimony in her behalf from knowledgeable sources, and discounting unsubstantiated, emotional commentary, there still persists the question: "What caused her destruction?"

---

[1] *Richmond Daily Dispatch,* 21 Sep 1857, 1-2.

CHAPTER XV

The Hurricane and Other Causes of the Disaster

Hurricane:

There is scant officially recorded data available concerning the hurricane encountered by the *Central America* and all of the other vessels in the path of the storm.[1] It has not been recorded by the United States Weather Bureau as a major hurricane, but, as attested to by the amount of damage inflicted by it on many ships (the names of at least sixty-nine ships damaged, sunk or run aground were reported in the newspapers of the day), the storm was of great significance. On-shore coastal damage seems to have been somewhat limited, most of its impact having been at sea. There is a great deal of information from the reports of captains of damaged vessels, revealing the hurricane to have been of unusual force and that its path covered a wide area. Because of the lack of recorded data, its magnitude may have been underestimated. A measure of the tempest may be had from the damage reported and from the comments of many persons who experienced it.

Lorin Blodget, a well-known meteorologist of the day, published the results of his investigation in the Philadelphia *North American*. Mr. Blodget considered that few ships of any class could "run with a hurricane of this [rotary] character throughout its usual course from Key West to Norfolk with any prospect of surviving it," and, it was his opinion that "steamships are far less safe than sailing vessels under such ceaseless violence." He added: "If the *Central America* and *Empire City* had laid by for half a day, they would have been safe, since the storm ceased at Norfolk only one or two days"[2] after the steamers would have passed that point. The reports of vessels in the track of the storm confirmed the general position assigned to it. Storms of that nature

[1] Ivan Ray Tannehill, *Hurricanes*.
[2] *The New York Times*, 23 Sep 1857, 1-6.

descended on vessels without advanced warning, the lack of communications permitting no time for preparation.

Marshall Roberts, the owner and agent of the *Central America*, "manifested no fears on her account." Regardless of what he may have surmised, he spoke of her as one of the staunchest of vessels, and an excellent sea-boat, and had full confidence in her ability to weather the gale through which the other steamers passed in safety. None of the mid-nineteenth century vessels were one hundred per cent seaworthy, and they were far less immune to human error and natural disaster than are the ships of today.

A theory put forth in the *Baltimore Sun* of September 22, 1857, speculated that the *Central America*, about fifty miles ahead of the *Empire City*, met the full force of the gale, a hurricane with a circular motion. She "was caught in the very centre of the whirl. The outer edge of the whirlwind struck her on Wednesday, the 9th, the time when the *Empire City* first experienced it . . . ."

The *Washington Intelligencer* reported: "The effects of the storm have spread far and wide. Every day brings us tidings of some new disaster or narrow escape." The British steamship *Indiana*, enroute New York from Bremen, Prussia, encountered the hurricane on September 15th at 44° 30' N latitude, 53° 30' W longitude (south-east of Newfoundland), and narrowly avoided losing her boats from the davits.

Captain McGowan said: "the storm was one of the most severe gales of wind that I ever witnessed, and continuing without interruption until Monday at 12 o'clock; the wind, varying during the day from northeast to southwest, around by west, and blowing furiously from each point."

The captain of the steamer, *Maryland*, which arrived in Washington, D.C. from Norfolk via the Potomac River on September 17th, reported:[3]

> The late storm at Norfolk was of unparalleled violence. The wind, accompanied with rain, continued to blow so hard from Saturday evening to Monday evening that no steamboat dared to leave her moorings; and all the sailing vessels that could make that anchorage, took refuge in Hampton Roads.
>
> So violent was the gale that the staunch bay steamers plying between Norfolk, Hampton and Old Point were compelled to remain in the harbor and suspend their regular trips until its raging had abated. It has been very long since a storm anything like it in violence and destructiveness has been experienced in that region.

There were 200 to 250 vessels riding at anchor in Hampton Roads,

---

[3] *The New York Times*, 18 Sep 1857, 1-4.

"much effort and nautical skill" having been required to get them safely into port to wait out the storm.[4]

"The wind blew from N.E., and it is apprehended that many marine disasters will be the result," said the Captain of the *Maryland*. He saw a wreck in his passage up the river, a large sloop in tow of a schooner. She was entirely dismasted, her boats carried away, and her rigging entirely riddled.

One of the proprietors of the *Charleston News*, who was a passenger on the *Columbia*, a steamer that weathered the gale between New York and Charleston,[5] said:

> The *Columbia* lost her paddle-boxes, some of her deck load, and "a pair of fine horses. And now for eighteen hours did that tempest beat upon her . . . . Not only were the waves of the greatest magnitude and wildness, and the wind the most terrible hurricane, but, for hours, they came in cross directions . . . from S.E. giving the ugliest cross sea, and subjecting us to the double danger of swamping and capsize. At 10 P.M., the wind veered to ESE., and reached its height, but the seas thus more fully in its direction. Until 2 A.M., the climax of the terrible power of both prevailed, then slowly abated, and at 5 o'clock A.M. Saturday, the wind was down, leaving us on immense rolling waves.
>
> . . . At 9 A.M., the wind having shifted to the west and north or landward, was in a few minutes the most driving hurricane we had ever seen or conceived. It prostrated the awful seas which had come from the broad ocean and appeared to sweep its surface along in spray and foam with lightning power and velocity. For five hours it exhibited not even abatement enough to mark squalls—it was one great squall. Under it the sea gradually increased, and when at last the wind became more fitful, it had reached a surging power that made every timber quiver.
>
> The gale must have been a circular hurricane through which the *Columbia* passed, or which rather passed over her position. The outer portion of its whirl took her in one direction, then its centre being more or less still and vacuous enveloped her in the few hours lull, and again the opposite side striking her from still other directions produced the second storm, and turned her prow to all points of the compass in her struggle for preservation.

The *Columbia*'s master, Captain Berry, according to England's *Manchester Guardian*, October 5th, said the storm was "the most driving hurricane ever seen or conceived."

The *Richmond Daily Dispatch* on September 22nd, reported the storm in North Carolina: "In Warrenton, the tide was four feet higher than

---

[4] *New York Daily Tribune*, 18 Sep 1857, 5-3.
[5] *The New York Herald*, 18 Sep 1857, 1-2,3; *The New York Times*, 18 Sep 1857, 1-3.

usual high water. The whole of Water Street and a portion of the back of the town was inundated. A large shed and work-shop . . . was blown away . . . there was considerable loss of naval stores and destruction of buildings and fixtures.

Until 1857, according to separate reports, there were only two disasters at sea that parallel the loss of the *Central America*, the first being the *Amphitrite*,[6] the second the *Arctic*, a commercial passenger vessel.[7] In the years after the *Central America* sank, the greatest loss of life during the nineteenth century occurred on the *Sultana*.[8]

The *New York Herald* of September 22nd termed the 1857 hurricane "unexampled in violence and in the length of time it continued." The giant transatlantic steamer *Persia*, her course being far north of the track of the *Central America* and *Empire City*, had experienced the northern extent of the storm on Friday, September 11th, when her decks were swept.

On September 24th, the *Baltimore Sun* reported very conservatively, the entire list not being in, "the total number of lost and damaged vessels amounts to 48: steamers 6; ships 4; barks 9; brigs 7; schooners 22."

Proximate and Contributing Causes of the *Central America* Disaster:

All of the evidence on hand in 1990 was available in 1857, but it is not clear that all of it was thoroughly clarified by the investigating parties.

To whatever degree of blame he may or may not have been entitled, the beleaguered Ashby could probably never forget nor fully escape

---

[6] The *Amphitrite*, was described by the Philadelphia press as "the only disaster within our memory with a loss of life to equal the 1857 loss." More than 25 years earlier, the *Amphitrite*, with about 800 convicts on board, was lost off the coast of France. Most of them were handcuffed and linked two-and-two with fetters, and unable to save themselves. *The New York Times*, 18 Sep 1857, 1-3.

[7] In 1854, 35 lives were lost on the steamer *Arctic*, including a member of the family of *Central America*, First Officer Charles Van Rensselaer. He was the surgeon, Dr. Taylor, brother-in-law of Rev. Maunsell Van Rensselaer (brother of Charles). Devens, Our First Century, 608. *The Richmond Daily Dispatch*, 25 Sep 1857, 1. *The Baltimore Sun*, 24 Sep 1857, 2-3. *The New York Herald*, 26 Sep 1857, 8-2.

[8] On April 27, 1865, the *Sultana* was destroyed on the Mississippi, 8 miles north of Memphis, by a fire resulting from a boiler explosion, ostensibly an act of sabotage. On the crowded vessel were about 2,200 persons, including 15 women and children, 1,961 Union soldiers who had just been released from Confederate prison camps, and enroute home. More than 1500 lives were painfully taken, and the Memphis hospitals filled with the scalded and burned. Only two or three of the fifteen women and children survived. *The New York Times*, 2 May 1865, 5-1, quoting the *Memphis Bulletin*.

criticism for his part in the incident. His behavior toward some of the passengers demonstrated that he was not a mild-mannered gentleman. In the midst of his other problems, a former shipmate deemed the time appropriate to sue him for battery.[9] The chief engineer may have been an ill-tempered bully, but to accuse him of deserting his ship became another matter. The reunion of Tice and Ashby gave no indication of ill feeling on the part of the former, Tice fully supporting Ashby in his timely action "as soon as the leak was discovered." Tice said that Ashby informed him that "he was going to the brig *Marine* for boats and assistance," and he also heard Captain Herndon reiterate his order to Mr. Ashby to "obtain the boats of the brig as soon as possible."

Second Officer Frazer, Boatswain Black, Chief Engineer Ashby and Second Assistant Engineer Henry Keefer signed sworn statements in the form of a legal protest[10] to the underwriters, describing their activities within their own departments.

The *New York Times* editor recognized the significance of the observations and opinions of Thomas Badger. He "was accustomed to the sea and perfectly familiar with everything relating to the management of ships under all circumstances of danger and difficulty, and he was known, moreover, to have taken a very active and efficient part in the last arrangements on board the *Central America*."

At the height of the storm, a half hour after detecting no water in the ship, Badger said that two or three heavy lurches brought him back to the deck. Looking into the engine room he saw the engines moving very slowly, and "while he stood looking at them they stopped altogether." He looked into the lee bilge, saw no water there, and could not see any in the engine-room." He later saw water rapidly entering the steamer around the shaft, and thought this the principal opening through which

---

[9] Reported by the *Baltimore Sun*, quoting the *Cincinnati Daily Enquirer* of September 27, 1857: "An action is now pending against Mr. Ashby, . . . in conjunction with his second assistant, Mr. Keefer, . . . in the Supreme Court of Kings County, L.I., for assault and battery upon Mr. Woodhill, for a long time in the employ of the United States Mail Steamship Company, and for three years butcher on board the *George Law*. From the deposition made by Mr. Woodhill, it appears that in March last, at Aspinwall, on account of a slight quarrel between him and Ashby, the latter threatened to kill him; and, when on board, he and a person from Aspinwall, named Johnson, whose assistance he had procured, seized him and knocked him down, violently kicking and jumping upon him and dragging him by the hair over the deck of the vessel. In this, according to the complaint, he was assisted by the second assistant engineer, Keefer. After nearly murdering him, as alleged, he was rescued by the first assistant engineer, Mr. John Tice, who remonstrated strongly with Ashby. Ashby is a large, powerfully built man, and his opponent of a slight, active figure. Mr. Woodhill has held the damages at $5,000, and the case, it is expected, will be tried in the Supreme Court, Brooklyn, in October next."

[10] *New York Daily Tribune*, 18 Sep 1857, 5-3.

the water came in, although a large amount had come in through the dead-lights in the after cabin which *could not be closed.*"[11]

Badger's recollections, as well as those of other reliable witnesses, absolve the Chief Engineer from any dereliction of duty. He observed Ashby in the continuous process of taking counter-measures to correct or prevent damage to the vessel. The engineer discovered the leak in a timely fashion, and sprang to immediate action at the first sign of the faltering of the engines. He may have been prompted by Captain Badger in commencing the bailing of the steamer, but any criticism of his performance seemed primarily to involve judgmental errors in human relationships. In spite of all of the evidence in his favor, George Ashby continued in many future comments and writings to be the scapegoat and villain of the *Central America.*

The crew attempted to raise steam on the donkey-engine, which would drive the Worthington pumps, and the following may be a critical point of observation: *"The pumps would not operate under power from the donkey-engine."* Captain Badger did not know why the pumps would not function, but later Second Assistant Engineer Henry Keefer told him that the cock, which would allow pressure to pass to the pumps, *"had not been turned."*[12] That *valve was located down in the lee bilge,* and by the time it came to mind, "the water over it became so high and so hot that it could not be reached, no further attempt being made throughout the night to raise steam to work the pumps, or to repair them."[13] However, Chief Engineer Ashby stated that, on Saturday morning, "steam was again got on the donkey boiler and the pumps worked till the rapidly gaining water submerged them entirely."

There is no indication that any attempt had been made as the water cooled during the night to access the forgotten valve, and it may have been that that particular problem had not yet been recognized.

> In the morning [said Captain Badger] they got up steam enough to drive the donkey-engine, *but the* [Worthington] *pumps would not work.* Soon after, the engine stopped. The reason given was that the water level had risen so high as to *cover the steam-pipes leading from the boilers to the cylinders, and thus to cool the steam.* They then abandoned all attempts to get up steam.[14]

Badger concluded that the engines had stopped before any consider-

---

[11] *The New York Times,* 23 Sep 1857, No. 1876, 1-1.
[12] The valve allowed steam pressure to pass from the donkey boiler to the Worthington pumps.
[13] *The New York Times,* 23 Sep 1857, 1-1.
[14] All emphases are by the author.

able amount of water entered the vessel, and deemed that "this failure could not have been owing to the extinguishment of the fires by the water, but seems due to the lack of a proper supply of coal." There being "no means of judging whether this was the fault of the men whose business it was to pass it, the answer should be within the knowledge of the Engineer,—as it was his responsibility to see that coal was supplied to furnish all the steam that was needed."

Although responsibility for the engine room belonged to the chief engineer, he was not expected to be on duty there throughout each day, without rest. An assistant engineer always had supervisory responsibility in his absence, one of them (John Tice, Henry Keefer or George Buddington) being in charge during the period, on Friday, September 11th, that the engines stopped while Ashby rested in his cabin. This author found no record of Ashby's redirection of the blame for this failure, but, possibly with justification, neither was he willing to accept the responsibility for the loss of steam power, nor to admit to any human failure in the operation of the engine room.

The task of passing the coal in sufficient quantity became hopeless. First Assistant Engineer Tice, subsequent to his dramatic rescue, said: "As the ship listed, our coal barrows were useless—we passed coal in baskets and buckets with our gang, assisted by nearly all the waiters, who were sent by Captain Herndon to assist us."

In a sworn statement, Chief Engineer George Ashby said:[15]

> At nine A.M. I discovered that the ship was making considerable water . . . . We then started the starboard Worthington Pump and Bilge Injection, taking steam from the large boilers. This was about ten o'clock. The water in the ship was then quite hot from being in contact with the boilers, I suppose, and in consequence of her list was all in the starboard bilge. This pump took water and worked freely—still the water gained on us. I then inspected all the pipes and their connections, and found them tight. At about twelve o'clock the water overflowed the coal-bunker-floors, both forward and aft, water putting out nearly all our [oil] lamps . . .
>
> [The engine] having only the port fires to depend on [because of the list to starboard,] the steam was soon used up . . . The coal was wet and unusable, so the boiler was then fired with wood, which was supplied by tearing out the bunks and other fixtures of the ship. But the water rose so high that all the fires were extinguished; the engines stopped between four and five P.M.
>
> The Worthington pumps, which had been previously worked by

---

[15] *New York Daily Tribune*, 22 Sep 1857, 5.

steam from the main boilers, *were then worked by the donkey boiler*, and continued to work until about eight o'clock with several stoppages of a few minutes each, which were made necessary to free the feed-pipe of the boiler from obstruction . . . The donkey engine finally stopped [because] the feed-pipe had become so choked up that it was necessary to cut and repair it.

Since the pumps had worked earlier, the valve must have been closed when the clogged line was repaired, then neglected to be reopened. John Tice's comments were essentially the same as Ashby's.

As is often true in emergency situations, the problem is compounded by human error, or unrecognized factors, and, in this case, the simple procedure of opening the valve, allowing pressure to travel from the donkey boiler, on deck, to the pumps, in the bilge, was overlooked until too late. This oversight, even though the ship may not have been ultimately saved, significantly reduced the possibility that she may have remained afloat in the subsiding sea for a considerably longer period of time. This hypothesis must include the recognition that, without steam in the main boilers, the ship would still have been uncontrollable. But the fact that the water in the hold was hot when the valve was inaccessible indicates that the amount of sea water entering the vessel was not overwhelming at that time.

On October 17th, the *New York Times'* correspondent in Panama commented:

Certificates are published [on the *Central America*] . . . to prove her staunchness and excellent sea-going qualities. There can be no doubt that the *Central America* was one of the strongest and best built steamships that ever floated. She had, however, been on shore two or three times. Once about a year ago, on one of the Florida reefs [Pickle Reef, September 10, 1856], where she lay 16 hours, and once, some three months since she lay all night rubbing, and probably pounding on a coral reef just outside the entrance to Aspinwall . . . she was placed in dock . . . It is not improbable, however, that she might have been weakened or strained in one of these mishaps, so as to have led to the dreadful misfortune that the whole people are now mourning.[16]

---

[16] Running ashore on Caribbean reefs frequently occurred. In September 1857, the coal ship *Vespasian* had run on a coral reef in the same place, near Old Providence Island. Her captain remained behind with the vessel while crew-members made their way in open boats to Havana. *New York Daily Tribune*, 22 Sep 1857, 5. On November 10, 1857, *Star of the West* went ashore on the Florida Coast. Passengers were sent from stem to stern, larboard to starboard, in an attempt to move her by shifting the weight. At midnight, an anchor was dropped ahead, which, by help of the windlass, caused the ship to swing almost around. At 3 A.M., four boats of passengers were sent on shore, and 30 tons of water discharged from the boilers; a strong pull was made upon the anchor and both wheels put in motion. At 4 A.M., the steamer went off to deeper water, having been all night on the reef. On November 19, 1857, *Northern Light*, 23 hours out of Aspinwall, ran on a coral reef, where she remained for 8 or 9 hours. *Sacramento Daily Bee*, 19 Nov 1857, 1-1.

Ironically, grateful passengers had awarded Chief Engineer George Ashby a gold watch for his effort in extricating the vessel from the reef.[17]

A Committee of the Insurance Underwriters and several passengers justifiably criticized the absence of a carpenter from the vessel. Had there been such an individual on board, he may have had tools available to box the pumps, although there is no assurance that such a measure would have helped the situation.

The *Central America* was engulfed in the worst area of the most vicious hurricane in the memory of easterners and sea captains, and a violent lurch probably extinguished the first fire in her boilers. Ansel Easton quoted Captain Herndon as saying that the first fire was put out by the ship being "suddenly thrown on her side, when the smoke and steam became so suffocating that those below had to go on deck." Herndon added that the disaster had not been caused by a leak in the ship's hull "because the water in her was hot," his significant comment also being reinforced by the statements of others including Ashby, Tice and Badger. Initially, at least, any supposed damage to the hull had not caused a leak.

This thesis and supporting comments explain the sudden and unavoidable damage to the steamer, the inability of the coal passers to adequately supply fuel at the necessary moment and the fact that "Captain Herndon at no time directed blame to Chief Engineer Ashby" [Badger]. It also tends to confirm that the sinking of the vessel followed the development of more leaks caused by damage incurred while she lay battered in the trough. The submerged starboard deadlights, in addition to being left open, were particularly subject to damage, not only from the rough sea, but from floating objects within the ship, as witnessed on the *Empire City* during the storm.

On Monday, September 14th, two days after the *Central America* sank, another steamship, the *Norfolk*, (formerly the *Penobscot*) belonging to the Union Steamship Co. of Philadelphia, foundered in Chesapeake Bay. Although all passengers were saved, it is ironic that two steamers unable to weather the hurricane both sailed under new names. The effect upon public opinion became significant, and the loss of the *Central America* provided another lever for the opponents of the eastern mail steamship company.

On January 5, 1858, John M. Weeks and Henry B. Renwick, United States Local Inspectors at the Port of New York,[18] issued a statement in

---
[17] *The New York Times*, 17 Oct 1857, 2-1.
[18] *New York Daily Tribune*, 5 Jan 1858, 3-6.

regard to their investigation of the conduct of the licensed officers of the *Central America.*

The New York Board of Underwriters represented the insurers of the specie on board the *Central America,* and was consequently specifically interested in the causes of her loss and whether or not there was any wrong-doing or incompetency connected therewith. The Board appointed a committee of eight inspectors to investigate the causes.

The Local Inspectors found that "the testimony was clear and conclusive" that every possible effort had been made by the licensed engineers to prevent the quenching of the fires.

The donkey boiler was fired up at a sufficiently early date, and the assistant engineers in charge of the donkey pumps persevered in attempting to keep those pumps at work until compelled to be hoisted up because of being immersed in hot water.

The inspectors found that although the chief engineer had not been able to prove he was ordered away by Captain Herndon, this was not unusual considering the small number saved, and there were no grounds for an opinion that he was not ordered away. It was considered that he had been able to prove the language addressed to him by Captain Herndon after he was in the boat, and

> the tenor of that language leaves no doubt that he had either been ordered into the boat or had volunteered to take charge of her, and his offer had been accepted.
>
> After the main engines had ceased to work, and the donkey pumps had stopped on account of being submerged, the testimony proved that the engineers were actively engaged in stopping leaks, superintending pumping gangs, and constructing pumps.
>
> The result of the whole is to prove that the licensed officers did their duty.

The inspectors refrained from comment as to the causes leading to the disaster because the "law under which they act confines their inquiries to the conduct of the licensed officers."

The report, being a vindication of George E. Ashby, his certificates, which had been withheld pending the investigation, were returned to him, and he was again qualified to resume the practice of his profession. However, he remained plagued by ill feelings on the part of many people. Dr. Harvey, in May 1858, coincidentally met Ashby on the streets of New York, and learned that he had not been able to find a position as an engineer. The doctor's bitterness against the engineer was reflected in a comment to the New York papers in which he said he was "grateful" to hear the news.[19] Ashby soon entered the service of the United States Navy.

On January 16, 1858, the investigating committee of the Board of Underwriters[20] made public their report, the investigation having been "conducted with the sole desire to elicit truth and not incriminate anyone." The recommendations became a guide for future improvements in the construction, equipment, manning, and management of steamships, and were intended to aid in providing improved safety for passengers, as well as to elevate their confidence.

The Committee, chaired by M.C. Perry,[21] stated that it was well aware that all of their recommendations for reform or change would be strongly opposed. Nevertheless, they considered the proposed improvements to be plausible, and necessary to insure greater safety in ocean navigation.

The committee thought the most serious defect, "being common, it is feared—a want of proper organization in regard to the relative authority and duties of the officers and crew of the vessel, and each department appearing to be independent of the other, instead of all being strictly subordinate and responsible to the captain, as the legitimate and superior chief. This independence of action was thought to be the more observable in the department of the engineer." This was a criticism of the captain's method of controlling his crew, the captain not being able to defend his position in this regard. However, Ashby stated that he reported directly to Captain Herndon on all matters pertaining to his department.

Within nine categories, the investigators made many recommendations:

Large vessels should have at least four watertight cross bulkheads, with watertight doors to allow the passage of a coal car, and a railway constructed for that purpose.

Pipes should be "sufficiently strong and *their valves placed in view of engineers and firemen.*"[22] This comment indicates that the board had been made aware of the forgotten valve. There must be "positive access to the lower ends of the receiving pipes of the bilge and injection pumps."

All deck pumps and stationary pipes connected with the donkey

---

[19] *Sacramento Union* 16 Apr 1858, 2-3.
[20] *New York Daily Tribune*, 23 Nov 1857; 16 Jan 1858, 3-4.
[21] Captain Herndon served under Commodore Matthew Calbraith Perry during the war with Mexico.
[22] Author's emphasis.

pumps should be "enclosed in pump wells large enough for a small man to clear the lower openings." This is "boxing" the pumps, as referred to by young Henry O'Connor.

Other specific recommendations included detailed provisions for adequate life-boats, their manning and contents, including emergency gear.[23] A few suitable spars should be carried "for the construction of one or more rafts."

Probably with Captain Badger in mind, the board approved of the use of qualified passengers in an emergency.

"It is obvious," said the report, "that those who superintend the management of the vessel and the engines should be the last to desert their posts, though events occurring at times not far remote have shown that some of the engineers, instead of standing by their engines, have been the first to seek the boats." This comment may have been a last shot at Chief Engineer Ashby, but it particularly applied to the crew of the steamer *Arctic*.

Before the inspectors' recommendations were made public, the United States Mail Steamship Company announced[24] on October 2, 1857, that water-tight bulkheads and extra pumps for each compartment were being provided for all of their steamers. Fire and engine-rooms were all to be enclosed. The addition of these safeguards had already been completed for the *Granada*. The steamers of the USMSC then in service were the *Granada, Illinois, Northern Light, Star of the West, Empire City,* and the *Philadelphia,* the construction of a new steamer, *Moses Taylor,* being nearly completed.

About the causes of the disaster, Judge Alonzo Castle Monson wisely commented: "An indefinite number of hypotheses might be set afloat, but none of them be anywhere near the truth." However, that having been said, the proximate causes of her sinking were:

(1) A violent lurch extinguished the boiler fires.

(2) The intensity of the hurricane made it impossible to pass coal in sufficient quantities to maintain steam pressure.

(3) The leak which developed around the shaft allowed water to enter the boiler area.

---

[23] Probably because of the compartmentalization of her hull, recommendations for boats and rafts were ignored. The plans for life-boats to be carried by the British steamship *Titanic* in 1912 totaled 64. That number was finally reduced, so that when the "unsinkable" steamship sailed, she carried 16. There were 1,331 passengers lost when she sank on her maiden voyage; 2,227 were on board. Even with that high loss of life, which was 60% of the passengers, the percentage of life lost on the *Central America* was greater; 73.3% (435) of the passengers in the 1857 disaster were lost; 71.4% (53) of the crew died in the wreck.

[24] *The New York Times*, 2 Oct 1857, 3-2.

(4) Inability to maintain steam power made the ship unmanageable in the turbulent sea.

(5) Broken or open deadlights allowed more water to enter the ship than could possibly be bailed out.

Contributing causes:

(1) The neglected valve—opening it may have permitted water to be pumped out by the donkey engine, allowing the vessel to remain afloat for many more hours, conceivably long enough to save her.

(2) The hull of the steamer may have been weakened by previous damage. Adding this possibility for further leaks to that of the shaft and deadlights suggests the notion of a complexity of leaks.

(3) The foremast, having become entangled with the cathead and anchor, may have inflicted damage to the hull.

The results of the sinking of the *Central America* were three-fold:

(1) The loss of the steamship provided an impetus for the completion of a transcontinental railway, and may have been a major factor in accelerating its construction. The *New York Herald* said, "The disaster has revived the talk about a Pacific railroad. The *Evening Bulletin* of today [September 27, 1857] heads an article upon the subject, by saying pithily—'Over 500 lives would have been saved if we had a railroad to the Pacific.'"

(2) Improvements were made for the safety of steamships.

(3) It spurred the demise of the company, for upon the expiration of its government contract in 1859, the United States Mail Steamship Company ceased to exist.

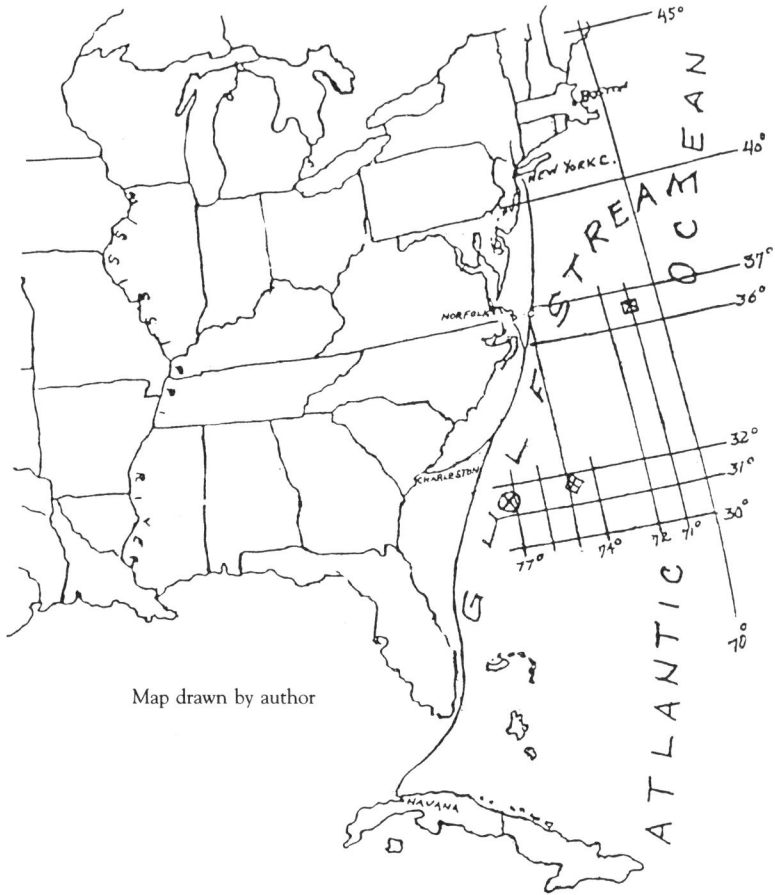

Map drawn by author

Position Report of Central America

⊗ The last position report, given by Captain Herndon to Captain Stone at 6:50 P.M., Septmeber 12th, was 31° 25' north latitude; 77° 10' west longitude. The given location was about 125 miles east-southeast of Charleston, on a bearing of approxmiately 125 degrees. The normal position for the steamer at that latitude was 75 miles from shore, so that with the gulf stream and other forces she had drifted about 50 miles east of course, and in the one and one-fourth hours she remained afloat, the final position must have been even farther to the east and north.

◆ Captain Burt's reported position of the steamer when she sank was 31° 40' N; 75° 50' W. This would place the vessel more than 200 statute miles east-southeast of Charleston at 8 P.M., September 12th, an eastward movement of 80 nautical miles (92 statute) in one hour and twenty minutes. To arrive at an accurate position may have been difficult; there is a wide margin of longitudinal error in one or both of them.

⊠ Captain Shearer of the *Mary* stated he picked up Tice, Dawson and Grant at 36° 41' N; 71° W.

CHAPTER XVI

Lost Specie and Treasure

The wreck of the *Central America* became part of another crisis that had been spreading across the country. A financial panic rocked the nation, excessive debt attributed to railroad construction investment being its chief cause.[1]

There were bankruptcies of railroads, peremptory sales of iron works, stoppage of cotton mills and other industrial establishments, business failures and distress in all classes of society, except for one, agriculture —which involved less than one-eighth of the total population. There was no unemployment insurance, no deposit insurance, and no Federal Reserve Board to regulate the money supply. *Central America* passenger Dr. Obed Harvey observed that "money is commanding 3 to 5 percent per month" in New York.[2]

A depreciation of stocks and panic in the stock market were thought to be the result of a shortage of money, "not procurable even at usurious rates of interest." Gold was the world's standard of value, the United States being on that standard, but sufficient quantities of the metal were not available.[3] The crisis had been developing since 1853, "ever since money became scarcer and interest higher every year."[4] The banks of New York depended heavily upon the gold shipments regularly arriving from California on the vessels of the USMSC.

Trade deficits, announced in reports of the Secretary of the Treasury, were cited to show that exports of *coin and bullion,* on no less than an annual average of 84 millions of dollars, had exceeded imports. Foreign

---

[1] "The amount of railroad indebtedness to the United States is frightful to contemplate," said the *Keokuk Daily Post,* Iowa, Oct 9, 1857, 2-2. The amount of specie in banks throughout the Union amounted in 1856 to only "$60,000,000. The amount of bank notes in circulation was $190,000,000." The *Post* listed more than 110 banks in 13 States and the District of Columbia which had been broken or had suspended specie payment.

[2] *The Mountain Democrat,* Placerville, California, 14 Nov 1857, 1-4.

[3] David Ricardo, 1772-1823, noted English political economist, said: "On extraordinary occasions a general panic may seize the country, when every one becomes desirous of possessing himself of the precious metals as the most convenient mode of realizing or concealing his property; against such panic banks have no security on any system." John J. Valentine, *Money, The Silver Question and Hard Times,* 154-5.

[4] *District of Columbia Intelligencer,* 1 Oct 1857, 3-2.

liabilities increased so that the *London Times* placed estimates of U.S. indebtedness to England alone at 100 million pounds (500 million dollars). This, "at seven and one half per cent, obliges us to pay, if called for, annually, a sum of 37 million 500 thousand dollars interest, nearly absorbing all the gold proceeds from California, which are thus virtually lost to us."

"Here then is the chief reason for the distress in money," said the *Times*, "it consists in the usual excess of imports of *foreign goods over exports of domestic produce*[5] to be paid for in hard coin, and in the interest of a colossal debt," blame being directed toward "an utterly fallacious commercial policy." This condition was bound to be repeated in later eras.

The lost shipment of gold on the *Central America* had its effect. The loss of any quantity of specie was a blow to the economy and to public confidence. As a temporary measure, a suspension of specie payments prevented a run on the banks.

Insurance houses promptly gave assurances that all would be made right, but "the information was received more in fear than in hope." The anticipation of an immediate demand of more than a million dollars from the different insurance companies became a front page news item. William Tecumseh Sherman said, "The absolute loss of the treasure went to swell the confusion and panic of the day."[6]

The daily *New York Herald* (then selling for two cents per copy) editorialized that while too much regret could not be expressed at the loss of human life by the foundering of the *Central America*,

> it must not be forgotten that the loss of the specie and mails will occasion much suffering. Aside from the great inconvenience to the mercantile community from the loss of the specie, there are hundreds of letters from miners in California to their friends or families here containing remittances, the loss of which will be deeply felt. Perhaps many families were depending on these receipts for the payment of rent, or the purchase of winter stores, the lack of which will occasion much suffering, and form no little proportion in the unfortunate results of this terrible calamity . . . . The sad intelligence of the loss of the *Central America* threw a gloom over the city, and had its ill effects on many happy homes.
>
> The stock market is feverish and all descriptions are lower. Gloom is depicted in every countenance, occasioned by the loss of life and property in the steamship *Central America;* also, the loss of the steamship *Norfolk,*

---

[5] Author's emphasis. An excess exporting of coin and bullion paid for an excess importing of goods and produce. This is a familiar situation, known as a trade deficit.

[6] Sherman, *Memoirs*, 135.

of this City, with one hundred thousand dollars worth of cargo. Those disasters and the previous panic in the money market make things look very bad here.

The insurance underwriters would bear the loss for the specie that went down with the steamer, and were therefore vitally interested in the cause of the disaster. The New York Underwriters somewhat assuaged public confidence when they promptly served public notice on September 19th 1857 that, upon presentation of the proper proofs, the claims against the respective companies would be paid without delay.[7]

The value of the shipment from San Francisco totaled $1,600,000, $550,000 of that amount being insured in New York, $950,000 in London, and $100,000 in Philadelphia.

The *London Daily News* noticed that the New York stock exchange had weathered the loss better than expected. It had been realized in New York that about two-thirds of the loss on board the *Central America* would be incurred by insurance companies of London, England.[8]

The estimated loss of $1,600,000 in specie (then about 320,000 English pounds) and an account of the loss of life and other details of the wreck were reported on October 3rd in England's *Manchester Guardian* and *London Daily News*. Both reported it remarkable that the *Central America* was the only vessel belonging to the steamship company, "ever lost on the return voyage, though the line has been operational since December 1848."

In California, because of the scarcity of coins, a pinch of gold dust from a miner's pouch often satisfied such purchases as admission to a minstrel show, or a shot of whiskey. From 1850 to 1854, gold dust had been a principal medium of exchange, the value erratically varying from about four dollars to twenty dollars an ounce, but stabilizing in 1854 to

---

[7] *The New York Herald*, 19 Sep 1857, 4-4. Those companies insuring the treasure on the vessel from Aspinwall to New York were:
The Atlantic Mutual Insurance Co., J.D. Jones, Pres.
The Great Western Insurance Co., Richard Lathers, Pres.
The Sun Mutual Insurance Company, A.B. Nelson, Pres.
The Union Mutual Insurance Company, F.S. Lathrop, Pres.
The Orient Mutual Insurance Company, Leopold Bierwith, Pres.
The Commercial Mutual Insurance Co., Daniel D. Smith, Pres.
The Mercantile Mutual Insurance Co., Ellwood Walter, Pres.
The New York Mutual Insurance Co., John H. Lyell, Vice Pres.
The Pacific Mutual Insurance Co., Alfred Edwards, Pres.

[8] For example, Wells, Fargo & Company, the largest shipper, was insured in London, where the company had a running policy of 1.1 million dollars in The Marine Insurance Co., Indemnity Marine, London Associated Corporation and Royal Exchange Associated Corporation. *The New York Times*, 19 Sep 1857, 1-2.

sixteen dollars per ounce.[9] Transportation costs increased the New York value to eighteen dollars.

The inconvenience of handling gold dust as a medium of exchange led to the establishment of a branch mint in San Francisco, which began producing gold coin in 1854.[10] The total amount of gold coin on the *Sonora* from San Francisco, transferred to the *Central America* at Aspinwall in the charge of Purser Edward W. Hull, was reported as 1.6 million dollars. However, later word from Aspinwall advised that a portion of the shipment, destined for England, went by another route. The shipments of B. Davidson, Abel Guy and others were shipped direct by the West India Mail steamer,[11] thus leaving a total specie shipment of $1,219,187.43. This was less than an average shipment carried by the vessel.[12]

The *New York Times* on October 5th, published a detailed list of consignees for the shipment from Aspinwall brought by the *Star of the West*.[13]

A report on October 17th gave the total to be $1,219,189, the *Central America* also being rumored to have taken in at Havana an additional $125,000 in specie, which, if correct, would increase the total shipment to $1,344,187.

All references concern relative money values of 1857, and therefore the losses involved do not at this time appear particularly large or devastating. To place them in perspective, however, the 1857 United States dollar at its inflated 1987 value would mean that an equivalent

---

[9] Hunt, *California*, 256.
[10] *Ibid.*, 256.
[11] *Daily Alta California*, 24 Oct 1857, 2-3.
[12] *The New York Times* periodical accounts.
[13] *The New York Times*, 5 Oct 1857, 1-1, 2.

Wells, Fargo & Co.	$260,300.00	Treadwell & Co.	10,027.92
Sather & Church	208,000.00	Crosby & Diblee	10,000.00
Tallant & Wilde	136,000.00	Spatz, Newhouse & Co.	10,000.00
Alsop & Co.	147,979.86	J. Saulnier & Co.	9,929.00
James Patrick & Co.	105,000.00	C.T. Meader	6,500.00
Lewis [Levi] Strauss	76,441.79	J.B. Thomas	5,120.00
E. Kelley & Co.	41,500.00	Geo. Howes & Co.	5,000.00
St. Losky, Levy & Co.	40,037.70	Z. Einstein & Bro.	4,000.00
Freeman & Co.	37,000.00	J. Guerin & Co.	4,000.00
D.O. Mills & Co.	34,000.00	Rutte & Co.	3,400.00
D.L. Ross & Co.	33,912.28	A.E. Sabattie & Co.	3,300.00
W.T. Coleman & Co.	29,590.00	E. & J. Rosenfeld	2,800.00
Parrott & Co.	25,836.10	E. Zahn	2,370.00
Pioche, Bayerque & Co.	21,000.00	Other shippers	55,442.48
Mark Brummagim & Co.	14,000.00		
Rousset, Auger & Co.	11,000.00	Total:	$1,324,189.13

shipment today would be valued at more than thirty millions of dollars, not including the rumored shipment of $125,000,[14] and takes into account an increase in value of an ounce of gold from $16[15] to $400.

There were many miners and people of financial means on board the steamship, and during that particular season of the year, large amounts of gold were carried by the passengers on their persons and in their baggage. Mrs. Thayer, for example, had taken the advice of others, and stored her money in her baggage.

The loss of more than the insured specie being recognized, the *New York Times* said: "Anyone who has observed [the passengers] landing at the piers must have been struck with the peculiar anxiety they bestowed upon their trunks, and the great difficulty always experienced in lifting and conveying them—two men usually necessary for this purpose." The reporter recalled that when a returned Californian was robbed in French's Hotel, New York City, about three thousand dollars were found in his trunk. An average of two to three thousand dollars per passenger may be a fair estimate of the amount each carried. Passenger Henry Kimball estimated that each passenger had from one to five thousand dollars.[16]

According to their own statements and those of witnesses, some passengers lost large sums of gold. Thomas Badger was seen to have emptied on the floor of the cabin the contents of a carpet-bag containing some seventeen to twenty thousand dollars in gold coin. Frank Jones, having observed the event, added that he saw many men thus relieve themselves of their treasure, hundreds of thousands of dollars thus thrown away.

James Birch, president of the California Stage Company, in addition to his life, lost seventy thousand dollars with the steamer.

Joseph Bassford had two thousand dollars in gold in a belt, which he

---

[14] *The New York Herald*, 19 Sep 1857, 1-1.

[15] According to Kellog and Humbert, assayers of Sacramento, California, in 1857, the value of an ounce of California gold differed according to its fineness—its approximation to pure gold. The actual market value of a bar of gold varied according to the amount of silver contained in it, and, for example, ranged from $15.50 per ounce at 750 fine to $19.63 at 950 fine. Gold was very seldom found in a state of absolute purity, the alloy in it being mostly silver and iron. The commonly quoted fineness for bars offered for sale in the California market was 880, valued at $18.19 per ounce. A refined bar to be received at the mint had to be over 990 fine, and possess the requisite for "toughness" for conversion into coin. A small amount of lead in an already refined bar would cause brittleness, and the process had to be repeated. New York calculations further took shipping and holding into consideration, thus increasing the price about two dollars per ounce. In view of the Kellog and Humbert table, the fact of a stabilized value of $16.00 per ounce may be questionable. *Sacramento Daily Union*, 15 Jun 1857, 1-5.

[16] *The Sacramento Daily Union*, 26 Oct 1857, 1-6.

lost, but Stephen Caldwell saved his twenty pounds of gold, which, for many workers, represented fifteen years of salary, enough to ensure years of comfort.[17] Willard Fletcher lost all of the gold he had mined. He had thought it would keep him in comfort for the rest of his days.

Among the sad stories of loss, that of two brothers named Horne,[18] from Missouri, affected many of the survivors. Henry Childs said that they had about four thousand dollars in a valise, which they brought on deck and placed between them. They clasped hands, taking seats on either side of it, and went down with the vessel. Both John and Anson Horne were lost.

> On Saturday, when death appeared close at hand and inevitable, treasure belts and bags were opened, and gold was scattered on the cabin floors, lest a few ounces or pounds of weight should decide their desperate contest with the waves. Full purses, containing in some instances two thousand dollars, were lying untouched on sofas. Carpet bags were opened by men, and the shining metal was poured on the floor and opened in contempt . . . . Two ladies brought out ten thousand dollars in twenty dollar gold pieces, and threw them down in the cabin, but no one wanted them. None of the ladies took more than two twenty dollar pieces with them.

There were exceptions to this statement.

The following table is based on the supposition that 400 male passengers lost an average of three thousand dollars each:

In hands of 400 passengers	$1,200,000
On freight	1,219,187
In hands of crew, at least	5,000
Total on board and lost	$2,419,187

Frank Jones reported that the insured specie on the steamer was "stowed away in the run, right along with the keelsons[19] of the ship and, before anything could be done to get it up, it was under water." Captain Badger said the gold was in an iron locker, and quickly covered with

---

[17] In 1857, the seamen and quartermasters of the *Central America*, making twelve trips to Aspinwall, earned $240 per annum; the boatswain, $360; the surgeon, $600; first officer, $900; chief engineer, $1500 and captain $1800. With salaries in that range, it is no wonder that Stephen Caldwell went to such effort to save his gold, which, at that rate, represented many years of salary.

[18] John and Anson Horne had gone to California in 1850. They bunked with Oliver Manlove, who said they had saved $6,000. Their father was a minister of the Gospel in Missouri. Manlove, *Autobiography*, Ch. 41, 44.

[19] Keelson: a longitudinal structure incorporated with the framing of a ship to stiffen it, above, and fastened to the keel.

water. With no possibility of saving it even if it could have been brought up on deck, the gold coin had to remain where it was stored, until such time as the resting place of the vessel could be discovered.

The steamer was a total loss to her company. Mr. Kirby, representative of the USMSC stated that the company preferred to save the cost of insurance, and had considered her loss highly unlikely.[20] The value of the steamship, a few years later, would have tremendously increased during the Civil War.

At 6:30 P.M., September 12th, as the *El Dorado* passed near the steamship, Captain Stone gave the position of the Central America, one-and-one-half hours before the vessel sank, at latitude 31° 25′, longitude 77° 10′, with a very heavy gale blowing from the northwest.

After the sinking, negotiations were attempted between the Boston Submarine Armor Company and the underwriters of the *Central America* to raise her hull, believed to lie in about 28 fathoms of water. The specie in her would "furnish ample inducement for the experiment, if her position can be accurately fixed."

"It appears that the Boston company [Submarine Armor] is working with submarine armor [diving gear], in raising treasure from the wreck of the *San Pedro*, a Spanish government vessel, sunk off Venezuela in 1815, with three million dollars on board." The *Richmond Dispatch* hoped that "some of our enterprising companies may find work at home in recovering the million and a half in gold so disastrously sunken in the *Central America.*"[21]

The wreck of the steamship holds much more than the gold alongside the keelsons, in her safe and in the trunks of the passengers. If sufficiently preserved, she may be a capsule of mid-nineteenth century history.

Boston Submarine Armor, finding the steamer had come to rest at a far greater depth than feasible, deferred indefinitely any attempt to recover the treasure of the *Central America*. I have found the position given by Captain Herndon to be very close to the eastern edge of the Continental Shelf, and with a strong wind from the northwest, the steamer may have dropped to an extreme depth. There is a rapid drop of from 3,900 to 18,150 feet below sea level.

An item on page two of the *Nevada Journal*, November 13, 1857, quoting the *New York Post*, recognized the probability of error in calculating the position of the *Central America* at the time she went down. The vessel, it was considered, may have sunk upon the second

---

[20] *The New York Times*, 19 Sep 1857, 1-4.
[21] *Richmond Daily Dispatch*, 24 Sep 1857, 1-4

sub-marine bench from the coast marked on Lieutenant Maury's charts as being from 1000 to 2000 fathoms [6 to 12 thousand feet] in depth. Some of the insurance companies were willing "to sell any claims of salvage upon it very low. The Atlantic Mutual Insurance Company would sell its claim at a low figure."[22]

"The difficulty of determining, in such a storm as that in which the *Central America* perished, the exact position of a vessel renders the chance of success extremely uncertain." The period of uncertainty extended to nearly one hundred thirty years. (See Appendix A.)

---

[22] *The New York Times,* 28 Sep 1857, 8-2.

CHAPTER XVII

Heroes of the Disaster

A SUMMING UP

A hero is defined as a person of distinguished courage, admired for brave deeds or noble qualities. The late Joseph Campbell[1] defined a hero as a personification of the heroes of mythology, one who responds to the call to adventure, one willing to sacrifice his life to save another. In these definitions of the term, there were many heroes on board the *Central America,* some of whom are identifiable.

The details of the fate of Commander Herndon can never be known. He had not slept throughout the period of the emergency, and had driven himself to the full extent of his physical capability, first, in keeping the steamer under control, then in effecting the rescue of the women, children and as many passengers as possible. In his slight frame he must have had little remaining of the energy necessary to save himself. Those not rescued had continued to drift in a north-easterly direction until, overcome by fatigue, they died on their section of debris or in their life-preservers, or slipped off into the sea.

Collective as well as individual heroism characterized this story of maritime emergency. Captain Herndon pursued his decision and intent to first assure the rescue of the women and children. At great risk to himself, his ship, and crew, Captain Burt rescued many passengers. The *extraordinary* efforts of the life-boat crews, at constant risk to their own lives were probably least emphasized. The composure displayed by both husbands and wives and most of the male passengers during the emergency drew the admiration of the country.

The *New York Times,* on September 19, 1857, said:

The most valuable life lost by the recent disaster is probably that of

---

[1] 20th Century philosopher, for thirty-eight years a noted professor at Sarah Lawrence University, Bronxville, New York; author of *The Hero's Journey.*

Lieut.[2] William Lewis Herndon, U.S.N . . . .a man of gifted intellect and resolute will. Modest and retiring in manner, it required a close observer or an intimate friend to discover all the rare qualities he possessed. His courage—the calm, deliberate, enduring courage of a truly brave man—has been conspicuous on many occasions. He has been tried severely, and never found wanting.

While very flattering, and probably in many respects accurate, it is not likely that Herndon would have wanted his life characterized as the most valuable lost. An example of his modesty can be found in thoughts he expressed during his Amazon exploration. Burdened with problems of commerce and navigation, he wrote, "Questions which I could not answer, and reflections which I could not keep back, crowd upon me. Oppressed with their weight, and the magnitude of the task before me, I turned slowly and sadly away, secretly lamenting my own want of ability, and sincerely regretting that the duty before me had not been assigned to abler and better hands."[3] He went on to perform admirably in the task he had been assigned. His attitude was not one of placing a higher value upon himself than he would on others.

Herndon was proclaimed a hero, not only by the newspapers of the country, but by all of his associates including those of the Navy, the steamship company, and most of the surviving passengers. His performance had been a classic example of the sea captain going down with his ship, as well as having been the individual most responsible for the rescue of the women and children. If heroes there must be, Commander Herndon was a man very much worthy of admiration, and a role model for young men of all generations. Ever ready to lay down his own life for the safety of others, and aware of his own probable fate, he encouraged to the end his passengers and crew. Posthumous honors came from various quarters.

The survivors publicly praising him for his conduct, bravery and generosity, included Thomas Badger, Angelina Bowly, Ansel and Adeline Easton, Jane Harris, Robert Hutchinson, Frank Jones, Barney Lee, Oliver Manlove, Annie McNeil, Henry O'Connor and Rosalie Pahud. Additionally, Ann Small could not speak of Captain Herndon without deep emotion. "I shall ever remember him with gratitude, I am

---

[2] The Navy promoted Herndon to the grade of Commander on September 14, 1855. (The grade was established about 1835). He was then placed on extended leave of absence to accept the position of master of the *Central America*, normally filled by naval officers in the grade of Lieutenant. On board his vessel he was captain, or commander, of the crew and, at one time or another, was referred to by any one of the above titles. After his journey on the Amazon, he became widely known as Lieut. Herndon. Navy Historical Center Archives.

[3] Herndon, *Exploration* . . . (1854), 60.

not surprised that he is among the lost, because I knew by his appearance when I parted from him that he would be the last man to leave the ship." Consul Ange Richon said he "acquitted himself like a true commander . . . took no sleep or rest . . . was busy day and night in doing all he could to assist in saving the steamer." First Mate Sherlock of the schooner *El Dorado* said: "When Captain Herndon hailed the schooner his voice was as steady as if he had the best vessel in the world under him, in a smooth sea;" and Thomas McNeish said, "I believe there was not a man left on board the ship but would have given his life if it could have saved the Captain."

When news of the *Central America* reached Washington and the Navy Department, Secretary of the Navy, Isaac Toucey[4], requested that Matthew Maury prepare a report of the loss of Commander Herndon and the steamer. Maury complied and, on October 19, 1857, based on statements of the survivors, addressed a four page narrative of the incident to the Secretary. He wrote: "The law requires every commander in the Navy to show in himself a good example of virtue and patriotism; and never was example more nobly set forth or beautifully followed."

Theodore Payne summed up the praise for Herndon:

> Captain Herndon was a gallant commander, a brave and kind-hearted gentleman. Throughout the trying scene his presence was everywhere on the ship. He was never at a loss to give an order or speak words of encouragement to cheer the noble spirits that were toiling around him. He had the highest confidence and esteem of all. It was the decree of Heaven for him to be thus removed. He died at his post doing duty. To him, as the instrument of Providence, I feel as if I owed my life, for if he had not told me to take the next boat I might probably have missed it; and as it was the last one that left the ship with passengers, my fate, I am fearful, would have been sealed. Boundless gratitude fills my heart, and I shall ever esteem it a high privilege to be the friend of the widow and child . . . . I am indebted to Captain Herndon for my life. He was all the time at the post on duty doing all that man could do in the trying hour. His voice was always heard above the roar of the storm, giving directions.[5]

In Washington, D.C., on September 25th, 1857, "the officers of the Navy and Marine Corps now in this city, between forty and fifty in number, held a meeting this evening to give an expression of their feelings at the untimely loss of, and to pay a respectful tribute to the

---

[4] Sec. Toucey had previously been a U.S. Senator of Connecticut and governor of that state.
[5] *Richmond Daily Dispatch*, 22 Sep 1857, 1-5.

memory of their late brother officer, Commander Herndon."[6] It was resolved that a monument be erected, commemorative of the circumstances of his death, "not only as due his memory, but to incite to emulation of his noble conduct."[7]

> What more appropriate action, [said the *New York Journal of Commerce*,] could be taken with reference to his death—choosing to perish as he did, at the post of duty, rather than make an effort for his personal safety—than to erect a suitable monument on Ocean Hill, Greenwood Cemetery, where a lot is reserved for heroes such as he, and thus, not only perpetuate the memory of the man, but of his deeds, for the contemplation of future generations, and as an incentive to lofty ambition. While the courageous offender against law, human and divine, is covered with dishonor, let the great and good be held in perpetual remembrance.

Ocean Hill became the site of the United States Naval Academy, Annapolis, Maryland, and the Herndon monument remains in its original position. Standing in front of the chapel, it is the only monument on the grounds that has never been moved.

On March 6, 1858, the General Assembly of Virginia requested Governor Wise to commission a gold medal to be presented "in the name of the commonwealth, to the widow of the deceased, as a testimonial of respect for a virtuous and brave man, and a noble and gallant officer."[8]

In May, 1858, a special act of Congress[9] awarded Mrs. Herndon $7,500 in financial assistance. The life of Commander Herndon addi-

---

[6] Herndon Monument Fund, *Report* . . .

[7] Funds for the monument were raised from contributions of officers of Navy units in individual donations ranging from one to five dollars. The fund permitted a contract to be let with Quincy Granite Railway Co. for a monument of Quincy granite, "cut in the best style, delivered at Annapolis and to be set up complete on or before 1 June 1859." The monument, a granite obelisk, "composed of a frustum of a pyramid, 18ft high, 4ft square at the base, 1 1/2ft square at the top, would rest on a plinth 3ft high, 6ft square at the base, and be further placed upon a solid masonry foundation 3ft deep, 7ft square. The word "Herndon" on front side of the shaft, cut in large raised letters, and on the opposite side, the words 'September 12, 1857,'—cut in large raised letters."

The total contract price for the monument was $1,161, with $1,340.85 immediately raised, the maximum contribution having been limited to five dollars. Matthew Maury, Lieutenants William Lewis Maury and John S. Maury contributed, as did the officers of Commander Herndon's old ship *Constellation*. Navy Historical Center Archives.

[8] A medal was subsequently struck by New York medalist F.R. Smith at a cost of $500, and delivered to Mrs. Herndon in New York, December 1858, by Major William Munford, Secretary of the Commonwealth of Virginia. Two bronze copies of the medal were made, one being sent to Secretary Munford, the other to Governor Wise, who passed his along to a Herndon relative. The face of the medal, between olive branches, bore the inscription: "Presented by Virginia to the widow of Captain William Lewis Herndon, United States Navy, as testimonial of respect for a virtuous and brave man, and a noble and gallant officer. 1858." Congressional Record #10904-3, 25 May 1866.

[9] Coulter, *Central America*, 481-2.

tionally had been insured by the New England Mutual Insurance Company for the sum of $5000.

Recalling the 1827 words of B.R. Wellford, of Fredericksburg, in recommending Herndon for appointment as a midshipman, he did indeed "reflect credit on the administration which introduced him into our navy."

Commander Herndon did not stand alone on the deck of the *Central America,* and he would willingly recognize the heroic acts of others.

The Men of the *Central America*

The collective chivalrous attitude of the men on board the steamer, and the control they exercised in ensuring the evacuation and rescue of the women and children was truly an example for all.

Most nineteenth century American men took pride in their courage, often expressed as "manliness," and "nobleness." The age of chivalry was very much alive, and the women were looked upon with great respect as their mothers, and mothers of their children, and therefore they were shielded and protected above all else. That was the attitude expressed by Herndon, the husbands, and, no doubt, it extended to his crew and the majority of the male passengers. It is a tribute to the men that they stood back, obeying the captain's order, even though most of them were armed, a common circumstance in that era.[10]

Mrs. Kittredge said: "As a whole there was never a nobler set of men than those on board the steamer, though among them were a few cowards. Most of the men worked till completely exhausted, and when the cry went forth, 'More men, more men,' they would forget fatigue, and up and at it again."

The *Daily Alta California,* on November 14th, reported: "Sentiments of gratitude for departed worth are among the most exalted traits of our nature, as ingratitude is certainly the basest and most despicable." And extolling the virtues of the men on the *Central America:*

> How much more appropriate does such an acknowledgment appear, having for its object the perpetuation of a gallant band such as those who assisted in the debarkation of every woman and child from the ill-starred *Central America*—generously choosing to go down with the sinking ship, rather than yield to the irrepressible, but natural, instinct of self-preservation. It is difficult to conceive of heroism superior to this; the strong and impetuous preserving their firmness, and cheerfully witnessing the rescue of the feebler sex from the fate for which they, with all their

---

[10] Soule, *Annals,* 631.

magnanimity, were reserved . . . . Whoever repeats the story of that shipwreck renews the fame of those devoted men.

The *Alta* believed the story of the men on the steamer to have "enlisted the attention of the women of America throughout its length and breadth," and expected gratitude, in some way, to be expressed by them.

"Here, in California, our ladies . . . . have proposed to obtain subscriptions to erect a monument, not alone to Lieutenant Herndon, but to all whose conduct on board the *Central America* render them worthy of the testimonial." A variety of proposals arrived at the newspaper office, "most of which are practicable and worth the attention of all who are disposed to encourage so worthy an object. The matter should be placed in a tangible and practical shape, before it can be seriously acted upon by the public." This movement did not materialize.

The male passengers of the steamer stood back so that the women and children could be evacuated. When the last of them was safely in the boat, a few men could no longer restrain themselves; 489 others remained to go down with the ship.

Deserving of special praise, Captain Thomas W. Badger's untiring efforts during the entire catastrophe contributed beyond measure in assisting Captain Herndon to direct the keeping of the steamer afloat as long as possible. He encouraged the passengers, and even before he could be hauled aboard the *Ellen,* urged Captain Johnsen to expedite the rescue of others. Badger was directly responsible for saving many of them. The *Central America* Fund Committee awarded him an engraved silver trumpet, with the inscription: "Presented to Capt. Thos. W. Badger by the '*Central America* Fund Committee' in token of their high appreciation of his conduct on board the steamer *Central America,* at the time of the loss of that ill-fated vessel. Peletia Perit, President; Lloyd Aspinwall, Secretary, New York, May 17, 1858."

Oliver Manlove said: "Captain Badger was of great assistance to Captain Herndon throughout the storm, assisted in organizing the gangs for bailing, cheered us all up with hope of ultimate safety until all hope was gone, and then gave us the aid of his nautical experience."

There, too, was high praise for the bravery of the officers. First Officer Charles W. Van Rensselaer, Second Officer James M. Frazer and Third Officer Charles A. Myers stood beside the captain as the *Central America* sank.

One of the finest tributes to the crew of the *Central America,* (and to the ship as well), appeared in the *New York Times* of November 9, 1857.

David Raymond, Quartermaster of *Central America*
From the *San Francisco Chronicle*

It came from a former officer of the steamer, William L. Maury, who at the time of writing served on the ship *Tornado*, and was written from Liverpool, England, on Monday, October 12, 1857. The three-page letter, addressed to the *Times* editor, is condensed as follows:

> Your columns have furnished me with the sad details of the loss of the *Central America*, . . . I feel it a duty to their memory and to their mourning relatives to add my humble tribute to their worth . . . .
>
> I would render my humble admiration to those noble souls who, alas!, have so soon met a watery grave. Captain Herndon—who can say aught against him—so good, so noble-hearted, so generous in regard to the faults of others—he was a man to whom any officer would have become attached. I remember upon one occasion when a difficulty had arisen, how kindly he called me to him, how candidly he showed me where I was wrong, how warmly he interested himself to have the matter looked upon in a proper light . . . .
>
> The *Central America* was an example to other ships in point of unity and concord among her officers. During the few months I was among them we were as brothers—the sorrow of one was shared by all—when one was happy all rejoiced. Esteeming our commander as we all did, each felt that he was one in a thousand . . . .
>
> To those who knew them I have but to mention Tennison—my noble-hearted friend; Van Rensellaer, my ever faithful shipmate; the names, . . . in the hearts of their surviving shipmates they are written in letters of gold! . . . What better proof does the world want of their character than their conduct during the frightful disaster? Not a dismayed countenance, not a faint heart among them—they nobly perished doing their duty. What a contrast to the conduct of others in like circumstances!
>
> Herndon, Van Rensellaer, Tennison, alas! you are lost to us and the world forever—but your eulogium is engraved on the hearts of your shipmates!

With a boat half full of water and no oarsmen willing to join him, Quartermaster David Raymond fought to return to the steamer to rescue another load of passengers. Raymond said he would go to the steamer "if she was 50 miles away," and that he "was above taking pay for such services." On November 9, 1857, he was recognized for his bravery with a medal, presented by the *Central America* Fund Committee, in "token of their appreciation for his humane and successful efforts toward saving the lives of those unfortunates cast adrift upon the ocean by the foundering steamer *Central America*." Theodore Payne praised him for "standing in his little boat [the Captain's gig], which was constantly being dashed against the brig and calling in vain upon his comrades who had deserted him . . . . Those who witnessed his exertions felt that he was truly a noble-hearted sailor."

Boatswain John Black and his crew returned in their nearly swamped boat to rescue more of the men, arriving just as the *Central America* sank. They spent nine hours in the life-boat in rescue operations after the many hours at work on the steamer in the effort to save her. They alone returned to the steamer a third time, thus making four trips from steamer to brig.

Maury had great praise for the life-boat crews:

> It was conduct the most loyal, noble, and true. Indeed, there was probably not enough said in the favor of those oarsmen, who had worked at bailing and other duties along with everyone else during the emergency, then fought the angry sea for miles, in waves as high as thirty feet, to carry their passengers to safety on the brig. They must have been gratified in knowing that their lives had been spared in the performance of their duty.

Praiseworthy is the stoicism of Billy Birch, who, bleeding from wounds, kept up the spirits of other men, inspiring their courage. In possibly his most significant performance, the comic and minstrel, injured by a fragment of the wreck, "managed to grasp and crawl onto a floating hatch window." Several others joined him, and were despondent. Nevertheless, Billy "was as cool as a cucumber. To keep up their spirits he mimicked the sea monsters, told humorous stories, in his own peculiar way, and on that frail bark, stretched on his back, . . . at midnight, tossed to and fro upon the angry waves of mid ocean, he not only showed himself a true philosopher, but inspired courage in others, nor did he cease his vivifying harangue until an overwhelming billow [temporarily] ceased his utterance."[11]

The Women of the *Central America*

Many survivors praised the bravery and stoicism of the female passengers. The husbands, in characteristic 19th century fashion, attempted, in most cases, to withhold from them as long as possible the facts of the dangerous plight they were in on the vessel. Nevertheless, they were aware of their situation, and in the face of danger, the harrowing transfer to the brig *Marine* and the loss of many of their husbands, fathers, sons or brothers, they remained calm throughout the ordeal and won the admiration of all.

Joseph Bassford said: "Some of the ladies behaved most generously

---

[11] *Frank Leslie's Illustrated Newspaper*, 3 Oct 1857, 286.

and nobly—several of them volunteering to take their places at the buckets; but the men, tired as they were, had too much gallantry to allow this. The offer of the ladies, however, to assume a portion of the trying toil gave renewed encouragement to the men." Bassford praised Mrs. Easton for her tending with food and wine to the men bailing the ship.[12]

"Some of the ladies, feeling for the men," said Virginia Birch, "learning that some of them were getting both disheartened and exhausted at the pumps, volunteered to give a helping hand. And the ladies would have worked, too, like good fellows if the chance had been given them," she said. Her husband, Billy, thought: "The females were especially marked by . . . fortitude and presence of mind," and Ange Richon said that what struck him most, "amid the scenes on board the *Central America,* was the calm self-possession and heroism of the ladies. They deported themselves with fearlessness. Many volunteered to help the exhausted men in bailing the steamer, but male pride would not permit them to do so."[13]

Hearing their story, Matthew Maury, being impressed, complemented them: "Calm and resolute themselves, they encouraged and cheered the men at the pumps and in the gangways [and volunteered to do] man's work in battling with the tempest."

Doctor Harvey praised "Mrs. Caruthers and Mrs. Marvin for their kind care and attention on the sick and suffering." And Mrs. Bowly summed up the situation for the ladies, saying:

> The ladies were in no worse spirits toward the end than they were at the beginning of the danger. In fact, we all appeared to grow more and more calm and resigned. Those that had no little children to take care of, nor to be anxious for, were quite as brave and hopeful as the men. But as for myself, I must confess that, being sick and weak, and with these two helpless little ones clinging to me, I became somewhat discouraged and disheartened. A few of the ladies showed no signs of fear, and kept up to the last. It was wonderful to see their composure. In fact, it was wonderful that we were not all frantic.[14]

There were eighteen married couples on board the *Central America.* Fourteen of the wives were widowed.

---

[12] *New York Daily Tribune,* 21 Sept. 1857, 6-7.
[13] *Daily Alta California,* 23 Oct 1857, 1-4.
[14] *New York Daily Tribune,* 21 Sep 1857, 5-6.

Rescue Vessels

The conduct and seamanship of Captain Burt of the brig *Marine*, and of Captain Johnsen of the bark *Ellen* were exemplary. With great skill, they and their crews maneuvered their damaged vessels to rescue the passengers.

"Captain Burt," said *Frank Leslie's Illustrated Newspaper*, "has obtained a lasting popularity from the prompt manner in which he came to the rescue of the wrecked passengers of the *Central America*, and will long be held in esteem as an honor to the commercial mariners of our country."

Of Captain Johnsen, Thomas Badger said that he "did everything that good seamanship and a humane heart could dictate to save as many as possible."

Major Clark spoke for all of the rescued men on board the *Ellen* when he bestowed "unbounded praise upon the conduct of Captain Johnsen, of the *Ellen*, for his exertions to save life, and the treatment extended to them all afterwards." Theodore Payne spoke for those on the *Marine*, saying: "We are under lasting obligations to Captain Burt and his officers, as well as his crew, for the kind attention paid us while on the *Marine*. Their efforts in our behalf were unceasing."

From Norfolk, Virginia, in a letter dated November 9, 1857, D^n. Robertson (Swedish consul) wrote in glowing terms to Ansel Easton of Captain Johnsen, saying that during the captain's sojourn in Norfolk, he, Robertson, had "formed the highest regard" for him. And "unassuming as he is, he is the embodiment of all that is good, and I trust he may have his reward from a higher source for the meritorious acts he has performed."

Ansel Easton made personal efforts and recommendations for awards to Johnsen and his crew. Robertson hoped that "when Congress meets, [Captain Johnsen will] get back the $950 paid at the Navy yard for his repairs." The *Ellen* was valued at $3000. He continued that he hoped the efforts of Easton "may be crowned with success in regard to the medals."

To President of the United States James Buchanan, on October 19, 1857, John Lorimer Graham (described by Addie as "a political and personal friend of the President"), of New York, wrote that he had "known Mr. Easton for many years as a most estimable man," described Mrs. Easton as "an amiable and an educated lady," and enclosed a letter from her, petitioning for an award for Captain Burt from President Buchanan, equal to that for Captain Johnsen. He elaborated on Addie's "remarkable self possession . . . devout religious encouragement and consolation in the hours of their extreme peril. Permit me to add," continued Graham, "that public sentiment highly approved the conduct of Captain Burt, commander of the Brig *Marine* . . . his bringing into Port . . . safely . . . 96 human Beings, attributable entirely to his coolness, seamanship and humanity, is under all the circumstances truly miraculous and in the highest degree praiseworthy." Conceding that Captain Johnsen "should receive the distinguished notice he has from the Executive," he concluded, "our people feel that in doing honour to one of a foreign Country we should not overlook our countryman who saved the greatest number of lives and won for himself universal praise for his manly conduct."

In a private reply to Graham for the President, and referring to the letter of Mrs. Easton, the U.S. Secretary of State wrote that he appreciated "as highly as any one can do the noble conduct of Captain Burt, . . . and should be highly gratified to carry to him a testimonial of public approbation. But the presentation of a memorial to Captain Johnsen seems to be entirely misunderstood in many of the papers." The Secretary went on to say that after a good while awards had finally been authorized only for "foreigners who have distinguished themselves by heroic conduct in rescuing from the dangers of the Sea," and "out of that fund the chronometer was purchased for Captain Johnsen." However, "It is applicable exclusively to foreigners and we have no authority to procure and deliver such a testimonial to an American Citizen, however meritorious may be his conduct. I am dear sir, truly yours, [signed] Lewis Cass."[15]

Many years later, Addie Easton said: "Captain Burt and Captain Johnsen were both true sons of the sea . . . brave, generous and kindly, and but for their timely and unselfish aid no one should have been saved to tell the story of the wreck. My husband's friendship and gratitude to them lasted throughout his life."[16]

The Easton and Graham efforts were a gratifying tribute to Captain Burt. He received an award of $600 and a gold watch. That the Fund Committee awarded him a speaking trumpet is very likely, though not confirmed.

Captain Johnsen's crewmen, Mate Gustav Jorgen Jacobsen and

---

[15] Sec. Cass had previously been a U.S. Senator from Michigan and Governor of Michigan Territory.

[16] Olmsted-Lincoln, *Wedding Journey*, 37.

Sailmaker C.A. Norlund distinguished themselves by heroic acts in the rescue of passengers, and were consequently awarded silver medals for their respective acts. Jacobsen's medal is presently in the possession of the Aust-Agder Arkivet in Arendal, Norway. That of Norlund was last known to be in the possession of a descendant, Sigmund Norlund, Oslo, in 1966. On the medals presented by the *Central America* Fund Committee was inscribed: " . . . in token of their appreciation of his humane efforts towards saving the lives of those unfortunates cast adrift upon the ocean by the foundering of the steamer *Central America*, September 12, 1857."

Other passing vessels and their masters assisted in sustaining those on board the *Marine* and *Ellen*: Captain Smith of the bark *Saxony*, the unidentified captain of the bark *Cuba*, Captain Post of the propeller *Thomas Swann*; the clipper *Euphrasia*, Captain Lanfare, gave water and provisions to the *Marine*, without which those on board would have been in a desperate condition. The last water was being rationed when the *Euphrasia* was sighted. The *Laura*, Captain Wilmsen, transported the last three survivors to New York after they were rescued by the *Mary*.

The *Marine*, Captain Burt, the *Ellen*, Captain Johnsen and the *Mary*, Captain Shearer were the only three vessels directly rescuing the passengers and crew members of the *Central America*. Of the 596 persons on board the steamship, 161 were rescued as follows: *Marine*, 109; *Ellen*, 49; *Mary*, 3.

Appendices

APPENDIX A

The Treasure of the Central America

Since the abandonment by the Boston Submarine Armor Company of the search for the *Central America*, this author's research has been unable to locate a record of any other recovery attempts prior to July 1987.

The task of recovery abandoned one hundred thirty years ago by Submarine Armor has now been accomplished. Advanced technology and ingenuity have permitted the development of equipment capable of exploring the ocean's depths. The remains of the *Central America* lie in the vicinity of the position report given by Captain Hiram Burt, at a depth of about 8,500 feet, about "160 miles off Charleston, South Carolina,"[1] and a coordinate taken by Captain Smith of the bark *Saxony*.[2]

In Columbus, Ohio, a group of investors, the Columbus-America Discovery Group,[3] with a fund of 12.7 millions of dollars, financed the expedition. The director and founder of the Group, Thomas G. Thompson, is a marine engineer, formerly of Battelle Memorial Institute.

Although the *U.S. News and World Report* of August 3, 1987, first announced the possibility that the remains of the steamer had been found, the identity of the underwater image had not been confirmed. The salvage group positively identified the wreck of the *Central America* in September 1988 when her bell was raised from the Atlantic Ocean floor. However, release of the news was withheld pending a legal decision in regard to the ownership of the gold and "a struggle with recalcitrant machinery and the multiple problems of mechanics and weather that plague any such expedition at sea." There were additional problems.

A principal competitor, the *SS George Law* Partnership of Boston, organized by "treasure hunter" Bert Webber,[4] operated from a Columbia University-leased NASA recovery vessel, the *Liberty Star*, which was manned by a technical crew from the University's Lamont Doherty Geological Observa-

---

[1] David Seanor, "The Law of Sunken Treasure," 50-2.
[2] Herb Cook, Jr., "Gold! Treasure Hunt on the High Seas," 42-2.
[3] Judy Conrad, historian for Columbus-America Discovery Group, official video and newspaper releases.
[4] Seanor, "Sunken Treasure," 52-2.

tory. William Ryan, senior research scientist of the observatory, claimed to have been in search of the *Central America* more than a year before the Columbus-America Group. He also asserted that, thinking Thompson to be working on a Navy project, he had shared technical data with Thompson and leased to him a winch. Ryan and his group had mistakenly imaged a shipwreck in her vicinity [according to the *ABA Journal*, May 1990, 52,] but had not succeeded in locating the hull of the steamer.

There ensued a jockeying for legal positions, planned by Discovery Group attorney Richard Robol, the object being to establish ownership of the treasure of the *Central America*. The "full story may not be known for a long while because the operational strategy has been found by the court to be proprietary information."

Robol devised a means through the international legal concept *competence de la competence*,[5] combined with the theory of *in rem* jurisdiction, (concerning a thing, as a legal proceeding for its recovery), as a means for the court to establish and protect its jurisdiction. As evidence, he needed an artifact, and suggested a lump of coal as an item "valueless but conclusive" to establish jurisdiction.

From the angle iron of one its runners, the undersea robot recovery vessel *Nemo* brought a piece of coal to the surface, where it was taped in styrofoam. To speed the process of getting it from site to shore, Thompson devised a means for an air pick-up reminiscent of the 1960s recovery of U.S. military satellites over the Pacific Ocean. The package of coal, fastened to the middle of a nylon cord stretched between Nemo's hoisting crane and a pipe extended by Thompson from a rubber raft, was then picked up by an aircraft equipped with a suspended pulley and grappling hook. The aircraft then delivered the parcel to shore, where it was presented to the Norfolk, Virginia, court of Judge Kellum, who then asserted jurisdiction over the site.

Skeptically questioning the jurisdiction of the court, Ryan accused the Columbus-America group of bluffing, saying the coal may not be from the *Central America*. Kellum issued a temporary restraining order to prevent further interference with the court, and issued an injunction making the site off-limits to all salvors but the Columbus-America organization. This gave the latter the advantage of being able to "work without interference through the summer of 1988."

During that period, Thompson equipped the robot with a "sophisticated sonar grid established for precise measurement of the wreck site." In October 1988, the recovery of the bronze bell of the steamer established positive identification, but much of the activity remained a closely guarded secret, including the finding of a gold bar and two gold coins in September 1988.

"United States District Court Judge Richard B. Kellum, Norfolk, Virginia, operating on the ancient precedents of admiralty law,"[6] awarded salvage rights

---

[5] "The jurisdiction to determine jurisdiction as a court, and that court's jurisdiction to protect its jurisdiction." Ibid., 53-1.

to Thompson's group, and extended federal protection to within a fifty mile radius of the site. Television and newspapers of the Associated Press, on September 14, 1989, announced the discovery location being variously reported at from 160 to 200 miles east of Cape Fear, North Carolina, and between eight and nine thousand feet below the surface of the sea. The ABA Journal placed it about 160 miles east of Charleston, South Carolina, but did not reveal the precise location.[7]

The salvagers and their gear are carried by a mother ship, the *Arctic Discoverer*, a "30 year old former Canadian icebreaker built with armor plate left over from World War II."[8] The equipment includes a computer-based imaging system and the robot *Nemo*, about the "size of a pickup truck and weighing eight thousand pounds," the weight increasing with added equipment. Aptly named after the submarine commander in Jules Verne's classic novel *Twenty Thousand Leagues Under the Sea*, Thompson reports that it is "the first unmanned, mechanical deep-ocean excavation vehicle—a submarine archaeologist equipped with cameras and sensors. The robot returns computer-generated sonar images, affording scientists a window on the ocean floor."[9]

Nemo has performed admirably at the task for which it was designed. The robot has great strength, the main arm being able to lift three hundred pounds when extended to its full length of fifteen feet; "the other arm has the same capability but only at a reduced length. Its sensitive, padded fingernails" allow it to "lift and recover a fragile teacup or a coin smaller than a dime" and it can

> sit on the ocean floor or hover over it, using thrusters to move about. The machine's built-in computers automatically shut down if a malfunction occurs.
>
> At the underwater site, the remains of the *Central America* structure have collapsed under the deep ocean pressure, and silt and biological goo has slowly covered the surface, [said Thompson.] The ocean floor is quite calm, with crystal-clear water and almost no disrupting currents.

A side-wheel is recognizable.

There are some unique tenants in the wreckage. Group oceanographer, Charles Herdendorf, believes researchers have discovered "two new invertebrates clinging to the SS *Central America*, . . . and an unusual sponge."[10]

Thompson said that on about September 5, 1989, "remote video images revealed a shiny cluster on the sodden beam . . . it was on one of the protruding beams in the wreckage, and some of the site analysts thought it was tube worms or some kind of biological growth, . . . a closer look found the beam layered with gold coins cemented together and to the worm-bitten beam by an iron oxide crust."

Thompson described the underwater scene as "a garden of gold. A bridge of

---

[6] *U.S. News and World Report*, 3 Aug 1987, 48.
[7] *ABA Journal*, May 1990, 50.
[8] *The Washington Post*, 14 Sep 1989, A26-1.
[9] Ibid.
[10] *The Crescent-News*, Defiance, Ohio, 18 Sep 1989, 3.

gold bars . . . [The bars, which had been stacked on the keelsons, remained cemented together after the wooden members had disintegrated] . . . There were rivers of gold coins, carpets of gold . . . .Bags that held gold dust were long gone, but the dust was stuck together. *Nemo* blew off silt, and a carpet of gold coins appeared before you."[11]

Among the items recovered, the largest minted bar weighs sixty-two pounds, and bears the stamp of the San Francisco Mint. To protect the coins, "molds about eighteen inches square are placed over sections of [the entire length of the] wreckage, and mixed silicon sprayed through a nozzle into the mold between the coins . . . " The silicon hardens in about thirty minutes, after which the "silicon block carrying as many as two hundred coins" is gently seized by *Nemo* and ninety minutes later arrives at the surface. "Many of the coins are lying in the rolls they were originally shipped in."[12]

Reminiscent of the 1857 gale that doomed the *Central America*, the September 1989 appearance of hurricane "Hugo," which had struck the eastern Caribbean with winds up to 114 miles per hour, delayed work on the salvage operation.[13]

The value placed upon the find varies from one hundred millions to one billion dollars, depending upon the amount of gold carried by the passengers, its condition, the numismatic value and the selling prices realized at public auction. The then newly minted coins, including uncirculated double eagle twenty dollar gold pieces,[14] are of considerable value,[15] their discovery being termed the most significant in the history of American treasure. The Discovery Group has promised that the venture will be a model of careful salvage and archaeology.

The more than two-hundred John W. Audubon drawings carried on the steamer by John Stevens were a significant loss. Unless they were placed in a sealed container, they have more than likely disintegrated. In this regard, no report has as yet been made.

Lloyds of London and other insurance claimants hold that the claims for the treasure of the heavily insured *Central America* were paid and the search has never been terminated. "We never abandoned anything," said an attorney representing some of the insurance companies.

Other seekers of a portion of the treasure were the Commercial Union Insurance Co., the Insurance Company of North America, the London Assurance Society and the Salvage Association of the United States.[16] Additionally, the South Carolina Marine Archaeological Trust, a handful of descendants of passengers, and the state of New York, made claims.

---

[11] *Los Angeles Times*, Apr 3, 1990, A17.

[12] *The Columbus Dispatch*, 18 Sep 1989, 2A.

[13] *Ibid.*, 1A.

[14] The largest of all regular United States issues of gold coins, weighing 516 grains.

[15] The ship carried mostly double eagles because one double eagle occupies less space than two eagles or four half eagles, though containing the same weight of gold. Walter Breen, "The S.S. *Central America*," 1130-3.

[16] *Los Angeles Times*, 3 Apr 1990, A17-2.

Saying that a whole new field of jurisprudence has been established as a result of this case, attorney Robol foresees the steamship affecting "law involving salvaging of outer-space debris and rights of private companies that have commercial ventures in space. He says he is arguing for the "law of achievements"—the belief that recovered abandoned property "restored to the stream of commerce" should belong to the finder,[17] or as some call it, "finders keepers."

On August 15, 1990, at Norfolk, Virginia, Judge McKellum ruled in favor of the Columbus-America Discovery Group. He rejected the claims of nine insurance companies, saying they had produced no documents showing they had insured the gold, and that the treasure had been "abandoned" because no attempts at recovery had been made since the sinking of the *Central America*.[18]

After the surprising announcement of the steamer's finding, several questions arose. Will the state of preservation of the wreck reveal any conclusive indication of the ultimate cause of her taking on more water than the bailing crews could handle? As occurred on the *Empire City* in the storm, will some of the deadlights (port-holes) be found broken? Can the valve between the donkey-engine and the pumps be located and found closed? The deterioration may be too great to resolve any of these questions.

November 11, 1990: The salvage group announced through the *Columbus Dispatch*, the recovery from the wreck of one of the Easton's trunks, containing a well-preserved issue of the July 20, 1857, *New York News*, a number of items of clothing and valuable personal pieces, including "Ansel's dog-head watch fob, a beautiful gold or bronze piece with ruby-red eyes." This latest recovery rekindles my hopes for the finding in this treasure trove of history Audubon's sketches of 1849, Lewis Wood's unpublished manuscript on the Vigilance Committee, and the dispatches of the Latin diplomats. There is much more gold, and there are many more treasures to be found in the trunks of the passengers. The protective depth and the possibility of air-tight containers may have done their work of preservation.

---

[17] Seanor, "Sunken Treasure," 54-3.
[18] *San Francisco Chronicle*, Aug 15, 1990.

APPENDIX B

Aftermath—Personnel

What became of the participants in the drama of 1857? Extensive research data from census reports, biographies and local histories tells some of the story.

Records of the United States Naval Archives in Washington, D.C., state that **George E. Ashby** entered the Navy in 1859 in the grade of fourth assistant engineer. During the Civil War he served on the steam gunboat *Mahaska* in the North Atlantic Blockading Squadron. By 1864, Ashby held the grade of acting first assistant engineer, ranking after the officer grade of lieutenant. Having honorably served, he resigned from the Navy on October 28, 1864, by which time there was no longer a necessity for an Atlantic blockade. He later resided for many years at 106 Waverley Avenue, Brooklyn, N.Y.

William H. Aspinwall, the Isthmus railroad developer and first president of the PMSC, by the time he resigned from the corporation in 1856, had become one of the richest men in New York. He had a keen interest in politics but never sought public office, preferring philanthropic activities. His obituary described him as "a good man, generous if not open-handed, lenient to debtors, and willing to meet bankrupt merchants more than half way."[1]

John W. Audubon, whose sketches of California went down with the steamer, died as the result of a severe cold and fever in 1862, at the age of 49. His brother, Victor, identifier of the frigate bird, died of injuries incurred by a fall in 1860, less than three years after his letter to the New York Herald.

After their 1857 arrival in New York, **Captain Thomas** and **Jane Badger** spent a few years on the 111-acre Badger family farm known as Red Bank, near Marionville, Virginia.

The New York fund committee awarded Captain Badger a large and massive solid silver trumpet, elaborately engraved with mementos of the disaster, and bearing the inscription: "Presented to Captain Thomas W. Badger in token of their high appreciation of his conduct on board of the steamer *Central America*, at the time of the loss of that ill-fated vessel. New York, May 17, 1858."[2] For the rest of his life he highly prized this award, which is preserved in the Virginia Historical Society Museum, Richmond, Virginia.

Thomas and Jane Badger returned to California in 1861. They purchased

---

[1] Malone, Vol. I, 396.
[2] M.W. Wood, *History of Alameda County, California* (Oakland, CA: n.p.), 557.

ten acres of land on an inlet of San Francisco Bay, in Brooklyn, which is now East Oakland. They developed the Oakland property into a show place of fancy gardens of local and tropical trees and flowers, laid out in lawns and walks. The local train to Clinton, Hayward and San Leandro stopped near there, and by ferry boat and train, many visitors came from all over the Bay Area to see their garden.

The Museum of Oakland, California, has displayed an interesting painting by Joseph Lee of a nineteenth century residence, the home of Captain and Mrs. Thomas W. Badger.

> The most important place of public resort [said the Oakland City Directory of 1878-79,] especially on Sunday is Badger's Central Park, East Oakland, where there are highly ornamental grounds, and a large pavilion for dancing, and all the attractions found at public gardens. The excellent road around Oakland has eight large livery stables, all of them doing a prosperous business.

In an old shack in Badger's Park, according to local historian Wm. E. McCann, writer "Jack London lived with an old Negro washerwoman, Mammy Davis, when Jack was eight or ten years old."

Under two California administrations, Badger held an appointment as Pilot Commissioner for the port of San Francisco. Additionally, he was Marine Surveyor for one of the principal insurance companies.[3]

From their home at Badger Park, they had a commanding view of the Oakland Estuary, an inlet frequented by many vessels. In December, 1890, a barquentine, looking for refuge from a storm, made her way up the estuary. She was the *Jane A. Falkenburg*. The Badgers had not seen her for thirty-three years before she anchored "almost directly in front of Mrs. Badger's windows."[4]

On New Years Day, Jane Badger presented to Captain and Mrs. Bowes a forty-foot flag "of cream white bunting, bordered with thirty-six stars," made by an old pioneer, C.H. Smith, who did all the letters and designs in bright red. Said Thomas: "It will be with great pleasure and deep feeling to me when I send this flag to the breeze on the *Falkenburg*, in honor of whom she was named, and in memory of him who modeled[5] her." Jane also presented a small painting by Joseph Lee, bearing the date, name etc., and representing the vessel lying opposite the Badger home.

"Mrs. Thomas Badger led the vanguard of business women in the county. When her husband opened Badger's Park, she was his able assistant, . . . and every day she accompanied her husband on his rounds. He looked after 'the talent' and she looked after the cash box. She was the first woman cashier in any of the activities of pioneer days in this county."[6]

At the age of seventy-two, after an illness of a year, Thomas Badger died in

---

[3] Frank Clinton Merritt, *History of Alameda County, California*, Vol I, (Chicago, IL: S.J. Clarke Publishing Co, 1928), 149.

[4] *San Francisco Examiner*, 26 Feb 1893, 5-1, 2.

[5] Captain Falkenburg created the model upon which the construction was based. *San Francisco Examiner*, 26 Feb 1893, 5-1, 2.

Oakland on November 21, 1899. The *Oakland Tribune* thought it an impressive coincidence that as he breathed his last, "the ship, *Jane A. Falkenburg,* laden with lumber from Puget Sound, was over-turned . . . . Waterlogged and abandoned, she ran aground off the Mendecino Coast."

Jane, also after a prolonged illness, followed Thomas less than three months later, on February 9, 1900, at age 65. "During Captain Badger's late illness last Nov, Mrs. B. grew worse and she has been confined to her bed most of the time since her late husband's death." Mrs. Badger's "generous and kindly disposition won for her many warm personal friends . . . . She was a pioneer of the State and city."[7] The Badgers had no direct descendants. They were buried in San Francisco with Charles A. Falkenburg. On the gravesite a massive stone monument bore a sculpture of the barquentine, *Jane A. Falkenburg*.

Joseph McDonald Bassford returned to his wife and their four sons in Benicia, California. Seven years later, they bought 80 acres of land, located a few miles west of Vacaville, and planted "the finest kind of fruit, and among the same is a choice variety of cherries . . . . He is one among the earliest shippers in the valley."[8] Joseph and Julia Sprague Bassford had eight children. Subsequent to Julia's death, Bassford married Catherine McGrasey, and they had three children.

In 1891, he was described as an "old pioneer, jovial and fond of a good time generally . . . . Although his whiskers are silvered by the frost of many winters, still his eyes retain that brightness which is peculiar to men who are fond of the rod and gun."

Daniel Beaver had made his "find and started for home," said fellow passenger **Charles A. Vose**.[9] Daniel's 21-year-old-son, Gideon, remained in California. Beaver's tavern and other property were sold to settle the estate. His wife, Catherine, raised their five younger children, and her youngest son, Pierce, cared for her until her death in 1885. Her relative, Elias Lyman Baldwin, prospered in California and became known as "Lucky Baldwin."

James E. Birch died before he could learn of the success of his stage route from San Antonio to San Diego. The second run was made in thirty-four days, and was expected to be reduced to less than thirty.

In February 1858, his widow, Julia Birch went to Sacramento, California, where she sold her interest in the mail transportation line. There she met her husband's friend, vice-president of the stage line, Frank Shaw Stevens. They were married on July 24, 1858.[10]

Julia (Chace) Birch Stevens died in Swansea, February 18, 1871. The silver cup, delivered to her at Swansea by George Dawson, remained encased on a

---

[6] Mollie Conners, *Pioneer Women of Alameda County* (Oakland, CA: *Oakland Tribune*, n.d.), 5.
[7] *Oakland Tribune*, 9 Feb 1900, 5-4.
[8] *A Memorial and Biographical History of Northern California*, (Chicago: The Lewis Publishing Co, 1891), 601.
[9] Letter from Dr. Stephen Beaver, a descendant.
[10] *Sacramento Union*, 15 Feb 1858; *Sacramento Bee*, 19 Mar 1858; *Sacramento Union*, 20 Oct 1858, 2-5.

Tiffany Silver Serving Tray of James Birch
Courtesy, University of California, Berkeley, Department of Materials Science and Mineral Engineering

pedestal in the Birch mansion until 1930, when the second Mrs. Frank Stevens (Elizabeth Richmond Case) died at Swansea. The unique Tiffany silver collection and the silver cup were willed to the University of California, where they are on permanent display at the Hearst Memorial Mining Building, Berkeley, California.

William and Virginia Birch. The *San Francisco Bulletin* of October 24, 1857, ran a story regarding Mrs. Birch. "Many of our readers, may not be aware that this woman is 'Jenny French,' a notoriously bad character of this city, to whom is attributed the murder of the German by Backus, and his sentence to the State prison—for it was to resent a supposed insult to this woman that the murder was committed." Since Charlie Backus was a fellow Minstrel of Billy Birch, readers assumed that Charlie had murdered a German who in some way had insulted Virginia Birch.

The case concerned Mr. Rodman W. Backus, an employee of Wells, Fargo and Company, who had "relatives and friends . . . highly connected and very respectable." At 7:30 one evening, he arrived at his boarding house to find his landlady, Margaret French, distressed because a man had attempted to break in. Backus chased the man, "Frederick Oldman (alias Simon), a known vagrant." Oldman drew a knife, whereupon Backus drew his revolver, "aimed low so as not to injure him fatally," but hit him in the head and killed him. Rodman Backus was charged with murder. He was tried, found guilty of manslaughter, and after several delays was finally sentenced on February 25, 1856 to 2 1/2 years in the State prison, and fined $3000. After serving in San Quentin Prison from May 19, 1856 to August 3, 1858, he was pardoned by Governor John B. Weller.[11]

Whether Margaret French was Jenny French, or whether Jenny French was Virginia Birch is not known.[12] Billy and Virginia returned to San Francisco in 1859, where Billy continued his theatrical career. In 1883, he and Charley Backus were proprietors of the San Francisco Opera House,[13] where Lotta Crabtree, a famous performer, was often billed with Billy.

At Broadway and 29th Street, New York City, on April 24th, 1890, three old friends met. They were R.M. Hooley, formerly of the San Francisco Minstrels, Tom Maguire, proprietor of Maguire's Opera House, San Francisco, and the third was William Birch, once a star of the then defunct minstrels. Billy was described as "a fattish little fellow with a merry twinkle in his eye and a mustache and goatee that are almost white."[14] To the New York press, Billy described at some length his experiences as a minstrel with Charlie Backus and Sam Wells, of whom he said, with his bass voice could imitate "a clap of indignant thunder, . . . which was about as good as the genuine article any day in the week."[15]

Birch made a fortune on the stage, much of it entertaining in the mining camps, and was conservative with his money, but said he "lost nearly all of it in the end. I had a friend in whom I misplaced my confidence to the tune of $200,000. Then I lost more in bad speculations." The year 1891 found him "back in harness and working at a salary I once would have spurned with a bitter scorn." Then, perhaps having in mind his experience on the *Central America*, he added, "but I suppose I ought to be thankful that I'm alive," and, too, he reflected on the loss by then of his two old partners, Backus and Wells.

---

[11] In 1887, writer James O'Meara somewhat sensationally discussed the Backus case. Some of the description of the event, according to the actual testimony, was a travesty. I have carefully reviewed the Transcript of Record of *The People vs Rodman M. Backus* (the defendant signed his name "W. Rodman Backus"), and found fundamental discrepancies between the court record and later writings, with the exception of the facts described in *San Francisco Daily Alta*, 25 Jan 1855, 2-2. It is notable that the file contains the testimony of one Margaret French, landlady of the Stouts Alley rooming house in which Backus lived. In the record of court proceedings there is no reference to "Jennie" French, and although there may have been more to the case than disclosed in court, I have found no way of connecting Margaret or Jenny French to Virginia Birch. Doyce Nunis, comp., *San Francisco Vigilance Committee of 1856: Three Views*, (Los Angeles: Los Angeles Westerners, 1971).

[12] *California Police Gazette*, 15 Oct 1859, 3-3, 6.

[13] *San Francisco Opera House Theatrical Notes*, bound volume in the Bancroft Library, Univ. of Ca., Berkeley: 10 Apr 1883.

[14] *San Francisco Theatre Research*, WPA Project 8386, Vol 2, Monograph III, Tom Maguire, Vol 13, "Minstrelsy," (Northern California, 1939). Lois Foster Rodecape, "Tom Maguire, Napoleon of the Stage," *Calif. Hist. Soc. Qtly.*, XX: 289-311 and XXI: 264-6.

[15] *San Francisco Call*, 6 Oct 1890, 3-5.

Billy was very fond of clams and fish of all kinds, and remarked that his wife, Virginia, knew how to cook them better than any chef. At his house on West Fourth Street, New York City, his family consisted of his wife and aged mother.

On April 20, 1898, the New York Times reported that "Billy Birch, the old-time California Minstrel died this afternoon in a small room on the top floor of 76 Seventh Avenue." He was "conscious to the last . . . his wife was with him, as were some of his fellow Elks, who bore the expense of his illness."

Naval records indicate that **John Black**, boatswain of the *Central America*, and whose life-boat transported the author's and many other person's ancestors to the *Marine*, served the Navy as a mate from 1864 until he resigned February 18, 1870. He resided in New York City until at least 1879.

Robert Turnbull Brown returned to Sacramento, California, where he continued his clothing business. Brown died about 1878, leaving his widow.

Hiram Burt, as master of the schooner *James Neilson*, enroute Truxillo, Honduras, went ashore on the reef at Sappoblo Keys, near Omoa. He and his crew were all desperately ill with fever taken at Omoa, and while in that condition on the reef, his ship was boarded by the crew of the Honduras schooner *Bolu de Ora*, who proceeded to dismantle and destroy the schooner.

The indomitable Burt crawled out of his berth, revolver in hand, and threatened to shoot the first man who dared cut another rope. The effect was immediate. Under his direction the *James Neilson* was gotten off the reef. The news report of the incident said: "Capt. Burt has had a very discouraging part to perform—extremely ill, without friends or means, in a strange country, where there is no Consul to assist him—he has succeeded in surmounting all obstacles, and has saved his vessel, which would have been destroyed."[16]

Hiram, a seventh generation American, died in Taunton on January 19, 1866 at the age of 53, leaving his widow, Frances D. (Hood) Burt.

In 1860, the **Casey twins**, then twenty-seven years of age, were farming in Sebastian County, Arkansas. **Randolph** and his wife, Lucinda, had two sons, as did **Jacob** and Nancy. The same value, eight hundred dollars, was placed on each Casey farm. In the 1870 census, Jacob's widow and four children, Randolph, his wife and five children were still on their farms. The adults and older children could neither read nor write.

Henry H. Childs: On September 27, 1857 [said *The New York Times* of the 28th,] at the Fourteenth Street Presbyterian Church, in New York City, pastor Asa D. Smith called upon Mr. Childs to make some remarks. Childs, a member of the church, briefly told his story, saying that while he was "floating on his plank that awful night," and when he thought he was "out of sight of any . . . [he heard] distinctly recited by another person, who evidently [like Childs] thought himself alone, the Lord's Prayer. The incident was touchingly told, and its recital thrilled the audience."[17] Henry continued in his New York

---

[16] Unidentified news clipping in Easton file. William Lee Burt, "Descendants of Richard Burt," (typewritten ms., n.d.), 94, 222.

[17] *New York Times*, 28 Sep 1857, 8-2.

City oils business. After the Civil War he was in New York City as a broker in the custom house. In 1883, he resided in New Brighton.[18]

Major Jacob Brown Clark,[19] went immediately from Baltimore to St. Louis, where he was interviewed by the *Missouri Republican* on September 24, 1857. After visiting with his brother, he returned to California, where in the Sacramento River floods of 1860-61, he again lost all his belongings. He served for a time as Sheriff of Sutter County, then moved to Colusa County, embarked in mining ventures and joined the Colusa Masonic Lodge. He was not married.

During his lifetime, Clark made five trips to his former home in Missouri. He died in Williams, California, in 1898, at age 87.

After recovering from his physical afflictions, **George Dawson**, delivered to Mrs. Julia Birch, the silver cup entrusted to him by James Birch. The cup was engraved, and later added: "Saved from steamer *Central America* lost 12th Sept. 1857."

Dawson returned to the mining town of Oroville, California. In mid-1858 he turned up in Victoria, British Columbia, and in September of 1860, traveling by canoe, he was reported drowned in the Gulf of Georgia while traversing from Victoria to the Fraser River, in Canada.[20]

In December 1857 Lieutenant **John D. Dement** returned to California on board the *John L. Stephens,* Captain Pearson. H.D. Barrows, a fellow passenger returning from his eastern visit, became acquainted with him, and was so interested in Dement's account of the *Central America* disaster that he made detailed notes of it in his diary.[21]

By 1860, Dement, with his brother, William C. Dement, and others, was involved in various enterprises, among them, the establishment of the Oregon City Woolen Mfg. Co.,[22] the second such mill in Oregon Territory, the other being the Willamette Woolen Mills at Salem. In the same year, the brothers, with Captain Hedges, built the stern-wheel steamer *Rival,* and placed her on the Portland to Oregon City route of the Willamette River.

William died in Oregon City, January 2, 1865, leaving his wife of 19 years, Olivia, and children. An early pioneer to Oregon, he had traveled west with the first large organized party, — "The Wagon Train of '43."[23]

On January 24, 1891, the Salem *Daily Oregon Statesman* reported the death of a pioneer, Colonel John D. Dement, at Portland, he "having been failing in health for some time." Dement, then 65 years of age, left his wife, Christine, and a son, Ralph M. Dement, a former police judge in Portland.

---

[18] New York City Directories.
[19] *William's Farmer,* 17 Sep 1898, 1-3, 4. *Marysville Pioneer Association Register,* 1869.
[20] Myrtle Archer, "The Sinking of the Central America," *California Highway Patrolman,* (Feb 1981), 6-32.
[21] Barrows, *Central America,* 70-75.
[22] Alfred L. Lomax, "Oregon City Woolen Mill," *Oreg. Hist. Qtly.*, XXXII, (Mar-Dec 1932): 240-5. James O'Meara, "Early Steamboating Era on the Willamette," Oreg. Hist. Qtly., XLIV, (Mar-Dec 1943): 142-3.
[23] James Willis Nesmith, *Two Addresses* (Ye Galleon Press, Fairfield, WA, 1978), 12.

Adeline and Ansel Easton canceled their trip to Europe, spent some time with relatives in New York, then returned to their home in San Francisco. In 1860, Ansel bought at a sheriff's sale fifteen hundred acres of land on the peninsula, south of San Francisco, where he and Adeline established their home. That land became all of North Burlingame and part of Hillsborough.[24] Addie's brother, Darius Ogden Mills bought another fifteen hundred acres just north of the Easton property, and his tract became the city of Millbrae. His bank became the Bank of California.

Their daughter, Jennie, and son, Ansel Mills, were born in San Mateo County. His son was only three when Easton died at Millbrae at the age of forty-nine, August 23, 1868.

In the California pioneer tradition, Jennie Easton married Colonel Charles F. Crocker, son of Charles Crocker, one of the "Big Four" who projected and completed the Union Pacific Railroad system. When Jennie Easton Crocker, died shortly after the birth of her daughter, Jennie Adeline Crocker, Addie Easton raised her and her brother, Charles.

In 1896, when the *San Francisco Chronicle* recounted the tragedy of 1857, Mrs. Easton was "sojourning in Europe," and in 1913 she was an Honorary Vice-President of the Panama Pacific Exposition in San Francisco.

In 1916, San Francisco newspapers reported that Mrs. Adeline Mills Easton, grandmother of Charles Templeton Crocker and Jennie Crocker Whitman, had died in Burlingame on June 12th, and was buried from St. Matthew Episcopal Church, San Mateo, which had been established in 1864 by her brother-in-law, Rev. Giles A. Easton. She was 87 years of age.

The Eastons had retrieved the ship's bell of the *Sonora* when she was salvaged, "had it inscribed with the account of their adventure," and donated it to St. Matthews Church.[25] It had rung on the morning she and Ansel were married, and it tolled from St. Matthew's during her funeral.

In 1922, Addie's grandson, Charles Templeton Crocker, was instrumental in the "reorganization and revitalization" of the California Historical Society.[26]

Nearly four decades after the wreck of the steamer, the story of **William Ede** appeared in the *San Francisco Chronicle*, February 23, 1896. He had gone to Wisconsin for his January 1858 wedding. He and his bride, Catherine, age 16, returned to San Francisco on the 1st of April of the same year. Ede became a successful roads contractor, and was treasurer of his Masonic Lodge for many years, residing with his family in San Francisco. He died there in 1899 at the age of 72.[27]

---

[24] *Qtly. of Calif. Hist.*, Vol XVII, 255. Alan Hynding, *From Frontier to Suburb, The Story of the San Mateo Peninsula*, (San Mateo: Star Publishing Co., 1982).

[25] In April 1986, during Sunday services, the bell disappeared. Myrtle "Cookie" Potter, *Childhood Years in My Burlingame Paradise, 1923-1987*, pamphlet, (Burlingame, [CA] Public Library: Dec 1987), 7. *The Church of St. Matthew, San Mateo, Its Growth and Its Ministry, 1864-1958*, (San Mateo, CA: n.p., n.d.), 4.

[26] *San Francisco Chronicle*, "This World," 30 Jul 1989.

[27] *History of Mission Lodge #169*, Free and Accepted Masons, Diamond Jubilee, 1863-1938, (San Francisco: n.p., 1938), 118. Mrs. Bernice Ede Campbell, "The Five Ede Brothers," Plumas Co. Hist. Soc. Pubn: No. 20, pg 19, and No. 30: "Abraham Ede."

In 1857, while at Norfolk, **Jane Fell** observed her 21st birthday. She and her two sons took the train to Baltimore and her home in Glasgow, Iowa. "Her destitute condition excited much sympathy at Burlington. A sum of money was raised for her benefit." [*State Gazette*]. Shortly after arriving home, her baby son died from exposure. In 1860, she married Daniel Fiedler and they had three daughters. She died in 1926 at age 90 and was survived by her daughters and son, **David Fell**.[28]

Willard F. Fletcher[29] lost all of his money in the shipwreck. In 1862, he again went West, spending short periods in Idaho, the Cariboo mines near Portland (Oregon), Nevada, Montana and, in 1865, Stockton, California, where he worked for four years as a moulder, then filled the duties of Chief of Police. Fletcher was a successful police officer. He organized the Stockton force, then in 1874, moved to Oakland, California, where, in 1877, he was appointed a member of the police force. He became captain of the force and held that position until April 1897, when he was appointed Chief of Police of Oakland. He was a Mason for thirty-five years, a Knight Templar and charter member of the Oakland Commandery.[30] His only son died in 1911. Fletcher died in Los Angeles, August 24, 1924, at age ninety-two.

James M. Frazer, "years later, named his son Herndon Frazer,"[31] after Commander Herndon. Frazer was awarded a gold watch.

Lieutenant Lardner Gibbon,[32] Commander Herndon's partner in the exploration of the Amazon, was born in Pennsylvania, about 1820, and resided in Philadelphia County at the time of his appointment as an acting midshipman, December 22, 1837. After serving for nearly two years at the Washington Naval Observatory, he was ordered to join Lieutenant Herndon in South America. Gibbon resigned from the Navy, May 15, 1857, lived for years in North Carolina, and died in Pennsylvania at over ninety years of age.

In New York, the Relief Committee requested **Dr. Obed Harvey** to remain for a few days and continue relieving the sufferers.

Harvey had in his possession a cane with a large and elaborately carved gold head set with gold quartz. "At the suggestion of a friend he had cut the head off and threw the stick away." He brought it safely through, and exhibited it at Barnum's, New York City, on September 21st. It was valued at $50.[33]

For the first time since the disaster, in San Francisco, June 15, 1858, there was a "joyful reunion" between Dr. Harvey and Second Officer James Frazer, when they met unexpectedly in the city. Their experience when adrift in the sea was recalled.[34]

---

[28] *Iowa State Democrat*, 3 Oct 1857, 1-4. *Keokuk Daily Post*, IA, 3 Oct 1857, 2-1. *Fairfield Ledger*, 14 Apr 1926, 2-5.
[29] Oakland Tribune, *Alameda County*, 202.
[30] *A History of the Masonic Widows' and Orphans' Home, Decoto, Alameda Co., CA*, (San Francisco: Lewis Roesch Co, 1898).
[31] Judy Conrad, *American Tragedy*, 3.
[32] Naval Historical Center Archives.
[33] *Richmond Daily Dispatch*, 22 Sep 1857, 1.
[34] *Daily Alta California*, 16 Jun 1848, 2-3.

The doctor returned to his home in Placerville, California, and from 1860 to 1863 served as State Senator (a Union Democrat) of El Dorado County, and Assemblyman representing Sacramento County, in 1863.[35]

In 1869, Harvey married Susan Mitchell Hall, of Connecticut, who, on April 27, 1855, had departed New York on the steamer *Northern Light* for Central America. With her mother and sister, she had proceeded to San Francisco from San Juan, by the Nicaragua route.[36]

On 3,000 acres of the Rancho Sanjon de los Moquelumnes, Obed Harvey founded the town of Galt, about fifteen miles south of Sacramento, California, where, at age 68, he died at his residence. He was survived by a son, and daughter, Genevieve Harvey. The eulogies of Dr. Harvey included a recollection of Judge Heacock entitled *A Touching Incident:*

> During the voyage the Doctor had given gratuitous medical attention to a man on board, then during the time of greatest peril, Harvey joined the other passengers in passing buckets. While at labor he happened to glance in his stateroom, and "saw the patient whom he had befriended trying to cut the gold top from a cane the Doctor greatly prized. The spectacle at such a time of what appeared to be gross ingratitude, as well as shameless cupidity, filled Dr. Harvey with amazement and disgust. Shortly afterward the patient went down with the ship. But great was the Doctor's surprise when he found the gold top of his cane in his own pocket, to where the doomed patient had found some chance to convey it. It then was plain that the poor fellow, himself despairing of escape from a watery grave, had given thought to his benefactor, laboriously hacking away at the cane until he succeeded in saving the gold top for its owner. The Doctor often said it was one of the most touching incidents of his "long life."[37]

The **William Lewis Herndons** had only one child, their daughter, Ellen, who, on September 19, 1857 was described by the *New York Times* as "a lovely young lady with one of the best singing voices in the country." On January 13, 1880, the serious illness of Mrs. Chester A. Arthur was announced. Ellen (Herndon) Arthur suffered from an attack of pneumonia, which quickly took her life at age 42. Three days earlier, her husband, then Governor of New York, was called to her side from a visit to Albany. She died at their home in New York City, and was removed to Albany for burial.[38]

It was suggested by her friends that "The shock and nervous tension caused by her bereavement and long sad journey," less than two years previously to bring from France the remains of her mother, had impaired her health. She had been visibly affected by it. Francis Elizabeth (Hansbrough) Herndon, the wife

---

[35] Hubert Howe Bancroft, *The History of California, 1849-50*, 271. Charles E. DeLong, "Journal of Charles E. DeLong -1857," *Calif. Hist. Soc. Qtly.*, X, Note 12, 287.

[36] Susan Mitchell Hall, "The Diary of a Trip from Ione to Nevada in 1859," Intro. by Genevieve Harvey, *Calif. Hist. Soc. Qtly.*, XVII: 75-80.

[37] *Sacramento Bee*, Jan 23, 1894, 1-1, quoting the *San Francisco Bulletin.*

[38] *The New York Times*, 16 Jan 1880.

of Commander Herndon, died April 5, 1878, while on a visit to Hyeres, France, on the Mediterranean coast.

Ellen had been married to General Arthur since her father's birthday, October 25th, 1859. Among her friends, she was known as "an amateur vocalist of most extraordinary merit, and as a genial, accomplished lady and devoted wife and mother."

Mrs. Arthur left two children, Chester Alan Arthur Jr., born July 25, 1865, and Ellen Herndon Arthur, born November 21, 1871.[39] Her first child, William Lewis Herndon Arthur, died in 1863 at the age of thirty-one months.

For his remaining years, President Arthur mourned his wife, and to Herndon's brother, Brodie, remarked: "Honors to me are not what they used to be." In the White House, he daily had a fresh bouquet of flowers placed before Ellen's portrait.[40] Arthur died November 18, 1886, at the age of 56.

According to folklore, [the town of] Herndon, Virginia, was named after Commander William Lewis Herndon . . . . A meeting was held by local residents to choose an acceptable name and, according to town legend, a survivor of the *Central America* happened into the meeting. He told the group about the heroism of the ship's captain, and those at the meeting declared the new name to be Herndon.[41]

Aaron R. Holcomb, the forty-year-old black saloon cook of the *Central America* lived with his wife, Ann, and five children in New York City, where he was employed as a cook. He died about 1900.

Jabez Howes returned to San Francisco to continue his partnership with his brothers George and Henry. Their firm, George Howes & Co. developed into a prosperous shipping business, which played a major role in the San Francisco trade for about three decades.

The Howes brothers owned a large fleet of sailing vessels including two famous clipper ships, the *David Crockett* and *Young America*. The latter has been described as one of the *"many splendid products of the yard of William H. Webb in New York City."*[42] In spite of the *Central America* disaster, the Howes apparently had no misgivings whatsoever regarding the quality of shipbuilding by the Webb yard.

Jabez pursued a life of financial success and ease. He was a gentleman seaman, enthusiastic yachtsman, and was particularly interested in racing. He was a life member of the Pacific Yacht Club, and transported his personal yacht, *Annie*, around the Horn on the *Three Brothers*, formerly the U.S. Navy steamer *Vanderbilt*, which the brothers converted into a giant clipper ship.

---

[39] Wilson, *Presidents*, 233.
[40] Barbara Crookshanks, "Portrait of a Romance—Nell Arthur," Fredericksburg *Times*, (Aug 1984), 15.
[41] Office of the Town Clerk, Herndon, Virginia, *Citizen's Guide*, 1. Herndon Chamber of Commerce, *Herndon Handbook* (Herndon, VA: 1988).
[42] Karl Kortum, *An Old San Francisco Firm* (San Francisco: 1977). Sanderson, *An Ocean Cruise . . .* , (San Francisco: H.S. Crocker & Co, for Pacific Yacht Club, 1884).

Reverses overtook the three brothers. From the shipping business Jabez Howes worked into insurance and finally became the agent of the Dumbarton Land and Improvement Company. He died in 1897, leaving a widow and two step-daughters.[43]

Gustav Jorgen Jacobsen,[44] mate of the *Ellen*, was, in 1857, a young man of 21 years. Born on the island of Hisoy, south of Arendal (Captain Johnsen also resided on Hisoy), he had passed his examination as mate at the age of 19. Jacobsen died in 1916.

Captain Anders Johnsen. Through the Swedish consul, Mr. Robertson, the captain asked for permission to have repairs made on the *Ellen* at the Portsmouth Navy Yard.[45] By direction of the Secretary of the Navy, this work was done at U.S. government expense. Johnsen had avoided the embarrassment of what he considered undue praise for his dramatic rescue of the passengers, and said that he felt the good he did was sufficient reward.

On October 7, 1857, President James Buchanan recognized the humane performance of Captain Johnsen and awarded him "a magnificent gold pocket chronometer and chain, which is said to be one of the best the world can produce." said the *New York Times*. "Aside from its intrinsic value at a cost of about $350," the circumstances surrounding its presentation would add greatly to its value, "and will be regarded, in some sense, as a testimonial from the whole people, in the person of their Chief Executive." The captain being at Portsmouth, Virginia, the award was presented there by S.T. Sawyer, Collector of Customs, in a ceremony at Mechanics Exchange. The following inscription was engraved on the cover of the chronometer:

> The President
> of the
> United States
> To
> Captain A. Johnson,
> Norwegian Barque Ellen,
> for his humane, prompt, zealous and
> successful efforts, in rescuing persons from the wreck of the
> steamer "Central
> America."
> 1857.

Reported simply as A. Johnson, the captain's name was repeatedly misspelled. The disposition of the chronometer is not known by the Norsk Sjofartsmuseum, Oslo, Norway.

---

[43] *San Francisco Call*, 31 Jul 1897, 14-5. *San Francisco Examiner*, 31 Jul 1897, 7-2.

[44] Dannevig, *Vi Menn*, Norway, Mar 1966, 26-7. *Agderposten*, Arendal, Norway, 3 Aug 1965. Jac. Worm-Muller, *Den norske sjofarts historie* (The Norwegian Maritime History); *Arendal, fra fortid til nutid* (a local history of Arendal), published by The City of Arendal, Kristiania, (1933).

[45] *Baltimore Sun*, 24 Sep 1857, 2-3, quoting *Portsmouth Transcript*.

On October 22, 1857 from Norfolk, Virginia, Captain Johnsen wrote the following letter to Ansel Easton:[46]

> Dear Sir: Having completed my repairs and all my accounts being settled up and being about to leave for England, I feel that I must again express to you my extreme thankfulness & sense of great gratitude for the benevolent & kindly interest you have manifested in my behalf, in times to come I shall look back to the circumstances that brought us together with mingled feelings of pain & pleasure, with painful because so many of our fellow creatures were called before their God, almost unwarned & in so short a period of time, with pleasure because I was the humble instrument in God's hands by which so many of my fellow beings were rescued from a watery grave, your name and that of your estimable lady will be names that I shall always remember in my journey through life with feelings of interest & hoping that you may enjoy health & happy for many a year to come, believe me, Yours sincerely, A. Johnsen.

Added to Johnsen's letter was a note by D^n. Robertson saying that the captain had "never ceased talking about you [Easton] since his return. His vessel is now in order, & I trust he will reach his destination in safety. He is a most deserving man."

In about 1920, Ansel Mills Easton, son of Addie and Ansel Ives Easton, wrote his recollection that a few days before Christmas, 1881, Captain Johnsen, visiting New York City, was walking along Broad Street "when he came face to face with a skyscraper, 12 stories in those days. He saw inscribed over the entrance, 'Mills Building'."

Johnsen found the office of D.O. Mills, introduced himself, and asked, "Are you related to Adeline Mills Easton?" When Mills replied that he was her brother, the captain asked to know all about the Eastons, whom he had not seen for 24 years. The following day, Johnsen met the younger Ansel, who was spending the Christmas holidays with his uncle. Easton said: "I shall never forget that day; how we checked and double checked over the wreck of the *Central America,* and he told me how my father, through the State Department had President Buchanan sign a testimonial for his services in saving the lives of forty-nine passengers. The following week he sailed and that is the last I ever heard or saw of him again."

According to the Norsk Sjofartsmuseum in Arendal, Captain Johnsen died sometime in the 1880's, the 1881 visit probably being his last to the United States.

Frank A. Jones has neither been found in the city directories nor censuses of New York or California, nor positively identified in Kentucky. The many professional gamblers sailing with the gold rush steamers often used fictitious names to preserve their identities. Frank made repeated steamer trips. Was the personable Jones one of these? Or was he truly Frank Jones: wealthy Kentucky

---

[46] Adeline Easton preserved the letter, now at the San Mateo Co. Hist. Assoc. Archives.

planter, New York socialite, gambler? *Index to the Argonauts of California*, by Haskins, reveals that F.A. Jones, a member of the Green River Mining Company, arrived in California from Kentucky on April 22, 1849. Was he Frank A. Jones?

Mrs. Almira Mead Kittredge returned to Santa Cruz and her husband, Dr. Francis M. Kittredge. Their son, Ruel W. Kittredge, during the Civil War, enlisted in the cavalry service, and on February 28, 1863, at age 23, died of exposure-induced consumption. On September 4, 1866, the California Society of Pioneers elected Dr. Kittredge to membership;[47] he died in 1879, at age 69. Almira Kittredge died in 1885, at 68. The family is buried under a sizeable monument in the Old Cemetery (Evergreen), Santa Cruz, California.

George Law, after leaving the United States Mail Steamship Co., continued in successful business enterprises, including the acquiring of the Brooklyn and Staten Island ferries. He died in his 5th Avenue residence on November 18, 1881, at the age of 75.

We are indebted to **Frank Leslie** and his illustrator, **Frederick Anderson**, for many drawings depicting the catastrophe of the *Central America*. It is coincidental that Mr. Leslie's funeral occurred in New York, the day before that of Ellen Arthur.[48]

On Thursday, October 22, 1857, the San Francisco Courts adjourned "out of respect for" attorney **Rufus A. Lockwood**, lost with the *Central America*. **Mrs. Harriet Hill Lockwood**, **Rose Alice**, **Rufus, Jr.**, and **Harriet** returned to their large farm at Lafayette, Indiana, where Harriet remained until her death, about 1897. Her husband had named her the sole heir and executrix of his estate. This included a bond for the sum of one hundred thousand dollars by John C. Fremont to said decedent in the month of September, 1857, payable out of profits from the Mariposa mine in California. Mrs. Lockwood is "not believed to have collected on the debt of Major General John C. Fremont."[49]

The 1907-8 City Directory of Lafayette, Indiana lists Rufus A. Lockwood, Jr., occupation collector, and wife, residing at 1101 Tippecanoe Avenue.

Oliver Perry Manlove returned to his father's Muscoda, Wisconsin, home, where he farmed. He entered the army in November 1863, was assigned to Co. H, 37th Wisconsin Regiment, and in 1864 participated in a battle at Petersburg, VA. At the huge explosion under the Confederate fort, his unit was ordered to advance around the crater. "It was death to advance, death to retreat and death to remain where we were." They lost 4000. 1600, including Manlove, were taken prisoner at Petersburg, July 30, 1864, and confined at Danville prison.

After he returned home, he married Carrie Carrel and raised two sons, Norman C. and Howard P. Manlove. He engaged in literary pursuits and

---

[47] *Daily Alta California*, 4 Sep 1866, 1-4.
[48] *The New York Times*, 16 Jan 1880.
[49] Hastings, *Lockwood*, 97-110.

contributed to several journals, among which were the *Waverly Magazine* and *New York Weekly*. He was active in civic affairs, a member of the first board of Muscoda High School (1877) and served as town assessor for two years.[50]

Manlove later resided in Park Rapids, Hubbard County, Minnesota. In 1901, on reading an item from *The Bee*, a Sacramento, California, newspaper, concerning *Central America* passenger Mary E. Swan, he promptly wrote to the Sacramento paper. At the request of *The Bee*, he prepared, at age 70, an account of his recollections of the disaster, and his story appeared in the February 1, 1902, edition of the paper. In 1915, at age 84, he wrote his autobiography based on his journals, letters and recollections.

Amanda Marvin departed New York City for Chicago by rail, on September 28, 1857, in charge of Mr. Bryant, of the St. Paul and Fond du Lac Railroad. She had been provided with $50 cash in addition to clothing and trunks valued at $250. At Corning, upstate New York, the train was derailed, her trunks destroyed, and their contents almost ruined. She proceeded to her Buffalo (or Chicago) home with new trunks provided by the railroad company.[51] In 1860, a Mrs. Amanda Marvin resided in Hector, Schuyler Co., New York.

Commander **Matthew Fontaine Maury**, in desperately hoping to save the Union, devised a "New Jersey Plan" in which he proposed for that state to act as mediator between North and South. Although "contrary to his wishes and better judgment,"[52] Maury gave his services to his State of Virginia when she left the Union during the Civil War. In 1862, he was sent on a mission to England. The year 1865 found him in Mexico, where Maximilian, Archduke of Austria and Emperor of Mexico, to promote colonization of Mexico, appointed him Imperial Commissioner of Colonization and naturalized him.[53] When this plan faltered, he returned to Virginia. During his later years, Commander Maury was Professor of Physics at the Virginia Military Institute. He died at Lexington, Virginia, February 1, 1873.

Captain John N. McGowan:[54] At the commencement of the Civil War, commanding the steamer *Star of the West*, McGowan was sent to the relief of General Anderson and the small garrison at Fort Sumter. In trying to effect a landing on January 9, 1861, to supply the garrison with food, he was fired upon by a battery on Morris Island, obliging him to abandon the attempt and put to sea. The first gun of the Civil War was fired at the *Star of the West*, Captain McGowan.[55]

In 1862, McGowan organized and directed the operations of the Mosquito

---

[50] *History of Grant County, Wisconsin* (1881), 804, 967. Costello N. Holford, *History of Grant County, Wisconsin*, (Lancaster, WI: The Teller Print, 1900). Manlove, *Autobiography*.
[51] Jack Finney, *Forgotten News* (Garden City, NY: Doubleday & Co, 1983), 276.
[52] Reddick, *Herndon, Maury* . . . , 59. *Descendants* . . . *Fontaine*, 128-30.
[53] *The Mexican Times* (English), 11 Nov 1865, 2-1.
[54] Naval Historical Center Archives. Lewis R. Hamersly, comp., *The Records of Living Officers of the U.S. Navy and Marine Corps*, (Philadelphia: J.B. Lippincott & Co., 1878).
[55] Long, E.B., *The Civil War Day by Day*, Garden City, 1971, 5 Jan thru 11 Jan 1861. Navy Hist. Center Arch.

Fleet (second line of defense of coast line) in Chesapeake Bay, and in June of 1863, then as a Navy captain, commanded the Revenue Cutter *Cuyahoga* in search of the Confederate States bark *Tacony*, which had been attacking Northern shipping.

He retired in 1871, and died at Elizabeth, New Jersey, January 18, 1891, at age eighty-five, survived by his son, Rear Admiral John N. McGowan, Jr.

After a visit with his brother in New York City, **Judge Monson**[56] returned to Sacramento, California. The law firm of Monson & Sunderland was in Latham's Building, 53 and 55 J Street. In 1860, he sat on the governor's Board of Commissioners to Select Plans for a State Capitol Building at Sacramento, and in 1861 presided over the California Pioneer Society, in Sacramento.

In 1865, Monson returned to New York where he was president of a law firm at 40 Wall Street. He revisited Sacramento in 1892, and at age eighty died at his New York City residence of Bright's disease on January 1, 1902.

C.A. Norlund: A sailmaker on the *Ellen*. For voluntarily plunging into the black sea to save several passengers, Norlund was awarded a silver medal. In 1966 the medal was in the possession of a descendant, Sigmund Norlund, of Olso, Norway.[57]

Mrs. Eleanor O'Connor and her son, **Henry**, tarried briefly in New York after the wreck until contact was made with **Louis Bonneau's** aunt, Mrs. Jane Dees, who thanked Mrs. O'Connor "most heartily for her care of him during the trying scenes on board the *Central America* and afterwards," as reported by the *New York Herald*.

On October 3, 1857, the *New York Irish Weekly* reported: "One night last week, the steamer *New World*, then the largest paddle-wheel steamer built (385 feet in length), ran into a fleet of canal boats, Mrs. O'Connor and son, two of the rescued passengers of the *Central America*, were on board at the time of the occurrence. Their terror was very great, which is not to be wondered at, after their recent escape." They were interviewed at their home by the *Albany Evening Journal* on September 23, 1857. In 1865, Mrs. Ellen O'Connor lived in Albany, N.Y. Her twenty-five year old son, attorney Henry T. O'Connor, boarded with her.

Madame Rosalie Pahud, and her three children, traveled to Paris. She died in 1860 at the age of 37, and was buried in Hoboken, New Jersey. Francois invested in a promising but unsuccessful gold mining enterprise, and was a partner in one or more mining claims. The Swiss adventurer then proceeded to Mountain Ranch, Calaveras County, California, where records of 1860 find him as Frank Pahud, miner, and for some time he resided at Gold Hill, then Utah Territory. In the 1860s, concurrent with Matthew Maury's association there, he was a purveyor of goods and supplies to Maximilian, the

---

[56] *Sacramento, CA City Directory*, 1861-2; *New York City Directory*, 1876-1900; *Sacramento Bee*, 3 Jan 1902, 4-5. *Sacramento Union*, 21 May, 1860, 3-1.

[57] Letter to N.E. Klare, 14 Feb 1989, from Else Marie Thorstvedt, Norsk Sjofartsmuseum, Oslo, Norway.

Augustine Pahud Renault,
Piedmont, CA, 1934
Courtesy, Author Family
Collection

Austrian emperor of Mexico. He was killed at Mazatlan, Mexico, in 1865, either by bandits, or by opponents of the Maximilian regime.

The orphaned children, **Augustine, Edouard,** and their **younger brother**, name unknown, resided in New York. Edouard married and eventually settled in Bordeaux, France, where he died in 1922. His two daughters returned to New York. At age twenty-two, Augustine Pahud returned alone to San Francisco, in the vain hope of determining precisely what had befallen her father. There she met and married Louis J. Renault. Augustine and Louis Renault had eight children, six of whom grew to adulthood, all surviving the San Francisco earthquake of 1906. On November 11, 1941, Augustine died at age ninety-three. Based on current information, she was the last survivor of the great shipwreck of 1857. Two of her long-lived daughters lived beyond age one-hundred, and the third to nearly ninety-three years.

Theodore Payne,[58] remained in New York with his wife, Nancy, and sons, Theodore F. and Warren R., until February of 1861, when they departed for the return trip to California. After a layover at Acapulco, Mexico, they arrived in San Francisco on Friday, April 4th. Payne was taken suddenly ill on Saturday while sitting in the room of his business partner, Mr. Dewey, removed to his apartment in the Oriental Hotel. His condition gradually grew worse, and he became delirious. His physician, Dr. Gray, reported the *Daily Alta California,* "found that he was taken with Panama fever of a malignant type—the symptoms increased in virulence, and terminated in his death, Tuesday, April 9, 1861 . . . .The fever of which he died he must have taken at Acapulco, where he went on short stay of the [steamer] *Cortes* there."

---

[58] *California,* 1900, 227. Pendleton, *San Francisco Fire Co.,* 94.

In 1900, Payne was recalled as "a man of many parts, and diversified talents," and one of the best known and "most widely respected citizens" of San Francisco's early days. He "always threw the weight of his influence into the scale for honest government, and purity in politics, and the administration of justice."[59] He earned the esteem and respect of his community, and, because of these and many other favorable comments, I consider him to have been a most reliable witness in the support of George Ashby.

Susan Pettorous, the nurse employed by Mrs. Thayer, according to the *New York Times* on 1 Oct 1857, remained in New York City to file for letters of administration for her husband's estate, valued at $4,000, a considerable sum. He had accumulated the money in California, as a storekeeper. **Charles** and Susan had been married in San Francisco.

Mrs. Pettorous asked to have the hearing delayed because she had hoped that her husband might be rescued. He was not. Meanwhile, Margaret Davidson appeared on the scene, claiming she was married to Charles in 1843, and presented a marriage certificate as proof. Evidence indicated, however, that Margaret had since remarried without knowing the status of Charles. The disposition of the estate is unknown.

William Plass returned to New York, married, had a child and in 1860 worked as a farm laborer.

Albert Priest returned to his wife, Teressa, and resided at Jamaica, Long Island, New York, in 1860.

In 1860, **Jacob Quincer**, his wife Catharine and two sons resided at Watertown, New York, where he was employed as a baker.

David Raymond was awarded by the *Central America* Fund Committee a medal for his "humane and successful efforts toward saving the lives of those unfortunates cast adrift upon the ocean by the foundering of the steamer *Central America.*" An accompanying likeness of him and of his medal appeared in the *San Francisco Chronicle* of February 23, 1896. By 1863 Raymond had settled in San Francisco, where he was employed by the Pacific Mail Steamship Company, married and became the father of five children, all born in California. Later years he worked as a guard for PMSC until his death on November 14, 1888. He was buried from the Golden Gate Masonic Lodge.

Marshall O. Roberts, after the government allowed the USMSC contract to expire, estimated the company had lost two million dollars, and attempted to recover the loss on the grounds there had been no added subsidy for direct service to Aspinwall. Although rejected by the Court of Claims, litigation eventually led to an award to Roberts of $1,031,000, through a Supreme Court decision (Roberts vs. U.S. 92 U.S. 41, & II Court of Claims, 774).

During the Civil War he made nearly "three million dollars from a half dozen steamships," by leasing and selling them to the government. His activities "were investigated by Congress in 1866 and 1868, with no results."[60] The *New*

---

[59] Pendleton, *San Francisco Fire Co.*, 2.
[60] Malone, Vol. XVI, 12.

York Times, 29 Apr 1865, reported his contribution of ten thousand dollars to a fund for Mrs. Abraham Lincoln. He was active in politics, and rated as one of the leading Republican contributors. In 1880, Roberts attended the funeral of Ellen Herndon Arthur, and died the same year on September 11th, at Saratoga Springs, New York.

According to the Beaver family history, **Joseph Schuler** was from Hamilton, Ohio, and was severely criticized by the local people for having gotten into the life-boat with the women and children.

After their reunion on the *Empire City*, the Seeger family returned to their home in St. Louis, Missouri. The names of **Benn Seeger**, his wife, **Mary**, their California-born sons, **John** and **William**, Missouri-born daughters, Josephina and Theresia, appeared in the 1860 census. Seeger was a bar keeper. In 1870, his name was listed as **Bernhard Seeger**, employed as a teamster; son John was apprenticed to a butcher and the five younger children were in school. In 1900, William was employed as a brewery collector, had a wife and two children.

The San Francisco jewelry company of **Samuel S.** and George C. **Shreve**, an uncle nearly Sam's own age, has since 1852 continued to operate as a major firm in the manufacture of fine jewelry. It was said to have no equal in the United States, with the exception of New York's Tiffany, the makers of James Birch's silver collection. Located at 110 Montgomery Street, Shreve's was later removed to Grant and Post Streets, its present location.[61] The Shreve family is no longer associated with the firm.

Ann Small. The *Sacramento Union* of June 22, 1858, published the *Newburyport Herald* announcement of the death of Mrs. Ann Keziah P. Small. The ailing Mrs. Small lived only nine months after she delivered her husband's parcel of papers to the owner of the *Augustine Heard*. In 1874, her daughter, Miss **Anna P. Small**, attended a private school.

A Boston obituary states that ailing **Julius Stetson** died January 28, 1860 at the age of 24. He was survived by his parents.

Mary E. Swan, widow of Samuel, returned to California, where she remarried. Forty-four years later, in 1901, the story of the *Central America* adventure of Mary E. (Swan) Cook appeared in the *Bee* of Sacramento, California, where she was visiting her son, Frank Cook, of 418 Fifteenth Street, Sacramento. The *Bee* story found its way to Park Rapids, Minnesota, and the residence of Oliver Perry Manlove, who then sent his comments to the *Bee*.

In a fire which destroyed the town of her residence, Willits, Mendocino County, her husband was severely burned. Blood poisoning ensued and Mr. Cook died in 1880. "So this woman," said the *Bee*, "who was present at the birth of the Empire of the West, has felt the hand of Fate in two tragedies."

Mrs. Mary Swan Cook had six children. They were the daughter with her on board of the *Central America*, and five Cook sons who were born in California

---

[61] John S. Hittell, *San Francisco*, 88.

after 1859. She died on February 20, 1912 in Sonoma County, California, at the age of 78.[62]

Lucy W. Phillips Thayer: The *New York Daily Tribune* of September 22, 1857, said: "Mrs. Thayer leaves this morning with her two children for South Boston. She has for some time past spent alternate years in San Francisco and South Boston, but thinks that she shall never venture on a California steamer again. She is thoroughly tired, but will not give up at any rate until she reaches home. Her children do not seem affected at all."

Mrs. Thayer, **Lizzie** and **Herbert** returned safely to husband and father, Benjamin B. Thayer, in San Francisco. In October 1862, Lucy gave birth to Benjamin, Jr. Benjamin, Sr., a chemist, was, in 1875, California State Assayer,[63] and later, manager of Apothecaries Hall, corner Market and New Montgomery. He then became the manager of the Guadalupe quick-silver mine, San Jose, and died while there, March 3, 1885, at age 57.

Lucy Thayer survived the San Francisco earthquake of 1906 and fire, and her name last appeared in records of 1919, at which time she was more than 85 years old. Her daughter, Lizzie, married Dexter W. Knapp. Her son, Herbert P., resided in San Francisco until 1925. In 1908, Benjamin, Jr. became the President of Anaconda Copper Mining Co., Butte, Montana.

John Tice. When the steamship *Emily B. Sonder* foundered in the mid-Atlantic on December 10, 1878, her Chief Engineer, John Tice was lost with her. He had lived at 639 Leonard Street, Brooklyn, New York, having survived for 21 years after his dramatic rescue from the life-boat, nine days after the *Central America* sank.[64]

On November 6, 1857, the *Nevada Journal* reported: "A letter received in this city by Mr. B. Van Hagan from his friends at home, stated that **Mrs. I.N. Van Hagan**, one of the unfortunate passengers by the *Central America*, was not expected to live. The 1860 Census indicates that Hannah Van Hagan survived and lived at Vestal Town, Broome County, New York, with a Miller family and seven-year-old little girl, named California.

William Henry Webb, constructor of the *George Law*, sold his shipyards in about 1866. Under his management, many ships of war were built for the United States and foreign governments. In 1890, the year of his death at the age of 74, buildings for an academy and home for shipbuilders were erected at Fordham, New York, and later became the Webb Institute of Naval Architecture.[65]

---

[62] State of California *Death Index, C-E 1905-29*, Vol II, Department of Public Health, Sacramento, CA: n.d., Co. File #6593. Re CA State file no. 12-06593.

[63] Cooke & Lecount, *S.F. Directory*, 1860. *The San Francisco Morning Call*, Mar 4 1885, 2-2. Winfield Scott Downs, ed., *Encyclopedia of Biography*, (Vol 5, American Historical Society, Inc., New York, 1936), 411.

[64] The New York Times, 28 Dec 1878, 1-5.

[65] *Encyclopedia Americana*, 1944 ed., s.v. "Webb, William H."

APPENDIX C

Passengers and Crew

Passengers

In researching this disaster we have resurrected various passenger lists and estimates of the number of people aboard the *Central America* on her final voyage. Estimates of the total number on board ranged from 483 to 600, in addition to the crew.

The passenger lists were either inaccurately made, or they were badly garbled when transferred to the newspapers. This was evidenced by various spellings of the names, and inaccuracies as to the port where boarded. In comparing San Francisco and Aspinwall lists, there were omissions and additions of names, variations in the number of children, and duplications on single lists. The *Baltimore Sun*, on September 23, 1857, sagely commented: "All the lists are unavoidably inaccurate. A complete record of the lost will probably never be made on earth."

On September 28, 1857, Eastern newspapers regretfully reported: "It is said that the Panama agent of the U.S. Steamship line has no duplicate of the passenger list of the *Central America,* and we shall have no means of knowing the number and names of the passengers until the return of the California steamer after the news of the disaster reaches San Francisco, which will be two months hence." Their frustration is difficult to imagine.

A copy of the passenger list actually arrived in New York Port Quarantine from Aspinwall, October 10th, with the steamer *Northern Light*, Captain E.L. Tinklepaugh. Although there were many errors and omissions in its transmission by telegraph to the media, it appeared in the *New York Times* on October 16th. Accuracy depended in a good measure on the skill of the East Coast telegraph operators and reporters, and the spelling of the names varied among the different newspapers. Errors of omission, persons listed but not on board and duplications were found.

At least one passenger was reported lost, but was very much alive for another nine years. He was E. Morris Earl, a 49'er, whose name appeared on the passenger list of both the *Sonora* and *Central America*. However, he had at the last moment sold his ticket to someone else, and later made the journey on the *Star of the West*.

William Newman's name appeared among the passengers listed as lost on the *Central America*. He had resided for a number of years in Nevada County,

California, and was "regarded generally as a half-witted fellow."[1] Actually, Newman had had a mental breakdown, believed to have been brought on by the rigors of western life, and he yearned to return to his family.[2] Wealthy relatives pursuaded him to return home, and made arrangements with Hiram Stinchfield,[3] an acquaintance from Evansville, Indiana, to pay his passage and take charge of him.

Stinchfield purchased steerage tickets for himself and Newman, kept them in his pocket, and escorted the passenger on board. In the crowd they got separated. The ticket man came around and, finding Newman without a ticket, put him ashore. Stinchfield could not be located. Newman was in San Francisco when the steamer sank. Hiram Stinchfield was lost.

Three others on the list were Delano, A., Sheldon, B. and Hawley, A.; they were probably not on the ship. Alonzo T. Delano was a miner, Wells-Fargo agent and a well-known writer of stories and adventures of the 49'ers, known as "Old Block." Bishop Sheldon was an early hotel keeper near Mokelumne Hill and later a partner with his brother in Mark Sheldon's wholesale produce business in San Francisco, where they continued to live. Records reveal that they died in 1874 and 1902, respectively. Aaron Hawley was listed as a produce merchant from Bridgeport, Connecticut, the same as the Frederick Hawley family. However, nothing was said about him in any of the newspapers. We have deleted the three names from the list.

The Ellis family was not included; a Smith family was. There was no mention of the Smith wife and children being saved, but detailed information is available on the Ellises. We have concluded that the Ellises bought the Smith's tickets.

We have entered in our computer data base all of the available names gathered from a number of passenger lists, United States censuses and other sources. These have been carefully examined, and all information concerning individuals was compared. Some assumptions were made.

The list includes the through passengers from San Francisco and those boarding at Aspinwall and Havana. The names of those known to have debarked at Havana have been deleted. This list represents our best efforts, the compilation being particularly time-consuming and tedious. In the opinion of this author, it is the most accurate passenger list available. Nevertheless, it is recognized that the list can never be completely accurate. The author would

---

[1] *Santa Cruz Sentinel*, 7 Nov 1857, 2-1.

[2] Joseph P. Elliott, *A History of Evansville and Vanderburgh County, Indiana* (Evansville, IN: Keller Printing Co., 1897), 432-34.

[3] Stinchfield, age 33, had married Sarah McCrary when he was not quite 17 years old. He was 5'10", weighed 150 pounds, light in complexion. They lived with their five young children in Evansville, IN, where he was engaged in different occupations until February 1854. He then went to California, where two of his younger brothers, George and Moses, had preceded him. He engaged in mining at Nevada City, Montezuma Hill in Nevada County, on the North fork of the Yuba river, and at Eureka, Sierra County. The last heard from him was at Panama where he wrote to a brother in California before sailing on the *Central America*. Elliott, 432-34.

welcome the receipt of any additional information, which can be supplied via the publisher.

On board the *Central America* were 491 passengers, 105 officers and crew, including 3 men working their passage from Aspinwall, totaling 596 persons. Of these, 161 were saved: 101 were men, 32 women, 28 children. All of the women and children were saved, with the exception of one boy, eleven-year-old Ricardo Ollague, from Lima, Peru. Mr. G. Hahn and Mr. W. Watson each had a son who was lost. We assume that they were adults.

The first class cabins were occupied by 104 persons, 20 of them being women, 23 children. There were 55 in second class cabins, including 4 women and 3 children. Traveling in steerage were 332, including 8 women and 3 children.

LIST OF PASSENGERS

This list contains the following information: last name, title, first name, middle name, age, and home state. These facts are followed by letter codes which give two important bits of information: If the passenger was saved, the name of the ship which rescued them (M = Marine; E = Ellen; My = Mary), and an "S" = statement concerning passenger. Alternative spellings of a name are given in parenthesis.

FIRST CABIN

Aker, Mr. S.
Alston, Mr. A.J., 29, GA.
Ayulo, Mr. Enrique, Peru, E, S.
Badger, Mrs. Jane A., 22, MA, M, S.
Badger, Captain Thomas W., 30, VA, E, S.
Beach, Mr. Henry D.
Birch, Mr. James E., 28, MA.
Birch, Mrs. Virginia, M, S.
Birch, Mr. William, 26, NY, E, S.
Bokee, Mr. F. A., MA.
Bowly, Mrs. Angelina M., NY, M, S.
Bowly, Son Charles M., 2, NY, M.
Bowly, Daughter Isabella, 1, CA, M.
Brown, Mr. Peter.
Brown, Mr. Robert Turnbull, 36, NY, E, S.
Caruthers, Mrs. Eliza G., MA, M, S.
Childs, Mr. Henry H., NY, E, S.
Dement, Lieutenant John D., 31, DC, E, S.
Dobbin, Mr. John V., NC.
Doud, Mr. A.
Dyer, Captain Walter G., England.
Easton, Mrs. Adeline Mills, 28, NY, M, S.
Easton, Mr. Ansel Ives, 38, NY, E, S.
Ellis, Infant, OH, M.
Ellis, Son Alvin A., 2, OH, M.
Ellis, Dr. Alvin, 34, OH.
Ellis, Son Charles D., 4, OH, M.
Ellis, Daughter Lillie, 1, OH, M.
Ellis, Mrs. Lynthia Powers, 36, OH, M.
Esquerra, Mr. Pasqual, Spain, (Parieul)
Fallon, Mr. Thomas
Farmer, Mr. Marcellus, 35, NY.
Farnham, Mr. G. A. (C.)
Fell, David, 3, IA, M.
Fell, Son, 1, IA, M.
Fell, Mrs. Jane, 20, IA, M.
Fell, Mr. John, IA.
Forster, Mr. James A., 35, PA, E, S.
Gibbs, Dr. Charles, 32, MA.
Harvey, Dr. Obed C., 32, IL, E, S.
Hawley, Son Charles DeForest, 2, CT, M.
Hawley, Mrs. Elizabeth DeForest, 29, CT, M, S.
Hawley, Mr. Frederick S., 35, CT.
Hawley, Son William, 5 mos, CT, M.
Hirshfield, Mr. Edward
Howes, Mr. Jabez, 25, MA, E.
Jones, Mr. Frank A., KY, M, S.
Kittredge, Mrs. Almira Mead, 39, MA, M, S.
Lasinsky, Mr. M.
Lockwood, Mrs. Harriett Hill, 45, IN, M, S.
Lockwood, Dau. Harriett Maria, 9, M.
Lockwood, Dau. Rose Alice, 15, IN, M.
Lockwood, Son Rufus Albert, 12, IN, M.
Lockwood, Atty Rufus A., 46, IN.
Lowe, Mr. Charles A., 29.
Marvin, Mrs. Amanda, IL, M, S.
Marvin, Captain William H., IL.
McCarty, Mr. Charles, M. S.
McNeil, Mrs. Anna Maria Mullen, 19 NY, M, S.
McNeil, Mr. William, 33, NY.
McWilliams, Mr. E. (Williams)
Meteyer, Mr. M.
Monson, Judge Alonzo Castle, 32, NY, M, S.
Montgomery, Mr. G. Washington, 35, PA.
Moore, Mr. C.
O'Neil, Mrs. OH, M, S.

O'Neil, Mr. Thomas, OH.
Ollague, Mr. Adolfo, 27, Peru.
Ollague, Boy Ricardo, 11, Peru.
Pahud, Son, 3, NYC, M.
Pahud, Dau. Augustine Rosalie, 9, NY, M, S.
Pahud, Son Henri Edouard, 7, NY, M
Pahud, Mme. Rosalie Marie, 34, NY, M, S.
Parker, Mr. S. F., MA.
Payne, Mr. Theodore, 40, NY, M, S.
Priest, Mr. Albert, 60, NY, M.
Richon, Mr. Ange, France, M, S.
Ridgway, Mr. George G., 31, PA, S.
Saroni, Mr. Charles S., MA.
Sawyer, Mr. N.
Seguin, Senor Jose, DC, Peru.
Sellamer, Mr. J.
Shreve, Mr. Samuel Stillman, 27, M
Small, Mrs. Ann Keziah P., MA, M, S
Small, Dau. Anna, 2, MA, M.
Smith, Miss Elizabeth, M.
Smith, Mr. F. M. B., NY.
Tayloe, Mr. Charles, 27, NC.
Thayer, Son Herbert P., 2, MA, M.
Thayer, Dau. Lizzie A., 6, MA, M.
Thayer, Mrs. Lucy W Phillips, 25, MA, M, S.
Thomas, Mrs. Frances A., M.
Thorne, Mr. J. A., PA.
Tirado, Senor Nicolas M., Peru.
Travis, Child #1, NY, M.
Travis, Child #2, NY, M.
Travis, Dr. James E., NY.
Travis, Mrs. Mary Ann, NY, M, S.
Van Hagan, Child, NY, M.
Van Hagan, Mrs. Hannah, 30, NY, M.
Van Hagan, Mr. I. N., NY.
Vose, Mr. Charles A., 25, NH, E, S
White, Mr. Milton D.
Yanney, Dr. Henry P., 33, NY.

SECOND CABIN

Adams, Mr. William A., 27, MD, M, S.
Barchman, Mr.
Barlow, Mr. Otis
Bassford, Mr. Joseph McDonald, 35, NY,
Bonneau, Boy Louis, 3, CA, M.
Blum, Mr. Charles C. (Baum)
Carpenter, Mr. Frank
Clow, Mr. James C., 26, PA.
Davis, Mr. Lee
Dean, Mr. Henry, CT.
Dorsey, Mr. Laurence, PA.
Edmann, Mr. Robert (Erdman)
Fallon, Son James, 3, CT, M.
Fallon, Mr. Lawrence, CT.
Fallon, Dau. Winifred, 17, CT, M, S.
Fisk, Mr. Noble (Fish)
Gittermann, Mr. M.
Gould, Mr. George, NJ. (Guild, Gall, Gaul)
Graffus, Mr. William
Griffiths, Mr. C. W.
Harrell, Mr. J. N. (Harnett)
Harris, Infant, 1, M.
Harris, Mrs. Jane, M, S.
Hemmel, Mr. William
Holland, Mr. P., PA.
Hutchinson, Mr. George W., NJ.
Jameson, Mr. R. L.
Kent, Mr. Charles
Kent, Mr. Horace L. Jr., VA.
Lee, Mr. George, PA.
Levich, Mr. Robert, England.
Maloney, Mr. Thomas
Manott, Mr. George. (Manor)(Marrat)
McCarthy, Mr. J., NY. M, S.
McCarty, Mr. Peter (McChardy)
Morris, Mr. T.(L). J.
Mullen, Mr. J. W.
Munger, Mr. J. N.
O'Connor, Mrs. Eleanor, NY, M, S.
O'Connor, Mr. Henry T., 17, NY, E, S.
O'Neil, Mr. James
Olfur, Mr.
Osborne, Mr. William N., 45, IN, E, S.
Plass, Mr. William, 21, NY, M.
Raassi, Mr. D. B.

Redding, Mrs. Ann, NY, M.
Reed, Mr. J. F.
Richman, Mr. R.
Stevens, Mr. John O., 32, NJ.
Strauss, Mr. E.

Tompkins, Mr. Isaac N.
Tompkins, Mr. James W.
Watson, Son, England
Watson, Mr. W., England. (Robinson)
Wheelwright, Mr. Samuel G., 42, MA

STEERAGE

Adams, Mr. H.
Amour, Mr. A. (Amn)
Anderson, Mr. B. A., 22, AL.
Anderson, Mr. H. G.
Anderson, Mr. J. W.
Anthony, Mr.
Ash, Mr, F.(I.)
Bagwell, Mr. Wiley
Bailey, Mrs. Mary, M.
Ball, Mr. P. R.
Ball, Mr. T. B.
Barber, Mr. T. S., 35, RI.
Barr, Mr. F.
Barr, Mr. N.
Beashler, Mr. Henry
Beaver, Mr. Daniel, 56, OH.
Bedell, Mr. H. H.
Bell, Mr. W.
Berks, Mr. C.
Berry, Mr. H. Andrew, 31, PA.
Berry, Mr. W. G., 37, PA.
Blackman, Mr. J. H.
Blanton, Mr. Thomas R., 21, MO.
Boynton, Mr. J., 35, ME.
Brainard, Mr. G. W.,25, IL.
Bride, Mr. Patrick
Bride, Mr. Thomas, M, S.
Browning, Mr. W.
Brush, Mr. Gabriel D., 32, NY.
Bruyn, Mr. George, NY, E.
Buchanan, Mr. J. L.
Buckaway, Mr. D.
Buctzendorff, Mr. (Bactenzorff)
Bullie, Mr. Peter, Canada.
Burdick, Mr. R.
Burns, Mr. William
Burt, Mr. E. H.
Butler, Mr. Patrick, RI.
Cabell, Mr. H. Y.
Caldwell, Mr. Stephen C., 27, NY, E, S.

Callahan, Mr. James K.
Capello, Mr. Joseph, Italy.
Carter, Mr.
Casey, Mr. Jacob M., 25, AR, E, S.
Casey, Mr. Randolph W., 25, AR, E, S.
Casta, Mr. Demecio, Italy.
Chaillan, Mr. Jean P.
Chapman, Mr. Daniel Hudson C., 42, MO.
Chapman, Mr. J.
Chase, Mr. William, MI, E, S.
Cherry, Mr. J. R. (Cheney)
Chort, Mr. J.
Christian, Mr. S. (Christman)
Christie, Mr. J.
Clark, Mr. D.
Clark, Major Jacob Brown, 46, MO, E, S.
Closer, Mr. A.
Colt, Mr. Benjamin P., IL.
Condos, Mr. E.
Crafts, Mr. John N.(W), 47, ME, E.
Cragen, Mr. Michael, WI.
Crider, Mr. E.
Crimins, Mr. Michael
Crist, Mr. A.
Crohan, Mr. H. W.
Cross, Mr. Joseph W.
Crowell, Mr. Alfred F., MA.
Cubbe, Mr. J. (Cobble)
Cummings, Mr. John, 32, IA, M, S.
Daley, Mr. L.
Darett, Mr. S. (Danbery)
Davidson, Mr., MD.
Dawson, Mr. George W. 35, NY, My,S
Denenburg, Mr. Henry.
Denour, Mr.John, PA. (Denaner)
Deshond, Mr. W. P.
Dezel, Mr. William (Delzan) (Delya)
Dixon, Mr. John, NY.
Dougherty, Mr. M., NY, M.
Dugan, Mr. Patrick

Eastman, Mr. A. W.
Eaton, Mr. William L.(S),
Ede, Mr. William, 30, WI, E, S.
Edwards, Mr. P.
Ewen, Mr. John D., 27, NY, E. (Edmond)
Falconer, Mr. W.
Farnham, Mr. R. C.
Fenner, Mr. W. R.
Festu, Mr. Gaitano, Italy, M, S. (Testher)
Finnegan, Mr. Peter A.
Fisher, Mr. D. Jr.
Fisk, Mr. M. H. (Fish)
Flangan, Mr. W.
Fletcher, Mr. Willard F., 20, ME, E, S.
Ford, Mr. E.
Forrest, Mr. D. W. (Foust)
Foster, Mr. John H.
Frank, Mr. H.
Frederick, Mr. Adolph, E, S.
Fredet, Mr. John (M)
Fryer, Seaman Thomas, M.
Gallaher, Seaman James, M, S.
Gardner, Seaman Alexander, M, S.
Garrison, Mr. R. L.
Geary, Mr. William W., England, M,
Gehan, Mr. Samuel L., 30, ME. (Gahn)
George, Mr. John, 30, E, S.
Gilkey, Mr. Charles, 30, ME.
Gilkey, Mr. James B., 27, ME.
Goodnow, Mr. George F., 28, ME.
Goostree, Mr. A. J.
Gorley, Mr. W. (Gorbey)
Gray, Mr. M., M.
Green, Seaman William, NY.
Greenlee, Mr. A.
Gushee, Mr. L.
Haag, Mr. E., IL, M.
Hahn, Son, OH.
Hahn, Mrs. Athros, OH, M.
Hahn, Mr. G.(J.), OH.
Halyard, Mr. Henry, Canada, E. (Halcon) (Ailord)
Hart, Mr. Joseph, OH
Hartman, Mr. Henry, Germany, E, S.
Heaton, Mr. Warren, OH. (Hanyan)
Hendrick, Mr. W. M.
Henry, Mr. F.
Hicks, Mr. T.
Hastings, Mr. H.
Hoadley, Mr. H. F.
Hoagland, Mr. J. F.
Hobert, Mr. William, MA. (Probert)
Hodge,, Mr. R.
Holland, Mr. Henry, 31, KY, M.
Horn, Mr. J. W.
Horn, Mr. R. H.
Horne, Mr. Anson, MO.
Horne, Mr. John D., MO.
Howe, Mr. J. D., MA.
Hughes, Mr. Robert, IL.
Hughes, Mr. T. R.
Hunter, Mr. John
Hussey, Mr. Benjamin F.
Hutchins, Mr. J. V., MA.
Hutchinson, Mr. Robert, VA, M, S.
Jackson, Mr. James, MD, E.
Jerome, Mr.
Johnson, Mr.
Jones, Servant Charles.
Jones, Mr. David, PA.
Jones, Mr. E. F.
Jones, Mr. John E.
Kay, Mr. J.
Keith, Mr. George
Kelly, Mr. John
Kerr, Mr. Bernard
Kerr, Mr. Johnson, 20, WV.
Kilburn, Mr. C.
Kimball, Mr. Henry, 41, NY, M, S.
Kirk, Mr. Christian
Klus, Mr. Jack
Knight, Mr. William, NY.
Kron, Mr. P. (Krow)
Lagan, Mr. Charles
Lean, Mr. P. (Lan)
Lebse, Mr. G.
Lee, Mr. Barney M., 27, PA, E, S.
Lee, Mr. William, Canada.
Leech, Mr. John, 47, MA.
Leonard, Mr. John, NY.
Lepper, Mr. N.
Lobman, Mr. John, WI.
Locke, Mr. C. Y., E.
Look, Mr. Prince W., 40, ME.

Look, Mr. Samuel W., 47, ME, E, S.
Loring, Mr. B., 27, NY.
Lowenthal, Mr. J.
Luckeman, Mr. E.(C)
Lugden, Mr. R. P.
Mack, Mr. A., NY.
Mahoney, Mr. Daniel, 47, PA.
Mangold, Mr. J.
Manlove, Mr. Oliver Perry, 25, WI, E, S.
Martin, Mr. Nicholas H., OR
Mathey, Mr. F. A. (Matty)
Maynard,, Mr.
McCabe, Mr. John B., NY, E.
McCormick, Mr. Cornelius
McCoy, Mr. M. L., M.
McGrenery, Mr.
McGugan, Mr. C. (McGagan)
McGuire, Mr. O.(A)
McLellan, Mr. J. (McLelland)
McNeish, Mr. Thomas, 24, PA, E, S.
Meron, Mr. E.(C) (Marin)
Merry, Mr. E. R. (Mary)
Meyers, Mr. John, MO.
Miller, Mr. Henry H.
Miller, Mr. L.
Mitchell, Mr. J. C.
Mitchler, Mr. Valentine
Montague, Mr. M. L.
Moore, Mr. Edward W., VA, E. (Edmond Morse)
Moran, Mr. D.
Moran, Mr. P.
Morris, Mr. J. J., 36, KY.
Morton, Mr. W. J.
Moseley, Mr. A., AR.
Murch, Mr. Stephen B., 30, ME.
Murphy, Mr. M.
Murray, Mr. F.
Murray, Mr. L.
Myrtle, Mr. Frank, Canada.
Narramore, Mr. G. (Manamire)
O'Connor, Mr. John, NY.
O'Fallen, Mr. J. N., M. (Fallens)
Ogden, Mr. Frederick
Ogden, Mr. R. W.
Olconnon, Mr. Thomas, IN.
Owens, Mr. Moses, 35, OH.
Owings, Mr. W. C.
Palmer, Mr. Benjamin, MO.
Parago, Mr. Francis
Payne, Mr. Thomas, CT.
Pettorous, Mr. Charles, NY.
Pettorous, Nurse Susan, NY, M.
Phillips, Mr., England.
Pomeroy, Mr. P.
Poole, Mr.
Pope, Mr. E., 36, MO.
Porter, Mr. Horace D.
Powell, Mr. John, KY.
Prince, Mr. R., ME.
Pritchard, Mr. C.
Pullen, Mr.
Quincer, Mr. Jacob B., 55, NY, E, S.
Ragland, Mr. James H.
Rahan, Mrs. F., IL, M.
Reed, Mr. Charles, NY, E.
Reed, Mr. R.
Reese, Mr. B.
Reese, Mr. William S., NY.
Revenna, Mr. Thomas, Italy.
Richards, Mr. Sam S. 41, MA.
Ridley, Mr. Billings H., ME, E.
Roberts, Mr. William (R.) E., MA.
Robertson, Mr., MA.
Robinson, Mr.
Ross, Mr. James H., OH, E.
Rudwell, Mrs. Mary Ann, England, M, S.
Rudwell, Mr. John, England.
Ruhle, Mr. J. (Rubb)
Rummell, Mr. Henry W., IL, E. (Brumwell)
Rutherford, Mr. Douglas, 37, WI, M, S.
Ryan, Mr. T. F.
Sackbower, Mr. Philip, PA.
Sanborn, Mr. J. W.
Sanborn, Mr. Nelson P.
Sawin, Mr. J.
Schmendmann, Mr. J.
Schuler, Mr. Joseph, OH, M.
Seeger, Mr. Bernhard, 33, MO, E.
Seeger, Son John, 3, MO, M.
Seeger, Mrs. Mary, 24, MO, M.
Seeger, Son William, 2, MO, M.
Shaw, Mr.
Shaw, Mrs. Carolyn, M.
Shepperd, Mr. George D.
Shipman, Mr. D. F.
Short, Mr. R.

Sibbot, Mr. H.
Sigel, Mr. T.
Simmons, Mr. C., 42, WI.
Simmons, Mr. F.
Simon, Mr. G.
Smith, Mr. Benjamin L.
Smith, Mr. David D., ME.
Smith, Seaman James.
Smith, Mr. James
Smith, Mr. P. S.
Snyder, Mr. P. H., PA.
Spaulding, Mr. M. A.(D.)
Spohn, Mr. Peter.
Spooner, Mr. Elijah, PA.
Sprout, Mr. William.
Stall, Mr. A. (Stahl)
Steer, Mr. George
Stetson, Mr. Julius, 21, MA, E, S.
Stevens, Mr. W., 36, NY,
Stewart, Mr. David, 24, OH. (Daniel)
Stinchfield, Mr. Hiram, 27, IN.
Strom, Mr. J. H.
Strueve, Mr. A.
Sullivan, Mr. James.
Swan, Daughter, 1, PA, M.
Swan, Mrs. Mary Ann, 23, PA, M, S.
Swan, Mr. Samuel B., 35, PA.
Tanner, Mr. John.
Taylor, Mr. John C., 26, NY, E, S.
Taylor, Mr. Robert, 38, WI.
Theberger, Mr. A.
Thomas, Mr. W. G., PA.

Tuck, Mr. Charles H., NY.
Unknown, Mr. Charley
Van Horn, Mr. J.
Van Meter, Mr. H. B. (W.B. Van Natter)
Van Ness, Mr., NY.
Van Nockin, Mr. Edward.
Van Reed, Mr. W.
Van Waldheim, Mr. F. G.
Vean, Mr. Antoine, Canada.
Villot, Mr.
Wade, Mr. Robert, Jr., 49, IN.
Wallace, Mr. James.
Weeks, Mr. J. L.
Welge, Mr. W.
Wells, Mr. E.
Wells, Mr. F. A., MA, E, S.
Wells, Mr. J. B.
Whalen, Mr. James.
White, Mr. R. J.
Whitney, Mr., NJ.
Wiley, Mr. E.
Wiley, Mr. John, 24, NY.
Willett, Mr. D.
Willett, Mr. T.(F.)
Wilton, Mr. Richard, 31, IL.
Wood, Mr. Lewis, 30, NY.
Woodworth, Mr. James, 25, IA.
Young, Mr. Donald.
Young, Mr. Leonard M., 28, OH.
Young, Mr. William, OH.
Zimmerman, Mr. C., (Zimmerlin)

THE CREW

According to public reports, there were 101 crew-men on board the steamer, but our information indicates there were 102 on the regular crew and 3 who were working their passage from Aspinwall. Twenty-eight were saved, most of those having manned the small boats for the transfer of passengers to the brig *Marine*.

Commander Herndon had accumulated many years as a naval officer on vessels at sea, including steam vessels, but his selection as master of the large luxury vessel *George Law/Central America* was a particularly desireable position for him.

The 29th Congress had in 1847 provided for each steamer of the mail service to receive on board four passed midshipmen to serve as watch officers. Records of the United States Navy contain no indication that any other of the steamer's officers had any prior U.S. Navy service, however, they had other qualifying experience on steam vessels of the mail steamship company.

The United States Navy authorized the following officer grades[4] during the period 1842-1853:

Captain	Master	Chaplain
Commander	Boatswain	Gunner
Lieutenant	Surgeon	Carpenter
Passed Midshipman	Passed Assistant Surgeon	Sailmaker
Midshipman	Assistant Surgeon	Master's Mate
	Purser	

Between 1854 and 1858, the following officer grades were added to meet steam Navy[5] requirements:

Chief Engineer	Second Assistant Engineer
First Assistant Engineer	Third Assistant Engineer.

In 1859, Secretary of the Navy Isaac Toucey gave comparative officer grades for engineers, proclaiming that chief engineers with more than twelve years of service would rank with naval officers in the grade of commander; those with less than twelve years, with the grade of lieutenant. First assistant engineers were ranked after the grade of lieutenant; second assistant engineers, followed the grade of master; and third assistant engineers ranked with midshipmen. Fourth assistant engineers were not included in the officer grades.

For each steamer trip of the USMSC, a crew list was prepared and authenticated, the list of 20 August 1857, for the *Central America*, being accomplished by the Clark Co., 118 South Street, New York, signed by Wm. Lewis Herndon, and authenticated by Jonah N. Clark, Public Notary, stating: "The above list contains the names of all the Officers and Crew of the said steamship together

---

[4] Edward W. Callahan, ed. *Officers of the U.S. Navy and Marine Corps, 1775-1900* (New York: E.R. Hamersby & Co., 1901). United States Navy, "Officers' Ranks, U.S. Navy 1805-65," Typewritten, n.d.

[5] Frank M. Bennett, *The Steam Navy of the United States*, (Pittsburgh, PA: Warren & Co., 1897), 180-5.

with the places of their Birth and Residence, as far as he hath been able to ascertain the same." According to the list, New York was the birthplace and residence of every member of the crew.

Although the roster had been prepared near the departure date, there were a number of substitutions made for men who appeared on the original list. In comparing it with other crew lists of the same members, we found variations in the spelling of the names, as well as in other data, making difficult, if not impossible, the assurance of accuracy. The two lists under the new name, *Central America*, 6 July and 20 August 1857, were prepared by a Clark Co. representative, who included the age and a height estimate of each member, this data varying slightly between lists. The spellings of crew members' names have been resolved to the best of our ability through comparisons of available sources and references. On September 17, the Clark Co. presented to the *New York Times* for publication a corrected list of crew members.

The height of the crew members ranged from five feet six inches to six feet, with only two, Richard Reed and George Wilson, being the latter size. Most were in the five foot six to eight range, reflecting the average sizes of the American men of the 19th century. Ages ranged from 16 (Charles Boyd) to 56 (Lucy Dawson). The majority were in their twenties. Eighteen were identified as "colored."

LIST OF CREW

The following list, by position, contains the name and age of each crew member, as well as the code letter for the ship of rescue, if any.

Captain: Herndon, William Lewis, 44
   Captain's Man: Garretson, William, 30, M.

Officers:
   1st: Van Rensselaer, Charles W., 30.
   2nd: Frazer, James M., 27, E.
   3rd: Myers, Charles A., 30.

Purser: Hull, Edward W., 32.　　　　　Surgeon: Tennison, Joseph T., 35.

Boatswain: Black, John, 33, M.　　　　Ship's Storekeeper:
　　　　　　　　　　　　　　　　　　　　Hull, William H., 26.

Engineers:　　　Chief: Ashby, George E., 35, M.
1st Asst: Tice, John, 26, My.　　　　　4th Asst: Clark, Joseph, 30.
2nd Asst: Keefer, Henry, 28, E.　　　　Jones, William, 33.
3rd Asst: Buddington, George, 27.　　　McDonald, Donald, 21.
　　　　Engineers Storekeeper: Wigglesworth, William, 28.

SHIPS CREW:

Quartermaster:
   Frazier, Finley, 27, M.　　　　　　Long, Robert, 22, M.
   Jackson, William, 43, M.　　　　　Raymond, David, 27, M.

Seamen:
   Bourne, William　　　　　　　　　Lawrence, Samuel
   Brougham, Frederick, 21, M.　　　Matthews, Thomas
   Brown, Edward, 28, M.　　　　　　McLane, James, 21, M.
   Christy, Robert　　　　　　　　　Parker, Thomas, 26.
   Clark, James, 22, M.　　　　　　　Reed, Richard, 45, M.
   Davidson, John, 29, M.　　　　　　Travis, James, 26, M.
   Dorsey, John, 26.　　　　　　　　Waters, Francis, 29.
   Hodges, Edward, M.

Firemen:
   Bagley, Morgan, 24, M.　　　　　　Hetherington, Henry, M.
   Carr, Patrick, 28.　　　　　　　　Hyde, Martin
   Clark, John, M.　　　　　　　　　Jones, John, 25, M.
   Concklin, Bernard, 27.　　　　　　Smith, John, 26.
   Doyle, Edward, 27.　　　　　　　　Stuart, George, 23, M.
   Grant, Alexander, 25, My.

Coal Passers:
   Bell, Arnold, 21.　　　　　　　　　McCarty, Bartley, 21, M.
   Bell, Richard, 24.　　　　　　　　McConnin, John, 22.
   Callan, Christopher, 21.　　　　　Norris, James, 21.
   Gavin, Patrick, 21.　　　　　　　Yager, Herman, 26.
   Gillespe, John

Ash Men:
  Banks, John, 19.
  Brannan, James

Stewards:
  Ships: McBride, N.L., 26.
  Ladies: Dawson, Lucy, 56, M.
  Steerage: Yancey, James, 36.

Porters:
  Pennington, Charles, 26.
  Sarvent, William, 33.

Ship's:
  1st: Hardenbrook, Henry, 29, E.
  2nd: Prattis, Isaac, 28.
  3rd: West, James, 25.
Pastry: White, John, 27.

Butcher: Patterson, John
Silver Man: Roker, Philip, 24.
Tin Man: Myers, William
Scullion: Cornell, Charles, 18

Head: Breslin, James, 35.
  Brown, John, 30.
  Carroll, Patrick, 20.
  Clemens, Eli, 26.
  Dwyer, Michael, M.
  Freeman, John, 28
  Gaynor, Bartlett, 24.

Steerage Waiters:
  Blue, John, 40.
  Henry, James, 27.
  Holcombe, Henry, 27.

Mess Boy:
  Officer's: Gilbert, Richard, 35.
  Fireman's: Flynn, William, 19.

Evans, Patrick, 18.
Kinnelty, John, 18.

Cabin Boys:
  Boyd, Charles, 16.
  McEwen, Timothy, 21, E.

Barber:
  Gillead, Jacob, 30.

Cooks:
  Saloon:
    1st: Holcomb, Aaron, 40, E.
    2nd: Prattis, John, 24.
    3rd: Haney, John, 24.
  Baker: McLelland, William

Pantry Men:
  Hare, William, 31.
  Libbey, Elias, 21.
  Young, John

Waiters:

  McBeath, Archibald, 24.
  Morgan, John, 20.
  Nelson, Cyprian, 33.
  Nelson, Samuel, 25.
  Perkins, William, 22.
  Stevens, William, 26.

  Kelley, Peter, 34.
  Painter, Richard, 22.
  Wilson, George, 30.

Water Closet Boy:
  Nash, Isaac, 18.

Bibliography and Index

Selected Bibliography

BOOKS

Alameda County: The Eden of the Pacific. Oakland, CA: Oakland Tribune, 1898.

Audubon, John Woodhouse, and Hodder, Frank Heywood. *Audubon's Western Journal, 1849-1850.* Cleveland: Arthur H. Clark Co., 1906.

Bancroft, Hubert Howe. *Works.* Vol XXIII, *The History of California, 1848-1849.* Vol XXIV, *The History of California, 1849-1850.* Vol XXIX, *The History of Oregon, 1834-1848.* San Francisco: The History Company, 1888.

Banning, Captain William and George Hugh. *Six Horses.* London and New York: The Century Co., 1930.

Bennett, Frank M. *The Steam Navy of the United States.* Pittsburgh, PA: Warren & Co., 1897.

Boggs, Mae Helene Bacon. *My Playhouse Was a Concord Coach: An Anthology of Newspaper Items of California History.* Oakland, CA: Howell-North Press, 1942.

California, 1900: Fifty Years of Progress: Pg. 227. "Theodore Payne," n.p., n.d.

Callahan, Edward W., ed. *Officers of the U.S. Navy and Marine Corps, 1775-1900.* New York: E.R. Hamersby & Co., 1901.

Conrad, Judy, ed. *Story of An American Tragedy: Survivors' Accounts of the Sinking of the Steamship* Central America. Columbus, OH: Columbus-America Discovery Group, Inc., 1988.

Dana, Richard Henry. *Two Years Before the Mast.* New York: Collier & Son, 1909. Harvard Classics, Vol. 23.

Daughters of the American Revolution of California. *Vital Records from San Francisco Daily Bulletin, 1856-7.* Vol. I, San Francisco: 1943.

Descendants of John De La Fontaine. Fredericksburg, VA: n.p., n.d.

Devens, Richard Miller. *Our First Century.* Springfield, MA: Nichols & Co., 1882.

Drury, Clifford M. *San Francisco YMCA, 1853-1953: 100 Years by the Golden Gate.* Glendale, CA: Arthur H. Clark Co., 1963.

Encyclopedia Americana. 1944 ed., s.v. "Webb, William H."

Finney, Jack. *Forgotten News.* Garden City, NY: Doubleday & Co., Inc., 1983.

Gallucci, Mary McLennon and Alfred D. *James E. Birch.* Sacramento, CA: Sacramento Co. Hist. Soc., 1958.

Genealogies of Virginia Families. Vol. IV. Baltimore, MD: Genealogical Publishing Co, 1981.

Gibbons, Alice Tone. *My Pioneer Grandfather, John Henley Tone.* Stockton, CA: 1972, 1976.

Guinn, J.M. *History of the State of California and Biographical Records of Coast Counties of California.* Chicago, IL: Chapman Publishing Co., 1904.

Haskins, C.W. *The Argonauts of California.* New York: Ford, Howard & Hulbert, 1890.

Hasse, Adelaide R. comp. *Tentative Biography of Matthew Fontaine Maury, 1917,* with additions by Hugh A. Morrison. n.p., 1928.

Heitman, Francis B. *Historical Register and Dictionary of the United States Army, 1789-1903.* Vol. I, Washington, D.C: 1903.

Herndon, John Goodwin. *The Herndons of the American Revolution.* Lancaster, PA: Wickersham Printing Co., 1951.

Herndon Monument Fund. *Report of the Committee to Collect Funds and Procure and Erect A Monument to the Memory of the late Commander Wm. Lewis Herndon.* Washington, D.C: 1858.

Herndon, William Lewis and Lardner Gibbon. *Exploration of the Valley of the Amazon.* House of Representatives Exec. Doc. 53, 33d Congress, 1st Session. Washington, D.C: 1854.

Herndon, William Lewis. *Exploration of the Valley of the Amazon.* Intro. by Hamilton Basso, ed. New York: McGraw-Hill Book Company, Inc., 1952.

Heyl, Erik. *Early American Steamers.* Vol. 1, Buffalo, NY: n.p., 1953.

History of Grant County, Wisconsin. Chicago, IL: Western Historical Company, 1881.

History of Washtenaw County, Michigan. Chicago, IL: Charles C. Chapman & Co., 1881.

Hittell, John S. *A History of the City of San Francisco.* San Francisco: A.L. Bancroft & Co., 1878.

Holliday, J.S. *The World Rushed In.* New York: Simon & Schuster, 1981.

Hunt, Rockwell D. *California and Californians.* Vols. II and III, San Francisco: Lewis Publishing Co. 1930.

Illustrations of Santa Cruz, California, with Historical Sketch. Santa Cruz: Wallace W. Elliott & Co., 1879.

Jackson, Joseph H. *Anybody's Gold.* San Francisco: 1941.

Karsten, Peter. *The Naval Aristocracy.* New York: The Free Press, 1972.

Kemble, John Haskell. *The Panama Route, 1848-1869.* Berkeley, CA: De Capo Press, 1943.

SELECTED BIBLIOGRAPHY 263

Kortum, Karl. *An Old San Francisco Firm*. San Francisco: 1977.

Lewis, Oscar. *Sea Routes to the Gold Fields*. Sausalito, CA: Comstock Editions, Inc., 1987.

Lytle, William M. *Merchant Steam Vessels of the United States, 1807-1868: "The Lytle List."* Mystic, CT: Steamship Hist. Soc. of America, Publ. #6, 1952.

Malone, Dumas, ed. *Dictionary of American Biography*. Vols. I, VI, XII, New York: Charles Scribner's Sons, 1928-1935.

Manlove, Oliver Perry. "Autobiography of Oliver Perry Manlove." Typewritten ms., 1915.

Matthews, Frederick C. *American Merchant Ships, 1850-1900*. Salem, MA: Marine Research Society, 1930.

Maury, Matthew F. *The Physical Geography of the Sea*. New York: Harper and Brothers, 1857.

———. "Report on the Loss of the *Central America* and *Herndon*." No. 299-302: Report to the Secy. of the Navy. *U.S. Naval Inst. Proc.*, Vol. 54, No. 1, (Jan 1928), 84-87.

Minot, George, Esq., Ed. *Statutes at Large and Treaties of the United States of America*. Vol. IX, 1851, Vol. XI, 1859. Boston: Charles C. Little and James Brown.

Morison, Samuel Eliot. *"Old Bruin": Commodore Matthew Calbraith Perry*. Boston and Toronto: Little, Brown & Co., 1967.

Morrison, John H. *History of New York Shipyards*. Port Washington, New York: Kennikat Press, 1909, 1970.

Navy Historical Center Archives. Miscellaneous Original Handwritten Documents and Typewritten Biographies. Washington Navy Yard, Washington, D.C.

Narell, Irena. *Our City: The Jews of San Francisco*. San Francisco: Howell-North, 1981.

Neville, Amelia Ransome. *The Fantastic City: Memoirs of the Social and Romantic Life of Old San Francisco*. Ed. by Virginia Brastow. Boston & New York: Houghton Mifflin Co., 1932.

Olmsted-Lincoln, Nellie. *The Story of Our Wedding Journey*. San Mateo, CA: A.M. Easton Private Printing, 1911.

Otis, F.N., M.D. *Illustrated History of The Panama Railroad*. New York: Harper & Brothers, 1862.

Pendleton, Harry C. *History of the San Francisco Fire Company Department, 1849-1900*. San Francisco: Authority of Exempt Fire Co., 1900.

Rasmussen, Louis J. *Ships Passenger Lists*. Vols. I-IV. San Francisco Historic Records, Colma, CA: 1982.

Richards, John E. (Justice of the Supreme Court) "The Mystery Man." Typed attachment to letter from The State Bar of California, 31 Jan 1957, ed. by Berton J. Ballard, to editor, *San Jose Mercury Herald*. San Jose: n.d.

Ridgely-Nevitt, Cedric. *American Steamships on the Atlantic.* Dover, DE: Univ. of Delaware Press, 1981.

Rourke, Constance. *Troupers of the Gold Coast.* New York: Harcourt and Brace, 1928.

Salley, H.E. *History of California Post Offices, 1849-1976.* La Mesa, CA: Postal History Assoc., Inc., 1977.

San Francisco Theatre Research. WPA Project 8386, Northern California, Vol. 2, Monograph III, "Tom Maguire," Vol. 13, Minstrelsy, 1939.

Schuck, Oscar T. *Bench and Bar in California.* San Francisco: The Occident Printing House, 1889.

Sherman, William Tecumseh. *Sherman's Memoirs - Written by Himself.* Vol. I, New York City: D. Appleton & Co., 1875.

———. *Home Letters of General Sherman.* Edited by M.A. De Wolfe Howe. New York: Charles Scribner's Sons, 1909.

Soule, Frank. *Annals of San Francisco.* San Francisco: D. Appleton & Co., 1855.

Tannehill, Ivan Ray. *Hurricanes.* Princeton, NJ: Princeton Press, 1938.

Thompson and West. *History of Sacramento.* Oakland, CA: n.p., 1880.

United States Congressional Record. Nos. 33-23, 66-4, 86-13, 1964 & 1966. No. 10904-3, 25 May 1966. Washington, D.C.

United States Navy. "Officers' Ranks, U.S. Navy. 1805-65." Typewritten, n.d.

United States Navy. *Aspinwall Line.* Washington, D.C: Navy Yard, n.d.

Valentine, John J. *Money: The Silver Question and Hard Times.* San Francisco: H.S. Crocker Co., 1896.

Waters, Rev. Wilson. *History of Chelmsford [MA].* Lowell, MA: Courier-Citizen Co., 1917.

Webb, William H. *New Era in Shipbuilding.* New York: Webb Ship Yards, n.d.

———. *Plans of Wooden Vessels Built by William H. Webb, 1840-1869.* Vol. I, New York: n.p., n.d.

Wertenbaker, Thomas J. *Norfolk: Historic Southern Port.* Second Ed. edited by Marvin W. Schlegel, Durham, NC: Duke Univ. Press, 1962.

Wilson, James Grant. *The Presidents of the United States.* Vol. III. New York: Charles Scribner's Sons, 1914.

Wright, E.W., ed. *Lewis & Dryden's Marine History of the Pacific Northwest.* Seattle, WA: Superior Publishing Co., 1967.

DIRECTORIES

Bogardus. *San Francisco, Sacramento, Marysville Business Directory.* May and July 1850.

Brown, Nat. P. and John K. Dallison. *Nevada, Grass Valley and Rough and Ready Directory*. Vol. I. San Francisco, 1856.
Chicago City Directory. Chicago, IL., 1853.
Colville, Samuel. *Directory of the City of San Francisco*. Commercial Steam Presses, Monson, Valentine & Co., 1856.
———. *Directory of the City of Sacramento, CA*. 1853-4, 1854-5.
Cooke and LeCount. *Directory of the City of San Francisco*. 1850, 1852, 1854, 1856-7, 1860-61, 1879-83, 1893-4, 1910.
Directory of the City of Oakland, CA. 1875-9, 1885-7, 1896-1900.
Directory of Nevada City, CA. 1856.
Directory of the City of Sacramento, CA. John J. Murphy, 1861.
Directory of Tuolumne, Portions of Calaveras Co., Stanislaus and San Joaquin Co. Miner's & Business Men's Dir., 1 Jan. 1856.
Heckendorn & Wilson. *Miners & Business Men's Directory. General Directory of the Citizens of Tuolumne and portions of Calaveras, Stanislaus and San Joaquin Counties*. Columbia, CA: Printed at the Clipper Office, 1856.
Kimball, Charles P. *Directory of the City of San Francisco, 1850*. San Francisco: Journal of Commerce Press, 1850.
Langley, Henry G. *San Francisco Directory - 1858*. Commercial Steam Presses, S.D. Valentine & Sons, San Francisco, 1858.
Morgan, A.W. & Co. *San Francisco City Directory*. F.A. Bonnard, 1852.
Parker, James M. *The San Francisco City Directory*. San Francisco, 1852.
Rode, Charles R. *The New York City Directory*. 1851-2 and 1852-3. New York: Doggett & Rode.
The San Francisco City Directory. 1854 and 1856. Harris, Bogardus and Labatt.

MAGAZINE ARTICLES

Barrows, H.D. "The Foundering of the Steamship *Central America*." *Qtly. of the Hist. Soc. of Southern California* IV, (1926): 70-75.
Breen, Walter. "The S.S. *Central America*: Tragedy and Treasure." *The Numismatist*, Vol 105, No. 7, (July 1990).
Burch, Ralph. "California's First Stagecoach King." *Westward Magazine*, (Kaiser Steel, Oct.-Nov. 1961): 26-31.
Carey, Charles H. "Theodore Talbot Journals, 1843, 1849-52." *Oregon Hist. Qtly.*, XXX, (Mar.-Dec. 1929): 326-337.
Cook, Herb, Jr. "Gold! Treasure Hunt on the High Seas." *Columbus Monthly*, Columbus, OH, (Dec. 1989).
Cook, William J. "Dredging for Dollars." *U.S. News and World Report*, (3 Aug. 1987): 48.

Coulter, E. Merton. "The Loss of the Steamship *Central America*, in 1857." *Georgia Hist. Qtly.* (Winter, 1970).

Dannevig, Hartvig W. "Dadenbak Medaljen" *Vi Menn*, Norway, (Mar. 1966): 26-7.

Hall, Susan Mitchell. "The Diary of a Trip from Ione to Nevada in 1859." *California Hist. Soc. Qtly.*, XVII: 75-80.

Hastings, Robert P. "Rufus A. Lockwood." *California Hist. Soc. Qtly.*, XXXIV, (June. 1955): 97-110, 239-63, 333-40.

Heite, Edward F. "Scientist on the Bridge." *Virginia Cavalcade*, Vol. XV, No. 4, (Spring 1966).

Kramer, William M. and Norton B. Stern. "The Search for the First Synagogue in The Golden West." *Western States Jewish Hist. Qtly.* Vol. 7, (Oct. 1974): 3-4.

L'Illustration, Journal Universal, Vol. XXX, No. 766, 31 Oct. 1857, Bureaux rue Richelieu 60, Paris: 297.

Parker, John F. "Millions in Gold Glittered as the *Central America* Sank." *New Bedford Standard Times*, 7 Sep. 1980.

Reddick, James P. Jr. "Herndon, Maury and the Amazon Basin." *U.S. Naval Inst. Proc.* Vol. 97, No. 815-820, (Mar. 1971) 56-63.

Ridgely-Nevitt, Cedric. "The United States Mail Steamer *George Law*." *The American Neptune*, X, (1950).

Rigler, Captain Frank V., USN (Ret). "William Lewis Herndon." *Shipmate* (Sep. 1974).

Seanor, David. "The Law of Sunken Treasure." *American Bar Assoc.*, (May 1990).

Van Nostrand, Jeanne Skinner. "Audubon's Ill-Fated Western Journey," Recalled by the Diary of J.H. Bachman. *California Hist. Soc. Qtly.*, XXI, No. 4: (Dec. 1942).

LETTERS

Beaver, Daniel, Lynda and Stephen to the author, Oct. 1989.

Benjamin, Theodosia to the author, Stockton, CA, 10 Oct. 1988.

Cass, Lewis to John Lorimar Graham, Washington, D.C., 24 Oct. 1857.

Easton, Adeline Mills to Jenny Page, her sister, Metropolitan Hotel, NY, 4 Oct. 1857.

Easton, Ansel M., typewritten copy of note describing his 1881 visit with Captain Johnsen, undated.

Graham, John Lorimar to His Excellency James Buchanan, President, New York, 19 Oct. 1857.

Herndon, William Lewis, Letters of recommendation for warrant as midshipman, to The Honorable Samuel Lewis Southard, Secretary of the Navy, Washington, D.C. From: Sombe [unreadable], Fredericksburg, VA, 3 Oct. 1827; Leadon, Thomas, Fredericksburg, VA, 23 Nov. 1827; Mercer, Hugh, Fredericksburg, VA, 23 Nov. 1827; Roberts, William I., Fredericksburg, VA, 25 Nov. 1827; Wellford, John T., Fredericksburg, VA, 25 Nov. 1827; Wellford, B. R., Fredericksburg, VA, 29 Nov. 1827.

Johnsen, Captain to A.I. Easton, Esq., Norfolk, VA, 22 Oct. 1857, includes note by D^n Robertson.

Maury, Matthew Fontaine to The Honorable Isaac Toucey, Secretary of the Navy, Washington, D.C., 19 Oct. 1857.

Norsk Sjofartrsmuseum, Norway, Else Marie Thorstvedt, Librarian, to the author, 14 Feb. 1989.

Robertson, D^n to A.I. Easton, Metropolitan Hotel, NY, 9 Nov. 1857.

Sherman, W.T. to D.O. Mills, New York, 18 Sep. 1857.

Wade, Dale to the author, Oct. 1989.

NEWSPAPERS

In the course of research, we have reviewed items contained in at least 127 newspapers. Specific references for all of those used may be found in the text and footnotes. We have primarily used information from the major newspapers of San Francisco and Sacramento, California; New York City, New York; Richmond, Virginia; Washington, D.C.; and Panama City, Panama.

Index

Acapulco (Mexico): 57
Adams, William: 100
Alabama (steamer): 152
Alsop, Richard: 22
Alston, A.J.: crushed, 95; tended by Dr. Harvey, 96; washed overboard, 107
Amazon: exploration of, 31-34
Amazon (ship): 168
Amphitrite (ship): loss of, 184
Anaconda Copper Mining Co: 244
Anderson, Frederick: 238
Andrews, John: 48
Arctic (steamer): 89, 168, 184
Arctic Discoverer (salvage ship): 221
Arthur, Chester Alan: 151, 235
Ashby, George E: 64; reports conditions to Herndon, 68-69; responsibilities, 70; enforces work procedures, 77, 79; draws knife, 82, 98; 89; swamped with life-boat, 95; 97, 99; departs steamer, 100; orders crew back into lifeboat, offers money to oarsmen, 101; requests lifeboat from Captain Burt, 101; 131, 139, 140, 143; widely condemned, 155; defends actions, 156; description, 156; defended by passengers, 157; support from the Isthmus, 158; letter to *Baltimore Transcript*, reports to USMSC, 159; 160; takes survivors in carriage, 165; 166, 176, 178, 184; signs protest, 185; 186; statement on conditions, 187; awarded gold watch in 1856, 189; vindicated by inspectors, 190; 225
Aspinwall House (Panama City): 59
Aspinwall (Panama): 19, 21, 22
Aspinwall, Lloyd: 22, 208
Aspinwall, William H: 21, 225
Astoria (Oregon): 21
Atalanta (steamer): sights wreckage, 148
Atlas (brig): 168
Atkins, Elisha: 85
Atlantic Mutual Insurance Co: 202

Audubon, John Woodhouse: 52, 153, 225
Audubon, Victor: identifies frigate bird, 153, 225
Augustine Heard (ship): 58, 243
Aust-Agder Arkivet (Arendal, Norway): 215
Ayulo, Enrique: 59; braces for plunge, 109; shares board with McNeish, 124; 137; takes pilot boat, 138; 143, 147, 160; comments on the *El Dorado,* 161

Backus, Charlie: 44, 229
Backus, Rodman M: 228-29
Badger, Capt. Thomas W: 46, 63; checks vessel, 67; sees ship free of water, 68, 75; sees Herndon on paddle-box, 105; obtains board, 107; 111; sees hundreds floating, 114; sights a bark, 119; urges Johnsen to first rescue others, 123; with Easton, first account to Johnsen, 124; 126; takes pilot boat, 138, 143, 155; comment on Ashby, 159-60, 163, 179; on causes of disaster, 185-87; defends Ashby, 189; threw gold on floor, 199; on storage of treasure, 200; awarded silver trumpet, 208; 213, 225-27
Badger, Jane A. Fitzgerald Falkenburg: 46; helps Fell children, 78, 92; talks with Herndon, 79; tries to rescue husbands gold, 82; 83; almost crushed, 91; 130-31, 225-27
Badger's Park (Oakland, CA): 226
Bagner, Mrs. R. N: 143
Bailey, Mary: 94
Baldwin, Elias Lyman ("Lucky Baldwin"): 227
Bank of California: 232
Banks, John: on raft, 168; last seen, 169
Barbacoas (Panama): 22
Barks: see *Cuba, Ellen, Laura, Sarah A. Nickel, Saxony, Tacony, Vespasian*
Barnum's: Hotel (Baltimore, MD), 150; Museum (New York City), 233
Barr, F: 171

Barrows, H.D: 60
Bartlett, Edwin: 22
Bassford, Joseph McDonald: 54-55, 63, 72; joins in chants, 80; sees passengers drinking, 88; in fourth boat-load to brig, 95; 99;loses gold, 100; 130-131, 133; 148; accuses Garretson, 152; blames Ashby, 155; $2000 in gold, 199; 211, 227
Bates, Dr: 40
Battelle Memorial Institute: 219
Battery Hotel: 166, 176
Beaver, Daniel: 51, 94
Beaver, Gideon: 228
Beaver, Dr. Stephen: 227
Beef and pork barrels: 80
Ben Franklin (steamer): 136
Berry, Captain: Master of *Columbia*, 183
Birch, James E: 47-48, 100, 108; silver collection, 175; $70,000 in gold, 199
Birch, Julia Chace: 48; awaits husband, 153; 174, 227
Birch, Virginia: 44; takes pet canary, 86; 128, 131, 143; gives interview, 149; 156, 212, 228-29
Birch, William: marriage, 44; describes entertaining in mining camps, 46, 72; helps wife to boat, 86; seeks James Birch, 100; 108; entertains on raft, 118; 137; takes pilot boat, 138; 143; note in bottle, 154; 211, 212, 228-29
Bishop, William: finds Birch bottle, 154
Black, John: 75; in charge of first life-boat, 86; 88-90, 95, 98, 100-101, 102, 104, 107, 110; makes last lifeboat trip, 127; signs protest, 185; praised, 211
Blodget, Lorin (meteorologist): 181
Bluff, Harry: 30, see Maury
Board of Underwriters report: 191
Bokee, F.A: arrives from Hong Kong, 53; carries Hawley son, 92; 171
Bonneau, Louis: 57, 94, 240
Bonneau, Thomas and Ann: 57
Boston Submarine Armor Company: possible search for *Central America* gold, 201; 219
Bourne, William: 59
Bowes, Capt: 226
Bowly, Angelina: boards lifeboat, 94; saves food for her children, 132; 212
Bowly, Isaac McKim: 94
Boyd, Mr: 153
Brazil cruise: 30
Bride, Patrick & Thomas: 98
Brigs: see *Atlas, Epervier, Marine, Mary, Mungo Park*

Brougham, Frederick: 140
Brown, Capt: 148
Brown, Edward: 93
Brown, Peter: 52
Brown, Robert Turnbull: 43-44; satisfied with steamer, 67; 73; works at pumps, 80; 108-09; joined by Dement, 113; ties ropes to hatch cover 117; 118; last rescued, 126; 137; takes pilot boat, 138; 143, 148, 155, 160; comments on the *El Dorado*, 161; 231
Brush, Gabriel: 59; offers James Birch life-preserver, 108
Buchanan, President James: 145, 213
Buddington, George: seen on raft, 168
Burt, Captain Hiram: 85, 88; hauls aboard women and children, 90; 93; shares possessions, 127; calls men to account, 130; supports Ashby, 158; esteemed by many, 213; 214, 219, 230
Butterfield Overland Mail Co: 145

Caldwell, Stephen C: 108; twenty pounds of gold, 116; rescued, 125; 199-200
Calhoun, Capt: 152
California: routes to, 15; real estate values, 39; Society of Pioneers, 238-39; 240
California (steamer): 21
Callao (Peru): 58
Call, Richard Keith: 30
Cambria (ship): 168
Campbell, Joseph (philosopher): 203
Cannon, Capt: 143
Cape Fear, NC: 221
Cape Hatteras, NC: 165
Cape Henry, VA: 133, 138
Capello, Joseph: 54
Carolina (steamer): 54
Carr, Patrick: 168
Caribou Mines (Oregon): 233
Caruthers, Eliza G: encourages young men, 95; commended by Dr. Harvey, 212
Casey, Jacob M: 109, 112; swims to hatchway, 118; rescued, 126; 230
Casey, Randolph: 109, 112; grabs plank, 117; answers call of *Ellen* crew, 123; 230
Cass, Lewis (Secretary of State): 214
Casta, Domecio: 54
Central America, The (steamer): 23; arrives at Aspinwall, 58; arrives Havana, 60; departs Havana, 63; crew, 64, 247, 256; excess steam pressure, 67; water reaches cabin floor, 72; boiler fires extinguished, 73; foremast cut away, 74; lists to port side, 77; hoist water from ship, 79; passengers form bailing lines,

INDEX

80; first lifeboat lowered, 86; 97; second cabin underwater, 105; plunges, 112; disaster news published in New York, 146; criticisms, 162; condition defended, 177; analysis of disaster, 192; results of sinking, 193; underwriters' report, 191-92; gold shipment insurers, 197; list of gold consignees published, 198; 201; rescue statistics, 215; 219-20, 235; possible last survivor, 241
Central America Relief Fund Committee: members, 150-51; 208, 209, 225, 233, 242
Chagres (Panama): 21
Chapman, Daniel Hudson C: 51
Charley (free black): 55
Charley (Jones' servant): 55
Charleston, SC: Charleston News, 183; 219, 221
Chase, William: 118, 123
Chauncey, Henry: 22
Cherokee (steamer): 23
Chesapeake Bay: 133
Childs & Dougherty: 66
Childs, Henry H: 66, 105; changes clothes, 108; 119; sees light of bark, 124; 138, 152, 160, 200, 230
Christy, Robert: 59
Churches: St. Matthews Episcopal (Burlingame, CA), 232; 14th St. Presbyterian, (New York City), 230; *see* San Francisco
City of Norfolk (steamer): 133, tows *Marine*, 138
Civil War: 239, 242
Clark, Major Jacob Brown: 53; thrown into sea, 109; drawn into whirlpool, 116; rescued, 126; 213; sheriff, 231
Clippers: *see David Crockett, Euphrasia, Mary Whitridge Three Brothers, Young America*
Clow, James C: 94
Columbia (steamer): 183
Columbus-America Discovery Group: 219, 222-23
Colon (Panama): 57
Committee on Finances (New York City): 146
Committee of the Insurance Underwriters: 189
Comstock, Samuel W: 22
Congressional Act of 1847: 19
Consignees: list of, 41
Cook, Frank: 243
Crescent City (steamer): 23, 48, 168
Crew of *Central America*: 64; salaries, 200; number, 247; by position, 256
Crocker, Col. Charles F: 232
Crocker, Jennie Easton and family: 232
Cuba (bark): dismasted, 138, 215

Cummings, John: 98
Cuyahoga (revenue cutter): 240

Dana, Richard Henry: 65
David Crockett (clipper): 235
Davidson, B: 198
Davidson, Margaret: 242
Davis, Mammy: 226
Dawson, George W: 48; helps construct raft, 110; 165; account of disaster, 169-72; description, 174; delivers silver cup, 174
Dawson, Lucy: cares for passengers, 68; falls into water, 87; injured, 90; dies, 133
Dean, Henry: helps Fallons and Redding, 91
Dean, John: 153
Dees, Jane: receives Louis Bonneau, 240
Dement, Lt. John D: 53; sleeps on deck, 104; moves to hurricane deck, 108; thrown by large sea, 110; surfaced by preserver, 112; 118-119; last rescued, 126; 152; family, 231-32
Dement, William C: 53, 231
Denison, Charles W: Purser of *Empire City*, 66; describes hurricane, 77; storm, 136; 138, 139, 141
Dobbins, James C: 162-63
Dobbin, John V. (Navy purser): 52, 80
Dougherty, M: 132
Dyer, Capt. Walter G: 108, 118

E. Townsend (schooner): sights wreckage, 148
Earl, E. Morris: 245
Easton, Adeline Mills: 42, 54, 65, 69, 70, 72; shares wedding wine and biscuits, 79; saves mementos, money, 91-2; 101-02; sees lights disappear, 112; returns watches, 130; 131; describes Lanfare, 133; 141-42; reunite with Ansel at Hotel, 142; 212-13, 232, 237
Easton, Ansel Ives: marriage, 41-42; 58; deplores steamer name change, 60; with Captain McGowan, 61; 92; note to wife, 102; siezed by Van Rensselaer, 113; 124, 126, 137; takes pilot boat, 138; 160; quotes Herndon on cause of leak, 189; recommends awards for Johnsen, 213; trunks salvaged, 223; 232
Easton Ansel Mills: meets Captain Johnsen, 237
Easton, Rev. Giles (brother of Ansel): pastor, St. Matthews Episcopal Church (San Mateo, CA), 232
Ede, Abraham: 112
Ede, William: struck by life buoy, 112; talks to Klus, 119; first rescued, 122; describes hospitality at Norfolk, 143; 161; wife 232
El Dorado (schooner): arrives on scene, 104;

none rescued by, 151; arrives at Boston, 159; comments on 159-61
Ellen (bark): damaged, 121; crewmen launch small boat, 122; enters Norfolk Harbor, 138
Ellis, Lynthia Powers: with children, in bunk, 128; 246
Ellis, Dr. Alvin: 128
Emily B. Sonder (steamship): 244
Empire City (steamer): 60-62; departs Havana, 63; weathers storm, 135; storm damage, 136, 137-38, 140, 148-49, 182
Epervier (brig): 29
Esquerra, Pasqual: 59, 65
Euphrasia (clipper): boarded by Payne, 132; 215
Evans, Patrick: seen on raft, 168
Explorer (steamer): 58

Falcon (steamer): 21; sights wreckage, 148
Falkenburg, Capt. Charles: fatal accident, 46, 227
Fallon, Lawrence: rescue of children, 91
Fallon, Winifred: with brother James, 82; sick, 91
Farmer, Chase & Co: 46-47
Farmer, Mr. & Mrs. Marcellus: 46, 153
Fell, Jane and John: 78, 124, 233
Ferguson (Mayor of Norfolk, VA): 142
Festu, Gaitano: 54
Fiedler, Daniel: 233
Fillmore, President Millard: 32
Financial panic: 195-96
Fletcher, Willard F: mans pulley ropes, 81; 110, 114; rescued, 125; comments on the *El Dorado*, 159; 200, 247
Florida: Territory of, 30; Cape, 66; Strait of, 63, 67
Food: turtle soup on *Sonora*, 55; Cuban orange, 62; hard crackers and water, 70; rations on the *Marine*, 131-2; provisions, 133; scarcity on *Ellen*, 137
Forster, James A: 63; notes lull in gale, 79; 108, 115; rescued, 124; declines money, 151
Foster, Stephen: 65
Frazer, James M: 64-66; on duty, 68; relieves Myers, 71; finds pump chamber burst, 80; increases water discharge, 81; hails brig *Marine*, 85; 89, 107-08; observes sinking, 110, 115, 123; mounts ladder to bark, 124; declines money, 151; signs protest, 185; 209, 233
Frazier, Finley: in charge of second life-boat, 86; takes boat to *Marine*, 91; 98; returns, 103; 107

Frederick, Adolph: sees Herndon, 119; 137; ill at Savannah, 151; 152
Fredericksburg, VA: 29
Fremont, Col. John C: 50, 238
French, Jenny & Margaret: 228-29
Frigates: *see* Constellation, Guerriere
Fryer, Thomas (*Vespasian* crewman): 62

Gallaher, James (*Vespasian* crewman): 62
Gallatin (revenue cutter): 135
Galt, CA: 234
Gambling on steamers: 54-55
Gardner, Alexander (*Vespasian* crewman): 62
Gardner, Capt: 32
Garretson, William: 69; delivers message, 72; conveys order to ladies, 85; 131; answers charge, 152
Geary, William: 69, 98, 155
George Law (steamer): launched, 23; renamed *Central America*, 23; description of, 23-26; called a condemned ship, 162; 185; Boston partnership, 219
George, John: 109-10, 124, 155-6
Georgia (steamer): 143
Gibbon, Lt. Lardner: 33-35, 233
Gibbs, Dr. Charles: 95-96
Gilbert, Richard: 168
Gillead, Jacob D: 169-70
Gold: discovery in California, 15; shipment, 41; consignees, 198; value of, 199; 200
Gold Hill (Utah Territory): 240
Golden Gate (steamer): 22-23
Gopher Hill (Plumas Co, CA): 56
Gorgona, Panama: 22
Graham, John Lorimer: 213
Graham, William Alexander (Secretary of the Navy): letter to Herndon: 33
Grant, Alexander: 110, 165; account of disaster, 168; joins Tice in life-boat, 171; reunion with wife, 175-76
Grass Valley, CA: 54
Gray, Col. A.B: *Empire City* passenger, 61; 63, 135; describes storm, 136; 137
Gray, Captain Alfred G: 63
Greeley, Horace: 46
Green River Mining Co: 238
Green, William (*Vespasian* crewman): 62
Greene, Capt: tows Marine, 133; 139, 141; defends position, 153 Guadalupe Quicksilver Mine (San Jose, CA): 244
Gulf Stream: 165, 168
Guy, Abel: 198

Hahn, Athros: 98

INDEX 273

Hahn, G: 98, 247
Hampton Roads: 136, 182
Harris, Jane: 73, 87, 90
Harvey, Dr. Obed C: 66, 72; tends Alston, 95; 108, 115-16; moves Alston to deck, 107; 123; shares door with Frazer, 124; finds medicine chest, 126; 155, 160, 190, 195; praises Caruthers and Marvin, 212; founds Galt, CA, 233; wife and daughter, 234
Havana, Cuba: 60-61
Hawley, Elizabeth DeForest: 49, 72, 77, 91-92; describes transfer of children, 93; sees passengers drinking, 88; praises Capt. Burt, 129; 131
Hawley, Frederick S: departs with family: 49; 72, 91; helps wife, 92
Hawser: 105
Heacock, Judge: 234
Herdendorf, Charles: 221
Herndon, Capt. William Lewis: biography, 29-36; sails from New York, 37; departs Aspinwall, 59; 65, 68; alerts passengers & directs crew, 69-71; 72, 76; orders distress signal, 77; 78-79; orders flares, 83; orders life-boats lowered, 86; checks for weapons, 89; 93; orders officers to remain on steamer, 95; 97, 99; orders to Ashby, sends Payne to *Marine*, 100; orders Black away from sinking steamer, 102; requests Stone's assistance, 104; 105, 107; on wheel guard, 108; last order, 110; 111; seen in water, 119; 146; friends lament loss, 148; 151, 184; quoted, 189; praised by survivors, 204; Navy tribute, 205; monument, 206; 234, 254
Herndon/Arthur family: 235
Herndon, Dabney, Esq: 29, 136
Herndon, Elizabeth Hull: 29
Herndon, Ellen: 35; consoled by fiance, Chester Arthur, 151; 153, 235
Herndon, Francis Elizabeth Hansbrough: 35, 150-51; receives Garretson, 153; 206, 235
Herndon, VA: 235
Heydenfeldt, Judge: 40
Hisoy, Norway: 236
Holcomb, Aaron R: 235
Hollister, Mr: 166
Hooley, R.M: 229
Hornby, Admiral: 33
Horne brothers: 200
Howard House (Aspinwall): 59
Howes, Jabez: 72, 137, 152
Howland, G.G. and S.S: 22
Huanuco, Peru: 34
Hudson, David: 52

Hull, Purser Edward W: 61; injured, seen in the water, 166; 199
Hull, William H: 61
Hunter, Lt: 36
Hurricane: 181 and following; Hugo, 222
Hutchinson, Robert: 78, 104, 155

Ijurra, Don Manuel: 34
Illinois (steamer): 48, 192
Independence (ship): 30
Indiana (steamship): 182
Insurance underwriters: 197
Isthmus of Panama: crossing, 16; railroad charter: 21
Ives, Lt. Joseph Christmas: heads Colorado River expedition, 58

Jacobs, Mr: refused passage at Havana, 62
Jacobsen, Gustav Jorgen (*Ellen* helmsman): 121; rescues men, 123; medal awarded, 215; 236
James Neilson (schooner): 230
Jane A. Falkenburg (barquentine): 46, 226-27
John L. Stephens (steamer): 54
Jefferson (revenue cutter): 30
Johnsen, Captain Anders (master of *Ellen*): changes course, 121; sails for Norfolk, VA, 126; 138, 150; expenses reimbursed, 151; comment on *El Dorado*, 161; 213, 236
Jones, Frank A: 54-55; gives watch to Addie Easton, 72; 77-80; 100, 103, 132, 148, 198-200, 237

Keefer, Henry: 80, 185
Kellog & Humbert, assayers: 199
Kellum, Judge Richard B: 220, 223
Kimball, Henry: 80, 102, 199
Kinnelty, John: 168, 171
Kirby, Mr. (of USMSC): 201
Kittredge, Almira Mead: 47, 70, 78, 82-83, 86; cares for Anna Small, 93; 95-96, 128, 130, 132, 141; describes generosity at Norfolk, 142; 157, 207
Kittredge, Dr. Francis M: 47
Kittredge, Ruel W: 238
Klus, Jack: 119
Knapp, Dexter W: 244

Lacy, Rev. (Minister of First Congregational Church): 49
Lanfare, Capt. William: 132, 215
Laura (bark): 165, 174, 215
Law, George: 19, 23, 238
Lee, Barney M: 66; describes rising storm, 67; 97, 100, 105; swept off by wave, 110, 115

Lee, George: 53
Lee, Joseph: 226
Lee's Gardens: 53
Le Fort (battleship): sunk, 154
Lemosey, Mr. (Norfolk telegraph office): 150
Lenea, J.C: 62
Leonard, Mrs. Abraham F: 143
Leslie, Frank: 238
Levich, Robert: 52
Lewis, Capt. William: 29
Lewis, Jack: 119
Life-boats: 21, rescue trips, 103; number on ship, 167
Livingstone, Dr. David: 146
Lloyds of London: 222
Lockwood, Harriet: 70, 238
Lockwood, Harriet Hill: 50, 127, 131, 238
Lockwood, Rose Alice: 93-94, 238
Lockwood, Rufus A: 51, 238
Lockwood, Rufus A., Jr: 238
London, Jack: 226
Long, Robert: 93, 96-97
Look, Prince: 137
Look, Samuel W: 137, 152
Louisiana (steamer): 143
Luce, Capt: 168

Magnolia Saloon (Nevada City, CA): 66
Maguire, Thomas: 44, 229
Mahaska (gun boat): 225
Mahoney, Daniel: 66-67, 97
Mameluke Hill, CA: 51
Manlove, Oliver Perry: describes food, 55; describes squall, 57; 62; describes fears, 69; meets boyhood friend, 88; observes drinking, 89; 97, 105; secures life preserver, 110; 114, 122; walks Norfolk streets, offered clothes, 138; 143, 155, 209; family, 238
Manzanillo, Mexico: 57
Maryland (steamer): 182-83
Marine (brig): sighted, 83; approaches the *Central America*, 85; contacted by Herndon and Frazer, 85; damaged, 88; transfer to, 90; scant accomodations, 127; conditions on, 131; becalmed 133; in tow, 138
Marvin, Amanda: 72, 78; pulls Fallon children through hatch, 82; 95; describes rope chair, 96; offers to help Capt. Burt, 130; describes food on brig, 132; 141, 157, 239
Marvin, Capt. William H: helps form bailing lines, 78; sends wife with money and jewelry, 95; 101
Mary (brig): rescues last three survivors, 172
Mary Whitridge (clipper): 53

Matachin, Mexico: 58
Matthews, Thomas: 59
Maury, Lts. John S. and William Lewis: 206
Maury, Matthew Fontaine: 30; scientific contributions, 31; 75; describes Herndon, 152; compiles report, 205; praises crew and women, 211-12; 239
Maximilian (Ferdinand Maximilian Joseph): Emperor of Mexico, 239-40
McBride, (Steward) N: 72
McCann, William E: 226
McCarty, Charles (*Golden Gate* engineer): 52; assists Ashby, 77; 80, 99, 131
McGowan, Capt. John N: 27; boards *Central America*, 60; 61, 63, 135; reports storm to USMSC, 136; ordered to search for *Central America*, 137; takes *Ellen* and *Marine* survivors on board, 138; 139; angry with Ashby, 140; 141, 239, 240
McGuire, James C: 30
McIlvane, Bowes R: 19
McKinstry, Lt: 27
McNeil, Anna Mullen: notes sea-sickness, 83; 87, 91, 132, 153, 156
McNeil, William: 44; insists wife go, 87
McNeish, Thomas: 104, 109; rescued, 124
Mechanics Exchange (Portsmouth, VA): 236
Melvina (schooner): 152
Memphis Navy-Yard: 30
Mexican War: 53
Miller: blocks passageway, 82
Miller, Jane: marries Fell, 78
Mills, Darius Ogden: 42, 232, 237
Miners: 51
Mint: *see* U.S. Mint
Missouri Volunteers: 53
Mokelumne Hill, CA: 54
Monson, Judge Alonzo C: 40, 65-66, 70, 77-78, 89, 99, 101, 131, 192, 240
Monson & Sunderland: firm of, 240
Montgomery, G. Washington: 63
Monument: for Herndon, 206; California proposal for, 208
Morgan Iron Works: 24
Morrell, Paul: 40
Morris, Commodore: 21
Morris, Robert H: 66
Moses Taylor (steamer): 192
Mosquito Fleet: 239
Mountain Ranch, CA: 240
Mullen, Anna Maria: marriage to McNeil, 44
Munford, Major William: medal to Mrs. Herndon, 206
Mungo Park (brig): sights *Central America*, 147

INDEX

Myers, Charles A. (third officer): 64; sets storm spencer, 71; 73; launches lifeboats, 86; 89, 108, 110, 209

Nashville (steamer): 152
National Hotel (Norfolk, VA): 141-42
National Observatory: 30
Navy memorial committee: 206
Navy Yard (Norfolk, VA): 213
Nemo (robot submarine): 220-21
Neville, Amelia Ransome: 21
New England Mutual Insurance Co: 207
New Jersey Plan (by M. F. Maury): 239
Newman, William: 245
New York Board of Underwriters: 191
New York City: Metropolitan Hotel, 147; Astor House, Earle's Hotel, Girard House, Merchant's Hotel, 153; Castle Gardens, 165; French's Hotel, 199; Columbia Unversity, 219; 14th St. Presbyterian Church, 230; Mills Building, 237
New York Times: Panama City, 158-59; defends Ashby and steamer, 188
Newspapers: *see* cities, bibliography
Nicaragua news: 145
Nichols, Capt: sights debris, 147
Norfolk, VA: epidemic of 1855, 136; 141; kindness of citizens, 142
Norfolk (steamer): name changed from *Penobscot*, 189
Norlund, C.A: 123; medal awarded, 215; 240
Norsk Sjofartsmseum, Arendal, Norway: 237
North Atlantic Blockading Squadron: 225
Northern Light (steamer): 188, 192, 234, 245

Ocean Hill (Greenwood Cemetery) (Annapolis, MD): 206
Ollague, Adolpho and Ricardo: 59, 130, 247
O'Connor, Eleanor: 55; sees passengers drinking, 88; bailed lifeboat, 127; reunited with son, 139; 240
O'Connor, Henry T: describes weather, 57; discusses "box pumps," 81; 94, 110, 114, 124, 139, 140, 240
O'Keefe, David: 88
O'Meara & Painter (San Francisco, CA): 55
O'Meara, James: 229
O'Neil, Mrs. Thomas: 94
Oregon Territory: first military unit to, 53
Oregon City Woolen Manufacturing Co: 231
Osborne, William: 108, 118; rescued, 125

Pacific Mail Steamship Co: 21, 40, 242
Pacific railroad: 193

Pacific Squadron: 32
Pacific Yacht Club (San Francisco, CA): 235
Pahud, Augustine: 48, 70; helps mother, 86; possible last survivor, 241
Pahud, Henry Edouard: 48, 86, 241
Pahud, Francois: 38; stays in San Francisco, 48, 240
Pahud, Madame Rosalie: boards with children, 48, 55; observes storm, 66; asked to write families, 86; 90; praises Capt. Burt, 128; 131; notes food supply waning, 132; 133, 148, 204, 240
Panama City, Panama: 57-58
Panama Railroad: 21-22, 39, 58
Para, Brazil: 34
Passengers: boarding at Aspinwall, 59; into lifeboats, 86-87, 91-94, 96, 99, 103; drinking, 88; five board the *Empire City*, 138; listing of, 245, 247-248
Payne, Theodore: 49, 67; helps last ladies into life-boat, 98; takes Herndon's watch, 99; 101; praises courage of ladies, 128; 129, 131; boards *Euphrasia*, 132; asks Captain Greene for tow, 133; 139, 141; describes reunion, 142; reports to Roberts, 150; delivers watch to Mrs. Herndon, 151; 158; summation, 205; 210, 213, 241-42
Perit, Palatia: *Central America* Fund Committee chairman, 151, 209
Perry, Commodore Matthew Calbraith: 31, 191
Persia (steamer): 184
Petersburg, VA: Civil War battle losses, 238
Pettorous, Charles: 48, 242
Pettorous, Susan: 48, 91, 242
Philadelphia (steamer):192
Pilot-boat: engaged by five passengers, 137-38
Plass, William: 97, 242
Point Conception, CA: 55
Polk, President James Knox: 19
Portsmouth Navy Yard, VA: 236
Post, Capt: offers passage to Charleston, 138; 215
Postmouth (sloop-of-war): 52
Potomac (steam frigate): 35
Priest, Albert: 54, 99, 131; wife Teressa, 242
Priest, Lee & Co: 53-55
Protest: signed by Frazer, Black, Ashby and Keefer, 185
Pulaski House (Savannah, GA): 152

Quincer, Jacob: 51, 109; sees men in sea, 117; saves two men, 123; and Catherine, 242
Quincy Granite Railway Co: 206

Rahan, Mrs. F: 96

Railroad indebtedness: 195
Ravenna, Thomas: 54
Raymond, David (Quartermaster): with life-boat crew, 93; 97-98; returns to brig, 101-02; 104; pleads with oarsmen, 107; medal presented, 209, 210; 242
Reaney, Neatie Co: 58
Redding, Ann: 58, 91, 94
Reed, Charles: 55
Reed, J.F: 109, 117
Relief Fund Committee: see Central America Relief Fund Committee
Renault, Augustine Pahud: 163, 241
Renwick, Henry B: 189
Revenue Cutters: see Jefferson, Gallatin, Cuyahoga
Revenue Cutter Service: 135
Richon, Ange: 59, 77, 104, 205, 212
Ridgely-Nevitt, Cedric: 24
Ridley, Billings H: 137, 152
Robol, Richard: 220
Roberts, Marshall O: 19, 23, 99; receives dispatches, 149; defends company and ship, 162; 181, 242
Roberts, William I: 29
Robertson, Mr: 51
Robertson, D: 213, 236-37
Rudwell, John: 54, 98
Rudwell, Mary Ann: 54; pleads with Herndon, 98; 101
Rummell, Henry: 54
Rutherford, Douglas: 98, 155
Ryan, William: 220

Sacramento, CA: 54
Saint Paul and Fond du Lac Railroad: 239
Sampson, Henry: 174
San Andreas, CA: 93
San Antonio and San Diego mail: 48
San Francisco, CA: 17, 20; description in 1857, 37-38, 41-42, 44, 51, 53, 55, 57, 222, 241-42, 244; Steamer Day, 39; 47; Vigilance Committee, 49; newspapers comments, 178-79; Dumbarton Land & Improvement Co, 236
San Francisco (steamer): 79
San Francisco Minstrels: 44
San Jacinto (steam frigate): 35
San Pedro (ship): 201
Sandwich (Hawaiian) Islands: 32
Santa Cruz, CA: 238
Santa Cruz (steamer): 46
Santos, Mrs. A: 143
Sappoblo Keys: 231
Sarah J. Nickel (bark): sights debris, 148
Saroni, Archer & Co: 53

Saroni, Charles S: hat manufacturer, 53
Saxony (bark): 137; takes five survivors, 138, 215
Sawyer, S.T: 236
Schenck, Capt: 152
Schooners: see *El Dorado, E. Townsend, Melvina, James Neilson*
Schuler, Joseph: 94, 243
Scott, Gen. Winfield: 30
Secretary of the Navy: 20
Seeger, Benjamin (Bernhard): family reunited, 139
Seeger, Mary: with two sons, 139
Seeger family: 243
Seguin, Jose: 59
Seminole Indian war: 30
Sharp, Mrs. Charles: 143
Shaw, Carolyn: 98
Shearer, Capt. Colin: delivers survivors to bark *Laura*, 165; sees life-boat, 172; rescues Dawson, Grant and Tice, 172
Sherlock, Mr. (mate of *El Dorado*): 104; 176
Sherman, William Tecumseh: letter about disaster, 147; describes Johnsen and story of bird, 150; comments on panic; 196
Ships: see *Independence, Augustine Heard, Tarolinta, Amazon, Cambria, Amphritrite, Vespasian, Spanish, San Pedro*
Shipyard: 24
Shreve & Company (San Francisco, CA): 243
Shreve, George C: 44, 243
Shreve, Samuel Stillman: 44, 65, 243
Silver cup: 48
Simmons, Mr: 148
Simson, Robert: 52
Side-wheel: found, 221
Slaves to California: 55
Slocum, Capt: sights debris, 148
Sloo, Albert G: 19
Sloops-of-war: see *Vandalia, Postmouth*
Small, Ann: 58, 93-94, 101, 132, 243
Small, Anna P: 58, 93, 243
Small, Capt. Benjamin: 58
Smith, Rev. Asa D: 230
Smith, Capt: shares provisions, 137; first report of disaster, 138; 215
Smith, C.H: 226
Smith, David: 110
Smith, Elizabeth: 91
Smith, F.M.B: 59
Smith, F.R: 206
Smith, James (*Vespasian* crewman): 62
Smith, L.W: 59
Sonora (steamer): 22-23; description, 38-39;

INDEX 277

departs San Francisco, 40; 55; arrives Panama, 57; 232
Soulé, Frank: 37
Southern Literary Messenger: 30
Spanish (ship): 201
Star of the West (steamer): 188, 192
Steamers: in service in 1850's, 23; ticket prices, 39; *see Alabama, Arctic, Atalanta, Ben Franklin, Carolina, California, Central America, Cherokee, City of Norfolk, Columbia, Cortez, Crescent City, Empire City, Explorer, Falcon, George Law, Georgia, Golden Gate, Illinois, John L. Stephens, Louisiana, Maryland, Moses Taylor, Nashville, New World, Norfolk, Northern Light, Persia, Philadelphia, Potomac, San Francisco, San Jacinto, Santa Cruz, Sonora, Star of the West, Sultana, Thomas Swann, Tobega, Yankee Blade*
Steamships: *see Indiana, Titanic, Emily B. Sonder*
Stephens, John L: 22
Stetson, Julius: meets Osborne, 118; rescued, 125; 243
Stevens, John O: 52
Stinchfield, Hiram: 245
Stock market panic: effected by loss of *Central America*, 196
Stone, Captain Samuel D: master of *El Dorado*, 104-05; reports position of hurricane and *Central America*, 159, 201; publicly condemned, 160; statement, 160; 176
Storm: 68; reports of, 182-84
Stowe, Harriet Beecher: 65
Sultana (steamer): loss of, 184
Survivors: 127-28, 130-31, 141; last three arrive Castle Garden, 165; numbers rescued, 215
Sutter's Fort (CA): 54
Swan, Mary Ann: 96, 130; saves food for baby, 132; 149, 243
Swan, Samuel B: 96

Tacony (bark): 240
Tarolinta (ship): 40, 51
Tayloe, Charles: PMSC second mate, 52
Taylor, John C: 82; swept into rigging, 111; 126
Taylor, President Zachary: 32
Tazewell, Mrs. Littleton Waller: 143
Telegraph to Marysville, CA: 145
Tennison, Dr. Joseph T: 27, 61, 64, 66; treated by Dr. Harvey, 107
Thayer, Benjamin B: 48
Thayer, Benjamin B., Jr: 244
Thayer, Herbert and Lizzie: 244
Thayer, Lucy Phillips: boards with children, 48; takes children to second boat, 92; gold in baggage, 199; 244

Thomas Swann (steamer, propeller): 138, 215
Thomas, Frances: 87, 131
Thompson, Thomas G: 219-21
Thorne, J: 59
Three Brothers (clipper): 235
Tice, John (Assistant Engineer): 64; fires donkey boiler, 70; describes crew labors, 102; 109, 165; account of disaster, 166-67; escorted by Ashby to hotel, 176; speaks against *El Dorado*, 176; 184, 187; final tragedy, 244
Tiffany & Company (N.Y.): 175, 228, 243
Tierra Blanca Mission (Brazil): 34
Tinklepaugh, Capt. E.L: 245
Tirado, Nichollas: 59
Titanic (steamship): 192
Tobega (steamer): 57
Tone, John H. "Jack": 52
Tooten, George M: 22
Toucey, Isaac (Secretary of the Navy): requests report by Maury, 205; 254
Trans-Atlantic cable: 145
Trautevine, John C: 22
Travis, James (seaman): 93, 97, 103
Travis, Dr. James: 53, 96
Travis, Jane: 95, 132
Treasure: insurance of, 197
Tribute: to the men, 207; to Herndon and crew, 210; to the ladies, 211; to rescuers, 213
Tucker, John W: 48
Twain, Mark (Samuel Clemens): inspired by Herndon's Amazon report, 35

Union Steamship Co: 189
United States District Court, Norfolk, VA: 220
United States Mail Steamship Co: 19; complaints against, 21; safety record, 23; steamships, 24; 148; comes under fire, 162; 178, 192; demise of, 193; 242
United States Mint: San Francisco, 37-38; 41, 222
United States Naval Academy: 206
United States Navy: steamship requirements, 19; grades of, 30, 254; orders to Herndon to Amazon, 33
United States Weather Bureau: 181
U.S. News and World Report: recovery announced, 219

Valentine, Charles: 52
Valparaiso, Chile: 32
Vanderbilt, Cornelius: 149
Van Hagan, I.N: 71-2, 83
Van Hagan, Hannah (Mrs. I.N.): 244
Van Ness, T.V: 153
Van Rensselaer, Charles Watkins (First Officer):

27, 64; orders pumps rigged, 73; 74; lowers gig, 93; 97; allows Monson to board boat, 99; 108, 110, 113, 209
Vandalia (sloop-of-war): 31-32
Verne, Jules: 221
Vespasian (bark): wrecked in Bahamas, 62, 188
Vessels: types in service in 1850s, 16; of steamship companies, 23; in direct rescue, 215
Virginia, General Assembly of: 206
Vose, Charles A. 227

Wade, Robert, Jr: 51
Walker, General William: 59, 145
Walters, Mr. Bray B: 141
Warrenton, NC: 183
Washerwoman Lagoon (San Francsico, CA): 42
Webb Institute of Naval Architecture: 244
Webb, William H: 20, 163, 235
Weeks, John M: 189
Wellford, B.R: 29, 206
Wells, F.A: rescued, 123
Wells, Sam: 229
West India Mail Steamer: 198

White, Mr: 108
Whiting, Capt. R.L. (master of *Sonora*): 40
Willamette Woolen Mills (Oregon Territory): 231
Willey, Rev. Samuel H: 42
Wilmsen, Captain: receives survivors, 165-66, 215
Wilson, George: 176
Wilson, Mrs. George: 176
Wilton, Richard: 89
Wise, Henry A. (Governor of Virginia): 206
Witnesses: reliable, 157
Wood, Lewis: manuscript on Vigilance Committees, 52, 223
Woodhill, Mr: 185
Worthington pumps: 24, 68; still operating, 75
Wortley, Lady Emmeline Stuart: 16

Yacht: *see* Annie
Yankee Blade (steamer): 55
Yanney, Dr. Henry P: 53
Yerba Buena: *see* San Francisco
Young America (clipper): 235

Henry Johnson

The enormous waves created by the hurricane had subsided when Henry Johnson, having strapped himself to a cabin door, was swept from the Central America into the sea. As he drifted along in the Gulf Stream, constantly striving to keep his head above water, hoping and praying to see a sail which could come to his rescue, his thoughts drifted to the events and experiences of his fifty-seven years of life.

Born a slave, on Christmas Day in the year 1800, Henry Johnson had the good fortune to be a member of the household of Henry Foxall, a kindly gentleman who, Henry recounted, treated him as a son, and promised him his freedom for his twenty-first birthday.

When he was twelve years of age, young Henry's mother was allowed to hire him out to General Walter Smith, of Georgetown, and he was "large enough to ride on horse-back with him." The brigadier commanded the militia at the battle of Bladensburg, and, on retreating, left Henry on the field, where he was captured by British Captain Patrick, and witnessed the burning of "the Capitol and President's House."

When questioned as to whom he belonged, "I told I belonged to my mother," he wrote. "If I had said I belonged to Mr. Foxall, they would have carried me off to England, for he was the man they wanted to hurt." Foxall, he said, "made the first big gun in the United States." He "begged so hard" to see his mother, that they let him go.

When the old gentleman died, Johnson was given his freedom at about the age of sixteen years, and, at seventeen, he sailed as cabin boy for Commodore Porter, on a four-year cruise. He then returned to serve as a footman for Mrs. Foxall, and in 1924, drove her to meet General Lafayette at Bladensburg. They escorted the general, he said, to the General Smith's in Georgetown.

Henry Johnson, enjoying an excellent reputation for his dependability, manner and intelligence, was soon hired for duty at the White House, Washington, D.C., where he prided himself on serving a number of prominent individuals of the day, naming Henry Clay and John C. Calhoun among them.

Johnson and his wife left the White House to accept service with the William Lewis Herndon family, and when Herndon received his appointment as Captain of the steamer *George Law*, he took Henry with him, either as a crew member or in steerage, on a number of his trips to the Isthmus. His name appears on the August-September voyage list of third class passengers of 1857.

Johnson recalled that "a great gale came up . . . that tore the ship all to pieces . . . not a man was allowed to leave until the women and children had been lowered into the boats.

"I stood close to Captain Herndon all of this time . . . after all the crew were off, he said: 'Now you go and shift for yourself.' I begged him to come with me. We were great friends, and I could not bear to leave him, but he said, 'No, I must stand by the ship.'

Herndon shook Johnson's hand, and the latter, tearing off a door, had hardly strapped himself to it when a huge sea swept him off the ship. "Before long I saw the ship go down with my captain," he said.

The Last Survivor

For three days and nights, Henry Johnson floated on his door, wondering whether death would come either by starvation or drowning. He did not elaborate on the sighting, whether the vessel passed close enough for crewmembers to spot him in the sea, or whether he managed to wave an item of clothing to attract their attention, but he related that he had been "picked up by a brig headed for 'Rio Janeiro'," where, being unable to find a ship bound for the United States, he sailed to Bremen, Germany, and from there to Liverpool and London, England, where he got passage to the States.

Johnson, said "I had gold in my pocket when I was lost at sea, but I had to throw it away as it was too heavy. The muscles of my feet were injured by being so long in the salt water, and I have been lame ever since."

He highly regarded Herndon, saying: "I never waited on a better man then Captain Herndon; he would not leave his ship because he thought it was his duty to stay there; he would do anything for me, and always wanted me with him. Oh, how much I have been through since I lost my captain, and how sorry he would have been."

On his arrival in New York, Henry visited an astonished Mrs. Herndon, who believed he had been lost at sea. "She had the greatest confidence in me;" he said, "many a time I had carried her little daughter to school in my arms when it was raining. That little girl [grew up, and] married Mr. Arthur, who became President of the United States after [her death]."

In his diary, accomplished in his nintieth year, he noted that he had "seen all of the Presidents excepting General Washington, and have waited at many of the State dinners in the White House." And it was there that he met his wife, whose mother had been Martha Washington's maid. Mrs. Washington had given her a table and other items, which she kept until her death, four years before Johnson wrote his account. "She was taken away," he lamented, "and I am left alone."

Some years after the publishing of *The Final Voyage of the Central America, 1857*, the above story came to my attention. I am indebted to Mrs. Cleo McAllister for a copy of the diary of Mr. Henry Johnson, obtained from the memorabilia of Dr. Obed Harvey, passenger/physician on the ill-fated vessel.

Author.

ADDENDUM

Ten Years Later and Beyond

During the years following the Columbus-America Discovery Group's finding of the sunken treasure and remains of the famous steamship, the organization was unfortunately involved in a number of years of litigation. Insurance underwriters doggedly pursued in the courts their claim to the recovered treasure.

Appeals traveled all the way to the United States Supreme Court. "This is the second round of appelate proceedings in this case," it was stated in the October Term, 1995, record of the court, this final appeal having emanated from the Atlantic Mutual Insurance Company, et al.

Ultimately, the extreme efforts and expertise of the salvage organization were recognized, as was the right of the underwriters to some percentage of the gold recovered. "We are hazarding but little to say that Columbus-America would, and will, receive by far the largest share of the treasure," it was said in Supreme Court record No. 95-415, September 1995.

The final decision on the percentage of distribution to the Underwriters and Columbus-America Discovery Group, being remanded by the high court to the U.S. Court of Appeals for the Fourth Circuit, finally the United States District Court for the Eastern District of Virginia, Senior Judge Richard B. Kellam.

When asked by attorneys for a delay in proceedings, Judge Kellum objected to any unwarranted delays, wryly saying "these days I don't even buy green bananas." The good judge may have known that illness may soon take his life, which it did soon after his final decision.

On June 14, 1995, the final decision awarded the salvage group ninety percent of the treasure, and the underwriters ten percent, with the stipulation that the latter must prove ownership. Eventually, the share to the salvage group became over ninety-two percent of the gold treasure, the insurance companies' share being sold in New York City by the well-known Christy's Auction House.

This had been no simple procedure. The very expensive, exhausting litigation, for both parties, had involved many thousands of pages of testimony, depositions, video tapes, extensive court proceedings and presentations of arguments by both sides of the issue. Costs amounted to many millions of dollars.

The *Federal Reporter* rather neatly summed up the entire exercise, saying:

"What Thompson and the Columbus-America Discovery Group have accomplished is by any measure extraordinary. We can say without hesitation that their story is a paradigm of American initiative, ingenuity, and determination. Almost as extraordinary, perhaps, have been the efforts of the district judge [Kellum], who has intrepidly waded through the morass of records and filings, and who has consistently evidenced good humor, notwithstanding the occasional contentiousness among the parties. He is to be commended."[1]

The Discovery Group's *Nemo* raised from the depths of the Atlantic about three tons of gold in the form of bars, specie (coin), nuggets, and dust, and news of the largest shipment of California gold ever to have been recovered became the subject of media reports and television documentaries.

Most of the coins are 1857-S mint-state double-eagles (twenty-dollar gold pieces) from the San Francisco Mint and five private mints, those being Blake & Co., Justh & Hunter, Harris Marchand & Co., Kellog & Humbert, and Henry Hentsch. Their maintained brilliance is the result of non-exposure to the elements for a 140 year period of time. The largest gold bar of the treasure weighs an astounding more than eighty pounds.[2] Referred to as *the Eureka bar*, the huge yellow brick, along with most of the treasure raised from the steamer, was purchased for the sum of one hundred million dollars by a consortium of companies called the California Coin Group, represented by John Albanese, Q. David Bowers, Larry and Ira Goldberg, and Dwight Manley, the latter describing the gold as "the ultimate numismatic treasure. There is no second," he said, "... This is it. There is nothing in the history books to compare with it." Notable retailers of the treasure have been Blanchard and Co., Bowers and Merina, and David Hall's North American Trading. The great bar, testing at .903 fine and measuring 10" × 4-1/2" × 2-1/2", after being placed on exhibit at various locations throughout the United States, has been sold by the authorized agents of the treasure, a world brokerage firm, Michael Cambrini, president, Monaco Financial Corporation, of Newport Beach, California, for the sum of eight million dollars.[3]

---

[1] Federal Reporter, 3d Series.
[2] The 1857 face value is seen stamped on the bar as $17,433.57 by Kellog & Humbert Assayers and weighing 933.94 ounces.
[3] *Coin World*, February 7, 2000.

In this year of 2002 A.D., nearly one hundred forty-four years after its loss on the historic Goldrush steamship, and after the efforts of the many people and organizations involved, the remaining treasure of gold bars, coins, nuggets and dust, is being marketed by the authorized agents as unique investments in items from America's historic past.

In this continuing saga, and notwithstanding the tremendous expense involved, perhaps other historical artifacts may be resurrected from the Atlantic grave of the sunken steamer, *Central America*. Along with the stories of bravery in the face of danger and certain death, these artifacts will be appreciated by future generations as representing a remarkable though tragic event in United States history.